D1175042

COWLES FOUNDATION

for Research in Economics at Yale University

Monograph 14

COWLES FOUNDATION

For Research in Economics at Yale University

The Cowles Foundation for Research in Economics at Yale University, established as an activity of the Department of Economics in 1955, has as its purpose the conduct and encouragement of research in economics, finance, commerce, industry, and technology, including problems of the organization of these activities. The Cowles Foundation seeks to foster the development of logical, mathematical, and statistical methods of analysis for application in economics and related social sciences. The professional research staff are, as a rule, faculty members with appointments and teaching responsibilities in the Department of Economics and other departments.

The Cowles Foundation continues the work of the Cowles Commission for Research in Economics founded in 1932 by Alfred Cowles at Colorado Springs, Colorado. The Commission moved to Chicago in 1939 and was affiliated with the University of Chicago until 1955. In 1955 the professional research staff of the Commission accepted appointments at Yale and, along with other members of the Yale Department of Economics, formed the research staff of the newly established Cowles Foundation.

A list of Cowles Foundation Monographs appears at the end of this volume.

Studies in Econometric Method

Edited by
Wm. C. Hood and
Tjalling C. Koopmans

New Haven and London, Yale University Press

Library
I.U.P.
Indiana, Pa.

330.182 H761s
c. 1

Copyright © 1953 by Cowles Commission for Research in Economics.
Third printing, July 1970.
All rights reserved. This book may not be
reproduced, in whole or in part, in any form
(except by reviewers for the public press),
without written permission from the publishers.
International standard book number: 0-300-01366-3 (cloth),
0-300-01367-1 (paper)
Printed in the United States of America by the
Carl Purington Rollins Printing-Office
of the Yale University Press.
Distributed in Great Britain, Europe, and Africa by
Yale University Press, Ltd., London; in Canada by
McGill-Queen's University Press, Montreal; in Mexico
by Centro Interamericano de Libros Académicos,
Mexico City; in Australasia by Australia and New
Zealand Book Co., Pty., Ltd., Artarmon, New South
Wales; in India by UBS Publishers' Distributors Pvt.,
Ltd., Delhi; in Japan by John Weatherhill, Inc.,
Tokyo.

CONTRIBUTORS TO THIS VOLUME

S. G. Allen, Jr., *Stanford University and Cowles Commission*
Jean Bronfenbrenner, *U. S. Department of Commerce*
Herman Chernoff, *Stanford University and Cowles Commission*
Nathan Divinsky, *University of Manitoba*
M. A. Girshick, *Stanford University*
Trygve Haavelmo, *University of Oslo and Cowles Commission*
Wm. C. Hood, *University of Toronto and Cowles Commission*
Tjalling C. Koopmans, *Cowles Commission and University of Chicago*
Jacob Marschak, *Cowles Commission and University of Chicago*
Herman Rubin, *Stanford University and Cowles Commission*
Herbert A. Simon, *Carnegie Institute of Technology and Cowles Commission*

ACKNOWLEDGMENTS

Most of the research underlying the contributions to this volume was supported by a generous grant from the Rockefeller Foundation.

Chapter II is reprinted from *Econometrica* (Vol. 17, April, 1949, pp. 125–144); Chapter IV is reprinted from the *Journal of the American Statistical Association* (Vol. 42, March, 1947, pp. 105–122); and Chapter V is reprinted in part from *Econometrica* (Vol. 15, April, 1947, pp. 79–110). Acknowledgment is made to the editors of these periodicals for permission to reprint.

Messrs. D. Waterman, J. G. C. Templeton, and E. Goldstein have rendered valuable assistance in the preparation of Chapter X.

Thanks are due also to Mrs. Jane Novick, formerly Editorial Secretary of the Commission and now an editorial consultant, for careful preparation of the manuscript for the press and for handling production of the volume through to its publication, and to Mr. Samuel Zahl, who assisted in proofreading and in preparing the indexes.

MAIN PRINCIPLES OF NOTATION

The following principles concern notation common to several chapters. Remaining differences among chapters arise from reprinting or from the specific aims of individual authors. Some chapters, especially Chapter X, utilize additional specialized notation, the principles of which are not stated here.

$\mathrm{A}, A; \mathrm{B}, B$	Greek and Latin capitals can be distinguished by the fact that all Greek capitals are vertical, all Latin capitals italicized.
$\alpha, \mathrm{A}, \gamma, \lambda, \pi, \Pi$	Known or unknown constants (parameters) are denoted by Greek characters.
a, A, c, l, y	Quantities subject to a probability distribution are denoted by Latin characters.
$\alpha, a; \Pi, P$	Unknown parameters and their estimates are denoted wherever possible by corresponding Greek and Latin characters.
$g = 1, \ldots, G; k = 1, \ldots, K;$ $t = 1, \ldots, T$	Latin characters (lower case) are also used as subscripts for numbering of variables, equations, or observation periods. In such cases the range of the subscript is often from 1 to a maximum denoted by the corresponding Latin capital letter.
$\mathfrak{S}, S; \mathfrak{F}, F$	German letters denote sets. Elements of a set are usually denoted by the corresponding Latin capital. (Chapter III is an exception.)
f, F, Q	Used to denote probability density functions.
$\mathcal{E}$	An operator denoting the operation of taking a mathematical expectation.
$\boldsymbol{A}, \boldsymbol{\Pi}; \boldsymbol{\alpha}, \boldsymbol{y}$	Matrices are denoted by capital letters, vectors by lower case letters. Submatrices are denoted by the same capitals with affixes; subvectors and scalar elements of matrices and vectors are denoted by corresponding lower case letters with affixes.
$\rho(P)$	The rank of the matrix P.
Σ, Ω	Covariance matrices of structural and reduced-form disturbances, respectively.
M	Used with various affixes to denote a matrix of moments of the observations.
$\mathrm{A}, \mathrm{B}, \Gamma$	Matrices of coefficients of structural equations.
Π	Matrix of coefficients of reduced-form equations.

x, y, z	Used frequently with various subscripts to denote observed variables.
u, v	Used with various subscripts to denote disturbances. Frequently u denotes disturbances associated with structural equations and v denotes disturbances associated with reduced-form equations.
G, K	The number of jointly dependent variables (or of equations) and the number of predetermined variables, respectively, in the structure.
$\Delta, \Delta\Delta; *, **$	Used as affixes to refer respectively to the dependent variables with unrestricted and zero coefficients and the predetermined variables with unrestricted and zero coefficients in a given structural equation.
I, II	When used as subscripts these symbols refer to sets of structural equations.

PREFACE

Econometrics is a branch of economics in which economic theory and statistical methods are fused in the analysis of numerical and institutional data. The studies assembled in this volume discuss in an expository style some problems of statistical method in econometrics.

In the application of statistical methods to economics two broad problems of economic analysis must be faced. The first is that the scope for experimentation is limited. Broadly speaking, economic history can only be observed as it is lived, uninfluenced for purposes of scientific inquiry. The second is that analysis must seek to answer questions concerning the effects of specific policies of governments, private firms, or individuals. From the studies assembled here it appears that, under these circumstances, the application of statistical methods to a given set of observations must lean heavily on preconceptions as to the nature and persistence of behavior relationships, i.e., conceptions not derived from (but possibly in part tested or screened by) the observations analyzed.

If these preconceptions were to specify all of the variables entering into each relationship of interest and if all of these variables were observed without error, there would be no need for "statistical" inference in the sense of methods dealing with observations subject to random variation. In reality, unobserved random variables need to be introduced to represent "shocks" in behavior relations (i.e., the aggregate effects on economic decisions of numerous variables that are not separately observed) and "errors" of measurement. The choice of assumptions as to the distribution of these random variables is further complicated by the fact that the behavior equations in question are often aggregated over many firms or individuals. The implications of this fact have been insufficiently explored so far.

In order to make scientific progress in a complicated situation it may be useful to proceed stepwise, introducing the various complications successively rather than simultaneously. For this reason the present volume is concerned largely with "shock models" that neglect errors of measurement. In this manner we face first certain statistical problems connected with the nonexperimental character of economics and arising from the simultaneous validity of several behavior relationships. It should also be mentioned that a number of studies of "error models" are available (see Chapter VI, footnote 7) and that some work on "shock-error models" has been started (see Chapter VI, footnote 6). To guide continuing studies, we believe that further fundamental research on the objectives and strategy of model construction will be needed. In particular, the consequences of incorrect specification need to be explored, both as a general methodological problem and in particular cases. This volume contains two case studies of specification error (Chapters VIII and IX).

The present monograph is devoted in part to an exposition of some of the problems treated more technically in Cowles Commission Monograph 10, *Statistical Inference in Dynamic Economic Models*. Some of the chapters in this category are reprinted journal articles (see Acknowledgments for details). It also contains several new studies representing the fruits of continuing research, as noted in the following review of the contents.

Chapter I by Marschak serves as an introduction to the book. It discusses the relation of economic theory to statistical method in econometrics and illustrates the uses of econometrics in deciding policy questions and in making predictions.

In Chapter II (reprinted), the concept and the criteria of identifiability of the parameters of economic behavior—a precondition for their estimation—are discussed by Koopmans. The problem of identifiability has been discussed in a variety of terminologies by quantitative workers in economics, psychology, sociology, and other fields. It is presented here in relation to a simple class of econometric models.

Chapter III by Simon throws new light on the concept of a complete model. This is accomplished with the aid of the notion of a causal ordering of variables and of equations. In addition, interesting connections between these basic ideas and the concept of identifiability are explored. The argument is put in terms of nonstochastic models and is developed most fully for the linear case.

Chapter IV by Haavelmo, by now a classic of econometric literature, illustrates the use and misuse of the least-squares method of estimation in terms of simple models involving the consumption function. The derivation of consistent maximum-likelihood estimates is illustrated for the simple case of systems containing one or two "just identifiable" equations and one identity.

In Chapter V (also reprinted) Girshick and Haavelmo present a brief discussion of maximum-likelihood estimation procedures and apply them to sets of equations pertaining to the demand for and supply of food. The portions of the original article that dealt with computational procedures have been deleted in this reprinting since an entire chapter (X) giving a detailed exposition of the subject of computation of maximum-likelihood estimates has been included in this volume.

Chapter VI by Koopmans and Hood consists of a systematic exposition of the large-sample theory of maximum-likelihood estimation in one particular "shock model" specifying linear equations and normally distributed disturbances. It also discusses tests of (a) the validity of the restrictions on, and (b) the identifiability of, a structural equation in this model. While previously published work contained in Monograph 10 and in Anderson and Rubin [1949, 1950] was drawn upon heavily in the preparation of this chapter, the application of the device of stepwise maximization of the likelihood function has been introduced here as a unifying element in the exposition.

In Chapter VII Rubin and Chernoff show that the methods and results of Chapter VI may be applied under much more general conditions, including cases of nonlinear relationships, to give estimates that still possess certain desirable large-sample properties. Except for brief abstracts, the research underlying this chapter has not been published previously.

The next two chapters, also new, deal with particular cases of specification error. A point made in Chapter VII is illustrated in Chapter VIII by Allen in terms of a simple two-equation model. The problem provides an example of specification error leading to an underestimate of the sampling variance of estimates, but not to asymptotically biased estimation.

Chapter IX by J. Bronfenbrenner gives several examples of specification error, again in terms of two-equation systems. The type of error discussed here, arising from incorrect choice of predetermined variables, results in large-sample bias of estimates.

In the last chapter (X) Chernoff and Divinsky give details of a variety of computation procedures for obtaining maximum-likelihood estimates of simultaneous economic relations. To illustrate the discussion a selection of worksheets exhibiting the more important steps in each procedure is reproduced. This chapter is based on considerable experience acquired after Monograph 10 was published.

An explanation of the main principles of notation common to several chapters is provided on pages xiii and xiv. Remaining differences in notation are due to reprinting or are motivated by the specific purposes of individual chapters. A list of references is given at the end of the volume, in which the references given with the reprinted articles are repeated.

THE EDITORS

January, 1953

TABLE OF CONTENTS

Chapter I

ECONOMIC MEASUREMENTS FOR POLICY AND PREDICTION

By Jacob Marschak

Page

1. Useful Knowledge

Knowledge is useful if it helps to make the best decisions.

To illustrate useful knowledge we shall take an example from the century-old elementary economics of the firm and of taxation. Such examples are admittedly crude (or, if the reader prefers, neat) compared with the complex actual world since their very purpose is to isolate the essentials of a problem by "idealizing reality." Later sections (beginning with Section 5) will deal with ways of eliminating at least some of the legitimate realistic objections.

What kinds of knowledge are useful (A) to guide a monopolistic firm in its choice of the most profitable output level and (B) to guide the government in its choice of the rate of excise tax on the firm's product? Let q represent quantity produced and sold per unit of time; p, price including tax; θ, tax per unit of product; γ, total cost of producing and selling q units. To fix ideas, suppose that the demand for the product of the firm is known to be (approximately) a linear function of the price and that all costs are known to consist of fixed charges. (This is almost the case with hydroelectric plants.) Write for the demand curve

$$p = \alpha - \beta q \qquad (\beta > 0). \tag{1}$$

The firm's profit (net revenue) per unit of time is

$$r = (p - \theta)q - \gamma, \tag{2}$$

or, using (1),

$$r = (\alpha - \theta - \beta q)q - \gamma = -\beta q^2 + (\alpha - \theta)q - \gamma. \tag{3}$$

CASE A: If the firm knows α, β, and θ, it can use equation (3) to compute the difference between the profits that would be attained at any two alternative output levels. To choose the most profitable output of all, it therefore suffices to know α, β, and θ. It happens in our example, as in most discussions of classical economics, that the functions involved are differentiable,[1] so that the best output level, say $q = \hat{q}$, can be found by putting $dr/dq = 0$. Hence

$$\hat{q} = (\alpha - \theta)/2\beta. \tag{4}$$

CASE B: Assume that the government knows that the firm maximizes its profit. What other knowledge is useful to the government? This depends on its aims:

CASE B_1: Suppose, first, that the government, which collects from the firm the tax revenue T,

$$T = \theta\hat{q}, \tag{5}$$

wants to maximize this revenue by the proper choice of the excise-tax rate θ. Then, by equations (4) and (5),

$$T = \theta(\alpha - \theta)/2\beta. \tag{6}$$

Therefore, if the government knows α, it can compute the ratio between the tax revenues resulting from fixing any two alternative excise rates. This ratio is independent of β. Hence, to make the best decision (i.e., to choose the value of θ that will bring in the highest tax revenue) it is sufficient for the government to know α. In fact, the best value of θ is $\hat{\theta} = \alpha/2$.

CASE B_2: Suppose, on the other hand, that the government wants to goad the monopolist into maximum production, provided that a fixed tax revenue $T = T^*$ can be collected. The best tax rate is found by solving the (quadratic) equation (6) for θ with T^* substituted for T. The equation will have two real roots, say θ_1 and θ_2 (which, in a limiting case, may coincide), provided that T^* is not too large. Since, by equation (4), q is larger the smaller θ is, and since the government was assumed to be

[1] But see Section 5.

interested in high output, it will choose the smaller of the two real roots, say $\theta_1 < \theta_2$. If T^* exceeds a certain level T_0, the roots will be not real (i.e., a tax revenue $T^* > T_0$ is unattainable). We thus conclude that if the government knows α and β it can choose the best value of θ for any desired and attainable level T^* of tax revenue.

We can sum up as follows:

CASE A: Desired: maximum r. Decision variable: q. Useful knowledge: the form of relations (1) and (2) and the values of the parameters α, β, θ.

CASE B_1. Desired: maximum T. Decision variable: θ. Useful knowledge: the fact that profits are maximized, the form of (1) and (2), and the value of α.

CASE B_2. Desired: maximum q for given $T = T^*$. Decision variable: θ. Useful knowledge: same as in Case B_2, plus the knowledge of β.

2. STRUCTURE

In all of our examples so far, useful knowledge pertains to certain economic relations. In Case A the firm has to know something about relations (1) and (2). Relation (1), the demand equation, describes the behavior of buyers. The form and the coefficients (α, β) of this relation depend on social and psychological facts, such as the frequency distribution of consumers by tastes, family size, income, etc. Relation (2), the profit equation, registers the institutional fact that the tax rate is fixed at θ, and the fact (reflecting the technology of the firm as well as the price and durability of its plant and the interests and rents stipulated in its contracts) that the total cost consists of given fixed charges, γ. With respect to the decision problem of Case A, relations (1) and (2) are called *structural relations* and are said to constitute the *structure;* they involve constants (α, β, θ, γ) called *structural parameters*. In Case B the assumed structure includes, in addition to (1) and (2), the assumption of profit maximization, which results in relation (4); and definition (5) may also be counted as part of the structure. If (1) or (2) or both had included a definite pattern of change—say, a linear trend—this would also be a part of the structure.

In each of the problems studied the form of the structural relations and the values of some (not necessarily all) of their parameters prove to constitute useful knowledge. However, we shall presently see that under certain conditions other kinds of knowledge, possibly more easily attained, are sufficient to make the choice of the best decision possible.

3. Maintained Structure and Change of Structure

We shall show that the knowledge of structure is not necessary if the structure is not expected to have changed by the time the decision takes its effect.[2] Again consider Case A. Assume that the form of the structural relations (1) and (2) and the values of coefficients α, β, γ are known to have been unchanged in the past and to continue unchanged in the future, and make three alternative assumptions about the tax rate θ:

Case A′: θ has not changed in the past and is not expected to change.

Case A″: θ has not changed in the past but is expected to change in a known way.

Case A‴: θ has changed in the past.

Suppose that in the firm's past experience, of which it has records, it had tried out varying levels of output q and obtained varying profits r. In Case A′ it can tabulate the observations of q and r in the form of a schedule, or fit an empirical curve, and use the table or the curve to predict future profit r for any given output q. It can therefore choose its most profitable output without knowing any of the structural parameters α, β, γ, θ.

True, knowledge of the form (not the parameters) of relation (3) may help in filling the gaps in the empirical schedule (if the observations are few) by suggesting that a quadratic rather than some other relation be fitted to the data on r and q. Remember that output q was assumed to be controlled by the firm independently of any other variables and to determine, for given values of the structural parameters (α, β, γ, θ), both the profit r and the price p. Accordingly, r and p are said to be "jointly dependent" on q, an "independent" variable. Independent variables are also called "exogenous" ("autonomous," "external"); and the jointly dependent variables, "endogenous" ("induced," "internal").[3] There are as many jointly dependent variables as there are structural relations—in our case, two. Solving the structural relations (1) and (2) for the two jointly dependent variables we obtain the "reduced form" of the system: two relations predicting, respectively, p and r from q. In our case the relation predicting p happens to coincide with one of the structural relations [viz., (1)]. The other equation of the reduced form (viz., the one

[2] See Chapter II, Section 8, of this volume and Hurwicz [1950b].

[3] A slight change in definition will be convenient later, when dynamic systems with lagged endogenous variables are introduced. See Section 9.

predicting r) is a quadratic equation,

$$r = \lambda q^2 + \mu q + \nu, \tag{7}$$

say, whose coefficients are related to the coefficients of the structural equations as follows:

$$\lambda = -\beta, \qquad \mu = \alpha - \theta, \qquad \nu = -\gamma. \tag{8}$$

If the structural relations (1) and (2) are assumed to retain in the future the same (linear) form and the same values of parameters as in the observed past, the firm can predict r for a given q by fitting a quadratic equation (7) to past observations on output and profit. It can thus determine empirically the parameters λ, μ, ν of the reduced form without having to pay any attention to the manner [described by equations (8)] in which these parameters are related to the demand and cost conditions. In fact, as already mentioned, the firm may display an even stronger disregard for "theory." If the number of observations is large while the firm's confidence in the linearity of the relations (1) and (2) and hence in the quadratic nature of (7) is small, it may prefer to rely altogether on some purely empirical fit.

Case A″ is different. Although the same schedule as in Case A′ will describe the past relation between output and profit, this schedule will not help in choosing the most profitable output under the new tax rate. If the firm could conduct a series of experiments under the new tax rate, varying the outputs and observing the profits, it could discard the old schedule and construct a new one to be used in decision-making. But such experiments take time.[4] In our case these experiments are not

[4] Strictly speaking, if the form of the new schedule is known, one needs only as many observations as there are unknown parameters of the schedule. Thus, three observations, and therefore a delay of three accounting periods, will suffice to determine the new quadratic schedule that replaces (7) when the tax rate is changed. If the form of the new schedule is not known, the output that results in maximum profit under the changed schedule can be found by trial and error, the number of necessary trials depending on the firm's skill in hitting from the beginning an output level near the optimal one and in varying the output level by amounts not too large and not too small. This skill is equivalent to some approximate knowledge of the properties of the new schedule—equation (9) of the text—in the neighborhood of the optimal point and is therefore enhanced if the firm has approximately the kind of knowledge to be discussed presently (viz., some knowledge of old structural relations and of the change they have undergone).

However, the full significance of the delay that occurs when, without knowing the structure, one estimates empirically a new reduced-form schedule (such as the relation between the dependent variable r and the independent variable q after the tax rate θ has changed) cannot be gauged by the reader as long as we deal with the artificial assumption of *exact* economic relations such as constitute the usual economic theory. When, beginning with Section 7, random disturbances of rela-

necessary if the firm knows, in addition to the old observations, the form of relations (1) and (2) and both the old and the new tax rates, say θ and θ^*. Then the old schedule will be the reduced-form equation (7). The firm obtains the coefficients of (7) empirically from old observations. It knows them to be related to the structural parameters, by equations (8). Under the new tax rate θ^* the coefficient μ will be replaced by $\mu^* = \alpha - \theta^*$, while λ and ν will not be affected. Hence the new relation between profits and outputs will be

$$r = \lambda q^2 + (\mu + \theta - \theta^*)\, q + \nu. \tag{9}$$

The new schedule can thus be obtained by the firm from the old one by inserting the known tax change in a well-defined way.

We see that, in the case of a foreseen change in structure, the purely empirical projection of observed past regularities into the future cannot be used in decision-making. But knowledge of past regularities becomes useful if supplemented by some knowledge (not necessarily complete knowledge) of the past structure and of the way it is expected to change. In our case we can replace the old, empirically obtained schedule (7) by the new, not observed schedule (9) if we know (a) the mathematical form (viz., quadratic) of these schedules and the role played in them by the tax rate [this knowledge is derived from the knowledge of the form (not the coefficients) of the structural relations (1) and (2)], and (b) the amount of change of tax rate, $\theta^* - \theta$. Having thus obtained (9), and maximizing r, we can determine the best output, $q = \hat{q}$. In terms of the tax change and of the coefficients of the old, empirical profit schedule (8),

$$\hat{q} = (\theta^* - \theta - \mu)/2\lambda.$$

We now come to Case A‴, in which the tax rate θ was observed to vary independently in the past, θ being similar in this respect to the output q. In this case, both q and θ are exogenous variables, while α, β, γ are, as before, structural parameters and r is endogenous. From past observations on q, θ, and r, the firm can derive a double-entry table or fit an empirical surface to predict the profit r for any specified output q and tax rate θ. As in Case A′, it is not necessary to know the structural parameters, although knowledge of the form of the structural relations helps to interpolate gaps in the empirical table. Specifically, profit r is

tions and errors in the measurement of variables are introduced, the time-saving aspect of the knowledge of structural relations will appear in a more realistic light. See Section 8.

related to q and θ by an equation of the form

$$r = -\theta q + \lambda q^2 + \pi q + \nu, \tag{10}$$

whose parameters are related to the structural parameters as follows:

$$\lambda = \beta, \qquad \pi = \alpha, \qquad \nu = -\gamma. \tag{11}$$

If the firm has confidence in the form of the structural equations (1) and (2), it will be helped by the knowledge that equation (10) involves a product term $(-\theta q)$ in the two exogenous variables and a term (λq^2) quadratic in q. Thus, Case A‴ is analogous to A′ except that the reduced form now involves two exogenous variables (q, θ) instead of one (q).

Suppose, however, that a change in the social and psychological conditions is expected to change the demand equation (1). Suppose, for example, that the slope of the demand curve, which had maintained a constant value β during the past observations, is expected to obtain a new value, β^*, while the tax rate θ and the output q had both undergone observed variations during the observation period. With the demand curve thus changed, the coefficient λ in equations (10) and (11) will be replaced by $\lambda^* = \lambda + (\beta - \beta^*)$. Therefore, the old reduced-form equation (10) cannot be used to predict profits r from given values of tax rate θ and output q and to decide upon the best output level $\hat{q}$ unless one knows, in addition, the amount by which the demand parameter β is going to change. This case is analogous to Case A″, with β now playing the role that was played in Case A″ by θ, while q and θ play the role previously played by q alone.

To sum up: (a) for purposes of decision-making it is always necessary to know past and future values of all exogenous variables (i.e., of variables that determine the outcome in question and that were observed to change in the past); (b) if conditions that have not changed in the past are expected to change in the future, some knowledge of such conditions (called "structure") and of the nature of their change is necessary for decision-making.

The choice of the best decision presupposes that two or more alternative future values are tentatively assigned to a decision variable. If the decision variable has varied in the past, it is called an exogenous variable; if it has not, it is usually called a structural parameter. In Cases A′, A″, and A‴, q, an exogenous variable, was such a decision variable. In Case B of Section 1 the tax rate θ was a decision variable, the government being the decision-maker. If θ has varied in the past, and is thus an exogenous variable, the government has to know these variations in order to choose the best decision on the basis of past relations between

θ and the quantity that it tries to maximize. If θ has not varied in the past (for example, if θ was zero) and the government now tries to fix it at its best value, a structural change is planned. To determine the effect of such a change the government has to know something about the past structure. This knowledge may require more than the knowledge of the past tax rate itself. For example, it is seen from equation (6) that if the tax is to be introduced for the first time, the choice of the tax rate that will maximize the tax revenue will require knowledge of α, a parameter of the demand equation.

4. Controlled and Uncontrolled Changes

We have noted that a decision variable can be either a structural parameter or an exogenous variable. Structural parameters and exogenous variables that are decision variables can be called "controlled" variables, as distinct from "uncontrolled" variables (both exogenous and endogenous) and parameters. For example, the legally fixed quantity θ is uncontrolled from the point of view of the firm, though controlled from the point of view of the government. The psychological and social factors determining α and β and the technological and economic factors determining γ were here considered uncontrolled, though a different hypothesis (e.g., involving the effects of an advertising campaign designed to change buyers' tastes) might have been discussed instead.

In predicting the effect of its decisions (policies) the government thus has to take account of exogenous variables, whether controlled by it (the decisions themselves, if they are exogenous variables) or uncontrolled (e.g., weather), and of structural changes, whether controlled by it (the decisions themselves, if they change the structure) or uncontrolled (e.g., sudden changes in people's attitudes, in technology, etc.). An analogous statement would apply to the firm except that, for it, government decisions belong to the category of uncontrolled variables.

5. Some Definitions Extended

We shall now proceed, as promised in Section 1, to generalize our examples to meet realistic objections. One such objection is that in practice the decision is frequently qualitative, not quantitative. For example, the firm may have to decide in which of a limited number of eligible locations—each of them near a fuel source, say—it should build a plant; the government has to decide whether to abolish or continue rent control; etc. Such cases look superficially different from Cases A and B_1, treated in Section 1, where the decision-maker had to choose among a large (possibly infinite) number of values of a (possibly continuous) variable. Note, however, that in Case B_2 the choice had to be made between only two values (θ_1 and θ_2). In every case the decision-maker compares the outcome of alternative decisions, and these may or may not form a continuous set. It is obviously not essential whether the alternatives are identified as quantities (as in the examples of the previous sections), or by city names (as in the case of location choice), or by the words "yes" or "no" (as in the choice between maintaining and abolishing rent control). In every case the choice goes to the decision that promises the best outcome.

The extension applies, in fact, to all the variables (including the structural parameters), which we had previously introduced as continuous quantities. It has been claimed, for example, that in the interwar period businessmen's willingness to invest in plant and equipment depended, other things being equal, on whether the national administration happened to be Democratic or Republican. Should an economist take this hypothesis seriously, there is nothing against his regarding the party label of the administration as a two-valued variable and trying to explain certain "shifts" in the investment schedule as a function of that variable.

Similarly, fluctuations in the supply of a commodity according to the four seasons of the year can be conveniently treated by introducing into the supply schedule a four-valued exogenous variable called season. This is a more rational approach than the usual mechanical "seasonal adjustment" of individual time series, which does not use available knowledge as to which particular structural relations (such as the technological supply schedule for crops or buildings or the demand schedule for winter clothes) are affected by seasons.

Finally, consider a structural change that (unlike the changes discussed in previous sections) consists, not in changing a certain continuous parameter, such as the coefficient α of the demand equation (1), but in scrapping one equation and replacing it by another. Let the two equations be, respectively, $F = 0$ and $F^* = 0$, where F and F^* are functions involving, in general, several endogenous and exogenous variables and certain parameters. Form the equation $\delta F + (1 - \delta)F^* = 0$, where δ is a new structural parameter with the following values: $\delta = 1$ before the change, $\delta = 0$ afterwards. Then structural change is expressed by a change in the value of δ.[5]

These examples show that our previous description of structures and decisions in terms of variables (including parameters) is general enough

[5] For example, the introduction of price control, which will be discussed in Section 6, consists in scrapping the equation $q^s - q^d = 0$ in (13) and replacing it by the equation $p - \bar{p} = 0$.

if the concepts are properly interpreted. The corresponding generalization of mathematical operations involved is, in principle, feasible.

Some readers may find it more convenient to give the set of exogenous variables and structural parameters a more general name: "conditions." Similarly, the set of jointly dependent variables can be renamed "result." Conditions that undergo changes during the period of observation correspond to "exogenous variables." Conditions that remain constant throughout the observation period but may or may not change in the future constitute the "structure." Conditions that can be controlled are called "decisions." Given the conditions, the result is determined. The decision-maker ranks the various achievable results according to his preferences: some results are more desirable than others. The best decision consists in fixing controlled conditions so as to obtain the most desirable of all results consistent with given noncontrolled conditions.

For the economy as a whole, endogenous variables can be roughly identified with what are often called "economic variables." These are usually the quantities (stocks or flows) and prices of goods and services, or their aggregates and averages, such as national income, total investment, price level, wage level, and so on. The exogenous variables and the structural parameters are, roughly, "noneconomic variables" (also called "data" in the economic literature) and may include the weather and technological, psychological, and sociological conditions as well as legal rules and political decisions. But the boundary is movable. Should political science ever succeed in explaining political situations (and hence legislation itself) by economic causes, institutional variables like tax rates would have to be counted as endogenous.[6]

6. The Technician and the Policy-Maker

Outcomes of alternative decisions are ranked according to their desirability by the policy-maker, not by the technician.

Returning to Case B of Section 1, suppose, for example, that the government desires both a high tax revenue and a high level of production of the taxed commodity. The endogenous variable that is being maximized is thus neither the tax revenue (as in Case B_1) nor the output (as in Case B_2) but a function of the two; for example, this function may be

$$U = T + \omega\hat{q}, \tag{12}$$

where ω, a positive number, indicates the "weight" attached to the production aim relative to the aim of collecting revenue. The statement that the government maximizes U is a special case of the statement, made in

[6] See Koopmans [1950c].

Section 5, that the government ranks the possible results—here the possible pairs of values of T and $\hat{q}$—according to its preferences. We find that the best value of θ, in this sense, is $\hat{\theta} = (\alpha - \omega)/2$.

We can imagine a division of labor between the government (or some other decision-maker) and the technician. The latter is relieved of the responsibility of knowing the "utility function" such as (12). The technician is merely asked to evaluate the effects of alternative decisions (tax rates θ) separately upon $\hat{q}$ and T, as in equations (4) and (5). Clearly, knowledge of the structural coefficients α, β is useful for this purpose. This knowledge is even necessary if the tax is introduced for the first time (or if α, β, θ had all been constant throughout the observed past). The technician will thus try to estimate α and β. The decision-maker, on the other hand, need not formulate his own utility function—$U(T, \hat{q})$, say—completely and in advance. It suffices for him to make the choice only between the particular pairs of values of $(T, \hat{q})$ that the technician tells him will result from setting the tax at various considered levels.

An additional example will illustrate this role of the technician as separated from the decision-maker. The government (or the legislator) considers the possibility of guaranteeing some fixed price for a farm product. The technician is asked how many bushels will have to be purchased for storage at public expense at any given guaranteed price. Suppose that the technician knows the supply and demand functions which have so far determined the price in a free market:

$$\begin{aligned} q^s &= \alpha^s + \beta^s p, \\ q^d &= \alpha^d - \beta^d p, \\ q^s - q^d &= 0, \end{aligned} \tag{13}$$

where q^s is the quantity supplied and q^d is the quantity demanded by private people, and where p is the (varying) price at which demand and supply were equalized in previous years. Under the intended legislation this system would be replaced by

$$\begin{aligned} q^s &= \alpha^s + \beta^s \bar{p}, \\ q^d &= \alpha^d - \beta^d \bar{p}, \\ q^s - q^d &= g, \end{aligned} \tag{14}$$

where q^s and q^d are, as before, the supply and demand of private people, and where g is the amount to be purchased by the government when the price is fixed at $\bar{p}$. Hence

$$g = (\alpha^s - \alpha^d) + (\beta^s + \beta^d)\bar{p}. \tag{15}$$

If the technician can estimate the parameters (α^s, β^s, α^d, β^d) of the supply and demand equations, he can tell what alternative pairs of values of g and $\bar{p}$ are available for the policy-maker's choice. We can say that the latter maximizes some utility function $U(g, \bar{p})$ over the set of those available pairs of values. But this function is of no concern to the technician.[7]

7. Random Shocks and Errors

Exact structural relations such as equations (1) and (2) are admittedly unrealistic. Even if, in describing the behavior of buyers, we had included, in addition to the price and to the quantity demanded, a few more variables deemed relevant (such as the national income, the prices of substitutes, etc.), an unexplained residual would remain. It is called "disturbance," or "shock," and can be regarded as the joint effect of numerous separately insignificant variables that we are unable or unwilling to specify but presume to be independent of observable exogenous variables. Similarly, numerous separately insignificant variables add up to produce errors in the measurement of each observable variable (observation errors). Shocks and errors can be regarded as random variables. That is, certain sizes of shocks and observation errors are more probable than others. Their joint probability distribution (i.e., the schedule or formula giving the probability of a joint occurrence of given sizes of shocks and errors) may be regarded as another characteristic of a given economic structure, along with the structural relations and parameters we have treated so far.

If at least some of the variables are subject to observation errors it is impossible to predict exactly what the observed value of each of the endogenous variables will be when the observed values of exogenous variables, together with the structure, are given. But it is possible to make a prediction in the form of a probability statement. The probability that the observation on a certain endogenous variable will take a certain value, or will fall within a certain range of values, can be stated, provided that the probability distribution of observation errors of the variables is known. Similarly, no exact predictions, but, in general, only probability statements, can be made if at least one of the structural relations is subject to random disturbances (shocks), even if all observations are exact. Few economic observations are free of errors; few economic relations are free of shocks. The quantities that we want to pre-

[7] In the above case of "protecting the farm income," g is nonnegative and $\bar{p}$ is chosen to be at least equal to the price p that satisfies equations (13) of the free market. Equations (13) and (14) can also describe the introduction of rent control, with $\bar{p} \leqslant p$ and with government-financed housing being denoted by $-g$.

dict (viz., the endogenous variables) are therefore random variables. Prediction consists in stating the probability distribution of these variables.[8]

As an example, replace the supply and the demand equations in (13) and (14) by equations involving shocks (random "shifts," in the economist's language) u^s and u^d but not errors of observation. In particular, equations (14) become

$$\begin{aligned} q^s &= \alpha^s + \beta^s \bar{p} + u^s, \\ q^d &= \alpha^d - \beta^d \bar{p} + u^d, \\ q^s - q^d &= g; \end{aligned} \tag{16}$$

accordingly, equation (15) must be replaced by

$$g = (\alpha^s - \alpha^d) + (\beta^s + \beta^d)\bar{p} + (u^s - u^d). \tag{17}$$

Suppose that the shocks are known to have the following joint distribution (as already remarked, it must be independent of the observable exogenous variables; that is, in our case, independent of $\bar{p}$):

$$\begin{aligned} &\text{the probability that } u^s = 1 \text{ and } u^d = 1 \text{ is } 3/6, \\ &\text{the probability that } u^s = 1 \text{ and } u^d = -5 \text{ is } 1/6, \\ &\text{the probability that } u^s = -2 \text{ and } u^d = 1 \text{ is } 2/6. \end{aligned} \tag{18}$$

Then $(u^s - u^d)$ is distributed as follows:

$$\begin{aligned} (u^s - u^d) &= 0 \text{ with probability } 3/6, \\ (u^s - u^d) &= 6 \text{ with probability } 1/6, \\ (u^s - u^d) &= -3 \text{ with probability } 2/6. \end{aligned} \tag{19}$$

That is, to predict the amount g which the government will have to purchase if it fixes the price at $\bar{p}$, the technician will use the same function of $\bar{p}$ as in equation (15), *plus* a random quantity which takes values 0, 6, or -3, with respective probabilities 3/6, 1/6, 2/6. Our example shows how, given the values of exogenous variables ($\bar{p}$ in our case) and given the structure [which now includes the probability distribution of shocks u^s, u^d along with the structural relations (16) and their parameters], the technician can state the probability distribution of each endogenous variable (g in our case). He can state with what probability each endogenous variable will take any specified value, or a value that will belong to any specified set of numbers or any specified interval.

[8] See Hurwicz [1950b] and Haavelmo [1944, Chapter VI].

Instead of a discrete probability distribution of u^d and u^s, such as (18), we might have assumed a continuous probability distribution. For example, let u^d and u^s be jointly normally distributed, with zero means, with a correlation coefficient $\rho = 0.6$, and with respective standard deviations $\sigma_d = 3$ and $\sigma_s = 5$ crop units. Then the term $u^s - u^d$ in (17) has a normal distribution with zero mean and with variance equal to $\sigma_d^2 + \sigma_s^2 - 2\rho\sigma_d\sigma_s = 16$ and standard deviation equal to $\sqrt{16} = 4$. Hence the odds are approximately 1:2 that the necessary government purchase g will have to exceed or fall short of the value given in (15) by more than 4 units.[9] The values of α^s, α^d, β^s, β^d, σ_s, σ_d, ρ constitute the structure, assuming that the structural equations (16) are linear and that the distribution of u^s and u^d is normal. The knowledge of the structure permits the prediction of the endogenous variable g, given the exogenous variable $\bar{p}$.

Such is the nature of statistical prediction. It is perhaps not too well understood in parts of economic literature. Too often economic theory is formulated in terms of exact relations (similar to alleged laws of natural science), with the frustrating consequence that it is always contradicted by facts. If the numerous causes that cannot be accounted for separately are appropriately accounted for in their joint effect as random disturbances or as measurement errors, statistical prediction in a well-defined sense becomes possible.

This is not to say that the interval within which a variable is predicted to fall with a given probability may not be large. If it is so large that widely differing policies appear to yield equally desirable results, the prediction becomes useless as a means of choosing the best decision. However, provided the technician has used the best available data and the most plausible assumptions, he cannot be blamed for the disturbances inherent in complex processes such as human behavior, weather, crops, new inventions, and for the errors that have occurred in measuring their manifestations. It is quite possible that some of the structural relations of our economy are, by their very nature, subject to strong random fluctuations. Should it be true, for example, that the investment decisions of entrepreneurs are essentially made in imitation of the decisions of a very few leaders who, in turn, are affected by conditions of their personal lives as much as by economic considerations, then the prediction of aggregate investment could be made only within a very large prediction interval, unless one is content with assigning a very small probability to the success of the prediction. This fact would merely be a

[9] When the sample is small, this calculation must be modified somewhat to account for errors of estimation in σ_d, σ_s, ρ. We disregard this here as technical and irrelevant to our discussion.

consequence of a certain structural characteristic of the economy, and the technician would merely have recorded it faithfully.

Note that any function of endogenous variables, and therefore also the utility of a given policy [such as U in equation (12)], now becomes a random variable. Its distribution depends on the structural relations, on the distribution of disturbances and errors, and on the values of exogenous variables, the structural relations and exogenous variables being partly controlled by the policy-maker himself. He will prefer certain probability distributions of utility to others and will choose the best decision accordingly. In particular, he can choose that decision which maximizes the long-run average (the mathematical expectation) of utility. This may result in his preferring policies with a narrow range of possible outcomes to policies with a wide range of possible outcomes; that is, he may "play for safety."

8. The Need for Structural Estimation

The results of Section 3 extend themselves with added force to the now generalized probabilistic (stochastic, statistical) concept of economic structure. The determination of relevant unknowns will now be called "estimation."[10] Generalizing the example used in Section 3, replace the demand and profit equations (1) and (2) and the resulting reduced-form equation (7) by, respectively,

$$p = \alpha - \beta q + u, \tag{1'}$$

$$r = (p - \theta)q - \gamma + v, \tag{2'}$$

$$r = \lambda q^2 + \mu q + \nu + w, \tag{7'}$$

where u, v, w are random shocks and where, corresponding to equations (8) of Section 3,

$$\lambda = -\beta, \qquad \mu = \alpha - \theta, \qquad \nu = -\gamma, \qquad w = uq + v. \tag{8'}$$

The shock variables u, v represent, respectively, random shifts in demand behavior and in the total cost and are independent of exogenous variables such as q and θ. As an example, u and v may depend partly on random fluctuations of the general price level (so that u and v are correlated) and partly on numerous other causes specific to the demand or to the cost formation. Let u, v be normally distributed with zero means, and call their variances σ_u^2 and σ_v^2 and their correlation coefficient ρ. Then w, the random term in the reduced-form equation (7′), will be, by (8′), normally distributed with zero mean and with variance

$$\sigma_w^2 = q^2\sigma_u^2 + \sigma_v^2 + 2q\rho\sigma_u\sigma_v. \tag{20}$$

[10] See Chapters VI and VII.

Suppose, as before, that a certain change in the structure (viz., a known change in the tax rate θ) is expected by the firm. It has to choose the best new level for its output. This may be defined as the output level that yields, under the new tax rate, the highest mathematical expectation of the profit (or, more generally, the highest mathematical expectation of some utility function of profit, possibly giving different weights to a dollar lost and a dollar gained). To find the best new output level we need to know, as in Section 3, the relation that will correspond to (7′) under the new structure. (This knowledge will now have to include the distribution of w in addition to some of the coefficients λ, μ, ν.) The case for estimating the old structure and inserting its known change, and against relying upon experiments to be made under the new structure, is now even stronger than it was in Section 3, where all relations were assumed to be exact.[11] Even though we have assumed that the firm knows the (quadratic) form of equation (7′) and that it knows the (normal) form of the distribution of w for given q, it will not suffice now to have just as many observations under the new structure as there are unknown parameters of the reduced form. To achieve a degree of precision necessary for practical action one may need a large number of observations on q and r under the new structure. This number is larger, the larger σ_w. Therefore, by (20), the larger the quantities σ_u, σ_v, ρ, and q are, the more observations are needed. The required delay would impede the making of decisions. On the other hand, the old structure (the old tax rate) may have prevailed during a long enough period to make possible a sufficiently precise estimation of the old structural equations (1′) and (2′) (i.e., of their coefficients and of the distribution of parameters σ_u, σ_v, ρ) from data on r, p, and q. Hence λ, μ (under the old as well as the new value of θ), and ν can be estimated, by (8′), and the standard deviation for any given q can be estimated, by (20).[12]

It is not claimed, to be sure, that the available data for the past always provide a large enough sample to estimate the old structure with precision that is sufficient for practical decision. In fact, it will be remembered from the previous section that the random disturbances of some economic relationships may well be so large as to make even the full knowledge of the old structure (including the knowledge of the distribution of those disturbances) useless for practical decisions. In this case even an infinitely large sample would be useless. All that is claimed in the present section is this: Whenever a given change in structure is expected or intended, the attempt to predict the outcome of alternative

[11] See footnote 4.

[12] For some other aspects of experiments vs. nonexperimental observations, see Marschak [1947a, p. 292 ff.].

decisions under the new structure without taking into account experience collected under the old structure is either so lacking in precision or so wasteful of time as to be useless. It is more promising, though not always practicable, to base the choice of best policy upon an estimate of the old structure and on the knowledge of its expected or intended change.

9. The Time Path of Economic Variables; Dynamic Structures

We are usually interested in predicting the values of economic variables, not only for a single point or interval of time, but for a whole successsion of such points or intervals. We are interested in the path of the variable through time. As often pointed out by economists, the properties of the path (for example, the intensity of the oscillations of, or the rate of growth in, income) are of direct concern to the individual or the nation.

Suppose that the exogenous variables and/or the structure will undergo specified changes during the future period in question, and disregard for a moment any disturbances and errors. Then the value of each endogenous variable, being at any time exactly determined by exogenous variables, will change throughout the period in the manner prescribed by the relevant equation of the reduced form, such as equation (7) or (15).

Now introduce disturbances, such as u and v in (1′) and (2′), or u^s and u^d in (16), and errors of measurement. Assume either that their probability distribution, which can be regarded as a characteristic of the structure, is unchanged throughout the period or that it will undergo specified changes. Then the relevant equation of the reduced form will also involve random fluctuations, as exemplified in (7′) or in (17). Thus, for each future point of time it will be possible to make a statistical prediction as discussed in Section 7.

So far we have discussed changes in the exogenous variables or in the structure and the presence of random disturbances and errors as the only explanations of the change of economic variables over time. If this were true, no economic trends or oscillations of endogenous economic variables would be generated except by trends and oscillations in specifiable exogenous variables (such as climate, population, technology, domestic political balance, the state of foreign economies, armaments, wars, demobilizations) or else by random variations of the joint effect of numerous other external forces for which we are unable to account separately. Accordingly, in the examples studied so far, all observed values of endogenous variables would remain constant if the exogenous variables and the structure did not change and if disturbances and errors were not present. All paths would be straight lines parallel to the time axis.

Many economists have been dissatisfied with this picture of economic changes. Many if not most business cycle theories imply that economic fluctuations would take place even if external conditions remained constant and no random shocks existed.

This is consistent with the observation, neglected in all of our previous examples, that relations describing human behavior, technology, or legal rules must often involve not only a set of contemporary variables but also their rates of change (time derivatives, or differences between successive values of a variable) or their cumulated values (integrals or sums over time). For example, net investment may be related to the rate of change in annual consumption and also to the existing capacity (i.e., to the cumulated past net investment). To give another example, building construction lags behind building plans, and both may play a role in a system of structural relations. Even supposing that the exogenous variables and the structure are constant and that random disturbances are absent, such a system would generate variations of endogenous variables through time. The paths of these variables will depend on their initial values and in general will not be parallel to the time axis, except possibly for a particular set of initial values (called "equilibrium values") which, if attained, are maintained. We call a structure that would admit variations of observed endogenous variables, even if exogenous variables did remain constant and if there existed no random disturbances, a "dynamic structure."

As an example, we may modify the market system (13) into the "cobweb" case familiar to economists and often used to illustrate the so-called "period analysis" of business cycles.[13] Suppose that the suppliers of grain determine output in response to the price that prevails one year before the harvest, and suppose that the demanders set the price at which they are willing to absorb the whole (perishable) crop immediately after harvest. Thus, transactions take place only once a year, and the prices and quantities obey the following relations:

$$q_t = \alpha^s + \beta^s p_{t-1} \quad \text{(behavior of suppliers)}, \tag{21}$$

$$p_t = \alpha^d + \beta^d q_t \quad \text{(behavior of demanders)}, \tag{22}$$

where the subscript indicates time. Let $\alpha^s = 0, \beta^s = 2, \alpha^d = 1, \beta^d = -\frac{1}{4}$, and suppose that the initial crop $q_0 = 1$. By previous definitions (Section 3), these five quantities can be regarded as structural parameters or, equally well, as exogenous variables that happen to remain constant during the whole period in question. The two endogenous variables, p_t and q_t, will trace certain paths, or time schedules, that we can obtain

[13] See Leontief [1934], Lundberg [1937], and Samuelson [1947, Chapter XI].

as follows. By equation (22), $p_0 = 1 - \frac{1}{4}q_0 = \frac{3}{4}$. Then, by (21), $q_1 = 2p_0 = \frac{3}{2}$; by (22), $p_1 = 1 - \frac{1}{4}q_1 = \frac{5}{8}$; by (21), $q_2 = 2p_1 = \frac{5}{4}$; and so on. In our numerical case q_t and p_t happen to oscillate around $\frac{4}{3}$ and $\frac{2}{3}$, respectively, approaching these constants as time goes on ("damped oscillations"):

(23)

t	0	1	2	3 $\cdots \to \infty$
q_t	1	48/32	40/32	41/32 $\cdots \to$ 4/3
p_t	24/32	20/32	22/32	21/32 $\cdots \to$ 2/3.

(Note that if, at some time $t = T$, the price and quantity were to be artificially set at $\frac{2}{3}$ and $\frac{4}{3}$, respectively, then the demand equation (22) would be satisfied. Also, by putting $t = T, T + 1, \cdots$ in (21) and (22), we see that $q_T = q_{T+1} = q_{T+2} = \cdots$, and $p_T = p_{T+1} = p_{T+2} = \cdots$. That is, the values $\frac{2}{3}$ and $\frac{4}{3}$, if attained, are maintained. They are the equilibrium price and quantity.)

The time schedule (23) expresses each endogenous variable as a function of time, a discrete function in our case. We have been able to predict the values of endogenous variables at each point of time from their values in the preceding point of time, using the fact that in equation (21) an endogenous variable was related to the lagged value of another endogenous variable. Another method for obtaining the time schedule (23) is to transform (21) and (22) into equations expressing each endogenous variable in terms of its own previous value, predicting q_1 from q_0, q_2 from q_1, etc. These equations are

$$q_t = \delta + \epsilon q_{t-1}, \tag{24}$$

$$p_t = \gamma + \epsilon p_{t-1}, \tag{25}$$

where $\epsilon = \beta^d\beta^s$, $\gamma = \alpha^d + \beta^d\alpha^s$, $\delta = \alpha^s + \beta^s\alpha^d$. Note, moreover, that if we replace t by $t - 1$, equation (24) becomes $q_{t-1} = \delta + \epsilon q_{t-2}$. Hence, substituting into the original (24), we have $q_t = \delta(1 + \epsilon) + \epsilon^2 q_{t-2}$; and, by repeating the procedure, $q_t = \delta(1 + \epsilon + \epsilon^2) + \epsilon^3 q_{t-3}$, and, in general,

$$q_t = \delta(1 + \epsilon + \cdots + \epsilon^{n-1}) + \epsilon^n q_{t-n} \quad (n = 1, 2, \cdots). \tag{26}$$

Thus, the current value of an endogenous variable can be predicted from any of its preceding values. In more general cases it can be predicted from combinations of these values. The form (24), (25) into which we have put the dynamic structural system (21), (22) exemplifies a set of "final equations," in Tinbergen's terminology.[14] Each final equation is a difference equation (or, in other cases, a differential, or possibly a mixed difference-differential-integral equation), possibly of high order, in a single variable, with a corresponding time schedule or path, such as those in (23), as its solution.

As still another, and the most direct, way to obtain the time schedule (23), we can express q_t (or p_t) in a form[15] involving only the initial values of the endogenous variables. In (26), put $n = t$:

$$q_t = \delta \cdot \frac{1 - \epsilon^t}{1 - \epsilon} + \epsilon^t q_0 . \tag{27}$$

Using (27), q_t is predicted from the following quantities, considered as given: the structural parameters, which determine δ, ϵ; the initial value q_0 ; and time.[16] In fact, (27) is the equation of the time schedule for q_t in (23); it is the solution of the "final equation" (24). Equation (27), together with the analogous one for price p_t , corresponds to the reduced form previously defined for static systems, since equation (27), like (7) or (13), relates an endogenous (or jointly dependent) variable to the independent quantities only. However, we have already mentioned other forms that can be used in a dynamic system to predict the future value of an endogenous variable. As the reader will remember, those other forms included as given the lagged values of the endogenous variable to be predicted or of other endogenous variables.

We can now readmit changes of exogenous variables in our example. Suppose that the intercept α^d of the demand curve is not a constant but a variable depending on the size of the population, and therefore determined outside of our system (21), (22). Suppose that α^d takes successive values α_0^d , α_1^d , $\cdots$. The demand equation (22) is replaced by

$$p_t = \alpha_t^d + \beta^d q_t . \tag{28}$$

The "final equations" change accordingly; (24) becomes

$$q_t = \delta_t + \epsilon q_{t-1} , \tag{29}$$

where $\delta_t = \alpha^s + \beta^s \alpha_{t-1}^d$. The reduced-form equation (27) becomes

$$q_t = \delta_t + \epsilon \delta_{t-1} + \cdots + \epsilon^{t-1} \delta_1 + \epsilon^t q_0 . \tag{30}$$

It is now, of course, impossible to predict the endogenous variable q from the constants (ϵ and q_0) only; one has to take account also of all

[14] Also called the "separated form" [Marschak, 1950, Sections 2.4.5 and 2.5.3].

[15] Also called the "resolved form" [Marschak, 1950, Sections 2.4.5 and 2.5.3].

[16] The equilibrium values are obtained, for $-1 < \epsilon < 0$, by putting $t = \infty$ Thus, in our numerical case ($\epsilon = \beta^d \cdot \beta^s = -\frac{1}{2}$, $\delta = 2$), we obtain $q_\infty = \frac{4}{3}$, which confirms (23). If $\epsilon = -1$, the oscillation has constant amplitude; if $\epsilon < -1$, the oscillation is "explosive." If $\epsilon > 0$, the path is nonoscillatory but converges to a constant if $\epsilon < 1$. Thus, equilibrium values for q exist only if $|\epsilon| < 1$.

the past values of the exogenous variables (δ and therefore α^d) if one uses the reduced-form equation (30). Alternatively, one can take into account only some of those past values but must then employ as additional predictors the past values of the predicted endogenous variable [as in (29)] or of other endogenous variables [as in (28) when combined with (21)].

Changes in exogenous variables will, of course, affect the time schedules of the endogenous variables. This fact is generally recognized in the case of annual seasons. But it is not always recognized with sufficient clarity by those who try to discover longer wave-like (so-called cyclical) regularities of the paths of economic variables without first eliminating the effects of noneconomic variables,[17] or try to predict future waves from the past ones without regard for possible changes in the noneconomic conditions.

Let us now replace observable exogenous influences by nonobservable random disturbances. Modify our example (21), (22) by letting the supply equation undergo random shifts. That is, replace α^s in (21) by $\alpha^s + u^s$, where u^s is a nonobservable random variable which we shall, to begin with, assume to have an unchanging probability distribution. For example, u_t^s may measure the effect of weather on crops in the year t, and we assume that weather in one year is independent of that in any of the preceding years but has the same probability distribution; this is a situation similar to that in which lots are drawn from a sequence of urns, lots of a given kind being present in each urn in the same proportion. To fix ideas, let this distribution be normal, with zero mean and variance σ_u^2. The distribution is now a part of the structure, which is described, in addition, by the following equations, with fixed values attached to each parameter denoted by a Greek letter and also to the initial values q_0, p_0:

(31) $$q_t = \alpha^s + \beta^s p_{t-1} + u_t^s \quad \text{(behavior of suppliers)},$$

(32) $$p_t = \alpha^d + \beta^d q_t \quad \text{(behavior of demanders)}.$$

The "final equations"[18] (difference equations in single endogenous variables) (24) and (25) now become "stochastic" (i.e., involve random variables). In particular, equation (24) is replaced by

(33) $$q_t = \delta + \epsilon q_{t-1} + u_t^s.$$

Each successive value of q is a random variable whose distribution depends on the value actually taken by q at the preceding point (or, generally, points) of time. The path of q (and also of p), instead of being a

[17] See Marschak [1949].

[18] This is the "separated form" of footnote 14.

sequence of constants as in (23), has become a "stochastic process." The equation of the path [viz., the reduced-form equation (27)] now becomes a "stochastic equation." The reader will easily obtain, by the same recurrent procedures as before,

$$q_t = \delta \cdot \frac{1 - \epsilon^t}{1 - \epsilon} + \epsilon^t q_0 + w_t, \tag{34}$$

where

$$w_t = u_t^s + \epsilon u_{t-1}^s + \cdots + \epsilon^{t-1} u_1^s. \tag{35}$$

Since $u_1^s, u_2^s, \cdots$ all have zero means, so has, by (35), w_t, the random component of q_t. Since $u_1^s, u_2^s, \cdots$ were assumed independent, the variance of w_t (and therefore of q_t) is the sum of the variances of $u_t^s, \epsilon u_{t-1}^s$, . . . and is therefore equal to

$$\sigma_{w_t}^2 = \sigma_u^2(1 - \epsilon^{2t})/(1 - \epsilon^2). \tag{36}$$

As t increases, this variance approaches a constant, provided that the absolute value of ϵ is smaller than one. (In our numerical example, $\epsilon = -\frac{1}{2}$ and $\sigma_{w_t}^2$ approaches $\frac{4}{3}\sigma_u^2$.) But q_t itself does not approach any equilibrium value. In this and other respects the path actually described by each endogenous variable will differ from the path (23) generated by the corresponding nonstochastic structure (21), (22). In fact, a stochastic structure may generate explosive oscillations even though the corresponding nonstochastic structure [such as (21), (22), with $\beta^s\beta^d = \epsilon = 1$] produces oscillations with a constant amplitude.[19]

However, the prediction procedure is similar to that of the nonstochastic case if the concept of prediction is appropriately modified (as in Section 7) in the sense of stating the probability that, at a given time, the endogenous variable in question will fall within a given interval. Analogously to the nonstochastic case, predictions can be made either from the structural quantities only [as in (34) and (36), where the predictors are δ, ϵ, q_0, and σ_u^2]; or from the past values of the endogenous variable that is being predicted [as in (33)]; or, more generally, from the past values of all endogenous variables.

If we now reintroduce changes in exogenous variables (such as α^d in a previous example), these will have to enter the equations used for prediction. In fact, under the conditions stated so far, the past values of endogenous variables play the same role as exogenous variables in that they are independent of present random shocks. In this case both the exogenous and the lagged endogenous variables determine the current values of the endogenous variables but are independent of them. They

[19] See Frisch [1933a] and Hurwicz [1945].

are, accordingly, called "predetermined," while the current endogenous variables are called "jointly dependent."[20]

This similarity between exogenous and lagged endogenous variables ceases to exist, however, if we drop our assumption that successive random shocks (the random supply shifts u_1^s, u_2^s, . . . due to weather in our example) are independent. If, for example, we consider not annual but daily weather records, the independence of successive shocks may have to be ruled out. Instead, these shocks u_1^s, u_2^s, . . . themselves may constitute a stochastic process, each shock depending on one or more of its predecessors. Since the lagged endogenous variable q_{t-1} depends on the shock u_{t-1}^s, and this is correlated with u_t^s, q_{t-1} is not independent of u_t^s. Therefore q_{t-1} is not predetermined. It is determined, jointly with $q_1, \ldots, q_{t-2}, q_t, q_{t+1}, \ldots$, by the exogenous variables, the coefficients of the structural equations [such as (31) and (32)], and the joint distribution of successive shocks entering all of the structural equations.[21] Whenever we use weekly or even quarterly instead of annual time series, we must be wary of predictions that use lagged endogenous variables as though they were exogenous.

The conclusions of the previous sections can now be generalized to the case of structures that are both stochastic and dynamic. Policy consists in changing those elements of the structure and those exogenous variables that are under the policy-maker's control. Given the values of the uncontrollable features of the structure and of the uncontrollable exogenous variables, the technician's task is to predict which stochastic processes will be generated by the various proposed policies. The variables that are thus predicted are the potentially observable (and hence possibly erroneous, because of measurement errors) values of some economic quantities of interest to the policy-maker. To make his best decision, the policy-maker ranks these alternative outcomes according to his preferences. For example, his objectives may include high income averaged over time, but also small intensity of variations in time, and, in addition, a high degree of predictability (small prediction intervals for a given probability level). These objectives may conflict, so he will rank the various combinations of average income, stability, predictability, etc. [for example, by ascribing to them weights analogous to 1 and ω in (12)].

As in the cases treated earlier, knowledge of past structure is necessary if the policies under consideration and the expected changes of uncon-

[20] Compare footnote 3. See Koopmans [1950c, Table, p. 406].

[21] In our example this joint distribution involves only $u_1^s, \cdots, u_t^s, \cdots$. The properties of this distribution, such as, for example, the ("serial") correlation coefficient between successive pairs u_{t-1}^s, u_t^s, must be considered part of the structure.

trolled conditions involve not only changes in exogenous variables but also changes in the structure itself.

10. "Steering Wheel" and Automatisms

To the extent to which economic fluctuations are regarded as an evil, policies can be suggested that will dampen such fluctuations. Through an appropriate change of controlled exogenous variables or controlled structural parameters, the jerky path described by national income and other economic aggregates in the last hundred years or so may be replaced by a smoother one in the future. In particular, jumps due to sudden changes of exogenous variables or to rare, but nonetheless possible, large random disturbances may be counteracted by the construction of appropriate "shock-absorbers." If the existing structure is known, one can attempt to find the extent to which a given and feasible change in the institutional characteristics of the structure would affect certain properties of the oscillatory path of an important economic variable, such as the wave frequency, or the so-called damping ratio between the amplitudes of two successive waves in the absence of new impulses. In this way Tinbergen [1939, p. 169] tried to measure the effect of increasing or decreasing the (properly defined) rigidity of wages or of prices upon the shape of the business fluctuations.

Economic history knows remarkable examples of stabilizing institutions. Possibly the best known is the unwritten law that is said to have ruled the conduct of the Bank of England during the nineteenth century. Any serious change in the balance of payments, as indicated by the outflow or inflow of gold, was counteracted by changes in the discount rate. More recently, in the discussion of the stabilization of employment and of the price level, institutional rules were proposed that would obligate the monetary or fiscal authorities to take specified measures that would nip deflations and inflations in the bud.

It has been argued that the formulation of such rules need not presuppose any knowledge of economic structure or, in particular, of its numerical characteristics. As Lerner [1941] put it, the motorist, ignorant of the car mechanism, steers his wheel quite successfully, responding instantaneously to changes in the surface and the direction of the road. Other economists have even suggested what we may call "pilotless" devices. Thus, income tax receipts, at a tax rate fixed once and for all, will rise and fall with money income, thus counteracting inflation or deflation. (Such automatisms have been called, e.g., by Hart [1945], "built-in flexibilities".) Again, it has been argued that the knowledge of economic structure is not necessary if one wants to stabilize the economy by such devices.

Library
I.U.P.
Indiana, Pa.
330.182 H761a c.1

Our previous conclusions (Sections 3 and 8) can be applied. There is a difference between changing the exogenous variables and changing the structure. If a certain rule of fiscal or monetary action in response to changes in national income or in price level has been tried out long enough, in various doses and with various delays, such experience can indeed suffice to determine when and how intensely the measure should be applied. If income tax has been operating in various situations and at various tax rates, it is possible to estimate the tax rate that would best fulfill the task of damping fluctuations of national income. In such cases we have merely to fit an empirical relation between, say, bank-reserve ratios or income-tax rates, on the one hand, and some measure of the violence of price or national income fluctuations on the other. The case is then indeed analogous to that of Lerner's motorist, or, for that matter, to the case of the firm that (as in Section 3) collected experience on the effect of output upon profit without ever bothering to explain this effect by the existing behavior of buyers, the cost structure, and the rate of the excise tax on the firm's product.

Suppose, however, that the institution in question is to be introduced for the first time. To fix in advance the rule of monetary action that will stabilize prices and national income most quickly and effectively, even within a large margin of error, it is necessary to know, for example, the lags and elasticities involved in the relation describing consumers' response to changes in national income, prices, cash balances, etc., and the lags and elasticities involved in other structural relations at a time when the institution was not in force. To experiment with the institution would require too much trial and error.[22]

11. Mathematics and Prediction

All of the foregoing was concerned with the logic of economic knowledge and of its uses. This logic is the same whether or not mathematical symbols are used. However, mathematical presentation is of great help in testing whether a set of structural relations proposed by a theorist is internally consistent and whether it can be determined numerically from observations. Mathematical presentation is hardly avoidable when appropriate statistical methods are to be applied to observations in order

[22] James Angell [1947, p. 291] sees here "the familiar problem of taking the right compensatory action *promptly* enough and in the right degree. . . . How much change in what indices should be the signal for how big a change in what fiscal and monetary operations, to offset or reverse a process of undesired general change which is *already* under way? Not only the nature of the actually current movement but the effects of the compensation measures themselves . . . must be gauged . . . if the result is not to be merely the imposition of a new set of 'artificial' or 'induced' fluctuations on those already operating."

to estimate the structure or (if no structural change is envisaged) to estimate its reduced form.

As stated in Section 7, the technician cannot be blamed if a certain kind of data results in a predicted range of values that is so wide, or has such a small probability attached to it, as to be useless. The mathematical method and result will merely reveal what otherwise might remain concealed. Mathematics does not suppress any information available for other methods, and it makes clearer when and how additional information must be used—for example, to extend the time series, to supplement them by cross-section data such as attitude surveys, or to insert additional knowledge on technology and institutions.

12. Conclusion[23]

This chapter has been concerned with the type of knowledge useful or necessary for determining the best policy. In particular, the circumstances were stated under which the choice of best policy requires the knowledge of "structure." Structure was defined as a set of conditions which did not change while observations were made but which might change in the future. If a specified change of structure is expected or intended, prediction of variables of interest to the policy-maker requires some knowledge of past structure. It follows that if among the policies considered there are some that involve structural changes, then the choice of the policy best calculated to achieve given ends presupposes knowledge of the structure that has prevailed before.

In economics, the conditions that constitute a structure are (1) a set of relations describing human behavior and institutions as well as technological laws and involving, in general, nonobservable random disturbances and nonobservable random errors of measurement; (2) the joint probability distribution of these random quantities.

Economic theories try to explain observed facts by postulating plausible human behavior under given institutional and technological conditions. To be consistent with facts, they should also introduce random disturbances and errors. Thus every economic theory susceptible to factual tests must describe a structure or a class of structures.

It follows that a theory may appear unnecessary for policy decisions until a certain structural change is expected or intended. It becomes necessary then. Since it is difficult to specify in advance what structural changes may be visualized later, it is almost certain that a broad analysis of economic structure, later to be filled out in detail according to needs, is not a wasted effort.

Thus, practice requires theory.

[23] See Marschak [1947b].

CHAPTER II

IDENTIFICATION PROBLEMS IN ECONOMIC MODEL CONSTRUCTION

BY TJALLING C. KOOPMANS[1]

I. INTRODUCTION

The construction of dynamic economic models has become an important tool for the analysis of economic fluctuations and for related problems of policy. In these models, macro-economic variables are thought of as determined by a *complete system of equations*. The meaning of the term "complete" is discussed more fully below. At present it may suffice to describe a complete system as one in which there are as many equations as endogenous variables, that is, variables whose formation is to be "explained" by the equations. The equations are usually of, at most, four kinds: equations of economic behavior, institutional rules, technological laws of transformation, and identities. We shall use the term structural equations to comprise all four types of equations.

Systems of structural equations may be composed entirely on the basis of economic "theory." By this term we shall understand the combination of (a) principles of economic behavior derived from general observation—partly introspective, partly through interview or experience—of the motives of economic decisions, (b) knowledge of legal and institutional rules restricting individual behavior (tax schedules, price controls, reserve requirements, etc.), (c) technological knowledge, and (d) carefully constructed definitions of variables. Alternatively, a structural

[1] I am indebted to present and former Cowles Commission staff members and to my students for valuable critical comments regarding contents and presentation of this chapter. An earlier version of this paper was presented before the Chicago Meeting of the Econometric Society in December 1947. This chapter is reprinted, with minor revisions and the addition of the sixth example in Section 2, from *Econometrica*, Vol. 17, April, 1949, pp. 125–144. Boldface numbers in brackets refer to the list of references at the end of the chapter.

equation system may be determined on the dual basis of such "theory" combined with systematically collected statistical data for the relevant variables for a given period and country or other unit. In this chapter we shall discuss certain problems that arise out of model construction in the second case.

Where statistical data are used as one of the foundation stones on which the equation system is erected, the modern methods of statistical inference are an indispensable instrument. However, without economic "theory" as another foundation stone, it is impossible to make such statistical inference apply directly to the equations of economic behavior which are most relevant to analysis and to policy discussion. Statistical inference unsupported by economic theory applies to whatever statistical regularities and stable relationships can be discerned in the data.[2] Such purely empirical relationships when discernible are likely to be due to the presence and persistence of the underlying structural relationships, and (if so) could be deduced from a knowledge of the latter. However, the direction of this deduction cannot be reversed—from the empirical to the structural relationships—except possibly with the help of a theory which specifies the form of the structural relationships, the variables which enter into each, and any further details supported by prior observation or deduction therefrom. The more detailed these specifications are made in the model, the greater scope is thereby given to statistical inference from the data to the structural equations. We propose to study the limits to which statistical inference, from the data to the structural equations (other than definitions), is subject, and the manner in which these limits depend on the support received from economic theory.

This problem has attracted recurrent discussion in econometric literature, with varying terminology and degree of abstraction. Reference is made to Pigou [**16**], Henry Schultz [**17**, especially Chapter II, Section IIIc], Frisch [**4**, **5**], Marschak [**15**, especially Sections IV and V], Haavelmo [**6**, especially Chapter V]. An attempt to systematize the terminology and to formalize the treatment of the problem has been made over the past few years by various authors connected in one way or another with the Cowles Commission for Research in Economics. Since the purpose of this article is expository, I shall draw freely on the work by Koopmans and Rubin [**14**], Wald [**19**], Hurwicz [**7**, **8**], Koopmans and Reiersöl [**13**], without specific acknowledgment in each case. We shall proceed by discussing a sequence of examples, all drawn from econometrics, rather than by a formal logical presentation, which can be found in references [**14**], [**7**], and [**13**].

[2] See T. C. Koopmans [**12**].

2. Concepts and Examples

The *first example*, already frequently discussed, is that of a competitive market for a single commodity, of which the price p and the quantity q are determined through the intersection of two rectilinear schedules, of demand and supply respectively, with instantaneous response of quantity to price in both cases. For definiteness' sake, we shall think of observations as applying to successive periods in time. We shall further assume that the slope coefficients α and γ of the demand and supply schedules respectively are constant through time, but that the levels of the two schedules are subject to not directly observable shifts from an equilibrium level. The structural equations can then be written as:

$$(1) \quad \begin{cases} \text{(1d)} & q + \alpha p + \epsilon = u \quad \text{(demand)} \\ \text{(1s)} & q + \gamma p + \eta = v \quad \text{(supply)}. \end{cases}$$

Concerning the shift variables u and v we shall assume that they are random drawings from a stable joint probability distribution with mean values equal to zero:

$$(2) \qquad Q(u, v), \qquad \mathcal{E}u = 0, \qquad \mathcal{E}v = 0.$$

We shall introduce a few terms which we shall use with corresponding meaning in all examples. The not directly observable shift variables u, v are called *latent variables*, as distinct from the *observed variables*, p, q. We shall further distinguish *structure* and *model*. By a structure we mean the combination of a specific set of structural equations (1) (such as is obtained by giving specific numerical values to α, γ, ϵ, η) and a specific distribution function (2) of the latent variables (for instance, a normal distribution with specific, numerically given, variances and covariance). By a model we mean only a specification of the form of the structural equations (for instance, their linearity and a designation of the variables occurring in each equation), and of a class of functions to which the distribution function of the latent variables belongs (for instance, the class of all normal bivariate distributions with zero means). More abstractly, a model can be defined as a set of structures. For a useful analysis, the model will be chosen so as to incorporate relevant a priori knowledge or hypotheses as to the economic behavior to be described. For instance, the model here discussed can often be narrowed down by the usual specification of a downward sloping demand curve and an upward sloping supply curve:

$$(3) \qquad \alpha > 0, \qquad \gamma < 0.$$

Let us assume for the sake of argument that the observations are produced by a structure, to be called the "true" structure, which is contained in (permitted by) the model. In order to exclude all questions of sampling variability (which are a matter for later separate inquiry), let us further make the unrealistic assumption that the number of observations produced by this structure can be increased indefinitely. What inferences can be drawn from these observations toward the "true" structure?

A simple reflection shows that in our present example neither the "true" demand schedule nor the "true" supply schedule can be determined from any number of observations. To put the matter geometrically, let each of the two identical scatter diagrams in Figures 1A and 1B represent the jointly observed values of p and q. A structure compatible with these observations can be obtained as follows: Select arbitrarily "presumptive" slope coefficients α and γ of the demand and supply schedules. Through each point $S(p, q)$ of the scatter diagrams draw two straight lines with slopes given by these coefficients. The presumptive demand and supply schedules will intersect the quantity axis at distances $-\epsilon + u$ and $-\eta + v$ from the origin, *provided* the presumptive slope coefficients α and γ are the "true" ones. We shall assume this to be the case in Figure 1A. In that case the values of ϵ and η can be found from the consideration that the averages of u and v in a sufficiently large sample of observations are practically equal to zero.

However, nothing in the situation considered permits us to distinguish the "true" slopes α, γ (as shown in Figure 1A) from any other presumptive slopes (as illustrated in Figure 1B). Any arbitrary set of slope coefficients $\alpha^{\oplus}$, $\gamma^{\oplus}$ (supplemented by corresponding values $\epsilon^{\oplus}$, $\eta^{\oplus}$ of the intercepts) represents another, statistically just as acceptable, hypothesis concerning the formation of the observed variables.

Let us formulate the same remark algebraically in preparation for further examples in more dimensions. Let the numerical values of the "true" parameters $\alpha, \gamma, \epsilon, \eta$ in (1) be known to an individual who, taking delight in fraud, multiplies the demand equation (1d) by $2/3$, the supply equation (1s) by $1/3$, and adds the result to form an equation

$$q + \frac{2\alpha + \gamma}{3} p + \frac{2\epsilon + \eta}{3} = u^{\oplus}, \tag{4d}$$

which he proclaims to be the demand equation. This equation is actually different from the "true" demand equation (1d) because (3) implies $\alpha \neq \gamma$. Similarly he multiplies the same equations by $2/5$ and $3/5$ respectively, say, to produce an equation

$$q + \frac{2\alpha + 3\gamma}{5} p + \frac{2\epsilon + 3\eta}{5} = v^{\oplus}, \tag{4s}$$

different from the "true" supply equation (1s), but which he presents as if it were the supply equation. If our prankster takes care to select his multipliers in such a manner as not to violate the sign rules (3) imposed by the model, the deceit cannot be discovered by statistical analysis of any number of observations.[3] For the equations (4), being derived from (1), are satisfied by all data that satisfy the "true" equations (1). Moreover, being of the same "form" as equations (1), the equations (4) are equally acceptable a priori.

Our *second example* differs from the first only in that the model specifies a supply equation containing in addition an exogenous variable. To be definite, we shall think of the supply of an agricultural product as affected by the rainfall r during a critical period of crop growth[4] or crop

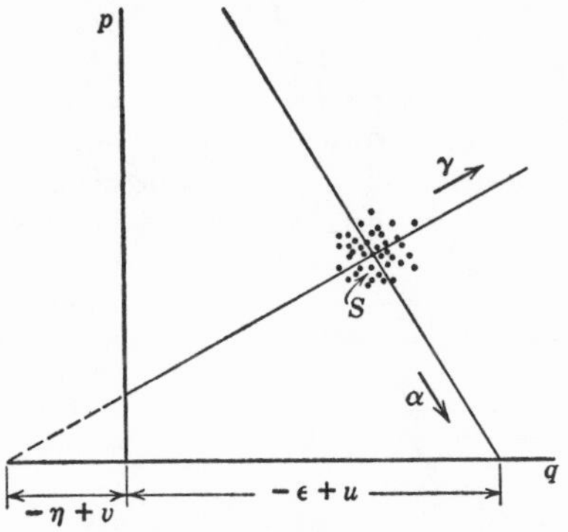

FIGURE 1A

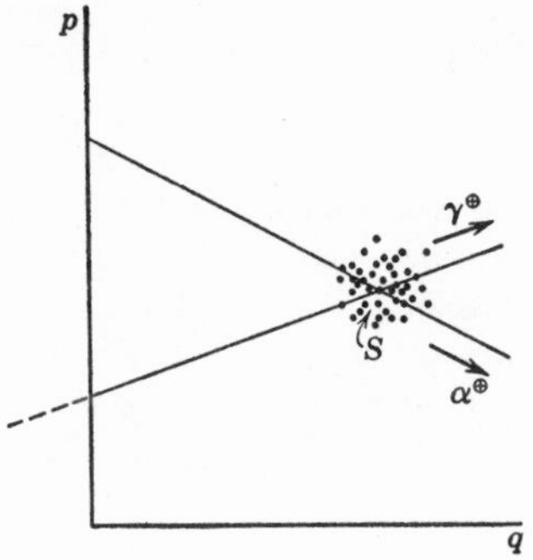

FIGURE 1B

gathering. This variable is called exogenous to our model to express the plausible hypothesis that rainfall r, while affecting the market of the commodity concerned, is not itself affected thereby. Put in mathematical terms, this hypothesis specifies that the disturbances u and v in

$$(5) \quad \begin{cases} \text{(5d)} \quad q + \alpha p \qquad\quad + \epsilon = u \quad \text{(demand)} \\ \text{(5s)} \quad q + \gamma p + \delta r + \eta = v \quad \text{(supply)} \end{cases}$$

are statistically independent[5] of the values assumed by r.

[3] The deceit could be discovered if the model were to specify a property (e.g., independence) of the disturbances u and v that is not shared by $u^{\oplus} = (2u + v)/3$ and $v^{\oplus} = (2u + 3v)/5$. We have not made such a specification.

[4] With respect to this example, the assumption of a linear relationship can be maintained only if we think of a certain limited range of variation in rainfall. Another difficulty with the example is that for most agricultural products, the effect of price on supply is delayed instead of instantaneous, as here assumed. A practically instantaneous effect can, however, be expected in the gathering of wild fruits of nature.

[5] It is immaterial for this definition whether the exogenous variable is regarded

It will be seen at a glance that the supply equation still cannot be determined from a sample of any size. If, starting from "true" structural equations (5) we multiply by $-\frac{1}{2}$ and $\frac{3}{2}$, say, and add the results to obtain a pretended supply equation,

$$q + \frac{3\gamma - \alpha}{2} p + \frac{3\delta}{2} r + \frac{3\eta - \epsilon}{2} = v^{\oplus} \tag{6s}$$

of the same prescribed form as (5s), any data will satisfy this equation (6s) as well as they satisfy the two equations (5).

A similar reasoning can *not* be applied to the demand equation in the present model. Any attempt to construct another pretended demand equation by a linear combination involving the supply equation (5s) would introduce into that pretended demand equation the variable r which, by the hypotheses underlying the model, does not belong in it.

It might be thought that, if r has the properties of a random variable, its presence in the pretended demand equation might be concealed because its "contribution" cannot be distinguished from the random disturbance in that equation. To be specific, if $\frac{4}{3}$ and $-\frac{1}{3}$ are arbitrarily selected multipliers, the disturbance in the pretended demand equation might be thought to take the form

$$u^{\oplus} = \frac{4u - v}{3} - \frac{\delta}{3} r.$$

This, however, would violate the specification that r is exogenous and that therefore r and $u^{\oplus}$ are to be statistically independent as well as r and (u, v). The relevance of the exogenous character of r to our present discussion is clearly illustrated by this remark.

Our analysis of the second example suggests (and below we shall cite a theorem establishing proof) that a sufficiently large sample does indeed contain information with regard to the parameters α, ϵ of the demand equation (it being understood that such information is conditional upon

as a given function of time—a concept perhaps applicable to a variable set by government policy—or as itself a random variable determined by some other structure involving probability distributions—a concept applicable particularly to weather variables. It should further be noted that we postulate independence between r and (u, v), not between r and (p, q), although we wish to express that r "is not affected by" p and q. The meaning to be given to the latter phrase is that in other equations explaining the formation of r the variables (p, q) do not enter. Precisely this is implied in the statistical independence of r and (u, v), because (p, q) is, by virtue of (5), statistically dependent on (u, v), and any role of (p, q) in the determination of r would therefore create statistical dependence between r and (u, v). On the other hand, the postulated statistical independence between r and (u, v) is entirely compatible with the obvious influence, by virtue of (5), of r on (p, q).

the validity of the model). It can already be seen that there must be the following exception to the foregoing statement. If in fact (although the model does not require it) rainfall has no influence on supply, that is, if in the "true" structure $\delta = 0$, then any number of observations must necessarily be compatible with the model (1) and hence does not convey information with regard to either the demand equation or the supply equation.

As a *third example* we consider a model obtained from the preceding one by the inclusion in the demand equation of consumers' income i as an additional exogenous variable. We assume the exogenous character of consumers' income merely for reasons of exposition, and in full awareness of the fact that actually price and quantity on any market do affect income directly to some extent, while furthermore the disturbances u and v affecting the market under consideration may well be correlated with similar disturbances in several other markets which together have a considerably larger effect on consumers' income.

The structural equations are now

$$
7)\quad \begin{cases} \text{(7d)} \qquad q + \alpha p + \beta i \qquad\qquad + \epsilon = u \qquad \text{(demand)} \\ \text{(7s)} \qquad q + \gamma p \qquad\qquad + \delta r + \eta = v \qquad \text{(supply)}. \end{cases}
$$

Since each of the two equations now excludes a variable specified for the other equation, neither of them can be replaced by a different linear combination of the two without altering its form. This suggests, and proof is cited below, that from a sufficiently large sample of observations, the demand equation can be accurately determined provided rainfall actually affects supply ($\delta \neq 0$), and the supply equation can be determined provided consumers' income actually affects demand ($\beta \neq 0$).

The *fourth example* is designed to show that situations may occur in which some but not all parameters of a structural equation can be determined from sufficiently many observations. Let the demand equation contain both this year's income i_0 and last year's income i_{-1}, but let the supply equation not contain any variable absent from the demand equation:

$$
(8)\quad \begin{cases} \text{(8d)} \qquad q + \alpha p + \beta_0 i_0 + \beta_{-1} i_{-1} + \epsilon = u \\ \text{(8s)} \qquad q + \gamma p \qquad\qquad\qquad\qquad + \eta = v. \end{cases}
$$

Now obviously we cannot determine either α or ϵ, because linear combinations of the equations (8) can be constructed which have the same form as (8d) but other[6] values $\alpha^{\oplus}$ and $\epsilon^{\oplus}$ for the coefficients α and ϵ.

[6] As regards $\epsilon^{\oplus}$ this is true whenever $\epsilon \neq \eta$. As regards $\alpha^{\oplus}$ it is safeguarded by (3).

However, as long as (8d) enters with some nonvanishing weight into such a linear combination, the ratio β_{-1}/β_0 is not affected by the substitution of that linear combination for the "true" demand equation. Thus, if the present model is correct, the observations contain information with respect to the relative importance of present and past income to demand, whereas they are silent on the price elasticity of demand.

The *fifth example* shows that an assumption regarding the joint distribution of the disturbances u and v, where justified, may open the door to a determination of a structural equation which is otherwise indeterminate. Returning to the equation system (5) of our second example, we shall now make the model specify in addition that the disturbances u in demand and v in supply are statistically independent, and that the standard deviation σ_u of u does not vanish. Remembering our previous statement that the demand equation can already be determined without the help of such an assumption, it is clear that in attempting to construct a "pretended" supply equation, no linear combination of the "true demand and supply equations (5), other than the "true" supply equation (5s) itself, can be found which preserves the required independence of disturbances in the two equations. Writing λ and $1 - \lambda$ for the multipliers used in forming such a linear combination, the disturbance in the pretended supply equation would be

$$(9) \qquad v^{\oplus} = \lambda u + (1 - \lambda)v.$$

Since u and v are by assumption independent, the disturbance $v^{\oplus}$ of the pretended supply equation is independent of the disturbance u in the demand equation (already found determinable) if and only if $\lambda = 0$, i.e., if the pretended supply equation coincides with the "true" one.

The foregoing reasoning depends essentially on the specification that σ_u in (5) is positive (which can be tested from observations). If σ_u were to turn out small in comparison with σ_v, values of λ could be found that are large enough to make

$$(10) \qquad \gamma^{\oplus} = \lambda\alpha + (1 - \lambda)\gamma, \qquad \eta^{\oplus} = \lambda\epsilon + (1 - \lambda)\eta$$

considerably different from γ and η in (5s), but also small enough to introduce only a slight correlation between $v^{\oplus}$ and u. In this case many observations would be needed for us to derive much benefit from the fact that the supply equation is in principle determinable. However, the question how many observations would be required is a sampling problem and as such is outside the topic of this chapter.

The opposite situation exists, of course, if σ_u is large and σ_v is small. This suggests a *sixth example* in which we do not specify independence of u and v, but instead add to the model of the second example the specification that σ_v not exceed a certain bound, given a priori,

$$\sigma_v \leqslant \sigma_0. \tag{11}$$

If in this case σ_u turns out to be much larger than σ_0, we have from (9)

$$\sigma_{v^\oplus}^2 = \lambda^2\sigma_u^2 + (1 - \lambda)^2\sigma_v^2 + 2\lambda(1 - \lambda)\sigma_{uv}, \tag{12}$$

where σ_{uv} denotes the covariance of u and v. The condition that this expression not exceed σ_0^2 may place on λ certain bounds, which we will not evaluate in detail but which may be narrow enough to allow $\gamma^\oplus$ and $\eta^\oplus$ in (10) only a limited range. In such circumstances, although γ and η cannot be determined with precision no matter how large the number of observations, finite and possibly narrow ranges within which these parameters are included can be determined with increasing precision as the number of observations grows.

We emphasize again the expository character of the foregoing examples. It has already been indicated that the income variable i is not truly exogenous. By assuming it to be so, we have held down the size of the equation system underlying our discussion, and we may as a result have precluded ourselves from seeing indeterminacies that could come to light only by a study of all relationships participating in the formation of the variables involved. It will therefore be necessary to develop criteria by which indeterminacies of the coefficients of larger equation systems can be detected. Before discussing such criteria for linear systems, we shall formalize a few of the concepts used or to be used.

3. The Identification of Structural Parameters

In our discussion we have used the phrase "a parameter that can be determined from a sufficient number of observations." We shall now define this concept more sharply, and give it the name *identifiability* of a parameter. Instead of reasoning, as before, from "a sufficiently large number of observations" we shall base our discussion on a hypothetical knowledge of the probability distribution of the observations, as defined more fully below. It is clear that exact knowledge of this probability distribution cannot be derived from any finite number of observations. Such knowledge is the limit approachable but not attainable by extended observation. By hypothesizing nevertheless the full availability of such knowledge, we obtain a clear separation between problems of statistical inference arising from the variability of finite samples and problems of identification in which we explore the limits to which inference even from an infinite number of observations is subject.

A *structure* has been defined as the combination of a distribution of latent variables and a complete set of structural equations. By a *complete set of equations* we mean a set of as many equations as there are endogenous variables. Each endogenous variable may occur with or without time lags, and should occur without lag in at least one equation. Also, the set should be such as to permit unique determination of the nonlagged values of the endogenous variables from those of the lagged endogenous, the exogenous, and the latent variables. Finally, by *endogenous variables* we mean observed variables which are not exogenous, i.e., variables which are not known or assumed to be statistically independent of the latent variables, and whose occurrence in one or more equations of the set is necessary on grounds of "theory."

It follows from these definitions that, for any specific set of values of the exogenous variables, the distribution of the latent variables (i.e., one of the two components of a given structure) entails or generates, through the structural equations (i.e., the other component of the given structure), a probability distribution of the endogenous variables. The latter distribution is, of course, conditional upon the values specified for the exogenous variables at each time point of observation. This conditional distribution, regarded again as a function of all specified values of exogenous variables, shall be the hypothetical datum for our discussion of identification problems.

We shall call two structures S and $S^{\oplus}$ (observationally) *equivalent* (or indistinguishable) if the two conditional distributions of endogenous variables generated by S and $S^{\oplus}$ are identical for all possible values of the exogenous variables. We shall call a structure S permitted by the model (uniquely) *identifiable* within that model if there is no other equivalent structure $S^{\oplus}$ contained in the model. Although the proof has not yet been completely indicated, it may be stated in illustration that in our third example almost all structures permitted by the model are identifiable. The only exceptions are those with either $\beta = 0$ or $\delta = 0$ (or both). In the first and second examples, however, no structure is identifiable, although in the second example we have stated that the demand equation by itself is determinate. To cover such cases we shall say that a certain parameter θ of a structure S is uniquely *identifiable* within a model if that parameter has the same value for all structures $S^{\oplus}$ equivalent to S contained in the model. Finally, a *structural equation* is said to be *identifiable* if all its parameters are identifiable.

This completes the formal definitions with which we shall operate. They can be summarized in the statement that anything is called identifiable that can be determined from a knowledge of the distribution of the endogenous variables, given the model (which is accepted as valid).

We now proceed to a discussion of the application of this concept to linear models of the kind illustrated by our examples.

4. Identifiability Criteria in Linear Models

In our discussion of these examples it has been possible to conclude that a certain structural equation is not identifiable whenever we are able to construct a different equation, obtained by linear combination of some or all structural equations, which likewise meets the specifications of the model. In the opposite case, where we could show that no such different linear combination exists, we could not yet conclude definitely that the equation involved is identifiable. Could other operations than linear combination perhaps be used to derive equations of the same form?

We shall now cite a theorem which establishes that no such other operations can exist. The theorem relates to models specifying a complete set of structural equations as defined above, and in which a given set of endogenous and exogenous variables enters linearly. Any time lags with which these variables may occur are supposed to be integral multiples of the time interval between successive observations. Furthermore, the exogenous variables (considered as different variables whenever they occur with a different time lag) are assumed not to be linearly dependent, i.e., in the functional sense.[7] Finally, although simultaneous disturbances in different structural equations are permitted to be correlated, it is assumed that any disturbances operating in different time units (whether in the same or in different structural equations) are statistically independent.

Suppose the model does not specify anything beyond what has been stated. That is, no restrictions are specified yet that exclude some of the variables from specific equations. Obviously, with respect to such a broad model, not a single structural equation is identifiable. However, a theorem has been proved [**14**] to the effect that, given a structure S within that model, any structure $S^{\oplus}$ in the model, equivalent to S, can be derived from S by replacing each equation by some linear combination of some or all equations of S.

It will be clear that this theorem remains true if the model is narrowed down by excluding certain variables from certain equations, or by other

[7] The criteria of identifiability to be stated would require amended formulation if certain identities involving endogenous variables were such that each variable occurring in them also occurs, in some equation of the complete set, with a time lag, and if this time lag were the same for all such variables. In this case, a complication arises from linear (functional) dependence among lagged endogenous (and possibly exogenous) variables.

restrictions on the parameters. Thus, whenever in our examples we have concluded that different *linear* combinations of the same form prescribed for a structural equation did not exist, we have therewith established the identifiability of that equation. More generally, the analysis of the identifiability of a structural equation in a linear model consists in a study of the possibility of producing a different equation of the same prescribed form by linear combination of all equations. If this is shown to be impossible, the equation in question is thereby proved to be identifiable. To find criteria for the identifiability of a structural equation in a linear model is therefore a straightforward mathematical problem, to which the solution has been given elsewhere [**14**]. Here we shall state without proof what the criteria are. They apply to the case where the additional specifications in the model take the form of (a) exclusions of specified variables from specified equations (or, more generally, specified homogeneous linear restrictions on the coefficients of specified equations) and (b) a rule of normalization (nonhomogeneous restriction) on each equation, to preclude the trivial multiplication of all coefficients of an equation by a constant. The latter type of restriction was implicitly introduced in the examples of Section 2 by giving to the variable q the coefficient 1 in each equation.

A *necessary condition* for the identifiability of a structural equation within a given linear model is that the number[8] of variables excluded from that equation (more generally, the number of linear restrictions on the parameters of that equation) be at least equal to the number (G, say) of structural equations, less one. This is known as the *order condition* of identifiability. A *necessary and sufficient condition* for the identifiability of a structural equation within a linear model, restricted only by the exclusion of certain variables from certain equations, is that we can form at least one nonvanishing determinant of order $G - 1$ out of those coefficients, properly arranged, with which the variables excluded from that structural equation appear in the $G - 1$ other structural equations. This is known as the *rank condition* of identifiability. (It can also be stated in more general form for the case of more general homogeneous linear restrictions.)

The application of these criteria to the foregoing examples is straightforward. In all cases considered, the number of structural equations is $G = 2$. Therefore, any of the equations involved can be identifiable through exclusion of variables only if at least $G - 1 = 1$ variable is excluded from it by the model. If this is so, the equation is identifiable provided at least one of the variables so excluded occurs in the other

[8] Again counting lagged variables as separate variables.

equation with nonvanishing coefficient (a determinant of order 1 equals the value of its one and only element). For instance, the conclusion already reached at the end of the discussion of our second example is now confirmed: The identifiability of the demand equation (5d) is only then safeguarded by the exclusion of the variable r from that equation if $\delta \neq 0$, that is, if that variable not only possibly but actually occurs in the supply equation.

5. The Statistical Test of A Priori Uncertain Identifiability

The example just quoted shows that the identifiability of one structural parameter, θ, say, may depend on the value of another structural parameter, η, say. In such situations, which are of frequent occurrence, the identifiability of θ cannot be settled by a priori reasoning from the model alone. On the other hand, the identifiability of θ cannot escape all analysis because of possible nonidentifiability of η. As is argued more fully elsewhere [**13**], since the identifiability of any parameter is a property of the distribution of the observations, it is subject to some suitable statistical test, of which the degree of conclusiveness tends to certainty as the number of observations increases indefinitely. The validity of this important conclusion is not limited to linear models.

In the case of a linear model as described in Section 4, the present statement can also be demonstrated explicitly by equivalent reformulation of the rank criterion for identifiability in terms of identifiable parameters only. By the *reduced form* of a complete set of linear structural equations as described in Section 4, we mean the form obtained by solving for each of the *dependent* (i.e., nonlagged endogenous) variables, in terms of the *predetermined* (i.e., exogenous or lagged endogenous) variables, and in terms of transformed disturbances (which are linear functions of the disturbances in the original structural equations). It will be argued more fully in Chapter VI, Section 1.6, that the coefficients of the equations of the reduced form are parameters of the joint distribution of the observations, and as such are always identifiable.

It may be stated here without proof that the following rank criterion for identifiability of a given structural equation, in terms of coefficients of the reduced form, is equivalent to that stated in Section 4 above: Consider only those equations of the reduced form that solve for dependent variables, specified by the model as occurring in (strictly, as not excluded from) the structural equation in question. Let the number of the equations so obtained be G^{Δ}, where $G^{\Delta} \leqslant G$. Now form the matrix $\Pi_{\Delta,**}$ of the coefficients, in these G^{Δ} equations, of those predetermined variables that are excluded by the model from the structural equation involved. A necessary and sufficient condition for the identifiability of that structural equation is that the rank of $\Pi_{\Delta,**}$ be equal to $G^{\Delta} - 1$. A proof of this condition is given in Chapter VI, Section 4.4. A direct proof of the equivalence of the two identification criteria is given in Chapter VI, Appendix A.

6. Identification through Disaggregation and Introduction of Specific Explanatory Variables

As a further exercise in the application of these criteria, we shall consider a question which has already been the subject of a discussion between Ezekiel [**2, 3**] and Klein [**9, 10**]. The question is whether identifiability of the investment equation can be attained by the subdivision of the investment variable into separate categories of investment. In the discussion referred to, which took place before the concepts and terminology employed in this article were developed, questions of identifiability were discussed together with questions regarding the merit of particular economic assumptions incorporated in the model, and with questions of the statistical method of estimating parameters that have been recognized as identifiable. In the present context we shall avoid the latter two groups of problems and concentrate on the formal analysis of identifiability, accepting a certain model as economically valid for purposes of discussion.

As a starting point we shall consider a simple model expressing the crudest elements of Keynesian theory. The variables are, in money amounts,

$$(13)\qquad \begin{cases} S & \text{savings} \\ I & \text{investment} \\ Y & \text{income} \\ Y_{-1} & \text{income lagged one year.} \end{cases}$$

The structural equations are:

$$(14)\quad \begin{cases} \text{(14id)} & S - I & & = 0 \\ \text{(14S)} & S & - \alpha_1 Y - \alpha_2 Y_{-1} - \alpha_0 & = u \\ \text{(14I)} & & I - \beta_1 Y - \beta_2 Y_{-1} - \beta_0 & = v. \end{cases}$$

Of these, the first is the well-known savings-investment identity arising from Keynes's definitions of these concepts.[9] The second is a behavior equation of consumers, indicating that the money amount of their

[9] These definitions include in investment all increases in inventory, including undesired inventories remaining in the hands of manufacturers or dealers as a result of falling demand. In principle, therefore, the "investment" equation should include a term or terms explaining such inventory changes. The absence of such

savings (income not spent for consumption) is determined by present and past income, subject to a random disturbance u. The third is a behavior equation of entrepreneurs, indicating that the money amount of investment is determined by present and past income, subject to a random disturbance v.

Since the identity (14id) is fully given a priori, no question of identifiability arises with respect to the first equation. In both the second and third equations, only one variable is excluded which appears in another equation of the model, and no other restrictions on the coefficients are stated.[10] Hence both of these equations already fail to meet the necessary order criterion of identifiability. This could be expected because the two equations connect the same savings-investment variable with the same two income variables, and therefore cannot be distinguished statistically.

Ezekiel attempts to obtain identifiability of the structure by a refinement of the model as a result of subdivision of aggregate investment I into the following four components:

(15a)
- I_1 investment in plant and equipment
- I_2 investment in housing
- I_3 temporary investment: changes in consumers' credit and in business inventories
- I_4 quasi-investment: net contributions from foreign trade and the government budget.

If each of these components were to be related to the same set of explanatory variables as occurs in (14), the disaggregation would be of no help toward identification. Therefore, for each of the four types of investment decisions, Ezekiel introduces a separate explanatory equation, either explicitly or by implication in his verbal comments. In attempting to formulate these explanations in terms of a complete set of behavior equations, we shall introduce two more variables:

(15b)
- H semi-independent cyclical component of housing investment
- E exogenous component of quasi-investment.

---

terms from (14) and from later elaborations thereof may be taken as expressing the "theory" that for annual figures, say, such changes can be regarded as random. Alternatively, investment may be defined so as to exclude undesired inventory changes, and (14id) may be interpreted as an "equilibrium condition," expressing the randomness of such changes by replacing the zero in the right-hand member by a disturbance w. The obvious need for refinement in this crude "theory" does not preclude its use for illustrative purposes.

[10] The normalization requirement that the variables S and I shall have coefficients $+1$ in (14S) and (14I) respectively does not restrict the relationships involved but merely serves to give a common level to coefficients which otherwise would be subject to arbitrary proportional variation.

In addition, linear and quadratic functions of time are introduced as trend terms in some equations by Ezekiel. For purposes of the present discussion, we may as well disregard such trend terms, because they would help toward identification only if they could be excluded a priori from some of the equations while being included in others—a position advocated neither by Ezekiel nor by the present author.

With these qualifications, "Ezekiel's model" can be interpreted as follows:

$$
(16)\begin{cases}
(16\text{id})\ S - I_1 - I_2 - I_3 - I_4 & = 0 \\
(16\text{S})\ S \qquad - \alpha_1 Y - \alpha_2 Y_{-1} \qquad - \alpha_0 & = u \\
(16\text{I}_1)\quad I_1 \qquad - \beta_1 Y - \beta_2 Y_{-1} \qquad - \beta_0 & = v_1 \\
(16\text{I}_2)\quad I_2 \qquad - \gamma_1 Y - \gamma_2 Y_{-1} - H \qquad - \gamma_0 & = v_2 \\
(16\text{I}_3)\quad I_3 \qquad - \delta_1 Y + \delta_1 Y_{-1} \qquad - \delta_0 & = v_3 \\
(16\text{I}_4\quad I_4 - \epsilon_1 Y - \epsilon_2 Y_{-1} \qquad - E - \epsilon_0 & = v_4
\end{cases}
$$

(16id) is the savings-investment identity. (16S) repeats (14S), and (16I_1) is modeled after (14I). More specific explanations are introduced for the three remaining types of investment decisions.

Housing investment decisions I_2 are explained partly on the basis of income[11] Y, partly on the basis of a "semi-independent housing cycle" H. In Ezekiel's treatment H is not an independently observed variable, but a smooth long cycle fitted to I_2. We share Klein's objection [**9,** p. 255] to this procedure, but do not think that his proposal to substitute a linear function of time for H does justice to Ezekiel's argument. The latter definitely thinks of H as produced largely by a long-cycle mechanism peculiar to the housing market, and quotes in support of this view a study by Derksen [**1**] in which this mechanism is analyzed. Derksen constructs an equation explaining residential construction in terms of the rent level, the rate of change of income, the level of building cost in the recent past, and growth in the number of families; he further explains the rent level in terms of income, the number of families, and the stock of dwelling units (all of these subject to substantial time lags). The stock of dwelling units, in its turn, represents an accumulation of past construction diminished by depreciation or demolition. Again accepting without inquiry the economic assumptions involved in these explanations, the point to be made is that H in (16I_2) can be thought to represent specific observable exogenous and *past* endogenous variables.

Temporary investment I_3 is related by Ezekiel to the rate of change in income. Quasi-investment I_4 is related by him partly to income[12] (espe-

[11] We have added a term with Y_{-1} because the exclusion of such a term could hardly be made the basis for a claim of identifiability.

[12] We have again added a term with Y_{-1} on grounds similar to those stated with respect to (16I_2).

cially via government revenue, imports), partly to exogenous factors underlying exports and government expenditure where used as an instrument of policy. The variable E in ($16I_4$) is therefore similar to H in that it can be thought to represent observable exogenous or past endogenous variables.

It cannot be said that this interpretation of the variables H and E establishes the completeness of the set of equations (16) in the sense defined above. The variable H has been found to depend on the past values of certain indubitably endogenous variables (building cost, rent level) of which the present values do not occur in the equation system (16), and which therefore remain unexplained by (16). The reader is asked to accept what could be proved explicitly: that incompleteness of this kind does not invalidate the criteria of identifiability indicated.[13]

Let us then apply our criteria of identifiability to the behavior equations in (16). In each of these, the number of excluded variables is at least 5, i.e., at least the necessary number for identifiability in a model of 6 equations. In order to apply the rank criterion for the identifiability of the savings equation (16S), say, we must consider the matrix

$$\begin{array}{cccccc} (I_1) & (I_2) & (I_3) & (I_4) & (H) & (E) \end{array}$$
$$(17) \qquad \begin{bmatrix} -1 & -1 & -1 & -1 & 0 & 0 \\ 1 & 0 & 0 & 0 & 0 & 0 \\ 0 & 1 & 0 & 0 & -1 & 0 \\ 0 & 0 & 1 & 0 & 0 & 0 \\ 0 & 0 & 0 & 1 & 0 & -1 \end{bmatrix}$$

There are several ways in which a nonvanishing determinant of order 5 can be selected from this matrix. One particular way is to take the columns labeled I_1, I_2, I_3, H, E. It follows that if the present model is valid, the savings equation is indeed identifiable.

It is easily seen that the same conclusion applies to the equations explaining investment decisions of the types I_1 and I_3. Let us now inspect the rank criterion matrix for the identifiability of ($16I_2$):

$$\begin{array}{ccccc} (S) & (I_1) & (I_3) & (I_4) & (E) \end{array}$$
$$(18) \qquad \begin{bmatrix} 1 & -1 & -1 & -1 & 0 \\ 1 & 0 & 0 & 0 & 0 \\ 0 & 1 & 0 & 0 & 0 \\ 0 & 0 & 1 & 0 & 0 \\ 0 & 0 & 0 & 1 & -1 \end{bmatrix}$$

Again the determinant value of this square matrix of order 5 is different from zero. Hence the housing equation is identifiable. A similar analysis

[13] Provided, as indicated in footnote 7, there is no linear functional relationship between the exogenous and lagged endogenous variables occurring in (16).

leads to the same conclusion regarding the equation ($16I_4$) for quasi-investment.

It may be emphasized again that identifiability was attained not through the mere subdivision of total investment, but as a result of the introduction of specific explanatory variables applicable to some but not all components of investment.[14] Whenever such specific variables are available in sufficient number and variety of occurrence, on good grounds of economic theory as defined above, the door has been opened in principle to statistical inference regarding behavior parameters—inference conditional upon the assumptions derived from "theory."

How wide the door has been opened, i.e., how much accuracy of estimation can be attained from given data, is of course a matter depending on many circumstances and to be explored separately by the appropriate procedures of statistical inference.[15] In the present case, the extent to which the exclusion of H and/or E from certain equations contributes to the reliability of estimates of their parameters depends very much on whether or not there are pronounced differences in the time paths of the three *predetermined variables* Y_{-1}, H, E, i.e., the variables determined either exogenously or in earlier time units. These time paths represent in a way the basic patterns of movement in the economic model considered, such that the time paths of all other variables are linear combinations of these three paths, modified by disturbances. If the three basic paths are sufficiently distinct, conditions are favorable for estimation of identifiable parameters. If there is considerable similarity between any two of them, or even if there is only a considerable multiple correlation between the three, conditions are adverse.

7. Implications of the Choice of the Model

It has already been stressed repeatedly that any statistical inference regarding identifiable parameters of economic behavior is conditional

[14] In fact, more specific detail was introduced than the minimum necessary to produce identifiability. Starting again from (14), identifiability can already be obtained if it is possible to break off from investment I some observable exogenous component, like public works expenditure P (supposing that to be exogenous for the sake of argument). Writing $Q = I - P$ for the remainder of investment, (14) is then modified to read

$$(14a)\qquad \begin{cases} S - Q - P & = 0 \\ S - \alpha_1 Y - \alpha_2 Y_{-1} - \alpha_0 & = u \\ Q - \beta_1 Y - \beta_2 Y_{-1} - \beta_0 & = v, \end{cases}$$

of which each equation meets our criteria of identifiability. The intent of this remark is largely formal, because (14a) is not as defensible a "theory" as (16).

[15] We are not concerned here with an evaluation of the particular estimation procedures applied by Ezekiel.

upon the validity of the model. This throws great weight on a correct choice of the model. We shall not attempt to make more than a few tentative remarks about the considerations governing this choice.[16]

It is an important question to what extent certain aspects of a model of the kind considered above are themselves subject to statistical test. For instance, in the model (16) we have specified linearity of each equation, independence of disturbances in successive time units, time lags which are an integral multiple of the chosen unit of time, as well as exclusions of specific variables from specific equations. It is often possible to subject one particular aspect or set of specifications of the model to a statistical test which is conditional upon the validity of the remaining specifications. This is, for instance, the case with respect to the exclusion of any variable from any equation whenever the equation involved is identifiable even without that exclusion. However, at least *four* difficulties arise which point to the need for further fundamental research on the principles of statistical inference.

In the *first* place, on a given basis of maintained hypotheses (not subjected to test) there may be several alternative hypotheses to be tested. For instance, if there are two variables whose exclusion, either jointly or individually, from a given equation is not essential to its identifiability, it is possible to test separately (a) the exclusion of the first variable, or (b) of the second variable, or (c) of both variables simultaneously, as against (d) the exclusion of neither variable. However, instead of three separate tests, of (a) against (d), (b) against (d), and (c) against (d), we need a procedure permitting selection of one of the four alternatives (a), (b), (c), (d). An extension of current theory with regard to the testing of hypotheses, which is concerned mainly with choices between two alternatives, is therefore needed.

Secondly, if certain specifications of a model can be tested given all other specifications, it is usually possible in many different ways to choose the set of "other" specifications that is not subjected to test. It may not be possible to choose the minimum set of untested specifications in any way so that strong a priori confidence in the untested specifications exists. Even in such a case it may nevertheless happen that, for

[16] In an earlier article [11] I have attempted, in a somewhat different terminology, to discuss that problem. That article needs rewriting in the light of subsequent developments in econometrics. It unnecessarily clings to the view that each structural equation represents a causal process in which one single dependent variable is determined by the action upon it of all other variables in the equation. Moreover, use of the concept of identifiability will contribute to sharper formulation and treatment of the problem of the choice of a model. However, the most serious defect of the article, in my view, cannot yet be corrected. It arises from the fact that we do not yet have a satisfactory statistical theory of choice among several alternative hypotheses.

any choice of the set of untested specifications, the additional specifications that are confirmed by test also inspire some degree of a priori confidence. In such a case, the model as a whole is more firmly established than any selected minimum set of untested specifications. However, current theory of statistical inference provides no means of giving quantitative expression to such partial and indirect confirmation of anticipation by observation.

Thirdly, if the choice of the model is influenced by the same data from which the structural parameters are estimated, the estimated sampling variances of these estimated parameters do not have that direct relation to the reliability of the estimated parameters which they would have if the estimation were based on a model of which the validity is given a priori with certainty.

Finally, the research worker who constructs a model does not really believe that reality is exactly described by a "true" structure contained in the model. Linearity, discrete time lags, are obviously only approximations. At best, the model builder hopes to construct a model that contains a structure which approximates reality to a degree sufficient for the practical purposes of the investigation. The tests of current statistical theory are formulated as an (uncertain) choice, from two or more sets of structures (single or composite hypotheses), of that one which contains the "true" structure. Instead we need to choose the simplest possible set—in some sense—which contains a structure sufficiently approximative—in some sense—to economic reality.

8. For What Purposes Is Identification Necessary?

The question should finally be considered why it is at all desirable to postulate a structure behind the probability distribution of the variables and thus to become involved in the sometimes difficult problems of identifiability. If we regard as the main objective of scientific inquiry to make prediction possible and its reliability ascertainable, why do we need more than a knowledge of the probability distribution of the variables to permit prediction of one variable on the basis of known (or hypothetical) simultaneous or earlier values of other variables?

The answer to this question is implicit in Haavelmo's discussion of the degree of permanence of economic laws [**6**, see p. 30] and has been formulated explicitly by Hurwicz [**8**]. Knowledge of the probability distribution is in fact sufficient whenever there is no change in the structural parameters between the period of observation from which such knowledge is derived and the period to which the prediction applies. However, in many practical situations it is required to predict the values of one or more economic variables, either under changes in structure that come about independently of the economist's advice, or under hypothetical changes in structural parameters that can be brought about through policy based in part on the prediction made. In the first case knowledge may, and in the second case it is likely to, be available as to the effect of such structural change on the parameters. An example of the first case is a well-established change in consumers' preferences. An example of the second case is given in Chapter I, Section 8. Other examples are contained in a contribution by Carl Christ to the discussion of a paper by Smithies [**18**] on business cycle analysis and public policy.

In such cases, the "new" distribution of the variables, on the basis of which predictions are to be constructed, can be derived from the "old" distribution prevailing before the structural change only if the known structural change can be applied to identifiable structural parameters, i.e., parameters that can be determined from a knowledge of the "old" distribution combined with the a priori considerations that have entered into the model.

REFERENCES

[**1**] J. B. D. Derksen, "Long Cycles in Residential Building: An Explanation," Econometrica, Vol. 8, April 1940, pp. 97–116.

[**2**] M. Ezekiel, "Saving, Consumption and Investment," *American Economic Review*, Vol. 32, March 1942, pp. 22–49; June 1942, pp. 272–307.

[**3**] M. Ezekiel, "The Statistical Determination of the Investment Schedule," Econometrica, Vol. 12, January 1944, pp. 89–90.

[**4**] R. Frisch, *Pitfalls in the Statistical Construction of Demand and Supply Curves*, Veröffentlichungen der Frankfurter Gesellschaft für Konjunkturforschung, Neue Folge, Heft 5, Leipzig: Hans Buske, 1933, 39 pp.

[**5**] R. Frisch, "Statistical Versus Theoretical Relations in Economic Macrodynamics," mimeographed document prepared for a League of Nations conference in Cambridge, England, July 18–20, 1938, concerning Tinbergen's work.

[**6**] T. Haavelmo, "The Probability Approach in Econometrics," Econometrica, Vol. 12, Supplement, 1944, also Cowles Commission Paper, New Series, No. 4.

[**7**] L. Hurwicz, "Generalization of the Concept of Identification," in *Statistical Inference in Dynamic Economic Models*, Cowles Commission Monograph 10, New York, John Wiley & Sons, 1950, pp. 245–257.

[**8**] L. Hurwicz, "Prediction and Least-Squares," in *Statistical Inference in Dynamic Economic Models*, Cowles Commission Monograph 10, New York, John Wiley & Sons, 1950, pp. 266–300.

[**9**] L. Klein, "Pitfalls in the Statistical Determination of the Investment Schedule," Econometrica, Vol. 11, July-October 1943, pp. 246–258.

[**10**] L Klein, "The Statistical Determination of the Investment Schedule: A Reply," Econometrica, Vol. 12, January 1944, pp. 91–92.

[**11**] T. C. Koopmans, "The Logic of Econometric Business Cycle Research," *Journal of Political Economy*, Vol. 49, 1941, pp. 157–181.

[12] T. C. Koopmans, "Measurement Without Theory," *The Review of Economic Statistics*, Vol. 29, No. 3, August 1947, pp. 161–172, also Cowles Commission Paper, New Series, No. 25.

[13] T. C. Koopmans and O. Reiersöl, "The Identification of Structural Characteristics," *Annals of Mathematical Statistics*, Vol. 21, June, 1950, pp. 165–181 (included in Cowles Commission Paper, New Series, No. 39).

[14] T. C. Koopmans, H. Rubin and R. B. Leipnik, "Measuring the Equation Systems of Dynamic Economics," in *Statistical Inference in Dynamic Economic Models*, Cowles Commission Monograph 10, New York, John Wiley & Sons, 1950, pp. 53–237.

[15] J. Marschak, "Economic Interdependence and Statistical Analysis," in *Studies in Mathematical Economics and Econometrics*, in memory of Henry Schultz, Chicago, The University of Chicago Press, 1942, pp. 135–150.

[16] A. C. Pigou, "A Method of Determining the Numerical Values of Elasticities of Demand," *Economic Journal*, Vol. 20, 1910, pp. 636–640, reprinted as Appendix II in *Economics of Welfare*.

[17] Henry Schultz, *Theory and Measurement of Demand*, Chicago, The University of Chicago Press, 1938.

[18] Smithies, A., "Business Cycle Analysis and Public Policy," with comments by J. M. Clark, L. Hurwicz, and C. Christ, in *Proceedings of the Conference on Business Cycles*, New York: National Bureau of Economic Research, 1951.

[19] A. Wald, "Note on the Identification of Economic Relations," in *Statistical Inference in Dynamic Economic Models*, Cowles Commission Monograph 10, New York, John Wiley & Sons, 1950, pp. 238–244.

CHAPTER III

CAUSAL ORDERING AND IDENTIFIABILITY

BY HERBERT A. SIMON[1]

Page

1. INTRODUCTION

In careful discussions of scientific methodology, particularly those carried on within a positivist or operationalist framework, it is now customary to avoid any use of the notion of causation and to speak instead of "functional relations" and "interdependence" among variables. This avoidance is derived, no doubt, from the role that the concept of causality has played in the history of philosophy since Aristotle, and particularly from the objectionable ontological and epistemological overtones that have attached themselves to the causal concept over the course of that history.

Empiricism has accepted Hume's critique that necessary connections among events cannot be perceived (and hence can have no empirical basis). Observation reveals only recurring associations. The proposition that it is possible to discover associations among events that are, in fact, invariable ceases to be a provable statement about the natural world and becomes instead a working rule to guide the activity of the scientist. He says, "I will seek for relationships among events that seem always to hold in fact, and when it occurs that they do not hold, I will search for additional conditions and a broader model that will (until new exceptions are discovered) restore my power of prediction." The

[1] I am indebted to Tjalling C. Koopmans for his valuable suggestions and comments on earlier drafts of this chapter, particularly with regard to the discussion of the relation between causal ordering and identifiability. A distinction between endogenous and exogenous variables similar to the concept of causal ordering here developed was made by Orcutt [1952]. For a discussion of the incorporation of the notion of causality in a system of formal logic, see Simon [1952].

only "necessary" relationships among variables are the relationships of logical necessity that hold in the scientist's model of the world, and there is no guarantee that this model will continue to describe the world that is perceived.

Even this narrower notion of causality—that causal orderings are simply properties of the scientist's model, properties that are subject to change as the model is altered to fit new observations—has been subjected to criticism on two scores. First of all, the viewpoint is becoming more and more prevalent that the appropriate scientific model of the world is not a deterministic model but a probabilistic one. In quantum mechanics and thermodynamics, and in many social science models, expressions in terms of probabilities have taken the place of completely deterministic differential equations in the relationships connecting the variables. However, if we adopt this viewpoint, we can replace the causal ordering of the variables in the deterministic model by the assumption that the realized values of certain variables at one point or period in time determine the probability distribution of certain variables at later points or periods.

The second criticism is in one sense more modest; in another, more sweeping. It has already been alluded to above. It is simply that "causation" says nothing more than "functional relationship" or "interdependence," and that, since "causation" has become encrusted with the barnacles of nonoperationalist philosophy, it is best to abandon this term for the others.

In view of the generally unsavory epistemological status of the notion of causality, it is somewhat surprising to find the term in rather common use in scientific writing (when the scientist is writing about his science, not about its methodology). Moreover, it is not easy to explain this usage as metaphorical, or even as a carry-over of outmoded language habits. For, in ordinary speech and writing the causal relationship is conceived to be an asymmetrical one—an ordering—while "functional relationship" and "interdependence" are generally conceived as entirely symmetrical. When we say that A causes B, we do not say that B causes A; but when we say that A and B are functionally related (or interdependent), we can equally well say that B and A are functionally related (or interdependent). Even when we say that A is the independent variable in an equation, while B is the dependent variable, it is often our feeling that we are merely stating a convention of notation and that, by rewriting our equation, we could with equal propriety reverse the roles of A and B.

The question, then, of whether we wish to retain the word "cause" in the vocabulary of science may be narrowed down to the question of whether there is any meaning in the assertion that the relationship between two variables in a model is sometimes asymmetrical rather than symmetrical. If the answer to this question is in the negative, there would seem to be good reason for abandoning "cause" in favor of its synonyms. If the answer is affirmative, the term "cause," carefully scrubbed free of any undesirable philosophical adhesions, can perform a useful function and should be retained.

It is the aim of this chapter to show how the question just raised can be answered in the affirmative and to provide a clear and rigorous basis for determining when a causal ordering can be said to hold between two variables or groups of variables in a model. Two preliminary remarks may help to clarify the approach that will be taken.

First, the concepts to be defined all refer to a model—a system of equations—and not to the "real" world the model purports to describe. Hence both Hume's critique and the determinism-indeterminism controversy are irrelevant to the question of whether these concepts are admissible in scientific discourse. The most orthodox of empiricists and antideterminists can use the term "cause," as we shall define it, with a clear conscience.

Second, it might be supposed that cause could be defined as functional relationship in conjunction with sequence in time. That is, we might say that if A and B are functionally related and if A precedes B in time, then A causes B. There is no logical obstacle to this procedure. Nevertheless, we shall not adopt it. We shall argue that time sequence does, indeed, sometimes provide a basis for asymmetry between A and B, but that the asymmetry is the important thing, not the sequence. By putting asymmetry, without necessarily implying a time sequence, at the basis of our definition we shall admit causal orderings where no time sequence appears (and sometimes exclude them even where there is a time sequence). By so doing we shall find ourselves in closer accord with actual usage, and with a better understanding of the meaning of the concept than if we had adopted the other, and easier, course. We shall discover that causation (as we shall define it) does not imply time sequence, nor does time sequence imply causation.

We conclude these introductory comments with two examples of relationships that "common sense" would regard as causal. First, the classical work of the biologists Henderson, Cannon, and others on homeostasis is replete with references to asymmetrical relationships among the variables. On thirst, Cannon [1939, pp. 62–66] states: "Thirst is a sensation referred to the inner surface of the mouth and throat, especially to the root of the tongue and the back part of the palate . . . . When water is lacking in the body the salivary glands are unfavorably affected . . .

[They] are therefore unable to secrete, the mouth and pharynx become dry and thus the sensation of thirst arises."

The causal chain clearly implied by this statement is

deficiency of water in body tissues→reduction in salivation→dryness of tongue and palate→stimulation of nervous system (sensation of thirst).

To this Cannon adds elsewhere:

→activity of drinking→restoration of water content of tissues.

It is difficult to think or write of these functional relationships as symmetrical, or as asymmetrical but running in the opposite direction. For example, if there is normal salivation but the saliva is prevented from reaching the tongue and palate, thirst is produced, but this neither reduces salivation nor produces a deficiency of water in the body tissues.

Similarly, in economics we speak of relations like

poor growing weather→small wheat crops→increase in price of wheat

and we reject the notion that by changing the price of wheat we can affect the weather. The weather is an "exogenous" variable, the price of wheat an "endogenous" variable.

2. Self-Contained Structures

The task we have set ourselves is to show that, given a system of equations and a set of variables appearing in these equations, we can introduce an asymmetrical relationship among individual equations and variables (or subsets of equations and variables) that corresponds to our common-sense notion of a causal ordering. Let us designate the relationship by an arrow, →. Then we shall want to construct our definition in such a manner that $A \rightarrow B$ if and only if A is a direct cause (in ordinary usage of the term) of B.

In the following discussion we shall seek mathematical simplicity by limiting ourselves to systems of linear algebraic equations without random disturbances. Later we shall indicate how the concepts can readily be extended to nonlinear systems, but a discussion of stochastic systems is beyond the scope of this chapter.

Definition 2.1: *A* linear structure *is a system of linear nonhomogeneous equations* (cf. Marschak [1950, p. 8]) *that possesses the following special properties:*

(a) *That in any subset of k equations taken from the linear structure at least k different variables appear with nonzero coefficients in one or more of the equations of the subset.*

(b) *That in any subset of k equations in which $m \geqslant k$ variables appear with nonzero coefficients, if the values of any $(m - k)$ variables are chosen arbitrarily, then the equations can be solved for unique values of the remaining k variables.*

In particular, a linear structure is an independent and consistent set of linear nonhomogeneous equations, independence and consistency being guaranteed by properties (a) and (b).[2]

DEFINITION 2.2: *A linear structure is* self-contained *if it has exactly as many equations as variables* (cf. Marschak [1950, p. 7]).

Because of (b), a self-contained linear structure possesses a unique solution—there is precisely one set of values of the variables that satisfies the equations.

A linear structure can be represented by the matrix of the coefficients (augmented to include the constant terms) of the equations of the structure. We have already required that the system be nonhomogeneous (that not all the constant terms be zero) and that a sufficient number of variables appear with nonzero coefficients in one or more of the equations in any subset of the structure.

DEFINITION 2.3: *A* linear model *is the class of all linear structures that can be obtained from a given structure by the substitution of new nonzero coefficients for the nonzero coefficients of the original structure* [*without, of course, violating* (*a*) *or* (*b*)].[3]

With these terms defined we can undertake to introduce the notion of a causal ordering of the variables, and a corresponding precedence ordering of the equations, of a self-contained linear structure. We shall

[2] It should be noted that Conditions (a) and (b), incorporated in Definition 2.1, are absent from the definitions of linear structure employed in other chapters. This slight difference in definition simplifies the exposition and should cause the reader little difficulty. The relevant theorems on independence and consistency will be found in Bôcher [1907, pp. 43–49]. Condition (a) can be omitted if we exclude from consideration certain exceptional sets of values of the coefficients of the equation system; in this case we can develop properties of the system, parallel to those described in the present chapter, which hold "almost everywhere" (see Koopmans, Rubin, and Leipnik [1950, p. 82]) in the space of these coefficients.

[3] Again this definition, for purposes of simplification, is somewhat narrower than in other chapters.

then see at once that all the linear structures belonging to the same linear model possess the same causal ordering. Hence, we shall see that the causal ordering is determined as soon as we know which variables appear with nonzero coefficients in which equations.

3. Causal Ordering

3.1. Consider any subset A of the equations of a linear structure (alternatively, a subset of the rows of the augmented coefficient matrix) and the corresponding subset α of the variables that appear with a nonzero coefficient in at least one of the equations of A. Let N_A be the number of equations in A, and n_α the number of variables in α. By (a), $n_\alpha \geqslant N_A$. If we extend Definition 2.2 to subsets of equations in a linear structure, then we may say:

Definition 3.1: *A subset A of a linear structure is* self-contained *if and only if* $n_\alpha = N_A$.

Definition 3.2: *If* $n_\alpha > N_A$, *we shall say that A is* sectional [Marschak, 1950, p. 7].

Now suppose that A and B are two subsets of equations of the same linear structure. We prove the theorem:

Theorem 3.1: *Let A be self-contained and B be self-contained. Then their intersection C (the set of equations belonging to both A and B) is self-contained.*

Designate by α the set of variables that appear in A, by β the set in B, and by γ the set in C; let $A \cap B$ designate the intersection of the sets A and B, and $A \cup B$ their sum (i.e., the set of elements belonging either to A or to B). Then the theorem states that if $n_\alpha = N_A$, $n_\beta = N_B$, and $C = A \cap B$, then $n_\gamma = N_C$.

Proof: Designate by N_S the number of equations in $(A \cup B)$, and by n_σ the number of variables in $(\alpha \cup \beta)$. Then we have

$$N_A + N_B - N_C = N_S . \tag{3.1}$$

Designate by $n_{(\alpha\cap\beta)}$ the number of variables belonging to both α and β. Then, similarly, we have for the sets of variables

$$n_\alpha + n_\beta - n_{(\alpha\cap\beta)} = n_\sigma . \tag{3.2}$$

But by hypothesis we have $N_A = n_\alpha$ and $N_B = n_\beta$, while, by (a), $N_S \leqslant n_\sigma$. Substituting these relations in (3.1) we get

$$n_\alpha + n_\beta - N_C = N_S \leqslant n_\sigma . \tag{3.3}$$

Finally, γ is included in $(\alpha \cap \beta)$ since if a variable is in γ it must appear in C, and hence in both A and B. Therefore, $n_{(\alpha \cap \beta)} \geqslant n_\gamma$. Employing this relationship together with (3.2), we get

$$n_\sigma \leqslant n_\alpha + n_\beta - n_\gamma , \tag{3.4}$$

whence, combining (3.3) and (3.4) and eliminating identical terms from both sides of the resulting inequality, we obtain

$$N_C \geqslant n_\gamma . \tag{3.5}$$

But since, by (a), $n_\gamma \geqslant N_C$, (3.5) implies

$$n_\gamma = N_C , \tag{3.6}$$

which proves the theorem.

DEFINITION 3.3: *We call those self-contained subsets of a linear structure that do not themselves contain self-contained* (*proper*) *subsets the* minimal self-contained subsets of the structure.

From Theorem 3.1 there follows immediately

THEOREM 3.2: *The minimal self-contained subsets A_i of the equations of a linear structure, and likewise the subsets of variables that appear in these minimal subsets of equations, are disjunct.*

That the subsets of equations are disjunct is obvious from Theorem 3.1. That the subsets of *variables* appearing in the several minimal self-contained subsets of equations are also disjunct follows from the observation that, if this were not so, the sums of minimal subsets with common variables would contain fewer variables than equations, contrary to (a). That is, let A and B be minimal self-contained subsets and let $C = A \cup B$. Then, since A and B are disjunct, $N_C = N_A + N_B$, while $n_\gamma = n_\alpha + n_\beta - n_{(\alpha \cap \beta)}$. But $n_\alpha = N_A$, $n_\beta = N_B$. Hence $n_{(\alpha \cap \beta)} > 0$ implies $n_\gamma < N_C$, which contradicts (a).

3.2. We can now decompose a self-contained linear structure A containing variables α into two parts: a part A', which is the sum of all the minimal self-contained subsets, $A' = A_1 \cup A_2 \cup \cdots \cup A_k$ (containing variables $\alpha' = \alpha_1 \cup \alpha_2 \cup \cdots \cup \alpha_k$); and a remainder, B. Since the A_i are disjunct, $N_{A'} = \sum N_{A_i}$. Similarly, $n_{\alpha'} = \sum n_{\alpha_i} = \sum N_{A_i}$. Hence $N_{A'} = n_{\alpha'}$, i.e., the number of variables appearing in A' is equal to the number of equations in A'. Further, if B is not null ("empty"), we must have $n_\beta > N_B$; otherwise B would be self-contained, contrary to its definition. Hence, at least one of the variables of α' must belong to β.

It is convenient to distinguish three cases:

I. A' consists of a single self-contained set, which coincides with the entire structure; i.e., the structure A contains no self-contained proper subset. In this case B is null, and we may say that the structure is completely *integrated.*

II. A' consists of one or more proper subsets of the structure and B is not null. In this case we may say that the structure is *causally ordered.*

III. A' consists of more than one proper subset of the structure and B is null. In this case we may say that the structure is *unintegrated.*

In all three cases we shall call the minimal self-contained subsets belonging to A' the (minimal) *complete subsets of zero order.*

DEFINITION 3.4: *If in Case II we solve the equations of A' for the unique values of the variables in α', and substitute these values in the equations of B [by (b) this is always possible], the linear structure we obtain is the* derived structure of first order, *a self-contained structure of N_B equations in $n_{(\beta-\beta\cap\alpha')} = N_B$ unknowns. We can now find the minimal self-contained subsets of the first derived structure, $B' = B_1 \cup B_2 \cup \cdots \cup B_m$* (complete subsets of first order), *and proceed as before, obtaining Case I, II, or III. If Case II holds, we repeat the process with the* derived structure of second order, *and so forth. Since the number of equations in the original structure was finite, we must finally reach a derived structure that falls under Case I or Case III.*

DEFINITION 3.5: *The minimal self-contained subsets of the derived structure of k-th order will be called the* complete subsets of kth order.

3.3. By the process just described we have arrived at a complete ordering of disjunct subsets of the equations of A, so that $A = A' \cup B' \cup \cdots \cup N$, where N, the derived structure of highest order, is either unintegrated or completely integrated. Each of the minimal complete subsets, of whatever order, reached in the process may be interpreted in either of two ways. The subset, taken by itself, may be regarded (as above) as a self-contained structure with as many variables as equations, the remaining variables having been eliminated by substitution after solution of the equations of the lower-order structures. Alternatively, it may be viewed as a *complete* subset, in which case the variables in question are not eliminated by substitution but are regarded as *exogenous variables*, the remaining variables (equal in number to the equations of the subset) being regarded as *endogenous variables.* (It will be clear that these terms are used in a sense relative to the complete subset of equations in question.[4])

Adopting the latter interpretation of subsets in the derived structures, it is clear that each complete subset of first order must contain at least one variable in α', for if it did not, the subset would be a complete subset of zero order. Similarly, each complete subset of kth order must contain at least one variable that appears in a complete subset of $(k - 1)$th order and that does not appear in any complete subset of order less than $(k - 1)$.

Since the concepts of endogenous and exogenous variables will play an important role in the following discussion, it will be useful to have for these terms a definition more formal than that just given.

DEFINITION 3.6: *If D is a complete subset of order k, and if a variable x_i appears in D but in no complete subset of order lower than k, then x_i is* endogenous in the subset *D. If x_i appears in D but also in some complete subset of order lower than k, then x_i is* exogenous in the subset *D.*

From our previous discussion (in particular, the paragraph following Theorem 3.2) it can be seen that each variable in a self-contained linear structure appears as an endogenous variable in one and only one complete subset of the structure, that it appears in no complete subset of order lower than the one in which it is endogenous, and that it appears in complete subsets of higher order (if at all) as an exogenous variable. Therefore, there exists a one-to-one correspondence between the complete subsets of equations and the subsets of variables occurring as endogenous variables in these equations.

We can now employ the distinction between exogenous and endogenous variables to define a causal ordering of the sets of variables endogenous to the corresponding complete subsets of equations.

DEFINITION 3.7: *Let β designate the set of variables endogenous to a complete subset B, and let γ designate the set endogenous to a complete subset C. Then the variables of γ are* directly causally dependent *on the variables of β ($\beta \rightarrow \gamma$) if at least one member of β appears as an exogenous variable in C. We can say also that the subset of equations B has* direct precedence *over the subset C.*

We have now partitioned the equations of a self-contained structure into disjunct subsets (the minimal complete subsets of various orders);

[4] This usage of "complete," "exogenous," and "endogenous" is consistent with Marschak's definition of those terms [Marschak, 1950, pp. 7–8].

we have similarly partitioned into disjunct subsets the variables of the structure (the sets of endogenous variables corresponding to the complete subsets of equations); and we have partially ordered these minimal subsets of equations and corresponding sets of variables by means of the (isomorphic) relations of direct precedence and direct causal dependence, respectively.

4. Analysis of Examples

4.1. Our first example is the simple one mentioned in the introduction to this chapter:

poor growing weather → small wheat crops → increase in price of wheat.

We may translate this into the form of a self-contained linear structure as follows: Let x_1 be an index measuring the favorableness of weather for growing wheat; x_2, the size of the wheat crop; and x_3, the price of wheat. We suppose the weather to depend only on a parameter; the wheat crop, upon the weather (we ignore a possible dependence of supply on price); and the price of wheat, on the wheat crop; and we suppose all relations to be linear. The resulting equations are

$$a_{11}x_1 = a_{10}, \tag{4.1}$$

$$a_{21}x_1 + a_{22}x_2 = a_{20}, \tag{4.2}$$

$$a_{32}x_2 + a_{33}x_3 = a_{30}. \tag{4.3}$$

Equation (4.1) contains only one variable and hence is a minimal complete subset of zero order, with x_1 as the endogenous variable. There are no other such subsets. Solving (4.1) for x_1 and substituting this value in (4.2) and (4.3), we get the derived structure of first order,

$$a_{22}x_2 = a_{20} - a_{21}(a_{10}/a_{11}), \tag{4.2a}$$

$$a_{32}x_2 + a_{33}x_3 = a_{30}. \tag{4.3a}$$

We see that equation (4.2a) is a minimal complete subset of first order, with x_2 as its endogenous variable. Solving (4.2a) for x_2 and eliminating x_2 from the third equation, we are left with a single equation as the minimal complete subset of second order. Applying Definition 3.7, we may write:

$$(4.1) \rightarrow (4.2) \rightarrow (4.3)$$

[read: "(4.1) has direct precedence over (4.2), and (4.2) over (4.3)"], and

$$x_1 \rightarrow x_2 \rightarrow x_3$$

(read: "x_1 is the direct cause of x_2, and x_2 of x_3").

4.2. A less trivial example, which also shows that our definitions correspond with common-sense notions of causality, is the structure whose coefficients are estimated by Girshick and Haavelmo in Chapter V, pages 107–110. In writing their system we omit the random terms and employ a different notation for the coefficients:

$$a_{11}y_1+a_{12}y_2+a_{13}y_3 \qquad\qquad +a_{18}z_8+a_{19}z_9=a_{10}\,, \tag{4.4}$$

$$a_{21}y_1+a_{22}y_2 \qquad +a_{24}y_4 \qquad\qquad +a_{28}z_8 \qquad =a_{20}\,, \tag{4.5}$$

$$a_{33}y_3 \qquad\qquad +a_{37}z_7 \qquad +a_{39}z_9=a_{30}\,, \tag{4.6}$$

$$a_{44}y_4+a_{45}y_5+a_{46}z_6 \qquad +a_{48}z_8 \qquad =a_{40}\,, \tag{4.7}$$

$$a_{52}y_2 \qquad +a_{55}y_5 \qquad\qquad +a_{58}z_8 \qquad =a_{50}\,, \tag{4.8}$$

$$a_{66}z_6 \qquad =a_{60}\,, \tag{4.9}$$

$$a_{77}z_7 \qquad =a_{70}\,, \tag{4.10}$$

$$a_{88}z_8 \qquad =a_{80}\,, \tag{4.11}$$

$$a_{99}z_9=a_{90}\,. \tag{4.12}$$

Analysis of this structure, which the reader may wish to carry out as an exercise, shows that there are four single-equation subsets of zero order: equations (4.9), (4.10), (4.11), (4.12), and one subset of first order: equation (4.6). The four remaining equations form a single subset of second order in the endogenous variables y_1, y_2, y_4, and y_5. In terms of equations, the precedence relations are

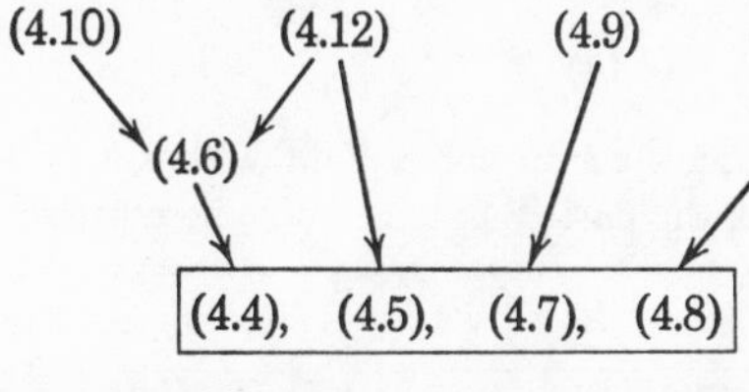

Interpreting this result in terms of the corresponding sets of variables, we find that Girshick and Haavelmo are asserting:

1. That food consumption (y_1), retail food prices (y_2), food production (y_4), and food prices received by farmers (y_5) are interdependent (members of the same minimal complete subset of second order) and directly causally dependent upon disposable income (y_3), last year's food prices received by farmers (z_6), time (z_8), and last year's disposable income (z_9).

2. That disposable income (y_3) is directly causally dependent upon net investment (z_7) and last year's disposable income (z_9).

4.3. We present, without interpretation, a final example:

$$\alpha_{11}x_1 + \alpha_{12}x_2 + \alpha_{13}x_3 + \alpha_{16}x_6 = \alpha_{10}\,, \tag{4.13}$$

$$\alpha_{24}x_4 + \alpha_{25}x_5 = \alpha_{20}\,, \tag{4.14}$$

$$\alpha_{32}x_2 = \alpha_{30}\,, \tag{4.15}$$

$$\alpha_{43}x_3 = \alpha_{40}\,, \tag{4.16}$$

$$\alpha_{51}x_1 + \alpha_{52}x_2 + \alpha_{53}x_3 + \alpha_{54}x_4 = \alpha_{50}\,, \tag{4.17}$$

$$\alpha_{66}x_6 + \alpha_{67}x_7 = \alpha_{60}\,, \tag{4.18}$$

$$\alpha_{71}x_1 = \alpha_{70}\,. \tag{4.19}$$

It can be shown that there are three complete subsets of zero order: equation (4.15) and variable x_2, equation (4.16) and variable x_3, and equation (4.19) and variable x_1. There are two complete subsets of first order: equation (4.13) and x_6, and equation (4.17) and x_4. Finally, there are two complete subsets of second order: equation (4.14) and x_5, and equation (4.18) and x_7. In this case each complete subset consists of one equation in one endogenous variable, and we can represent the precedence and causal partitioning alternatively as follows:

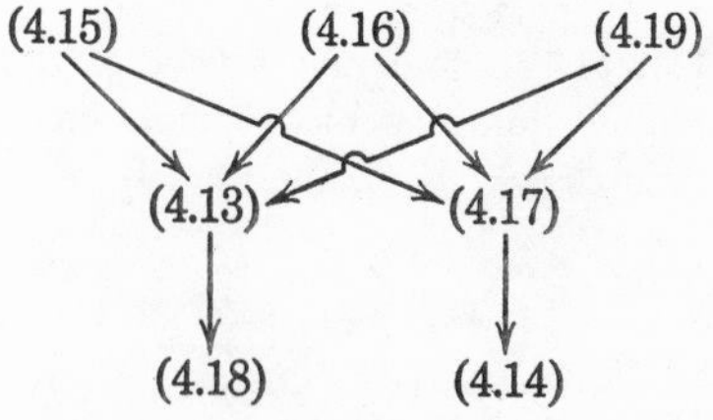

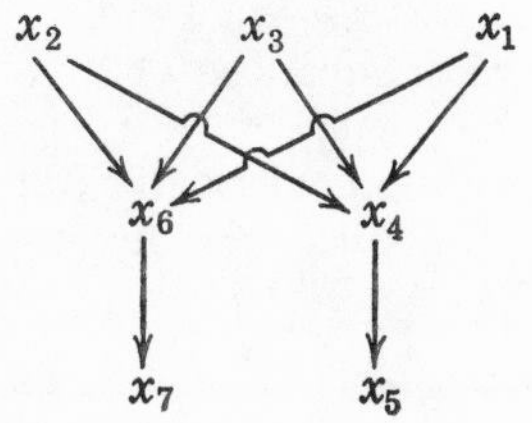

Reordering our equations to correspond with the order of the corresponding variables, the partitioning can also be represented as follows:

	x_1	x_2	x_3	x_4	x_6	x_5	x_7
(4.19)	×	0	0	0	0	0	0
(4.15)	0	×	0	0	0	0	0
(4.16)	0	0	×	0	0	0	0
(4.17)	×	×	×	×	0	0	0
(4.13)	×	×	×	0	×	0	0
(4.14)	0	0	0	×	0	×	0
(4.18)	0	0	0	0	×	0	×

In this table, nonzero coefficients in the matrix are designated by ×, zero coefficients by 0. The coefficients of the constant term are not displayed.

4.4. We see from this last representation that ordering the equations and variables according to their precedence and causal relations places the matrix in a canonical form that in a certain sense is as nearly triangular as the structural equations permit. This suggests that calculation of the causal relations in a structure may have some value in indicating the optimum arrangement of equations and variables in fixing the sequence of computation of their solutions. It would be easy to construct an electrical computing device which, even for very large structures, would rapidly locate the complete subsets from this matrix representation.

The blocks of zeros above and to the right of the main diagonal in the canonical form of the matrix show clearly also that our concept of causal ordering is essentially identical with the concept of unilateral coupling, employed in connection with dynamical systems.[5]

4.5. The blocks of zeros in the lower left-hand corner are really accidental properties of the particular partitioning we are studying—that variables of zero order appear only in equations of zero and first order, not in equations of second order.

The causal relation we have defined is a nontransitive relation—$\alpha \rightarrow \beta$ and $\beta \rightarrow \gamma$ does not imply $\alpha \rightarrow \gamma$. We may wish to introduce, among sets of endogenous variables, a transitive relationship meaning "directly or indirectly caused."

DEFINITION 4.1: *$\alpha \supset \gamma$ (read: "α is a cause of γ") if there exist β_1, $\beta_2, \cdots, \beta_k$ such that $\alpha \rightarrow \beta_1 \rightarrow \beta_2 \rightarrow \cdots \rightarrow \beta_k \rightarrow \gamma$. We may also speak of a relationship of* precedence *holding between the corresponding subsets of equations; for instance, $A \supset C$.*

5. CAUSALITY IN SYSTEMS NOT SELF-CONTAINED

5.1. We now proceed to show that it is essential that we assume a self-contained structure in order to introduce the notion of causal ordering.

Consider the structure used as an example in Section 4.3. Suppose that we omit equations (4.15) and (4.19) and replace them with

$$\alpha_{85}x_5 = \alpha_{80}\,, \tag{5.1}$$

$$\alpha_{99}x_7 = \alpha_{90}\,. \tag{5.2}$$

[5] As a matter of fact, the writer originally approached his problem from the standpoint of unilateral coupling (cf. Goodwin [1947, pp. 183–184]).

We then obtain the following causal structure:

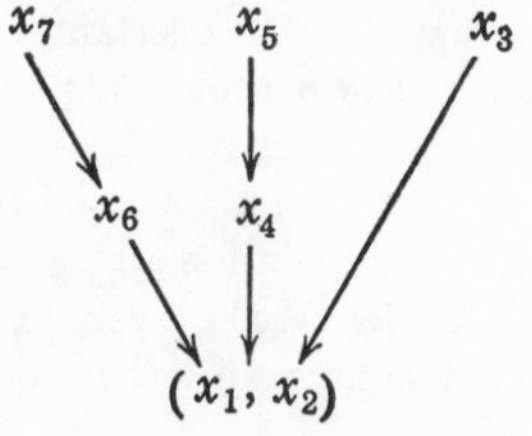

where (x_1, x_2) represents the complete subset of second order comprising the variables x_1 and x_2. We see that we have not only reversed the direction of causation between x_5 and x_7, on the one hand, and x_1 and x_2 on the other, but have also changed the relation of x_3 to the remainder of the structure. Hence we cannot speak of an "internal" causal structure among the variables of a sectional (not self-contained) structure apart from the particular self-contained structure in which it is imbedded. In our new case the canonical form of matrix is

	x_3	x_5	x_7	x_4	x_6	x_1	x_2
(4.16)	×	0	0	0	0	0	0
(5.1)	0	×	0	0	0	0	0
(5.2)	0	0	×	0	0	0	0
(4.14)	0	×	0	×	0	0	0
(4.18)	0	0	×	0	×	0	0
(4.13)	×	0	0	0	×	×	×
(4.17)	×	0	0	×	0	×	×

Of the five equations common to both structures, only equation (4.16) has retained the same order. Moreover, the complete subsets of equations are associated with subsets of variables different from those before.

5.2. In general, we can complete a sectional structure by adding an appropriate number of additional equations, and in general we can do this in a number of different ways. Each of the resulting self-contained structures is likely to have different causal relationships among its variables. One way to complete a sectional structure is to specify which variables are exogenous and to add a sufficient number of equations in which these exogenous variables alone occur [Marschak, 1950, p. 8].

6. Operational Significance of Causal Ordering

6.1. An important objection to our definition of causal ordering remains to be examined—the objection that it is essentially artificial, since the same set of observations could be represented by different structures with different causal orderings of the variables. Consider the following three sets of two equations each:

$$\begin{array}{ll}(6.1)\\(6.2)\end{array}\left.\right\} \qquad \begin{cases} a_{11}y_1 + a_{12}y_2 = a_{10} \,, \\ a_{21}y_1 + a_{22}y_2 = a_{20} \,; \end{cases}$$

$$\begin{array}{ll}(6.3)\\(6.4)\end{array}\left.\right\} \qquad \begin{cases} b_{11}y_1 \qquad\qquad = b_{10} \,, \\ a_{21}y_1 + a_{22}y_2 = a_{20} \,, \end{cases}$$

with $b_{11} = a_{11} - (a_{12}/a_{22})a_{21}$, $b_{10} = a_{10} - (a_{12}/a_{22})a_{20}$;

$$\begin{array}{ll}(6.5)\\(6.6)\end{array}\left.\right\} \qquad \begin{cases} b_{11}y_1 \qquad\qquad = b_{10} \,, \\ \qquad\qquad a_{22}y_2 = c_{20} \,, \end{cases}$$

with $c_{20} = a_{20} - (a_{21}/b_{11})b_{10}$.

All three sets of equations are satisfied by precisely the same set of values of y_1 and y_2 , namely,

$$(6.7) \qquad y_1 = b_{10}/b_{11} \,, \qquad y_2 = c_{20}/a_{22} \,.$$

Yet the causal ordering in the three sets is different. Equations (6.1) and (6.2) comprise a single minimal complete set of zero order. Equation (6.3) is a complete set of zero order, while (6.4) is a complete set of first order to which (6.3) is directly precedent. Equations (6.5) and (6.6) each constitute a complete set of zero order. The first structure is completely integrated, the second causally ordered, and the third unintegrated. If the three sets are to be regarded as operationally equivalent, because each can be obtained from either of the others by algebraic manipulation without altering the solution, then causal ordering has no operational meaning.

Closer inspection of the three sets of equations, (6.1)–(6.6), suggests a possible basis for distinguishing them even though they have an identical solution. Consider the first pair of equations. Suppose that equation (6.1) were altered (say, by a change in the constant term or one of the other coefficients). Then the values of both y_1 and y_2 would, in general, be altered. The same would be true if (6.2) were altered.

Consider next the second pair of equations. Suppose that equation (6.3) were altered. Again, both y_1 and y_2 would be changed in value. On the other hand, if (6.4) were altered, only y_2 would be affected and y_1 would remain unchanged.

Finally, consider the third pair of equations. Suppose that equation (6.5) were altered. This would change the value of y_1 but not of y_2. However, if (6.6) were altered, this would change the value of y_2 but not of y_1.

The principle illustrated by the example above can easily be generalized.

THEOREM 6.1: *Let A be a self-contained linear structure, let A_1 be a complete subset of order k in A, and let A' be a self-contained linear structure that is identical with A except for a single equation belonging to A_1. (We assume that the set of variables appearing in A_1 is unaltered.) Consider the (unique) solutions of A and A', respectively. Then (a) the values of all variables in A that are neither endogenous variables of A_1 nor causally dependent, directly or indirectly, on the endogenous variables of A_1 are identical with the values of the corresponding variables in A'; and (b) the values of all variables in A that are endogenous in A_1 or are causally dependent on the endogenous variables of A_1 are (in general) different from the values of the corresponding variables in A'.*

PROOF: We can solve the equations of a linear structure for the values of the variables appearing in a particular complete subset A_2 by (1) solving successively the complete subsets (starting with those of zero order) that have precedence over A_2, and finally (2) substituting in A_2 the values of all the exogenous variables appearing in A_2 and solving the equations of A_2 for the endogenous variables. Hence, altering an equation belonging to one of these complete subsets will, in general, alter the values of the variables in A_2; but altering an equation in a complete subset that does not have precedence over A_2 cannot alter the values of the variables in A_2.

6.2. Let us apply this notion to the example used in Section 4.1. The structure represented by equations (4.1)–(4.3) might be altered by changing any one of the three equations, each of which constitutes a complete subset.

I. If (4.1) is altered (e.g., rainfall is increased by sowing carbon dioxide crystals in clouds), this will also affect the wheat crop and the price of wheat.

II. If (4.2) is altered (e.g., a drought-resistant variety of wheat is introduced), this will affect the wheat crop and the price of wheat but not the weather.

III. If (4.3) is altered (e.g., a population increase shifts upward the demand schedule for wheat), the price of wheat will change but not the size of the wheat crop or the weather.

The causal relationships have operational meaning, then, to the extent that particular alterations or "interventions" in the structure can be associated with specific complete subsets of equations. We can picture the situation, perhaps somewhat metaphorically, as follows. We suppose a group of persons whom we shall call "experimenters." If we like, we may consider "nature" to be a member of the group. The experimenters, severally or separately, are able to choose the nonzero elements of the coefficient matrix of a linear structure, but they may not replace zero elements by nonzero elements or vice versa (i.e., they are restricted to a specified linear model). We may say that they *control directly* the values of the nonzero coefficients. Once the matrix is specified, the values of the n variables in the n linear equations of the structure are uniquely determined. Hence, the experimenters *control indirectly* the values of these variables. The causal ordering specifies which variables will be affected by intervention at a particular point (a particular complete subset) of the structure.

We see that, in addition to a language describing the linear model, we require, in order to discuss causality, a second language (a "metalanguage") describing the relationship between the "experimenters" and the model. The terms "direct control" and "indirect control" are in this metalanguage. Thus, in our metalanguage we have an asymmetrical relationship ($>$)—behavior of experimenters $>$ equation coefficients $>$ values of variables—that must be introduced in order to establish the asymmetrical causal relationship ($\rightarrow$).

In one sense we have moved our problem from the language of the original model to the metalanguage. In order to establish a causal ordering we must have a priori knowledge of the limits imposed on the "experimenters"—in this case knowledge that certain coefficients of the matrix are zeros. If the causal ordering is to have operational meaning it is necessary that, within these limits, the "experimenters" be able to alter at least some equation in each complete subset in some way.

7. Causal Ordering and Identifiability

The concept of identifiability has been introduced in Chapter II. In the present chapter no hint has been given thus far as to the relationship between identifiability and causal ordering. In fact, however, there appears to be a very close relationship between the two concepts, and it is the task of the present section to describe it.[6]

7.1. In Section 6 we sought an operational basis for the concept of causal ordering, a basis that would make of the ordering something more than an arbitrary property of a particular (and arbitrary) way of writing the equations governing certain empirical variables. We found that we could provide the ordering with an operational basis if we could associate with each equation of a structure a specific power of intervention, or "direct control." That is, any such intervention would alter the structure but leave the model (and hence the causal ordering) invariant. Hence, causal ordering is a property of models that is invariant with respect to interventions within the model, and structural equations are equations that correspond to specified possibilities of intervention.

The usual notion of operationalism requires us to associate with each *variable* of an empirical system a method (set of operations) for measuring it. The extended notion introduced in Section 6 requires us to associate with each *equation* a procedure (set of operations) for altering its constant term or coefficients. It is by virtue of such procedures that we can distinguish between "structural" and "nonstructural" sets of equations describing the same set of observations.

But it is precisely this same notion of intervention, and this same distinction between structural and nonstructural equations, that lies at the root of the identifiability concept.[7] As long as structure remains unaltered, identifiability is not required in order to estimate the parameters that are needed for prediction. When a recognizable change in structure occurs, however, identifiability of at least some of the parameters of the structural equations is necessary if correct predictions are to be made in the new structure. From these epistemological considerations we conclude that the conditions under which the causal ordering of a structure is operationally meaningful are generally the same as the conditions under which structural equations can be distinguished from nonstructural equations, and the same as the conditions under which the question of identifiability of the equations is meaningful.

[6] In addition to the logical connection, to be discussed in the text, between causal ordering and identifiability, it may be of interest to point to a number of historical connections. Pioneering work on identifiability was done by Ragnar Frisch [1934], who explored the problem discussed in Section 8.1 below. Other authors in econometrics began to use the concept of causality in their writings without explicit definition; for example, Haavelmo [1944, especially p. 22] and Wold [1949]. An explicit causal ordering for a special class of cases was introduced by Tinbergen [1940].

[7] See Marschak [1950, pp. 8–18], Hurwicz [1950b, pp. 266–273], Chapter I of this volume, and Section 8 of Chapter II.

7.2. Parallel with the epistemological relationship just described, we should expect to find a mathematical relationship between the two concepts. In this we are not disappointed.

Identifiability of a linear structure is obtained when certain a priori constraints are placed on the model. For complete identifiability of a structure these restraints must preclude the existence in the model of a different equivalent structure, that is (in linear models), a different set of equations whose members are linear combinations of the original equations.[8]

The simplest basis for identifiability is obtained if we can specify a priori that certain coefficients appearing in the model must be zero. But if the *j*th coefficient in the *i*th equation is zero, then the *j*th variable does not appear in the *i*th equation. Hence, these specifications may be regarded as determining which variables appear in which equations. In a self-contained structure specification of which variables appear with nonzero coefficients in which equations determines the causal ordering. (In the present section we shall restrict ourselves to a priori specifications of the kind just described.)

7.3. The argument just set forth may be restated in a more formal way, which will perhaps clarify further the operational status of the terms "causal ordering" and "identifiability." An important guiding principle in the relationship between mathematical models and empirical data is that a property of a mathematical model cannot be regarded as reflecting a property of the empirical world the model purports to describe unless this property is invariant under permissible (operationally nonsignificant) transformations of the equations specified by the model.

For example, in Newtonian mechanics it is meaningless to ask whether a body is at rest or in uniform motion in a straight line, for by a trivial transformation of the reference system the motion of the body can be transformed from the first state to the second.[9] It is meaningful

[8] The definition of identifiability from which this statement is derived (see Chapter II, Section 3, and Koopmans, Rubin, and Leipnik [1950, Definition 2.1.5.3]) refers to stochastic models. We shall see in Section 8 that the statement remains valid for an equivalent identifiability concept formulated for nonstochastic models [Marschak, 1950, Section 1.3]. In either case, the concept of identifiability always refers to a complete structure, whose equations may be a complete subset (Definition 3.5) of a (stated or unstated) structure consisting of a larger number of equations. The implications of this fact have not received sufficient emphasis in the literature on identifiability, and will be elaborated in Section 8.

[9] This is the classical problem of "absolute" versus "relative" motion. The notion of invariance under transformation as a necessary condition for a "real" property of a physical system has provided a leading motivation for the development of relativistic mechanics and other branches of modern physics. For the identification problems that arise in classical mechanics, see Simon [1947].

however, to ask whether the body is accelerated or unaccelerated since this property is invariant under transformation from one physically admissible reference system to another.

In the classical theory of systems of linear equations we are interested in properties of a system that are invariant under certain groups of transformations of the coefficients of its matrix. In particular, we may be interested in the solutions of any given system (the sets of values of the variables satisfying the system). These are invariant under elementary row transformations of the matrix.

DEFINITION 7.1: *Elementary row transformations of a matrix are those which (1) interchange rows of the matrix (i.e., reorder the equations), (2) add to a given row multiples of another row or rows, (3) multiply a row by a nonzero scalar. These all amount to premultiplication of the coefficient matrix by a nonsingular matrix.*[10] *The group of transformations thus generated we will call the R-transformations.*

DEFINITION 7.2: *Any two coefficient matrices that are obtainable from one another by R-transformations we will call R-equivalent.*

Concentration of interest on those properties (e.g., solutions) that are invariant under the group of R-transformations has led to the replacement of the notion of causality by the notion of mutual dependence. For, given a (consistent and independent) set of k linear equations in n ($n \geqslant k$) variables, then, in general, each variable belonging to any subset [Bôcher, 1907, p. 46] of k variables can be expressed as a function of the remaining $(n - k)$.

We have seen that the causal ordering in a linear structure is not invariant under the group of R-transformations (cf. Sections 6.1, 6.2). Hence, to give invariant meaning to this causal ordering we must restrict ourselves to a more limited group of transformations than the R-transformations.

DEFINITION 7.3: *We say that two coefficient matrices are structurally equivalent (S-equivalent) if the second can be obtained from the first by premultiplication by a nonsingular diagonal matrix (i.e., by row transformations of the third type only). The group of transformations thus admitted we shall call the group of S-transformations.*

It is clear that if only the S-transformations are admitted (multiplication of each equation by a constant), the positions of the zero and

[10] Albert [1941, pp. 24, 43].

nonzero coefficients cannot be affected. That is, the causal ordering of a linear structure and the identifiability of its several equations are invariant under the group of S-transformations but not under the wider group of R-transformations.

Now the operational significance of distinguishing between these two groups of transformations has already been suggested in Sections 6.2 and 7.1. If with each equation of a structure we associate a specific power of intervention, then, under S-transformations, this one-to-one correspondence between equations and interventions will not be disturbed—each equation will retain its identity. But, under R-transformations of types (1) or (2), the equations will be scrambled and combined. Suppose that the jth and kth equations belong to different complete subsets. If the jth equation is interchanged with the kth, the interventions will have to be correspondingly reordered; while if the jth equation is replaced by a sum of multiples of the jth and kth, the kth power of intervention will now not be associated with a single equation but with both the jth and the kth.

The definition of identifiability implies that a linear structure is completely identifiable if and only if the a priori restrictions on the model (e.g., the zeros of the coefficient matrix) are such as to permit only S-transformations upon the matrix. If the identifiable structure is self-contained, there will then be a unique causal ordering associated with it, and this ordering will be invariant under any transformations permitted by the a priori restrictions.[11]

8. Identifiability in Complete Subsets

The relationship, just explored, between causal ordering and identifiability casts some light upon the conditions under which the coefficients of a structure can be determined from data in the case of nonstochastic models. First, some preliminary explanations are necessary.

8.1. We suppose that we have a large number of observations of the simultaneous values of n variables entering in a linear model. Each observation may be regarded as a point in an n-dimensional space whose coordinates are the values of the n variables. We suppose, further, that the model specifies k equations ($k < n$) which are assumed to govern

[11] On the other hand, the causal ordering may be defined even if the structure is not completely identifiable. Since the causal ordering depends only on which subsets of variables appear in which complete subsets of equations, it will also be invariant over the group of R-transformations upon the equations of any complete subset.

the behavior of the variables; any single observation must satisfy the k equations. Under what conditions will the observations be sufficient to determine the unknown coefficients of all k equations, that is, the unknown structure within the model?

The answer to this question can be obtained from geometrical considerations. If each observation is to satisfy all the equations, all observations must lie in a hyperplane of not more than $(n - k)$ dimensions. This hyperplane must be the intersection of the k $(n - 1)$-dimensional hyperplanes representing the k equations. (For example, if there are three variables and two equations, each equation will be represented by a plane, and all observations will lie on the straight line that is the intersection of the two planes.)

Now if the observations do not lie in a hyperplane of *fewer* than $(n - k)$ dimensions, the criteria for identifiability of equations that have been derived for linear stochastic models[12] are also sufficient to assure unique determination of the coefficients of these equations in the present nonstochastic case. For a model satisfying these criteria restricts transformations of the equations to the group of S-transformations (which do not affect the location of the planes represented by the equations), and hence only one set of k admissible hyperplanes can intersect in the $(n - k)$-dimensional hyperplane defined by the observations. That is to say, any other set of k $(n - 1)$-dimensional hyperplanes intersecting in the same $(n - k)$-dimensional hyperplane must consist of linear combinations of the original set, and this possibility is ruled out by the a priori restrictions, specified by the model, that produce identifiability.

However, if the observations are "degenerate" [i.e., lie in a hyperplane of fewer than $(n - 1)$ dimensions], it may be impossible to determine all the coefficients of the structure. Hence, to insure the possibility of determining these coefficients we must require that the variables not be subject to any equations in addition to those of the structure.[13]

8.2. We shall now see how a knowledge of the causal ordering of a set of variables can be used to help determine whether the coefficients of a linear structure governing these variables can be determined. In the discussion of criteria for identifiability of a structural equation by a linear model, given in Chapter II and in Section 4.4 of Chapter VI, a necessary order condition and a necessary and sufficient rank condition for identifiability are derived. For simplicity, in the following discussion

[12] Chapter II, Section 4; Chapter VI, Section 4.4 and Appendix A.

[13] This requirement is a sufficient, but not a necessary, condition for determinacy. If the a priori restrictions are more than the minimum required for identifiability, determinacy may be present even if the variables are subject to additional, unknown restrictions. The problem under discussion here is the question of "confluence," first studied intensively by Frisch [1934].

we shall consider only the order condition. The exposition would be considerably complicated, and the results not materially altered, if the rank condition were included as well. In the following theorem we restate the order condition, which, in view of the discussion of Section 8.1, applies also to the present nonstochastic case.

THEOREM 8.1: *In a linear model with a priori restrictions in the form of exclusions of variables from equations, a necessary condition for the identifiability of the k-th equation of a structure A consisting of m equations in n variables is that at least* $(m - 1)$ *of the variables in A be excluded from the k-th equation.*

It follows immediately that, if A is a self-contained structure, the only equations belonging to it that are identifiable are those containing a single variable (i.e., the equations that constitute complete subsets of zero order). Hence, the prospects of determining the coefficients of a self-contained structure (unless it is made up entirely of one-variable equations) are nil as long as all observations are restricted by the entire system of equations. In fact, in a nonstochastic structure, repeated observations could in this case only produce the same set of values for all variables that was obtained in the first observation. This suggests that we shall need to intervene (see Section 6.2) to "relax" certain of the relationships in order to obtain observations adequate for determining the coefficients of the remaining equations.

In a self-contained structure A consider an identifiable complete subset S of k equations in n variables. [By Theorem 8.1, no equation of S contains more than $(n - k + 1)$ variables.] If we can produce a set of observations of the variables that satisfies these k equations, and no others independent of these, then we can determine the coefficients of S. Now let us add to S any number of additional equations of A which either (1) belong to complete subsets of the same or higher order than S, or (2) do not contain any of the variables of S. Designate by S' this structure (which includes S). Then the equations of S also satisfy the order condition of identifiability in this new system. For the number of variables in S' must exceed the number of variables in S by at least the number of equations added [by (a)]. None of these new variables appear in the equations of S. Therefore, the equations of S still satisfy the condition of Theorem 8.1 and hence, as far as the order condition is concerned, are still identifiable in S'. We have proved

THEOREM 8.2: *If each equation of a complete subset S of a linear structure A is identifiable in that subset, it also satisfies the order condition of identifiability in the larger set S′ that is formed by adding to S any equations of A which either (1) belong to complete subsets of the same or higher order than S or (2) do not contain any of the variables of S.*

By virtue of this theorem we see that in order to permit the determination of the coefficients of an identifiable complete subset of equations we need to relax, at most, the equations that are precedent to this subset. This theorem makes clear the point, referred to in footnote 8, that identifiability has reference to complete subsets of equations.[14] As a matter of fact, the condition of Theorem 8.2, while sufficient for the preservation of the order condition, is not necessary. Without pursuing the matter in detail, we may illustrate the situation with an example. Consider a complete subset S of k equations in k endogenous and m exogenous variables. Suppose the m exogenous variables to be endogenous to a complete subset T (of lower order of precedence) of m equations in $m + p$ $(p \geqslant m)$ variables. Then it is easy to see that, if an equation of S is identifiable in S, it is identifiable in the system consisting of S and T together. To guarantee that the order condition of identifiability will be satisfied when we add new equations to an identifiable complete subset we need merely make sure that we add as many new variables as equations.

8.3. The rationale of the identifiability concept with reference to a complete subset A_k of a self-contained structure A would appear to be the following. We suppose the equations of A_k of order k to be identifiable in A_k, and we wish to determine their coefficients. All the variables of A of order less than k that appear in A_k are exogenous variables relative to A_k. We now suppose that these variables can be arbitrarily varied (by relaxing the structural equations of order less than k) to produce a set of observations of the highest dimensionality consistent with the relations of A_k. This set of observations, together with the condition that the equations of A_k be identifiable, permits us to determine the coefficients.

It is to be noted that we have here again implicitly introduced the notion of an experimenter who, by his direct control over the parameters of the equations in A of order less than k (or by selection of observations provided by "nature"), can bring about independent variations in the variables that are exogenous to A_k. If this procedure is operationally meaningful, the experimenter, confronted with a self-contained structure

[14] In the stochastic case discussed in Chapter II, Section 3, and in Koopmans, Rubin, and Leipnik [1950, Definition 2.1.3.2] this is reflected in the stipulation that structures are regarded as equivalent only if they give rise to identical distributions of the observations for all values of the "exogenous" variables, i.e., exogenous with reference to the subset considered (Definition 3.6 above).

A, can partition the structure into its complete subsets and, isolating each of these from the whole, proceed to determine its parameters. This seems to correspond exactly to the procedure of a physiologist who (in the example used in the introduction) prevents an animal's saliva from reaching the palate and in this way explores the thirst mechanism.

In the stochastic case nature may provide some of the necessary variability of exogenous variables that escape experimental control. In fact, the discussion of identifiability of complete structures in the stochastic case is meaningful only if sufficient independent variation of "exogenous" variables is provided by nature.[15]

9. Causality in Nonlinear Systems

Thus far we have considered only the case of linear, nonstochastic structures. In this chapter the problem of causal ordering in the stochastic case will not be considered, but a few comments may be made on the nonlinear case.

We consider a system of functional relations of the form

$$\phi_i(x, \cdots, x_n) = 0 \qquad (i = 1, \cdots, n). \tag{9.1}$$

We assume further that the system has, at most, a denumerably infinite set of solutions. Now we can again decompose the system into complete subsets of equations of various orders, such that each subset contains as many variables not appearing in subsets of lower order as it contains equations. If appropriate conditions are imposed on our system, this decomposition will again be unique.

In our linear structure we assumed that an experimenter could directly control the parameters appearing in the equations. In the present case we assume that an experimenter can relax or modify any equation or set of equations in the system. In this way we have the same general relationship as in the linear case between the problem of defining the causal ordering and the problem of identification.

10. Conclusion

In this chapter we have defined a concept of causality that corresponds to the intuitive use of that term in scientific discussion. Causality is an asymmetrical relation among certain variables, or subsets of variables, in a self-contained structure. There is no necessary connection between the asymmetry of this relation and asymmetry in time, al-

[15] See footnote 13 above and also Chapter II, footnotes 7 and 13, from which it will be clear that "exogenous" as used in the sentence to which this footnote is appended corresponds to "predetermined" in the context of Chapters II and VI.

though an analysis of the causal structure of dynamical systems in econometrics and physics will show that lagged relations can generally be interpreted as causal relations.

In models specifying which variables are excluded from which equations, the concept of causality has been shown to be intimately connected with the concept of identifiability, although the conditions under which a self-contained structure possesses a nontrivial causal structure are somewhat weaker than the conditions under which it is completely identifiable.

A study of the operational meaning of the causal ordering (or of the concept of "structural" equations) appears to require a metalanguage that permits discussion of the relation between the structure and an experimenter who has direct control over some of the parameters of the structure. As the brief discussion of the nonlinear case implies, the distinction between parameters and variables can be disregarded if the former are regarded as exogenous variables (determined by a larger system) with respect to the latter. In this case the experimenter must be regarded as being able to relax or alter particular equations in this larger system.

Chapter IV

METHODS OF MEASURING THE MARGINAL PROPENSITY TO CONSUME[1]

By Trygve Haavelmo

1. Introduction

The marginal propensity to consume and its companion, the multiplier, are of central importance in modern theories of macroeconomics. The intense interest in these parameters derives largely from the importance that modern theories (and many older ones too) attach to the rate of investment as a primary factor in determining the levels of income and employment. In some theories investment is considered as an autonomous variable, an impressed force (e.g., Schumpeter's theory of innovations). Other theories, while operating with the notion of induced investment, imply nevertheless that current investment is, in part at least, an autonomous variable, its main determinants being such "external" factors as growth of population, new inventions, wars, etc., or *past* values of some other economic variables, such as profit, sales, or capital accumulation. It is in line with these ideas that attempts to derive, statistically, the marginal "propensity to invest" apparently have met with little success. The current view on the subject is probably well expressed in the following statement by Alvin H. Hansen: "Thus, the statistical data during the last two decades tend to support the thesis that the active dynamic factor in the cycle is investment, with consumption assuming a passive, lagging role."[2] Qualifying this statement somewhat, he continues: "For the most part, spontaneous expenditures—expenditures not caused by a prior rise in income

[1] Some of the methods discussed below were developed in connection with a study of the demand for agricultural products undertaken at the Department of Economics, The University of Chicago. The author is indebted to his colleagues at the Cowles Commission for many helpful suggestions. This chapter is reprinted from the *Journal of the American Statistical Association*, Vol. 42, March, 1947, pp. 105–122.

[2] Hansen [1941, p. 50].

—are likely to be made on investment goods or upon durable consumers' goods, but not upon other forms of consumption.

"It does not follow, however, that all investment is spontaneous. Much of it is, in fact, induced. It is, however, quite impossible to determine statistically what part is spontaneous and what part is induced."[3] Many economists would agree with Paul A. Samuelson's statement that "In behavior it [i.e., investment][4] is sporadic, volatile, and capricious. Its effective determinants are almost completely independent of current statistical factors (level of income, etc.)."[5]

If this is the current view on the role of investment, it is somewhat surprising to find that current attempts to derive statistically the marginal propensity to consume approach the problem by correlating consumers' expenditures with income.[6] This procedure is inconsistent with the view that investment is the autonomous determinant of income. We should, instead, take the regression of income *on investment*, to obtain the multiplier, and from this estimate of the multiplier we should derive the marginal propensity to consume. This idea, I am sure, is not new, but it might perhaps be useful to set down the arguments involved in somewhat more rigorous terms. I shall also give some numerical results, as illustrations.

2. Estimation of the Consumption Function When Investment Is an Autonomous Variable

In this section we shall be concerned with the following observable time series:

c_t = consumers' expenditure, in constant dollars per capita,

y_t = disposable income, in constant dollars per capita,

z_t = investment expenditures, in constant dollars per capita.

The term investment, as used here, is defined as the difference between disposable income and consumers' expenditure. (In terms of current statistical measurements by the U.S. Department of Commerce, investment, as defined here, would be equal to private net investment minus corporate savings plus Government deficits. Cf. Section 4 below.) This means that we impose the exact relationship

$$y_t = c_t + z_t. \tag{2.1}$$

[3] Hansen [1941, pp. 62–63].

[4] Author's remark.

[5] Samuelson [1943, p. 41].

[6] See, for example, Smithies [1945, pp. 4–6], Mosak [1945, p. 44], and others, too numerous to be mentioned here.

We assume further that the consumption function is a linear function of disposable income, but that this function is subject to random shifts. Let this function be

$$c_t = \alpha y_t + \beta + u_t \tag{2.2}$$

where α and β are constants, and u_t is the random element in consumers' behavior. The problem is to estimate the true values of α and β, by means of a certain number of observations of the time series c_t, y_t, and z_t. The u's are not observable.

The model, as it stands, is not complete. It does not determine the levels of income, consumption, and investment, even if we knew the true values of α and β. There are three variables, y, c, z, and only two equations, (2.1) and (2.2). For the same reason the model does not as yet tell us how to proceed statistically in order to estimate α and β. The model, as it stands, does not determine how the joint probability distribution of the observable variables c_t and y_t depends on α and β, and therefore does not determine the appropriate type of estimation formulae to be used. It is necessary to complete the model in such a way that the problem of estimating α and β becomes a well-defined statistical problem. For this purpose we add the following assumptions:

(a) The random variable u_t has expected value $\mathcal{E}(u_t) = 0$, and variance $\mathcal{E}(u_t^2) = \sigma_u^2$ for every value of t. The u's are serially uncorrelated, i.e., $\mathcal{E}(u_t u_{t-\tau}) = 0$ for $\tau \neq 0$.

(b) The time series z_t $(t = 1, 2, \cdots)$ is autonomous in relation to c_t and y_t. This condition is fulfilled if either

(b.1) the sequence z_t is a sequence of given numbers, in which case automatically $\mathcal{E}(z_t u_t) = z_t \mathcal{E}(u_t) = 0$, by (a), or

(b.2) each z_t is a random variable which is stochastically independent of u_t.

If assumption (b.1) is adopted we shall impose the condition that

$$\lim_{N\to\infty} m_{zz} \equiv \lim_{N\to\infty} \frac{1}{N} \sum_{t=1}^{t=N} \left(z_t - \frac{1}{N} \sum_{t=1}^{t=N} z_t \right)^2 = \bar{m}_{zz}, \tag{2.3}$$

where $\bar{m}_{zz}$ is a positive, finite number. Therefore

$$N m_{zz} \to \infty \quad \text{as} \quad N \to \infty. \tag{2.4}$$

Similarly, if assumption (b.2) is adopted, we shall assume that

$$\underset{N\to\infty}{\text{plim}} \frac{1}{N} \sum_{t=1}^{t=N} \left(z_t - \frac{1}{N} \sum_{t=1}^{t=N} z_t \right)^2 = \bar{m}_{zz} \tag{2.5}$$

where $\bar{m}_{zz}$ is positive and finite.[7] These assumptions are used in the analysis of the large-sample properties of the estimates discussed below.

Let us assume that conditions (a) and (b.1) are fulfilled. And consider either one of the following two relations derived from (2.1) and (2.2),

$$c_t = \frac{\alpha}{1-\alpha} z_t + \frac{\beta}{1-\alpha} + \frac{u_t}{1-\alpha} \tag{2.6}$$

$$y_t = \frac{1}{1-\alpha} z_t + \frac{\beta}{1-\alpha} + \frac{u_t}{1-\alpha}. \tag{2.7}$$

Under the assumptions made, each of these two equations satisfies the conditions of the Markoff theorem on least squares, when z_t is considered as the independent variable.[8] In the following we shall use the moment notations

$$m_{pq} = \frac{1}{N} \sum_{t=1}^{t=N} \left(p_t - \frac{1}{N} \sum_{t=1}^{t=N} p_t\right)\left(q_t - \frac{1}{N} \sum_{t=1}^{t=N} q_t\right) \tag{2.8}$$

$$m_p = \frac{1}{N} \sum_{t=1}^{t=N} p_t. \tag{2.9}$$

Using well-known formulae from ordinary regression theory, and writing b. u. est. as an abbreviation for "best unbiased estimate,"[9] we can then make the following statements:

$$\frac{m_{cz}}{m_{zz}} = \text{b.u. est. of } \frac{\alpha}{1-\alpha} \tag{2.10}$$

$$\frac{m_{yz}}{m_{zz}} = \text{b.u. est. of } \frac{1}{1-\alpha} \tag{2.11}$$

$$\frac{m_{zz}m_c - m_{cz}m_z}{m_{zz}} = \text{b.u. est. of } \frac{\beta}{1-\alpha}. \tag{2.12}$$

[7] "plim" means "the probability limit of." A statistic T_N, say, calculated from a sample of N observations, is said to have the probability limit A if the probability of $|T_N - A| > \epsilon$ approaches zero when N approaches infinity, for every fixed value of $\epsilon > 0$. A statistic T_N having this property is said to be a *consistent* estimate of A, or to converge stochastically to A.

[8] See, e.g., David and Neyman [1938].

[9] An estimate is said to be unbiased if its expected value is equal to the true parameter. An estimate is said to be a "best unbiased" estimate if its variance is smaller than that of any other unbiased estimate that is linear in the random variables involved.

We also have

$$(2.13)\quad s^2 = \frac{N}{N-2}\ \frac{m_{yy}m_{zz} - m^2_{yz}}{m_{zz}} = \text{an unbiased estimate of } \frac{\sigma_u^2}{(1-\alpha)^2}.$$

Under assumption (2.3) these estimates are *consistent*, that is, any one of the estimates (2.10)–(2.13) has the property that the probability of the estimate deviating more than an arbitrary ϵ from the true parameter approaches zero as N approaches infinity. Since α and β are continuous functions of $1/(1 - \alpha)$ and $\beta/(1 - \alpha)$ when $\alpha \neq 1$, we also know that the estimates, $\hat{\alpha}$ and $\hat{\beta}$, of α and β, derived[10] from (2.10) or (2.11), and (2.12), will have the following properties:

$$(2.14)\qquad \hat{\alpha} = \frac{m_{cz}}{m_{yz}} = \text{cons. est of } \alpha$$

$$(2.15)\qquad \hat{\beta} = \frac{m_{yz}m_c - m_{cz}m_y}{m_{yz}} = \text{cons. est. of } \beta.$$

The "estimates" of α and β obtained by the commonly used procedure of taking the least-squares regression of c_t on y_t do not possess this property. Let us denote these "estimates" by a and b, respectively. Then we have

$$(2.16)\qquad a = \frac{m_{cy}}{m_{yy}}$$

$$(2.17)\qquad b = \frac{m_{yy}m_c - m_{cy}m_y}{m_{yy}}.$$

These "estimates" a and b are not consistent estimates of α and β.

[10] In the present model, as well as in the model discussed in Section 4 below, the problem of obtaining estimates of the structural coefficients α and β from the regression coefficients in (2.10) or (2.11) and (2.12) happens to be particularly simple because we have exactly two independent equations defining the estimates of α and β, namely (2.10) and (2.12), or (2.11) and (2.12). [(2.10) and (2.11) give identical estimates of α.] In more general systems of structural equations the situation may be much more complicated: There may be more independent equations of the type (2.11)–(2.12) than there are structural parameters, or there might be too few such equations (as, e.g., in Section 3 below, if q_t is not observable). In such cases different, and—in general—much more laborious estimation procedures are required. For further discussion on this point, see Chapter VI of this monograph; in particular, Section 4.7.

This is seen as follows. Using (2.1) and (2.2) we obtain

$$a = \frac{\alpha m_{zz} + (1 + \alpha)m_{zu} + m_{uu}}{m_{zz} + 2m_{zu} + m_{uu}} . \tag{2.18}$$

From our assumptions it follows that $m_{zu} \to 0$ and $m_{uu} \to \sigma_u^2$ as $N \to \infty$. Thus, for sufficiently large samples, the statistic a approaches, stochastically, the limit

$$\operatorname*{plim}_{N\to\infty} a = \frac{\alpha + \dfrac{\sigma_u^2}{\bar{m}_{zz}}}{1 + \dfrac{\sigma_u^2}{\bar{m}_{zz}}} > \alpha \quad \text{when} \quad 0 < \alpha < 1. \tag{2.19}$$

Similarly, b will approach the limit

$$\operatorname*{plim}_{N\to\infty} b = \frac{\beta - \dfrac{\sigma_u^2}{\bar{m}_{zz}} \bar{m}_z}{1 + \dfrac{\sigma_u^2}{\bar{m}_{zz}}} < \beta \quad \text{when} \quad \bar{m}_z > -\beta. \tag{2.20}$$

Suppose now that we substitute assumption (b.2) for (b.1), letting the z's be random variables in repeated samples. Then the exact conditions of the Markoff theorem are no longer fulfilled. But under assumption (2.5) all the statements above concerning consistency and limit values of the estimates remain valid.

Thus, we reach the following conclusion: If investment, z_t, is an autonomous variable and if $0 < \alpha < 1$, $m_z > -\beta$, the least-squares regression of c_t on y_t leads to an "estimate," a, of α that has a systematic positive bias, and an "estimate," b, of β that has a systematic negative bias. If we believe that investment, z_t, is an autonomous variable we should rather use, in that case, the consistent estimates (2.14) and (2.15).

Confidence limits for the estimate of α by (2.14) may be derived in the following manner. Let us assume that the distribution of the u's is approximately normal and that the z's are not random variables. Then the ratio

$$t = \frac{\dfrac{m_{yz}}{m_{zz}} - \dfrac{1}{1 - \alpha}}{\dfrac{s}{\sqrt{N m_{zz}}}} \tag{2.21}$$

has the "Student" t-distribution, with $N - 2$ degrees of freedom. Choosing a certain level of significance, say 5 per cent, we obtain confidence limits for $1/(1 - \alpha)$. From these limits we can then derive confidence limits for α itself although, admittedly, this is not the only possible way of obtaining such confidence limits. The choice of confidence interval always depends, to some extent, on the type of statement one wants to make about the unknown parameter. (E.g., one might be more anxious to make a correct statement in the case where α is near to 1 than if α is smaller.)

3. Effects of Induced Investment

Suppose now that the hypothesis of investment, z_t, being autonomous is not true. Suppose that, instead, the variable z_t consists of two parts, one which is related to current income, and another, q_t say, which is autonomous. Assuming linearity, this alternative can be expressed as follows:

$$z_t = q_t + (\kappa y_t + \lambda + v_t). \tag{3.1}$$

Here the expression in parentheses represents the behavior of those investors whose investment policy depends on current income, y_t. κ and λ are constants, while v_t is a random element such that $\mathcal{E}(v_t) = 0$, $\mathcal{E}(v_t^2) = \sigma_v^2$, for every value of t, and also $\mathcal{E}(v_t v_{t-\tau}) = 0$, $\mathcal{E}(v_t u_{t-\tau}) = 0$, for $\tau \neq 0$. u_t and v_t may, however, be correlated, that is, $\mathcal{E}(u_t v_t) = \sigma_{uv}$ may be different from zero. We shall assume that the q's satisfy a condition of the type (2.3). Thus $\bar{m}_{qq}$ is obtained from (2.3) by substituting q for z.

Suppose, first, that the series q_t could actually be observed. Then one could obtain consistent estimates of α, β, κ, and λ, by the following procedure. From (2.1), (2.2), and (3.1) we derive

$$c_t = \frac{\alpha}{1 - \alpha - \kappa} q_t + \frac{\alpha\lambda + (1 - \kappa)\beta}{1 - \alpha - \kappa} + \frac{\alpha v_t + (1 - \kappa)u_t}{1 - \alpha - \kappa} \tag{3.2}$$

$$y_t = \frac{1}{1 - \alpha - \kappa} q_t + \frac{\beta + \lambda}{1 - \alpha - \kappa} + \frac{u_t + v_t}{1 - \alpha - \kappa}. \tag{3.3}$$

Under the assumptions made, these equations satisfy the requirements of the Markoff theorem on least squares, when q_t is taken as the independent variable. If we assume that the sequence q_t is a sequence of constants, we therefore have

$$(3.4)\qquad \frac{m_{cq}}{m_{qq}} = \text{b.u. est. of } \frac{\alpha}{1-\alpha-\kappa}$$

$$(3.5)\qquad \frac{m_{yq}}{m_{qq}} = \text{b.u. est. of } \frac{1}{1-\alpha-\kappa}$$

$$(3.6)\qquad \frac{m_{qq}m_c - m_{cq}m_q}{m_{qq}} = \text{b.u. est. of } \frac{\alpha\lambda + (1-\kappa)\beta}{1-\alpha-\kappa}$$

$$(3.7)\qquad \frac{m_{qq}m_y - m_{yq}m_q}{m_{qq}} = \text{b.u. est. of } \frac{\beta+\lambda}{1-\alpha-\kappa}\,.$$

These estimates are consistent. We therefore also have the solutions

$$(3.8)\qquad \frac{m_{cq}}{m_{yq}} = \text{cons. est. of } \alpha,$$

$$(3.9)\qquad \frac{m_{yq} - m_{cq} - m_{qq}}{m_{yq}} = \text{cons. est. of } \kappa,$$

$$(3.10)\qquad \frac{m_{yq}m_c - m_{cq}m_y}{m_{yq}} = \text{cons. est. of } \beta,$$

$$(3.11)\qquad \frac{m_{yq}(m_z - m_q) - (m_{yq} - m_{cq} - m_{qq})m_y}{m_{yq}} = \text{cons. est. of } \lambda.$$

It will be observed that expressions (3.8) and (3.10) are analogous to (2.14) and (2.15).

In Section 2 we compared the results, a and b, of the least-squares regression of c_t on y_t with the consistent estimates, $\hat{\alpha}$ and $\hat{\beta}$, under the assumption that z_t was autonomous. We found that a and b were not consistent estimates of α and β. Now, if a part of z_t is induced, the formulae (2.14) and (2.15) will, of course, not give consistent estimates either, the consistent estimates in that case being given by (3.8) and (3.10). It is of some interest to evaluate the large-sample bias that would result if we were to apply (2.14) and (2.15) in the present case, and to compare this bias with the large-sample bias involved in using (2.16) and (2.17). Let us consider, in particular, the estimates of α. Denote by a_1 the "estimate" of α given by (2.14) if z_t is defined by (3.1). And let a_2 be the corresponding "estimate" obtained from (2.16). Using (2.1), (2.2), and (3.1), and the properties assumed for the random variables involved, we find

$$\text{(3.12)}\quad \begin{aligned}\operatorname*{plim}_{N\to\infty} a_1 &\equiv \operatorname*{plim}_{N\to\infty} \frac{m_{cz}}{m_{yz}} \\ &= \frac{\alpha(1-\alpha)(\bar{m}_{qq}+\sigma_v^2)+\kappa(1-\kappa)\sigma_u^2+\kappa(1-\alpha-\kappa+2\alpha\kappa)\sigma_{uv}}{(1-\alpha)(\bar{m}_{qq}+\sigma_v^2)+\kappa\sigma_u^2+(1-\alpha+\kappa)\sigma_{uv}}\end{aligned}$$

$$\text{(3.13)}\quad \begin{aligned}\operatorname*{plim}_{N\to\infty} a_2 &\equiv \operatorname*{plim}_{N\to\infty} \frac{m_{cy}}{m_{yy}} \\ &= \frac{\alpha(\bar{m}_{qq}+\sigma_v^2)+(1-\kappa)\sigma_u^2+(1-\kappa+\alpha)\sigma_{uv}}{(\bar{m}_{qq}+\sigma_v^2)+2\sigma_{uv}+\sigma_u^2}.\end{aligned}$$

It is seen that neither of these expressions is, in general, equal to α. The bias depends on the unknown parameters. If we have some a priori knowledge about some of the parameters we can make more definite statements about the bias. Thus, if we assume that $0 < \alpha < 1$, $0 < \kappa < 1, 0 < (1 - \alpha - \kappa) < 1$, and that $\sigma_{uv} > 0$, we find that the bias of both (3.12) and (3.13) will be positive. If κ is small compared with α, and σ_{uv} also small, (3.12) will give smaller bias than (3.13), and so forth.

4. A More Explicit Model

In Section 2 we defined investment z_t in such a way that $y_t = c_t + z_t$. Before making a decision upon the use of this z_t as an autonomous variable, it might be worth-while to examine its content in terms of current statistics of the gross national product and its components.

In the terminology of the U.S. Department of Commerce, the gross national product and disposable income are defined as follows:[11] (For our purpose here the data should be interpreted as "per capita, in constant dollars.")

Gross national product = Government expenditures (excl. transfer payments) + gross private capital formation + consumers' expenditures.

Disposable income of individuals = gross national product − (total business taxes + personal taxes + employment taxes − transfer payments) − (depreciation and depletion charges + capital outlay charged to current expense + income credited to other business reserves − revaluation of business inventories + corporate savings).

The total of the five terms in the last parentheses might be termed "gross business savings," or "withholdings." From these definitions it follows that disposable income (y_t) − consumers' expenditures (c_t) = z_t = (Government expenditures + transfers − all taxes + gross private

[11] See, e.g., *Survey of Current Business*, May, 1942, p. 12.

capital formation) − gross business savings. Denoting the total of the four terms in the last parentheses above by x_t, and denoting gross business savings by r_t, we have

$$y_t - c_t = z_t = x_t - r_t. \tag{4.1}$$

The quantity x_t might be called "gross investment." Gross investment is, therefore, here defined as gross private capital formation plus Government net deficit. It might now be argued that it is this "gross investment" which is the exogenous, "dynamic" element, rather than z_t. (That is, one might say that z_t is composed of two parts, one, x_t, which is autonomous, and another, $-r_t$, which is induced.)

To reach a complete model under this hypothesis one has to introduce an additional hypothesis concerning the determination of r_t. Here there might be several possible alternatives. One might, for example, think of r_t as being a function of $(x_t + c_t)$. [The quantity $(x_t + c_t)$ could be called the "gross disposable income" of the private sector of the economy.] Another alternative would be to consider r_t as a function of profits, accumulated business savings, etc. As an illustration of the methodological problems involved in dealing, statistically, with such models let us here adopt the hypothesis that r_t is a linear function of $(x_t + c_t)$. This leads us to the following model:

$$c_t = \alpha y_t + \beta + u_t \tag{4.2}$$

$$r_t = \mu(c_t + x_t) + \nu + w_t \tag{4.3}$$

$$y_t = c_t + x_t - r_t \tag{4.4}$$

$$x_t = \text{an autonomous variable.} \tag{4.5}$$

Here (4.2) is a repetition of (2.2), while (4.3) is the "business-savings" equation. μ and ν are constants to be estimated, w_t being a nonobservable random variable. We assume that $\mathcal{E}(w_t) = 0$, $\mathcal{E}(w_t^2) = \sigma_w^2$, and $\mathcal{E}(w_t w_{t-\tau}) = 0$, $\mathcal{E}(u_t w_{t-\tau}) = 0$, for $\tau \neq 0$. We do not, however, assume that u_t and w_t are necessarily independent. The sequence x_t $(t = 1, 2, \cdots)$ is assumed to fulfill a condition of the type (2.3).

Because of (4.4) and (4.5) there are really only two "endogenous" variables involved. We may take these two variables to be c_t and y_t. Solving the system for c_t and y_t we obtain

$$c_t = \frac{\alpha(1-\mu)}{1-(1-\mu)\alpha}x_t + \frac{\beta - \alpha\nu}{1-(1-\mu)\alpha} + \frac{u_t - \alpha w_t}{1-(1-\mu)\alpha} \tag{4.6}$$

$$y_t = \frac{(1-\mu)}{1-(1-\mu)\alpha}x_t + \frac{(1-\mu)\beta - \nu}{1-(1-\mu)\alpha} + \frac{(1-\mu)u_t - w_t}{1-(1-\mu)\alpha}\,. \tag{4.7}$$

Under the assumptions made, both of these equations satisfy the requirements of the Markoff theorem on least squares, if x_t $(t = 1, 2, \cdots)$ is considered as a sequence of constants. Hence we have

$$\hat{A}_1 = \frac{m_{cx}}{m_{xx}} = \text{b.u. est. of } \frac{\alpha(1-\mu)}{1-(1-\mu)\alpha} \tag{4.8}$$

$$\hat{A}_2 = \frac{m_{yx}}{m_{xx}} = \text{b.u. est. of } \frac{(1-\mu)}{1-(1-\mu)\alpha} \tag{4.9}$$

$$\frac{m_{xx}m_c - m_{cx}m_x}{m_{xx}} = \text{b.u. est. of } \frac{\beta - \alpha\nu}{1-(1-\mu)\alpha} \tag{4.10}$$

$$\frac{m_{xx}m_y - m_{yx}m_x}{m_{xx}} = \text{b.u. est. of } \frac{(1-\mu)\beta - \nu}{1-(1-\mu)\alpha}\,. \tag{4.11}$$

These equations may, in turn, be solved, to obtain estimates, $\hat{\alpha}$, $\hat{\beta}$, $\hat{\mu}$, $\hat{\nu}$, of the structural parameters α, β, μ, ν, respectively. These solutions are

$$\hat{\alpha} = \frac{m_{cx}}{m_{yx}} \tag{4.12}$$

$$\hat{\beta} = \frac{m_{yx}m_c - m_{cx}m_y}{m_{yx}} \tag{4.13}$$

$$\hat{\mu} = 1 - \frac{m_{yx}}{m_{cx} + m_{xx}} \tag{4.14}$$

$$\hat{\nu} = \frac{m_{yx}(m_c + m_x) - (m_{cx} + m_{xx})m_y}{m_{cx} + m_{xx}}\,. \tag{4.15}$$

In a similar manner we might estimate σ_u^2, σ_w^2, and σ_{uw}. It will be noticed that the estimation formulae above are very similar to those of Section 3, although the present model has a different economic meaning.

If, as assumed, $Nm_{xx} \to \infty$ as $N \to \infty$, all the estimates above are consistent, by the same type of argument as that of Section 2.

An estimate of a parameter is in itself of little practical value unless it is accompanied by some measure of reliability. What we want is a "confidence region" for the unknown parameters: that is, if we consider all possible simultaneous values of the parameters as points in a parameter space, we want to construct a region, or set of points, which is a function of the observations, and which has a preassigned probability of covering the true, but unknown, parameter point. We shall indicate how such a region could be constructed in connection with the model above. We shall consider only the two "essential" parameters, α and μ.

Let us first make the assumption that u_t and w_t have a joint probability distribution which is approximately normal. As before, we assume that x_t is a fixed variable. Denote by A_1 the true value of the coefficient $\alpha(1-\mu)/[1-(1-\mu)\alpha]$ in (4.6), and by A_2 the true value of the coefficient $(1-\mu)/[1-(1-\mu)\alpha]$ in (4.7). And let $\hat{A}_1$ and $\hat{A}_2$ be the corresponding estimates, as given by (4.8) and (4.9). Under the assumptions made, the statistics $\hat{A}_1$ and $\hat{A}_2$ will be linear functions of normally distributed variables. $\hat{A}_1$ and $\hat{A}_2$ will therefore also be normally distributed. Their means will be equal to A_1 and A_2, respectively. The variance-covariance matrix of $\hat{A}_1$ and $\hat{A}_2$ will depend on σ_u^2, σ_w^2, σ_{uw}, α, and μ. It is then possible to obtain a joint confidence region for α and μ in the following manner.

Let σ_{11} and σ_{22}, and σ_{12} be the variances and the covariance of the residual random elements in (4.6) and (4.7), i.e.,

$$\sigma_{11} = \mathcal{E}\left[\frac{u_t - \alpha w_t}{1-(1-\mu)\alpha}\right]^2 \tag{4.16}$$

$$\sigma_{22} = \mathcal{E}\left[\frac{(1-\mu)u_t - w_t}{1-(1-\mu)\alpha}\right]^2 \tag{4.17}$$

$$\sigma_{12} = \mathcal{E}\left[\frac{u_t - \alpha w_t}{1-(1-\mu)\alpha}\cdot\frac{(1-\mu)u_t - w_t}{1-(1-\mu)\alpha}\right]. \tag{4.18}$$

If equations (4.6) and (4.7) are fitted to the data by the method of least squares, we obtain unbiased estimates, s_{11}, s_{22}, and s_{12}, of σ_{11}, σ_{22}, and σ_{12}, respectively. These estimates are

$$s_{11} = \frac{N}{N-2}\,\frac{m_{cc}m_{xx} - m_{cx}^2}{m_{xx}} \tag{4.19}$$

$$s_{22} = \frac{N}{N-2}\,\frac{m_{yy}m_{xx} - m_{yx}^2}{m_{xx}} \tag{4.20}$$

$$s_{12} = \frac{N}{N-2}\,\frac{m_{cy}m_{xx} - m_{cx}m_{yx}}{m_{xx}}. \tag{4.21}$$

Consider now the statistic T^2 defined by

$$T^2 = N m_{xx} \sum_{i,j=1}^{i,j=2} s^{ij}(A_i - \hat{A}_i)(A_j - \hat{A}_j) \tag{4.22}$$

where s^{ij} denotes the inverse of the matrix s_{ij}. The distribution of the statistic T^2 is known. More specifically $\{(N - 3)/[2(N - 2)]\}T^2$ has the F distribution with 2 and $N - 3$ degrees of freedom.[12] Choosing a certain level of significance, we find the corresponding value of F in Snedecor's table.[13] Let the corresponding value of T^2 be T_0^2. The set of points A_1, A_2 in the parameter space (A_1, A_2) for which $T^2 \leqslant T_0^2$ form the area of an ellipse with its center at $(\hat{A}_1, \hat{A}_2)$. This is a confidence region for the parameter point (A_1, A_2).

Since the transformation from the (A_1, A_2) plane to the (α, μ) plane is continuous, the confidence region derived for A_1, A_2 leads to a corresponding confidence region for α and μ. This transformation is given by the definition of A_1 and A_2. Expressing α and μ in terms of A_1 and A_2, we have

$$\alpha = \frac{A_1}{A_2} \tag{4.23}$$

$$\mu = 1 - \frac{A_2}{1 + A_1}. \tag{4.24}$$

In the next section we shall give some numerical illustrations.

5. Some Numerical Results

Some of the methods discussed in the preceding sections have been applied to U.S. data, partly for the period 1922–1941, partly for the period 1929–1941. The data used are given in Table 1.[14] Moments used in the calculations are listed in the appendix to Table 1. The numerical results given below are numbered so as to correspond to the theoretical formulae given in the preceding, theoretical sections. These results should, therefore, require little additional explanation.

[12] This fact was pointed out by Dr. T. W. Anderson. See also Wilks [1943, pp. 234–250].

[13] See Snedecor [1940, p. 184].

[14] It will be noticed that, in addition to reducing the figures to a per capita basis, we have used the Bureau of Labor Statistics cost of living index as a common deflator. By this procedure we do not, of course, mean to imply that the measure of "real investment" thus obtained is a good measure of the physical output of investment goods. The purpose of deflating the current-dollars series by the cost of living index is only to eliminate the effect of a scale factor in all prices, this scale factor being taken to be an autonomous variable. If we postulate that the absolute level of prices should not affect the real volume of consumption, investment, etc., we are—at least in point of principle—free to choose any price index as a common deflator.

TABLE 1

U. S. DATA USED IN STUDY

Year	(1) Disposable income, dollars per capita, deflated y_t	(2) Consumers' expenditure, dollars per capita, deflated c_t	(3) $z_t = y_t - c_t$	(4) "Gross investment" dollars per capita, deflated x_t	(5) Deflator: B.L.S. Cost of Living 1935–39 = 100	(6) U. S. population millions
1922	433	394	39	—	119.7	110.1
23	483	423	60	—	121.9	112.0
24	479	437	42	—	122.2	114.1
25	486	434	52	—	125.4	115.8
26	494	447	47	—	126.4	117.4
27	498	447	51	—	124.0	119.0
28	511	466	45	—	122.6	120.5
29	534	474	60	128	122.5	121.8
1930	478	439	39	97	119.4	123.8
31	440	399	41	81	108.7	124.8
32	372	350	22	45	97.6	125.6
33	381	364	17	45	92.4	126.3
34	419	392	27	66	95.7	127.1
35	449	416	33	78	98.1	128.0
36	511	463	48	103	99.1	128.9
37	520	469	51	98	102.1	129.6
38	477	444	33	83	100.8	130.7
39	517	471	46	105	99.4	131.7
1940	548	494	54	122	100.2	132.8
41	629	529	100	165	105.2	134.0
Sums:						
1922–41	9659	8752	907	—		
1929–41	6275	5704	—	1216	—	—
Means:						
1922–41	482.95	437.60	45.35			
1929–41	482.692	438.769		93.5385		

Second-order moments about mean:

1922–41:

$m_{yy} = 3249.65$ $m_{cy} = 2379.25$
$m_{cc} = 1794.35$ $m_{yz} = 870.40$
$m_{zz} = 285.55$ $m_{cz} = 584.90$

1929–41:

$m_{yy} = 4718.23$ $m_{cy} = 3413.69$
$m_{cc} = 2519.85$ $m_{yx} = 2159.62$
$m_{xx} = 1025.92$ $m_{cx} = 1537.85$

Sources of data.

Columns (1), (2), and (3): Years 1929–41 from *Survey of Current Business*, May, 1942, p. 12 Earlier years from unpublished estimates by the Department of Commerce. Deflated per capita, figures have been calculated by means of Columns (5) and (6).

Column (4): See (4.1) for definition of x_t. Years 1929–41 from *Survey of Current Business*, May, 1942, as revised in subsequent issues.

Columns (5) and (6): See, e.g , *Statistical Abstracts of the United States*. (Population figures for 1930–41 have been adjusted for underenumeration of children under 5.)

A. Numerical illustrations to Section 2. Applying formulae (2.11), (2.14), and (2.15) to the data given in Table 1, we obtain the following estimates:

$$\text{(2.11.a)} \qquad \frac{1}{1-\hat{\alpha}} = 3.048 \quad \text{(the "multiplier")}$$

$$\text{(2.14.a)} \qquad \hat{\alpha} = 0.672 \quad \text{(the marginal propensity to consume)}$$

$$\text{(2.15.a)} \qquad \hat{\beta} = 113.1.$$

Formula (2.13), for $N = 20$, gives

$$\text{(2.13.a)} \qquad s^2 = 662.82; \qquad s = 25.7$$

from which we obtain the standard error of $1/(1 - \hat{\alpha}) = s/\sqrt{20m_{zz}} = 0.341$. From tables of the t-distribution, and choosing 5 per cent as the level of significance, we find

$$\text{(2.21.a)} \qquad -2.101 \leqq t = \frac{3.048 - \dfrac{1}{1-\alpha}}{0.341} \leqq 2.101,$$

from which it follows that

$$2.33 \leqq \frac{1}{1-\alpha} \leqq 3.76.$$

The corresponding confidence interval for α is

$$0.57 \leqq \alpha \leqq 0.73.$$

For comparison, we have calculated the least-squares "estimates," a and b, obtaining

$$\text{(2.16.a)} \qquad a = 0.732$$

$$\text{(2.17.a)} \qquad b = 84.0.$$

As one might expect [see (2.19) and (2.20)], we find that $a > \hat{\alpha}$, and $b < \hat{\beta}$. Although the difference does not appear to be very large in terms of α, it is considerable in terms of the multiplier $1/(1 - \alpha)$, viz. 3.048 versus 3.731.[15]

B. Numerical illustrations to Section 4. Here we consider the model given by (4.2)–(4.5). We use data for 1929–1941 only, since the present model requires that the various terms add up in the manner defined by

[15] Although it is not the purpose of this chapter to improve upon economic theory, it is perhaps of interest to observe that, under the approach outlined

the U.S. Department of Commerce estimates of the gross national product and its components. Consistent data in this respect are available only from 1929. The results obtained are as follows:

(4.8.a) $\hat{A}_1 = 1.499$

(4.9.a) $\hat{A}_2 = 2.105$

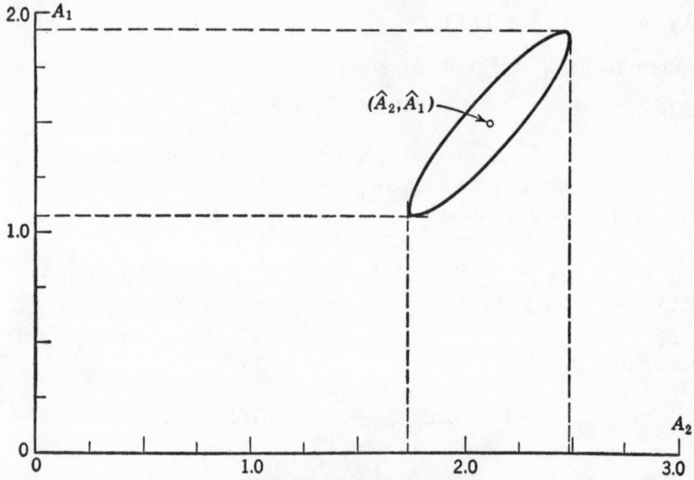

FIGURE 1—Joint confidence region for A_1 and A_2; level of significance, 5%.

(4.12.a) $\hat{\alpha} = 0.712$

(4.13.a) $\hat{\beta} = 95.05$

(4.14.a) $\hat{\mu} = 0.158$

(4.15.a) $\hat{\nu} = -34.30.$

The estimate of α is here slightly higher than that given by (2.14.a), while the estimate of β is, correspondingly, somewhat lower. (For comparison, we have also here calculated the least-squares regression of c_t on y_t. The "estimate" obtained for α was 0.723, which in this case happens to come rather close to the estimate α above.)

---

above, it is possible to show that last year's income also plays a role as a variable in the consumption function. By a method similar to that used above, treating y_{t-1} as a predetermined variable, one finds $c_t = 0.57y_t + 0.16y_{t-1} +$ const., while the least-squares estimate of this equation yields $c_t = 0.7y_t + 0.05y_{t-1} +$ const.

We shall derive a confidence region for α and μ. For this purpose we have calculated

$$s_{11} = 253.658 \tag{4.19.a}$$

$$s_{22} = 203.439 \tag{4.20.a}$$

$$s_{12} = 208.538. \tag{4.21.a}$$

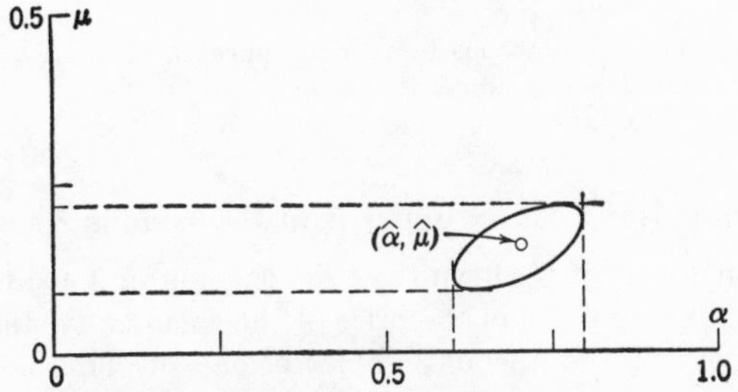

FIGURE 2—Joint confidence region for α and μ, corresponding to the region in Figure 1.

Now, $[(N - 3)/2(N - 2)]T^2$ has the "F"-distribution, $F_{2,N-3}$. In our case $N = 13$. Choosing the 5 per cent level of significance, we find from Snedecor's table that $F = 4.10$. The corresponding value of T^2 is then $T_0^2 = 9.02$. Using this and (4.19.a)–(4.21.a) we derive

$$\begin{aligned} 9.02 = 13337\,[&0.02507(A_1 - \hat{A}_1)^2 \\ &- 0.05139(A_1 - \hat{A}_1)(A_2 - \hat{A}_2) + 0.03125(A_2 - \hat{A}_2)^2], \end{aligned} \tag{4.22.a}$$

where $\hat{A}_1$ and $\hat{A}_2$ are given by (4.8.a) and (4.9.a). (4.22.a) represents an ellipse in the parameter space of A_1 and A_2. The area covered by this ellipse is the confidence region for A_1 and A_2. It is shown in Figure 1. The corresponding confidence region for α and μ is shown in Figure 2. This latter region was derived numerically by means of the transformations defining A_1 and A_2.

Chapter V

STATISTICAL ANALYSIS OF THE DEMAND FOR FOOD: EXAMPLES OF SIMULTANEOUS ESTIMATION OF STRUCTURAL EQUATIONS[1]

By M. A. Girshick and Trygve Haavelmo

1. Introduction: The Simultaneous-Equations Approach

In economic theory it is shown that the demand for a commodity can be considered as a function of the price of the commodity, the prices of other commodities, and the disposable income of the consumer. By analogy, we are led to the hypothesis that the total demand for the commodity may be considered a function of all prices and of total disposable income of all consumers. The ideal method of verifying this hypothesis and of obtaining a picture of the demand function involved would be to conduct a large-scale experiment, imposing alternative prices and levels of income on the consumers and studying their reaction. If we could produce a large number of observations in this way we should probably find that the data would not satisfy, exactly, any simple functional relationship. Let x_t be the tth observation of the

[1] This chapter is a reprinting of parts of an article which appeared under the same title in *Econometrica*, Vol. 15, April, 1947, pp. 79–110. In its original form the article contained an exposition of the theory of the limited-information method for estimating an equation and the computation procedure for obtaining these estimates. Since these topics are treated more extensively in Chapters VI and X of the present volume, the parts of the article devoted to them have been deleted from the version printed here. In particular, Section 3 and material from pages 100–108 of Section 4 of the original version have been deleted and minor compensating changes made. As stated in the original version, the present chapter contains some preliminary, and highly tentative, results of a project of quantitative research in agricultural economics of the Department of Economics of the University of Chicago and the Cowles Commission for Research in Economics. The authors gratefully acknowledge their indebtedness to colleagues at the U. S. Bureau of Agricultural Economics and the University of Chicago for helpful suggestions and constructive criticism. Special thanks are extended to Miss Selma Schweitzer and Mrs. Lois N. Shores. They have carried out most of the numerical work and have also helped to improve the exposition of the statistical methods involved. Needless to say, the authors assume all responsibility for the results presented.

quantity consumed, $p_{1t}, p_{2t}, \cdots, p_{nt}$ the corresponding prices of the n commodities in the market, and y_t income, and let $F(p_{1t}, p_{2t}, \cdots, p_{nt}, y_t; \alpha_1, \alpha_2, \cdots, \alpha_k)$ be a function containing k parameters $\alpha_1, \alpha_2, \cdots, \alpha_k$. Then we could write, in a purely formal way,

$$x_t = F(p_{1t}, p_{2t}, \cdots, p_{nt}, y_t; \alpha_1, \alpha_2, \cdots, \alpha_k) + u_t, \tag{1.1}$$

where u_t is a "residual." In order to operate with a reasonably simple function, F, with a finite number of parameters, α, it would be necessary to admit nonzero values of the u's. The relation (1.1) would be only a useless rewriting of the facts unless we could say something more about the properties of the u's. The u's must have some properties that are predictable *on the average.* A rational way of expressing this hypothesis is to assume that the u's are stochastic variables having certain characteristic distribution properties. The economic meaning of such a model is that, given a certain set of values of prices and income, consumers do not always behave in exactly the same way, perhaps because of the influence of other, neglected, variables or simply because the individuals are not absolutely consistent in their behavior.

If we were able to conduct an experiment as described we might take the values of the p's and of y to be a set of fixed, predetermined numbers, while the observations of x would be random variables, the stochastic properties of which would be defined implicitly by the stochastic properties assumed for the u's. On the basis of a set of observations and an assumed known form of the function F we might then be able to estimate the parameters α and also the parameters in the distribution of the u's.

Implicit in this statement is the assumption that there are no errors of measurement in the p's and y, in other words, that the observed values of the prices are the prices actually paid by the consumers and that the observations of y are correct measurements of their income.

But suppose it is not possible to carry out a rational experiment of the type described. Could we not assume that an "experiment" of a similar type is being carried out automatically by the market mechanism of the economy? Most of the numerical studies of demand functions have in fact been founded on this basis. It has been assumed that observed series of simultaneous values of consumer purchases, prices, and income represent data that are statistically of the same nature as those that one would obtain by an experiment of the type described. On this basis various types of demand functions have been fitted to observed data by choosing quantities consumed as the "dependent" variables and the prices and income as "independent" variables. There is a fundamental error in this approach. It leads to a logical contradiction: The demand function should, theoretically, be independent of the manner in which the prices and income are being fixed. But the "demand" function obtained by fitting the function (1.1) to market data for quantities purchased, prices, and income—as if they were the results of our hypothetical experiment—will depend on the nature of the other economic relations that, together with the demand function, determine the observable quantities, prices, and incomes. It is not always easy to see this intuitively. A simple example might be helpful.

Let x_t be a time series of the quantity consumed of a certain commodity and let p_t be the corresponding price series. And suppose that the demand function to be estimated is of the simple form

$$x_t = \alpha p_t + \beta + u_t, \qquad t = 1, 2, \cdots. \tag{1.2}$$

Suppose it is known that the u's are normally and independently distributed with $\mathcal{E}(u_t) = 0$, $\mathcal{E}(u_t^2) = \sigma_u^2$ for all values of t. We assume that x and p are observed without errors of measurement. Suppose that we try to estimate α and β by a least-squares regression of x on p. We shall show that the result of this procedure *will depend on the form of the supply function*. Let us assume two different alternatives for the supply function:

$$x_t = h_1 p_t + k_1 + v_t \tag{1.3a}$$

or

$$x_t = h_2 p_{t-1} + k_2 + w_t, \tag{1.3b}$$

where the v's and the w's are random residuals while the h's and the k's are constants.

Suppose, first, that (1.3a) is the true supply function. And let us assume that the v's are normally and independently distributed with $\mathcal{E}(v_t) = 0$ and $\mathcal{E}(v_t^2) = \sigma_v^2$ for all values of t. Let $\mathcal{E}(u_t v_t) = \sigma_{uv}$ be the covariance between u and v. Let, further, m_{xx}, m_{xp}, etc., denote second-order moments about the mean, and m_x, m_p, etc., the means of the variables, over the range $t = 1, 2, \cdots, T$. Then the regression of x on p yields a regression equation

$$x^{(\text{est})} = ap + b,$$

where

$$a = \frac{m_{xp}}{m_{pp}}, \tag{1.4}$$

$$b = \frac{m_x m_{pp} - m_p m_{xp}}{m_{pp}}. \tag{1.5}$$

Let us consider the estimate, a, that would be obtained for an infinite sample, so that we do not have the extra complications of sampling variations. In order to see what the formula (1.4) would mean under this condition we solve the two equations (1.2) and (1.3a) for x_t and p_t, obtaining

$$(1.6) \qquad x_t = A + U_t,$$

$$\text{where } A = \frac{\alpha k_1 - \beta h_1}{\alpha - h_1} \quad \text{and} \quad U_t = \frac{\alpha v_t - h_1 u_t}{\alpha - h_1},$$

and

$$(1.7) \qquad p_t = B + V_t,$$

$$\text{where } B = \frac{k_1 - \beta}{\alpha - h_1} \quad \text{and} \quad V_t = \frac{v_t - u_t}{\alpha - h_1}.$$

Equations (1.6 and (1.7) are called the *reduced form* of the system (1.2) and (1.3a). For an infinite sample we can replace the moments m_{xp} and m_{pp} by the covariance σ_{xp} and the variance σ_{pp} respectively, where, from (1.6) and (1.7),

$$(1.8) \qquad \sigma_{xp} = \frac{\alpha\sigma_v^2 - (\alpha + h_1)\sigma_{uv} + h_1\sigma_u^2}{(\alpha - h_1)^2},$$

$$(1.9) \qquad \sigma_{pp} = \frac{\sigma_v^2 - 2\sigma_{uv} + \sigma_u^2}{(\alpha - h_1)^2}.$$

From this we obtain a value for a that approaches, in the probability sense, the limit

$$(1.10) \qquad \frac{\alpha\sigma_v^2 - (\alpha + h_1)\sigma_{uv} + h_1\sigma_u^2}{\sigma_v^2 - 2\sigma_{uv} + \sigma_u^2}.$$

Whether this is an estimate of α in the sense that, apart from chance fluctuations arising in samples of finite size, it equals α, depends not only on α but on the value of the σ's and h_1. In fact, if the supply equation (1.3a) is true, and we have no other a priori information, it is impossible to estimate α or β by any method whatsoever. This is seen as follows: Let us multiply equation (1.2) by an arbitrary factor c and equation (1.3a) by $(1 - c)$ and add the two equations. This gives

$$(1.11) \quad x_1 = [h_1 + c(\alpha - h_1)]p_t + [k_1 + c(\beta - k_1)] + [cu_t + (1 - c)v_t].$$

This equation is of the same form as any one of the original equations, and the residual term $[cu_t + (1 - c)v_t]$ has exactly the same general properties as u or v, which are in any case not observable. By varying c we get an infinity of equations, any one of which can replace (1.2) or (1.3a) without any observable effect on the x's and the p's. Obviously the data do not contain any information by which to identify the particular equation (1.2).

Thus, if (1.3a) is the supply equation there exists no formula for estimating the parameters of the demand function (1.2). This cannot be seen from the specification of the demand function alone.

Let us now assume that (1.3b) is the true supply function instead of (1.3a). And let us again solve the system for x_t and p_t. We then obtain, as the *reduced form* of the system (1.2) and (1.3b), the following system:

$$x_t = h_2 p_{t-1} + k_2 + w_t \qquad \text{[equation (1.3b)]}, \tag{1.12}$$

$$p_t = \frac{h_2}{\alpha} p_{t-1} + \frac{k_2 - \beta}{\alpha} + \frac{w_t - u_t}{\alpha}. \tag{1.13}$$

Obviously p_{t-1} does not depend on u_t and w_t. It depends only on u_{t-1}, u_{t-2}, $\cdots$, and w_{t-1}, w_{t-2}, $\cdots$. By fitting each of the two equations (1.12) and (1.13) to the data by the method of least squares using p_{t-1} as the independent variable we can obtain estimates of the coefficients of the reduced form, viz., h_2, k_2, h_2/α, and $(k_2 - \beta)/\alpha$. We can get these estimates as accurately as we please by taking a sufficiently large sample, supposing the assumptions made to be valid over a sufficiently long period. From these four estimates we can in turn calculate the corresponding values of α and β. *But this method of estimating α and β could not have been deduced from the specification of (1.2) alone.*

Suppose that, in this second model, we should consider the regression of x on p, that is, the regression coefficients (1.4) and (1.5). Let us calculate what $a = m_{xp}/m_{pp}$ would be in the present model, assuming an infinite sample. From (1.12) and (1.13) we obtain

$$m_{xp} = \frac{h_2^2}{\alpha} m_{p_{t-1}, p_{t-1}} + \frac{1}{\alpha}(\sigma_w^2 - \sigma_{uw}), \tag{1.14}$$

$$m_{pp} = \frac{h_2^2}{\alpha^2} m_{p_{t-1}, p_{t-1}} + \frac{1}{\alpha^2}(\sigma_w^2 - 2\sigma_{uw} + \sigma_u^2). \tag{1.15}$$

Therefore,

$$a = \frac{m_{xp}}{m_{pp}} = \frac{\alpha(h_2^2 m_{p_{t-1}, p_{t-1}} - \sigma_{uw} + \sigma_w^2)}{h_2^2 m_{p_{t-1}, p_{t-1}} + \sigma_u^2 - 2\sigma_{uw} + \sigma_w^2}. \tag{1.16}$$

Obviously, this expression is not, in general, equal to α, nor is it, in general, equal to the expression (1.10).

These illustrations should be sufficient to show the difficulties encountered in devising estimation formulae for the estimation of a demand function on the basis of a specification of this function alone. This is, indeed, impossible if the supply function or other relationships involving the same variables are of such a form as to make the demand function unidentifiable. For the case in which identifiability is assured or hypothesized, estimation procedures requiring for their consistency very little beyond that hypothesis have been proposed by Wald [1950b]. However, these estimates must be regarded as rather inefficient whenever information about the form of other relationships in the model is available. Generally, if we wish to estimate any particular economic relationship on the basis of market data, we are materially helped by considering, simultaneously, the whole system of economic relations that together represent the mechanism that produces the data we observe in the market. Our examples above already indicate some of the tools of statistical technique that are available for dealing with problems of this nature. We shall attempt to set out the principles in somewhat more general terms.

Let $y_1(t), \cdots, y_n(t)$ denote n observable economic time series. Assume that these n series satisfy n linear stochastic lag relations involving m observable "exogenous" time series $z_1(t), \cdots, z_m(t)$, and n random, nonobservable residuals $u_1(t), \cdots, u_n(t)$ expressing the stochastic nature of economic behavior. To simplify the exposition we shall assume that there is only one type of lag term involved, namely $y_i(t-1)$, $i = 1, 2, \cdots, n$. But our results can easily be generalized to the case where other lags are involved. Let this system of relations be

$$(1.17) \quad \sum_{j=1}^{n} \alpha_{ij} y_j(t) + \sum_{j=1}^{n} \beta_{ij} y_j(t-1) + \sum_{j=1}^{m} \gamma_{ij} z_j(t) = u_i(t),$$

$$i = 1, 2, \cdots n; t = 1, 2, \cdots T.$$

It is assumed that the variables y and z are observable *without significant errors of measurement*, in other words, that these variables are measured according to their definition in our economic theory.

We make the following assumptions about the random elements $u_i(t)$:

$$(1.18) \quad \mathcal{E}u_i(t) = 0, \qquad i = 1, 2, \cdots, n; t = 1, 2, \cdots, T;$$

$$(1.19) \quad \mathcal{E}[u_i(t)u_j(t)] = \sigma_{ij}, \qquad i, j = 1, 2, \cdots, n; t = 1, 2, \cdots, T;$$

$$(1.20) \quad \mathcal{E}[u_i(t)u_j(t-\theta)] = 0, \qquad i, j = 1, 2, \cdots, n; \theta \neq 0;$$

$$(1.21) \quad z_j(t) \text{ stochastically independent of } u_i(t'),$$

$$j = 1, 2, \cdots, m; i = 1, 2, \cdots, n; t, t' = 1, 2, \cdots, T.$$

(1.19) says that simultaneous values of the n u's have a certain unknown n-by-n matrix of variances and covariances that do not depend on t. (1.20) means that there is no serial correlation in the u's. It is easily seen that the assumptions (1.20) and (1.21) imply that $y_j(t-1)$ and $u_i(t)$ are stochastically independent for all values of i and j.

The problem is to estimate the α's, the β's, the γ's, and the σ's from the observations of the y's and the z's at successive points of time $t = 0, 1, 2, \cdots, T$. From the form of the system (1.17), however, we see immediately that there is, in each equation, an arbitrary proportionality factor that we can never estimate from the data, because we cannot observe the u's and hence we do not know the scale of the σ's. One way of disposing of this arbitrariness is to impose a *rule of normalization*, e.g., by assuming that one of the α's in each equation is $= 1$. After this normalization there remain $n(n - 1)$ α's, n^2 β's, nm γ's, and $n(n + 1)/2$ σ's to be estimated from the data.

Now, let us consider the *reduced form* of the system (1.17). This is the system of equations obtained by considering the system (1.17), for any given value of t, as a system of n linear equations in $y_1(t), \cdots, y_n(t)$ and solving for $y_i(t)$ in terms of the lagged y's, the z's, and the u's. Obviously these solutions will be linear expressions in the variables $y(t - 1)$, the $z(t)$'s, and the $u(t)$'s. That is, the reduced form of (1.17) will be

$$y_i(t) = \sum_1^n \pi_{ij} y_j(t - 1) + \sum_1^m \pi'_{ij} z_j(t) + v_i(t), \qquad i = 1, 2, \cdots, n; t = 1, 2, \cdots, T, \tag{1.22}$$

where the π's are constants that depend on the α's, the β's, and the γ's in (1.17), while the v's are new random residuals that are simply linear combinations of the u's in (1.17). The v's therefore have stochastic properties that are exactly similar to those of the u's as given by (1.18) $-$(1.21). The variances and covariances of the v's will depend upon the variances and covariances of the u's and upon the α's. In particular, the v's will be stochastically independent of the variables $y(t - 1)$ and the variables $z(t)$. This follows from our assumptions about the u's. It can then be shown that by fitting each of the equations (1.22) to the data by the method of least squares, considering $y_i(t)$ as the dependent variable, the estimates p_{ij} and p'_{ij} obtained for π_{ij} and π'_{ij}, respectively, will possess certain optimal properties of "best estimates."

Obviously the system (1.22) is equivalent to the system (1.17) as far as the observations of the y's and the z's are concerned. Knowledge of the values of the π's and the parameters of the distribution of the v's would cover exhaustively all the implications of our theory as far as its observable consequences are concerned. This raises the following fundamental problem: To every system (1.17) there generally corresponds one and only one reduced form (1.22), that is, one and only one set of values of the π's and the variances and covariances of the v's. But does the converse also hold? That is, will the knowledge of the values of the π's and the variances and covariances of the v's determine uniquely the values of the α's, the β's, etc.? *This is the problem of identification.*

There are, altogether, $n(n + m)$ π's and $n(n + 1)/2$ variances and covariances of the v's. These parameters can be estimated from the data. Since these parameters are functions of the α's, the β's, the γ's, and the σ's our estimates provide us with $[n(n + m) + n(n + 1)/2]$ equations by which to calculate estimates of the original parameters. But from our counting above we found that, without additional restrictions upon the original parameters, there were $[n(n - 1) + n(n + m) + n(n + 1)/2]$ unknown parameters to be estimated. That is, there would be $n(n - 1)$ more unknown parameters than could be estimated from the data. We then say that there is *lack of identification* in the system. The only way of getting around this difficulty is to assume that we have some additional a priori information about the unknown parameters. The most frequently used type of assumptions of this kind is that some of the α's, β's, and γ's are known to be equal to zero, which means that some of the variables do not actually occur in all of the equations. By adding a sufficient number of such restrictions the system may become "*just identified*"; that is, having estimates of the π's and the variances and covariances of the v's we have exactly enough independent equations to determine the original, unknown parameters. If we have even more a priori restrictions than are required for this purpose, the system may become *overidentified*, that is, the estimates of the π's and the variances and covariances of the v's give us more equations by which to derive the original parameters than there are such unknown parameters. This happens, of course, only if we *neglect the extra restrictions* in estimating the π's and the variances and covariances of the v's. To take account of side restrictions upon the π's or the variance-covariance matrix of the v's in the process of estimating these parameters often leads, however, to very complicated computational problems. To get around this difficulty, certain short-cut methods have been worked out, whereby part of the a priori restrictions upon the coefficients are neglected, and therefore some statistical efficiency is given up, in return for simpler computational procedure. These methods, known as limited-information methods, will be explained in Chapters VI and X of the present volume.[2]

The notions of "lack of identification," "just identified," and "overidentified" can obviously be applied also to a single equation in the system (1.17), by considering whether or not the knowledge of the π's and the variance-covariance matrix of the v's allows us to derive uniquely

[2] See Chapter VI, Section 6, and Chapter X, Sections 3, 8, 9.

the parameters of that particular equation. Some of the equations in the system may be identifiable while others are not.[3]

It will be noticed that these properties of identifiability are formal properties of the system of equations that one is considering in each case. A careful analysis of these properties is necessary before one attempts to derive actual, numerical estimates.

In the following sections we shall discuss a tentative application of the various principles discussed above to a model of the connection between agriculture and the rest of the economy.

2. Macrodynamic Models Explaining the Demand for Food

We have pointed out that if one wants to study economic relations within one particular sector of the economy, one usually has to consider also the economic relations that govern the other sectors. But for practical reasons some simplification of the general theory is unavoidable. By methods of aggregation one has to try to reduce the number of the relations in which one is not directly interested to a minimum. The models below illustrate this principle.

A. The Demand for Food

If one divides total consumption into two groups, food and nonfood, one could say, by analogy from the microtheory of consumers' choice, that the per capita demand for food is a function of the price of food, the price of nonfood, and the per capita disposable income. Let c_1 denote annual per capita expenditure for food, and let p_1 be the price of food, p_2 the price of nonfood, P the total cost-of-living index, and r_t per capita disposable income. We may take $y_1 = c_1/p_1$ as an index of the volume of food consumption. Since P is a function of p_1 and p_2 we might consider the variables p_1 and P instead of p_1 and p_2. Let $y_2 = p_1/P$ denote the relative price of food and $y_3 = r/P$ the deflated per capita disposable income. Assuming the demand function to be a linear function of the relative price of food, y_2, and the "real income," y_3, we are then led to the hypothesis:

$$y_1(t) = \alpha_{12}y_2(t) + \alpha_{13}y_3(t) + \alpha_{10} + u_1(t), \tag{2.1a}$$

where the α's are constants and $u_1(t)$ is a random residual (a random "shift") for each value of t. The demand for food may be subject to a

[3] For a more detailed treatment of the problems of identification see Chapters II and VI, Section 4.4 and Appendix A, of this volume and also Chapters II, III, and IV of *Statistical Inference in Dynamic Economic Models*, Cowles Commission Monograph 10, New York: John Wiley & Sons, 1950.

trend due to changes in tastes, eating habits, etc., so that, alternatively, we might consider the demand

$$(2.1b) \qquad y_1(t) = \alpha_{12}y_2(t) + \alpha_{13}y_3(t) + \gamma_{11}t + \alpha_{10} + u_1(t).$$

Still another alternative would be that the consumption of food also depends, to some extent, on past income $y_3(t - 1)$, in which case we would write

$$(2.1c) \quad y_1(t) = \alpha_{12}y_2(t) + \alpha_{13}y_3(t) + \gamma_{11}t + \gamma_{12}y_3(t - 1) + \alpha_{10} + u_1(t).$$

The α's, the γ's, and the u's would of course have different interpretations in each of these three alternative equations. A similar remark applies to the various alternatives with respect to the other equations discussed below.

It will be noticed that in each of the three alternative demand equations there are three *simultaneous, or jointly dependent, variables*, that is, variables that have to be "explained" by other relations in the economic system, while the variables t and $y_3(t - 1)$ may be considered as *given* or predetermined in the sense that they are stochastically independent of the random variable $u_1(t)$. We assume that $\mathcal{E}[u_1(t)u_1(t-\tau)] = 0$ for $\tau \neq 0$, in other words, that there is no serial correlation in the residuals $u_1(t)$.

B. The Income Equation

In statistical studies of demand functions it has usually been assumed that income could be considered as a *given*, or independent, variable. In particular, it has been argued that, if the commodity in question represents only a small part of the budget, the repercussions upon income of variations in the demand for the commodity could be neglected. This hypothesis is obviously false. We could always split up total consumption into small subgroups by a sufficiently detailed specification of the various types of consumer goods. Obviously such a regrouping could not alter the fact that changes in the total consumer expenditures have a direct effect on income, income being the sum of consumers' expenditures and investment expenditures. We must therefore assume that income $y_3(t)$ depends to some extent on the random shifts $u_1(t)$ in the demand for food.

To arrive at an equation for income we must first derive the demand for all consumer goods. By our definition above this total demand is the sum of the demand for food and the demand for nonfood. Instead of considering the two equations, "demand for food" and "demand for nonfood," we might, however, equally well consider the pair, "demand for food" and "demand for all consumer goods." For the latter we may adopt the commonly accepted hypothesis that total per capita consumers' expenditure, deflated, is a linear function of real income, subject to random shifts. If $c(t)$ denotes per capita consumers' expenditure we therefore assume that

$$\frac{c(t)}{P(t)} = \alpha y_3(t) + \alpha_0 + u(t), \tag{2.2}$$

where $u(t)$ is a random residual that is the sum of the residual $u_1(t)$ in the demand equation for food and the corresponding residual in the demand function for nonfood. It will be noted that the prices p_1 and p_2 do not appear explicitly in this equation. This is equivalent to assuming that if the prices of individual commodities change there is no change in the relative allocation of income between present and future expected consumption (i.e., savings) except that which is brought about by the (real) income effect of the price change.

In order to derive an equation for income, y_3, we now adopt the hypothesis that investment expenditures measured in constant dollars represent an *autonomous variable*, an impressed force. We define the investment expenditures, $z(t)$, as

$$z(t) = \frac{I(t)}{P(t)} = y_3(t) - \frac{c(t)}{P(t)}, \tag{2.3}$$

where $I(t)$ is per capita investment expenditures in current dollars. From (2.2) and (2.3) we then derive

$$y_3(t) = \gamma_{31} z(t) + \alpha_{30} + u_3(t), \tag{2.4a}$$

where

$$\gamma_{31} = \frac{1}{1-\alpha}, \qquad \alpha_{30} = \frac{\alpha_0}{1-\alpha}, \qquad u_3(t) = \frac{u(t)}{1-\alpha}.$$

This might be called "the multiplier theory of income." There might be a trend in the consumption function (2.2), in which case we would obtain

$$y_3(t) = \gamma_{31} z(t) + \gamma_{32} t + \alpha_{30} + u_3(t). \tag{2.4b}$$

Furthermore, it is possible that the consumption function also depends on lagged income, in which case we would obtain

$$y_3(t) = \gamma_{31} z(t) + \gamma_{32} t + \gamma_{33} y_3(t-1) + \alpha_{30} + u_3(t). \tag{2.4c}$$

C. Supply of Food in the Retail Market

In order to arrive at an approximate model for the marketing chain for food products we propose to split the supply mechanism into two steps: namely the "supply by the farmers, demand by the commercial sector," and "supply by the commercial sector, demand by the consumers." In other words, we consider the whole commercial sector between the farmers and the consuming public as a "factory" buying raw materials from the farmers and supplying finished food products to the public.

Consider the supply of finished food products. In general, one might assume that this supply would depend on the retail price and the prices paid to farmers for crude foodstuffs. As an alternative to the variable "prices paid to farmers" in this supply function one might instead consider farm output of foodstuff, assuming that the farmer *has to sell* once the foodstuff has been produced, and that, therefore, prices paid to farmers may be considered as a residual share. One might also expect a trend in the supply equation, due to gradual change in processing and marketing technique. Since the commercial sector has the alternative of exporting instead of selling on the home market, and of importing food instead of buying from domestic farmers, the export and import prices might also enter the supply equation. In that case we assume, as an approximation, that the export and import prices are proportional, so that the "foreign" price can be represented by one price, the export price.

Let $y_4(t)$ denote the per capita supply of food by farmers to the commercial sector. (For simplicity we may consider—somewhat artificially perhaps—the farmers' own food consumption as also going through the commercial channels.) Let, further, $y_5(t)$ denote prices paid to farmers, and let $p_e(t)$ be the price of food in foreign markets. Both these prices should be considered as "normalized" by deflating them by the general cost-of-living index. Then we might consider the following alternative hypotheses regarding the retail supply of food:

$$(2.5a)\quad y_1(t) = \alpha_{22}y_2(t) + \alpha_{24}y_4(t) + \gamma_{21}t + \alpha_{20} + u_2(t),$$

$$(2.5b)\quad y_1(t) = \alpha_{22}y_2(t) + \alpha_{25}y_5(t) + \gamma_{21}t + \alpha_{20} + u_2(t),$$

$$(2.5c)\quad y_1(t) = \alpha_{22}y_2(t) + \alpha_{25}y_5(t) + \gamma_{21}t + \gamma_{22}p_e(t) + \alpha_{20} + u_2(t).$$

D. Supply of Foodstuffs by Farmers

For many farm products one might consider current output as a result of decisions based on *past* prices and other variables not related to the current market situation, such as weather, pasture conditions, available acreage, etc. The farmers have, on the other hand, undoubtedly some possibilities of almost instantaneous adjustment to the current price situation. They can speed up or slow down the feeding of livestock, put more labor, or less labor, into harvesting crops, etc.

Other products, such as vegetables or poultry, may have a period of production much shorter than a year. When we use annual data it would, therefore, seem necessary to include current prices as a variable influencing farm output of food. A trend might account for certain technological changes in technique of production, changes in the farm population, etc. We might then consider the following equation as an approximation to the farmers' supply equation:

$$(2.6a) \qquad y_4(t) = \alpha_{45}y_5(t) + \gamma_{41}t + \gamma_{42}y_5(t-1) + \alpha_{40} + u_4(t),$$

where the random residuals $u_4(t)$ might be expected to be large, particularly because we have no explicit variable accounting for the influence of the weather.

The supply equation (2.6a) does not explicitly take account of the effect of change in capacity, such as change in acreage, livestock, farm machinery, etc. One way of accounting for such changes might be to include last year's production as an additional variable, a "scale factor," for the output of the current year. This leads us to

$$(2.6b) \quad y_4(t) = \alpha_{45}y_5(t) + \gamma_{41}t + y_{42}y_5(t-1) + \gamma_{43}u_4(t-1) + \alpha_{40} + u_4(t).$$

If we were interested in a more detailed study of the determinants of food output, the equations (2.6a) or (2.6b) could probably not be considered as adequate behavioristic equations for the production policy of the farmers. It would be necessary to study production functions, principles of profit maximization, etc. The equations (2.6a) or (2.6b) must, to some extent, be considered as "derived" equations, the parameters of which are again functions of certain behavioristic parameters.

For the purpose of studying the demand for food one might even consider a much simpler hypothesis, namely

$$(2.6c) \qquad y_4(t) = \text{a predetermined variable.}$$

That is, we might think of farm food output as being practically independent of the current market situation. Such a hypothesis is obviously not strictly true. On the other hand, noneconomic factors, such as weather, together with lagged prices and other factors that do not depend on the current market situation, might be so dominant in determining current farm output that the errors of assuming that 1) α_{45} is zero and 2) $u_4(t)$ is uncorrelated with the u's in the other equations are not serious. Under these conditions it would be permissible, for the purpose of estimating the other equations in our system, to consider $y_4(t)$ as a statistically predetermined, or fixed, variable, without *explaining* how this variable itself is being determined in the system.

E. The Demand for Farm Food Products by the Commercial Sector

If $y_4(t)$ is not considered as a predetermined variable, it is necessary to study not only the supply function for farm food products but also the demand function for these products. We shall assume that the commercial sector demands farm food products for three purposes: 1) for processing and sale in the domestic retail market, 2) for export, and 3) for maintenance of, or changes in, commercial stocks. If we assume that the demand for stocks depends only on current prices, we may write this demand function as

$$(2.7a) \quad y_4(t) = \alpha_{52}y_2(t) + \alpha_{55}y_5(t) + \gamma_{51}t + \gamma_{52}p_e(t) + \alpha_{50} + u_5(t).$$

If we were to consider (2.5a) as the supply function for the retail market, we might even consider a much simpler demand function for farm food products, namely

$$(2.7b) \quad y_5(t) = \alpha_{52}y_2(t) + \gamma_{51}t + \alpha_{50} + u_5(t),$$

that is, we might assume that the price received by farmers is a "residual" which is a linear function of the prices obtained in the retail market. This then would have to be considered as a somewhat "superficial," institutional, equation, rather than a structural equation.

Above we have considered 5 groups of equations, namely [(2.1a), (2.1b), (2.1c)], [(2.4a), (2.4b), (2.4c)], [(2.5a), (2.5b), (2.5c)], [(2.6a), (2.6b), (2.6c)], [(2.7a), (2.7b)]. Choosing one equation from each of these groups, we have a system of 5 equations. It will be noticed that these five equations involve 5 simultaneous random residuals, denoted by u, and 5 simultaneous, observable variables, denoted by y. In addition, there are certain other variables, namely t, $z(t)$, and $p_e(t)$. These latter variables are statistically different from the y's, in the sense that, stochastically, they do not depend on the random residuals u. The same is, by assumption, true of the various lagged values of the variables y that occur in some of the equations. The variables $y(t - 1)$ are stochastically independent of the variables $u(t)$. Statistically, the variables $y(t - 1)$ can, therefore, be grouped together with t, $z(t)$, and $p_e(t)$ under the category of "predetermined variables,"[4] while the 5 variables $y(t)$ [except in the particular case (2.6c)] may be called "jointly dependent" variables, because their stochastic properties depend on the stochastic properties assumed for the random variables $u(t)$.

We may consider any one of the possible systems of five equations as a system determining the five jointly dependent variables $y(t)$ as functions of the five random variables $u(t)$ and the predetermined variables. This means that, for any given set of values of the predetermined

[4] See Chapter VI, Section 1.5.

variables, the joint distribution of the five jointly dependent variables $y(t)$, for any value of t, is given implicitly by the joint probability distribution of the five variables $u(t)$. *It is this joint probability distribution that must form the basis for the estimation of the unknown parameters, the* α*'s and the* γ*'s.* The statistical procedure involved will be explained in Chapter VI.

Suppose that, among the various alternative systems of five equations discussed above, there is one for which there exists a set of values of the parameters such that, for the assumed distribution of the u's, the resulting joint probability distribution of the y's is identical with the true distribution of the observable y's, for all values of the predetermined variables. Then we may say that the model is "true," in the sense that it is consistent with observations. Suppose, for example, that the model (2.1a), (2.4a), (2.5a), (2.6a), and (2.7a), together with a certain assumption concerning the joint probability distribution of the u's, represents a true model, by appropriate choice of the values of the parameters. In that case it is obvious that there exist an infinity of equivalent systems of equations that also represent "true" models. For example, by an arbitrary linear combination of two or more of the original equations we can derive a new equation that, together with four of the old equations, forms a true model. Why is it that we are interested in one particular member of this infinite set of true systems? It is because, in setting up the original model, we believe that there is one particular system of equations that is a system of *autonomous*, or *structural* equations, that is, equations such that it is possible that the parameters in any one of the equations could *in fact* change, e.g., by the introduction of some new economic policy, *without* any change taking place in any of the parameters of the other equations. If there is one system for which this is true, the other systems that can be derived from it will not have this property. The parameters of equations in derived systems will be functions of the parameters in two or more of the equations in the original system.

Suppose that we should succeed in deriving the *structural* equations of a model that is "true" in the sense discussed above and suppose also that these equations are identifiable, so that we could measure statistically the parameters involved. What could be the use of this knowledge? It would, first of all, help to satisfy a justified scientific curiosity. But we believe that such knowledge also could be of more immediate practical importance. The results could be used to judge, in advance, the effects of various policies that might be considered. If the policy considered represents a *known change* in the structure, e.g., a known absolute or relative change in one or more of the parameters or variables involved, and if the structure *before* the change is known, then obviously the structure *after* the change is also known, and we can compare the two. A variety of practical policies with regard to taxation, subsidies, etc., are precisely of this type.

It is clear, then, that the fundamental objective of statistical inference with respect to economic models is to derive estimates of the structural parameters. Knowing the structural parameters, all the relations implied by the model can be derived. In a sense these structural parameters play a role similar to that of the elements in chemistry.

3. Some Numerical Results

As an illustration,[5] the limited-information method has been applied to the estimation of the coefficients of each equation (taken one by one) of the following system of equations:

$$(3.1)\quad y_1(t) = \alpha_{12}y_2(t) + \alpha_{13}y_3(t) + \gamma_{18}z_8(t) + \gamma_{19}z_9(t) + \alpha_{10} + u_1(t),$$

$$(3.2)\quad y_1(t) = \alpha_{22}y_2(t) + \alpha_{24}y_4(t) + \gamma_{28}z_8(t) + \alpha_{20} + u_2(t),$$

$$(3.3)\quad y_3(t) = \gamma_{37}z_7(t) + \gamma_{39}z_9(t) + \alpha_{30} + u_3(t),$$

$$(3.4)\quad y_4(t) = \alpha_{45}y_5(t) + \gamma_{46}z_6(t) + \gamma_{48}z_8(t) + \alpha_{40} + u_4(t),$$

$$(3.5)\quad y_5(t) = \alpha_{52}y_2(t) + \gamma_{58}z_8(t) + \alpha_{50} + u_5(t).$$

These equations correspond to (2.1c), (2.5a), (2.4c) (omitting trend), (2.6a), and (2.7b), except that, for the sake of symmetry, we have here used the notations $y_5(t-1) = z_6(t)$, $z(t) = z_7(t)$, $t = z_8(t)$, and $y_3(t-1) = z_9(t)$. The following series were used for the model:

y_1 = Food consumption per capita published by the Bureau of Agricultural Economics. (An adjustment has been made in the official series for 1934 to exclude the quantity of meat purchased by the Government for relief purposes and distributed through noncommercial channels.)

y_2 = Retail prices of food products (*BAE*), deflated by the Index of Consumer Prices for Moderate Income Families in Cities, published by the Bureau of Labor Statistics.

y_3 = Disposable income per capita (Dept. of Commerce), deflated by the *BLS* Consumer Price Index.

[5] The model discussed here has been chosen primarily because it presents, in a simple form, almost all the particular statistical problems that have been discussed in the foregoing sections. Actually, we have carried out numerical work for a variety of different models, some of which might be more realistic than the one presented here.

y_4 = Production of agricultural food products per capita (*BAE*).

y_5 = Prices received by farmers for food products (*BAE*), deflated by *BLS* Consumer Price Index.

$z_6 = y_5(t-1)$ = Prices received by farmers for food products, lagged one year.

$z_7 = z(t)$ = Net investment per capita = Disposable income minus consumers' expenditures, based on Dept. of Commerce data, deflated by *BLS* Consumer Price Index.

$z_8 = t$ = Time.

$z_9 = y_3(t-1)$ = Disposable income per capita, lagged one year.

All the data are expressed in terms of index numbers (1935–39 = 100) except for time, z_8, which has the values, 1, 2, $\cdots$, 20. The analysis covers the period 1922 through 1941. The data are given in Table 1.

TABLE 1

DATA USED IN THIS STUDY

Calendar year	y_1 Food cons. per capita	y_2 Food prices ÷ by cost of living	y_3 Disp. income ÷ by cost of living	y_4 Food prod. per capita	y_5 Prices rec'd by farmers for food ÷ by cost of living	z_6 $y_5(t-1)$	z_7 Investment per capita ÷ by cost of living	z_8 Time	z_9 $y_3(t-1)$
1922	98.6	100.2	87.4	108.5	99.1	98.0	92.9	1	77.4
1923	101.2	101.6	97.6	110.1	99.1	99.1	142.9	2	87.4
1924	102.4	100.5	96.7	110.4	98.9	99.1	100.0	3	97.6
1925	100.9	106.0	98.2	104.3	110.8	98.9	123.8	4	96.7
1926	102.3	108.7	99.8	107.2	108.2	110.8	111.9	5	98.2
1927	101.5	106.7	100.5	105.8	105.6	108.2	121.4	6	99.8
1928	101.6	106.7	103.2	107.8	109.8	105.6	107.1	7	100.5
1929	101.6	108.2	107.8	103.4	108.7	109.8	142.9	8	103.2
1930	99.8	105.5	96.6	102.7	100.6	108.7	92.9	9	107.8
1931	100.3	95.6	88.9	104.1	81.0	100.6	97.6	10	96.6
1932	97.6	88.6	75.1	99.2	68.6	81.0	52.4	11	88.9
1933	97.2	91.0	76.9	99.7	70.9	68.6	40.5	12	75.1
1934	97.3	97.9	84.6	102.0	81.4	70.9	64.3	13	76.9
1935	96.0	102.3	90.6	94.3	102.3	81.4	78.6	14	84.6
1936	99.2	102.2	103.1	97.7	105.0	102.3	114.3	15	90.6
1937	100.3	102.5	105.1	101.1	110.5	105.0	121.4	16	103.1
1938	100.3	97.0	96.4	102.3	92.5	110.5	78.6	17	105.1
1939	104.1	95.8	104.4	104.4	89.3	92.5	109.5	18	96.4
1940	105.3	96.4	110.7	108.5	93.0	89.3	128.6	19	104.4
1941	107.6	100.3	127.1	111.3	106.6	93.0	238.1	20	110.7
Sum	2015.1	2013.7	1950.7	2084.8	1941.9	1933.3	2159.7	210	1901.0
Mean	100.755	100.685	97.535	104.240	97.095	96.665	107.985	10.500	95.050

Our findings can be summarized as follows:

A. Reduced Form Equations

$$\text{(3.6) Est. of } y_1(t) = -0.059y_5(t-1) + 0.040z(t) + 0.154y_3(t-1) - 0.041t + 87.932,$$

Multiple correlation: $R^2 = 0.7546$,

$$\text{(3.7) Est. of } y_2(t) = 0.241y_5(t-1) + 0.041z(t) - 0.052y_3(t-1) - 0.253t + 80.560,$$

$R^2 = 0.5865$,

$$\text{(3.8) Est. of } y_3(t) = 0.203z(t) + 0.367y_3(t-1) + 40.731,$$

$R^2 = 0.8833$,

$$\text{(3.9) Est. of } y_4(t) = -0.128y_5(t-1) + 0.062z(t) + 0.180y_3(t-1) - 0.487t + 97.923,$$

$R^2 = 0.5651$,

$$\text{(3.10) Est. of } y_5(t) = 0.649y_5(t-1) + 0.161z(t) - 0.287y_3(t-1) - 0.078t + 45.072,$$

$R^2 = 0.6549$.

B. The Final System of Structural Equations

$$\text{(3.1 est.) } y_1(t) = -0.246y_2(t) + 0.247y_3(t) + 0.051y_3(t-1) - 0.104t + 97.677 + u_1(t),$$

$$\text{(3.2 est.) } y_1(t) = 0.157y_2(t) + 0.653y_4(t) + 0.339t + 13.319 + u_2(t),$$

$$\text{(3.3 est.) } y_3(t) = 0.203z(t) + 0.367y_3(t-1) + 40.731 + u_3(t),$$

$$\text{(3.4 est.) } y_4(t) = 0.556y_5(t) - 0.300y_5(t-1) - 0.190t + 81.250 + u_4(t)$$

{this equation may also be written as

$$y_4(t) = 0.556[y_5(t) - y_5(t-1)] + 0.256y_5(t-1) - 0.190t + 81.250 + u_4(t)\},$$

$$\text{(3.5 est.) } y_5(t) = 2.883y_2(t) + 0.656t - 200.068 + u_5(t).$$

A theory of confidence intervals for the parameters has not yet been worked out. Such a theory is essential in order to judge the reliability of the estimates.

The residuals are given in Table 2.

TABLE 2

ESTIMATES OF THE RESIDUALS, $u(t)$

Year	$u_1(t)$	$u_2(t)$	$u_3(t)$	$u_4(t)$	$u_5(t)$
1922	0.14	−1.64	−0.60	1.74	9.64
1923	0.16	−0.64	−4.22	3.86	4.94
1924	0.90	0.19	−0.15	4.46	7.26
1925	0.53	1.48	−3.15	−8.12	2.64
1926	2.21	0.22	0.31	−0.02	−8.39
1927	0.78	0.31	−1.50	−0.56	−5.88
1928	0.29	−1.24	3.84	−1.49	−2.34
1929	−0.52	1.06	0.19	−3.83	−8.42
1930	−0.35	−0.20	−2.55	−0.16	−9.39
1931	0.30	0.60	−7.10	9.89	−1.11
1932	−0.22	1.86	−8.89	6.20	6.02
1933	0.33	0.42	0.39	1.89	0.74
1934	0.24	−2.40	2.58	−0.77	−9.31
1935	−1.75	0.30	2.86	−16.75	−1.75
1936	−1.86	0.95	5.92	−8.39	0.59
1937	−1.72	−0.55	1.89	−7.05	4.56
1938	−0.92	−0.81	1.14	6.00	1.77
1939	1.16	1.47	6.06	4.67	1.37
1940	0.65	−0.45	5.55	5.94	2.68
1941	−0.36	−0.92	−2.59	2.48	4.38

C. Comments

The main purpose in giving the numerical results above has been to illustrate, explicitly, the application of certain methods and principles set forth in the preceding sections of this chapter. Much careful research, both in the economic theory and in the statistics involved, is yet to be carried out before one can draw final, practical, conclusions from the results obtained.

To those familiar with multiple-correlation results obtained from agricultural data the most striking features of the results above are, probably, the relatively low values of the multiple-correlation coefficients (given under A), and the relatively large residuals (given in Table 2). A refinement of the economic model involved might improve these correlations. We should like to point out, however, that when one is searching for structural economic relations one cannot in general expect to find as high correlations as those obtained from a mechanical application of the method of multiple correlation to the variables in the structural equations. For the correlations obtained by the latter procedure are due not only to the occurrence of the same predetermined variables in the equations of the reduced form, but also to the intercorrelations between the residuals in these equations. The method of multiple correlation would produce higher correlations at the expense of a bias in the estimates of the structural coefficients involved.

Chapter VI

THE ESTIMATION OF SIMULTANEOUS LINEAR ECONOMIC RELATIONSHIPS

By Tjalling C. Koopmans and Wm. C. Hood[1]

[1] The authors are indebted to Herman Chernoff, John Gurland, and Herman Rubin for many valuable comments.

1. The Concept of a Complete Model

1.1 *The joint distribution of the observations.* The solution to a problem of statistical inference in any field must be based on a consideration of the process that yields the observations from which the inference is to be drawn. It is sometimes useful to think of the scientist and nature (in our case, society) as cooperating in the process of obtaining observations. Three aspects of the generation of observations may then be delineated. First there are the processes of nature whereby the quantities to be measured are generated. Then there is the control over these processes exercised by the scientist through experimental techniques. Finally there is the matter of measurement itself, the measurements being made by or for the scientist but their exactness not entirely controlled by him. In some fields the experimental control exercised by the scientist is a more significant factor than in others. In economics it is of much less significance than in most. But in all cases the choice and the usefulness of a method of estimation or of testing hypotheses depend on the character (assumed or known) of the process generating the observations.

Modern theories of statistical inference describe the generation of observations by the hypothesis that there exists for any given number T of observations an (unknown) joint probability distribution function $F_T(x)$ of as many variables $x = (x_1, x_2, \cdots, x_T)$ as there are observations, and that the observations actually obtained constitute one (multivariate) random drawing from this distribution. The extraction of knowledge about that distribution from the observations is aided by specifying a set $\mathfrak{F}_T$ of distribution functions, of which the distribution function $F_T(x)$ generating the observations is assumed to be an element. The set $\mathfrak{F}_T$ represents the a priori knowledge or hypotheses the statistician feels justified in specifying regarding the processes that yield the observations, either because he places confidence in these hypotheses or because he wishes tentatively to explore their implications. The latter wish may be motivated by the fact that the hypotheses made facilitate his reasoning and by the hope that some of the conclusions remain approximately valid under more general hypotheses.

We have used the term "multivariate random drawing" above to leave no doubt that we include cases in which $F_T(x)$ is such that "successive" observations $x_1, x_2, \cdots, x_T$ (which may again be multivariate themselves) are statistically dependent. The more common term "random sample" has sometimes been employed so as to imply the case of independence and constancy of the distribution functions of "successive" observations. In that case $\mathfrak{F}_T$ is specified to be such that every $F_T(x)$ in it can be written as a product

$$F_T(x) = f(x_1) \cdot f(x_2) \cdot \ldots \cdot f(x_T) \tag{1.1}$$

of T factors each of which is a value assumed by the same function, $f(x)$. From now on, however, we shall use the term "sample" for a multivariate drawing x from a distribution $F_T(x)$ without thereby implying either that a factorization (1.1) is prescribed by $\mathfrak{F}_T$ or that, where a factorization does exist, the functions $f_t(x_t)$ that enter into the factors are necessarily the same for different t. The case where the function $f_t(x_t)$ varies with t is of particular importance when "successive" observations $x_1, x_2, \cdots, x_T$ relate to successive points or periods of time.

1.2. *Structure and model.* It has already been argued in Chapter I (see Sections 3, 8, and 9) and Chapter II (see Sections 1, 3, and 8) of this volume[2] that the a priori knowledge about the distribution $F_T(x)$, embodied in the set $\mathfrak{F}_T$, must be derived from information or assumptions concerning the underlying economic *structure* whenever the purposes which statistical estimation is to serve include the prediction of the effects of economic policies or other given changes in structure. We shall now make this notion of a structure more specific by describing the types of structure to be considered in this chapter.

Let an economic theory specify the existence of a set of functional relations, each expressing an aspect of the economic behavior of a group of individuals, firms, or authorities. The variables entering into these relations consist of:

(a) A set of G "true" (*latent*) *endogenous* variables η_{gt} $(g = 1, \cdots, G)$, whose formation the theory is designed to explain. These differ only by errors of observation [listed under (d) below] from the *observed endogenous* variables y_{gt}.

(b) A set of $\bar{K}$ "true" (*latent*) *exogenous* variables ζ_{kt} $(k = 1, \cdots, \bar{K})$, which the theory regards as given for purposes of explaining the formation of the η_{gt}. These differ only by errors of observation [also listed under (d) below] from the *observed exogenous* variables $\bar{z}_{kt}$.

(c) A set of G *unobserved* (*latent*) variables u_{gt} $(g = 1, \cdots, G)$, to be called *disturbances* (or *shocks*), which represent the aggregate effects of additional unspecified exogenous variables on the economic decisions expressed by each relation.

(d) A set of $G + \bar{K}$ *unobserved* (*latent*) variables v_{gt} $(g = 1, \cdots, G)$ and w_{kt} $(k = 1, \cdots, \bar{K})$ representing errors of observation in the observed variables y_{gt} and $\bar{z}_{kt}$, respectively.

Examples of such equation systems have been given in Chapters I and II. We shall use vector notation[3] to represent by one symbol the members of each class of variables, as follows:

$$
\begin{aligned}
&y_t \equiv [y_{1t} \quad y_{2t} \quad \cdots \quad y_{Gt}], \qquad \bar{z}_t \equiv [\bar{z}_{1t} \quad \cdots \quad \bar{z}_{\bar{K}t}],\\
&u_t \equiv [u_{1t} \quad \cdots \quad u_{Gt}], \qquad v_t = [v_{1t} \quad \cdots \quad v_{Gt}],\\
&w_t \equiv [w_{1t} \quad \cdots \quad w_{\bar{K}t}].
\end{aligned}
\tag{1.2}
$$

The subscript t refers to the time point at which or period for which the variable in question (stock or flow, respectively, as the case may be)

[2] See also Koopmans and Reiersøl [1950].

[3] Matrices are denoted by capitals, vectors by small letters. Vectors are to be thought of as row vectors (one-row matrices) unless otherwise specified.

is measured. We shall employ a discrete notion of time,[4] choosing the unit of time so that the elementary period of observation is one time unit and letting stock variables with subscript t be measured at the beginning of the period of measurement of flow variables with subscript t.

With this notation, let the system of behavior equations be written

$$
(1.3)\qquad
\begin{aligned}
&h_1(\eta_t, \eta_{t-1}, \cdots, \eta_{t-\tau^\square}; \zeta_t, \cdots, \zeta_{t-\tau^\square}; u_{1t}; \alpha_1) = 0,\\
&\cdots\cdots\cdots\cdots\cdots\cdots\cdots\cdots\cdots\cdots\cdots\cdots\\
&h_G(\eta_t, \eta_{t-1}, \cdots, \eta_{t-\tau^\square}; \zeta_t, \cdots, \zeta_{t-\tau^\square}; u_{Gt}; \alpha_G) = 0
\end{aligned}
\qquad (t = 1, \cdots, T).
$$

Here the symbols h_g $(g = 1, \cdots, G)$ denote given scalar functions of the variables shown in parentheses, and the symbols α_g $(g = 1, \cdots, G)$ denote vectors of unknown behavior parameters (such as elasticities of supply or demand), assumed to be independent of t. The behavior equations are written in terms of the "true" endogenous and exogenous variables, which are connected with the observed variables by

$$
(1.4)\qquad y_t = \eta_t + v_t, \qquad \bar{z}_t = \zeta_t + w_t \qquad (t = 1 - \tau^\square, \cdots, 0, 1, \cdots, T).
$$

Both endogenous and exogenous variables are assumed to affect economic decisions with or without time lags, all lags being integral multiples of one unit of time. The longest lag occurring has been denoted $\tau^\square$. Finally, it is assumed that the system of equations (1.3) for any time t can be solved uniquely for the so-called *jointly dependent* variables η_{gt} $(g = 1, \cdots, G)$ of that time t whatever the values assumed by all other variables and parameters occurring in (1.3). If this were not true, the set of equations (1.3) would not represent a theory of the formation of the jointly dependent variables.

Let our economic theory specify further that there exists a joint distribution function of all latent variables occurring in (1.3),

$$
(1.5)\qquad Q(u_1, \cdots, u_T; v_1, \cdots, v_T; w_1, \cdots, w_T; \eta_{1-\tau^\square}, \cdots, \eta_0; \zeta_{1-\tau^\square}, \cdots, \zeta_0, \zeta_1, \cdots, \zeta_T).
$$

We do not need to include $\eta_1, \cdots, \eta_T$ in (1.5) since, by assumption, the values of these variables can be solved from (1.3) in terms of variables included in (1.5).

Now we shall speak of a *structure* S_T if we have assigned specific numerical values to the parameter vectors $\alpha_1, \cdots, \alpha_G$ in (1.3) and a specific

[4] For a discussion of a continuous notion see Koopmans [1950b].

function (given also by numerical parameters, or by a graph or table) Q in (1.5). A structure thus consists of two elements, a specific set of *structural relations*, (1.3) and (1.4), which permits determination of all observed variables from given values of all latent variables, and a specific joint *distribution of latent variables*. In particular, we speak of a *complete structure* because the structural equations (1.3) and (1.4) account for the formation of the values $y_1, \cdots, y_T$ of *all* endogenous variables in terms of latent variables whose distribution is given in (1.5).

Generally, the structure S_T is unknown, just as in the more usual formulation of estimation problems the distribution F_T of the observations discussed in Section 1.1 is unknown. In that discussion we used the notion of a set $\mathfrak{F}_T$ of distribution functions to represent the a priori knowledge or hypotheses concerning the generation of the observations. Similarly, we now introduce the notion of a set $\mathfrak{S}_T$ of structures S_T, also to be called a *model* $\mathfrak{S}_T$. A model is obtained if, for instance, we leave certain elements of the parameter vectors $\alpha_1, \cdots, \alpha_G$ in (1.3) unspecified, or restricted only as to sign or by other inequalities, and if we indicate a set $\mathfrak{Q}_T$ of distribution functions Q_T of latent variables (such as, for instance, the set of joint normal distributions of u, v, w with zero means). In particular, if all structures in the model are complete, the model itself is called *complete*. The model incorporates all of the a priori knowledge or hypotheses the statistician chooses to recognize as an aid in estimating that structure S_T which has generated the observations or in estimating those parameters of S_T in which he is particularly interested.

1.3. *The complete linear model without errors of observation*. We shall now describe a particular model for which estimation methods have been developed in detail. This model, which from now on we shall denote by $\mathfrak{S}_T$, assumes linear structural equations and disregards errors of observation. In Chapter VII methods are discussed for estimating the parameters of nonlinear structural equations, methods suggested by those for estimating linear equations presented in this chapter. A model with errors of observation is also considered in that chapter.

That errors of observation are disregarded in this chapter does not imply an a priori judgment that such errors are less important, in their effects on the choice of estimates and on the quality of these estimates, than disturbances in economic behavior.[5] This must be regarded as an

[5] It might be thought that with gradual improvement in the methods of data collection, errors of observation would after a lapse of time be less important than the random elements intrinsic to economic behavior. However, as Reiersøl has pointed out to one of the authors, as observations improve in accuracy and coverage, it will be possible to introduce more explanatory variables in each equation, thus reducing the variances of "unexplained" disturbances in behavior.

empirical question, to be settled by methods of inference based on models recognizing errors of observation as well as disturbances in behavior.[6] The emphasis on disturbances in this and other chapters of this volume must be regarded rather as a matter of tactics. "Shock-error models" are complicated. To prepare for their study one can develop many relevant concepts and methods from "shock models" without errors. Other studies[7] have been devoted to "error models" without shocks. Finally, even the models recognizing only shocks present a number of features perhaps specific to the measurement of economic relations, where variables are formed by the intersection of many behavior schedules. The implications of these features were pointed out clearly by Haavelmo [1943, 1944], whose penetrating analysis initiated the developments in methodology reported in this volume.

If we omit errors of observation and make the structural equations (1.3) linear, they can be written in the form

$$(1.6)\quad \begin{aligned} &\sum_{i=1}^{G} \beta_{1i0}\, y_{it} + \sum_{i=1}^{G} \sum_{\tau=1}^{\tau^{\square}} \beta_{1i\tau} y_{i,t-\tau} + \gamma_{10} + \sum_{k=1}^{\bar{K}} \sum_{\tau=0}^{\tau^{\square}} \bar{\gamma}_{1k\tau} \bar{z}_{k,t-\tau} = u_{1t}, \\ &\cdots\cdots\cdots\cdots\cdots\cdots\cdots\cdots\cdots\cdots \\ &\sum_{i=1}^{G} \beta_{Gi0} y_{it} + \sum_{i=1}^{G} \sum_{\tau=1}^{\tau^{\square}} \beta_{Gi\tau} y_{i,t-\tau} + \gamma_{G0} + \sum_{k=1}^{\bar{K}} \sum_{\tau=0}^{\tau^{\square}} \bar{\gamma}_{Gk\tau} \bar{z}_{k,t-\tau} = u_{Gt} \\ &\qquad\qquad\qquad\qquad\qquad\qquad (t = 1, \ldots, T). \end{aligned}$$

In order that, for any t, these equations can be solved for the variables y_{1t}, it is necessary and sufficient that[8]

$$(1.7)\qquad \det \mathrm{B}_0 = \det \begin{bmatrix} \beta_{110} & \cdots & \beta_{1G0} \\ \cdots & \cdots & \cdots \\ \beta_{G10} & \cdots & \beta_{GG0} \end{bmatrix} \neq 0,$$

a specification[9] that we shall incorporate in the model $\mathfrak{S}_T$.

We shall also make the model narrower in regard to the set $\mathfrak{Q}$ of distributions Q of latent variables (besides omitting observational errors). To introduce these further specifications we first write the distribution

[6] For a discussion of "shock-error models" see Anderson and Hurwicz [1947]. Further work, as yet unpublished, has been done on this subject by Reiersøl.

[7] Tintner [1945, 1946a, 1946b], Wald [1940], Geary [1948, 1949], Koopmans [1937].

[8] The symbol det R denotes the determinant associated with the square matrix R.

[9] This specification implies the requirement, stated in Chapter II, Section 3, that each endogenous variable appear without time lag in at least one equation.

of latent variables as the product of the conditional distribution of disturbances for given values of the exogenous variables and the marginal distribution of the exogenous variables. In this formulation we include with the exogenous variables, arrayed to form a vector $\bar{z}$, those values of the variables y_t pertaining to times $t = 1 - \tau^{\square}, \cdots, 0$ anterior to the period of observation, because their formation is not explained by (1.6). We then have

$$
\begin{aligned}
& Q(u_1, \cdots, u_T ; y_{1-\tau^{\square}}, \cdots, y_0 ; \bar{z}_{1-\tau^{\square}}, \cdots, \bar{z}_0, \bar{z}_1, \cdots, \bar{z}_T) \\
(1.8) \qquad & = Q^{(1)}(u_1, \cdots, u_T \mid y_{1-\tau^{\square}}, \cdots, y_0 ; \bar{z}_{1-\tau^{\square}}, \cdots, \bar{z}_T) \\
& \qquad \cdot Q^{(2)}(y_{1-\tau^{\square}}, \cdots, y_0 ; \bar{z}_{1-\tau^{\square}}, \cdots, \bar{z}_T).
\end{aligned}
$$

While any joint distribution of two sets of variables can be written in this way,[10] the advantage of doing so in this case arises from the next specification we shall make about the conditional distribution of the disturbances. We shall specify that this conditional distribution is in fact independent of the values given to the exogenous variables in its definition,

$$
(1.9) \qquad Q^{(1)}(u_1, \cdots, u_T \mid y_{1-\tau^{\square}}, \cdots, \bar{z}_T) = Q(u_1, \cdots, u_T).
$$

The meaning of this specification[11] is that we assume not only that the exogenous variables $\bar{z}$ are not affected by the endogenous variables y_t $(t = 1, \cdots, T)$ but also that there are no ulterior common causes in the generation of the exogenous variables $\bar{z}$, on the one hand, and of the disturbances u_t $(t = 1, \cdots, T)$, on the other, that create a statistical dependence between these two sets of variables.[12]

As has been pointed out by Hotelling in another context [1940, in particular pp. 276–277], the specification (1.9) makes it possible to put the study of the properties of estimates of the coefficients $\beta_{gi\tau}$, γ_{g0}, $\bar{\gamma}_{gk\tau}$, to be undertaken in this chapter, in a form independent of the distribution function $Q^{(2)}$. We need merely stipulate that, throughout the discussion of sampling properties of estimates, repeated "multivariate random drawings" as discussed in Section 1.1 relate only to the distribution $Q(u_1, \cdots, u_T)$ of disturbances. Sampling variation in these

[10] See Wilks [1943, Section 2.4] or Cramér [1946, Sections 21.4 and 22.1; especially equations (21.4.10) and (22.1.1)].

[11] In Chapter II, footnote 5, this specification is treated as part of the definition of an exogenous variable.

[12] The inclusion of $y_{1-\tau^{\square}}, \cdots, y_0$ among the exogenous variables $\bar{z}$ in this statement is based upon an anticipation of the next specification (1.10). Without this specification we should either have to omit the "anterior" values of y_t from (1.9) and treat these variables as endogenous or specify rather arbitrarily that the disturbances u_t $(t \leqslant 0)$ are independent of the disturbances u_t $(t \geqslant 1)$.

variables induces sampling variation in the endogenous variables y_t $(t = 1, \cdots, T)$, while the values assumed at all times by the exogenous variables $\bar{z}$ are held fixed. If in truth the exogenous variables $\bar{z}$ are subject to a probability distribution $Q^{(2)}$, we choose to study the sampling properties of our estimates in a particular subclass of all possible samples: viz., the class of those samples in which all exogenous variables $\bar{z}$ take on the same values as they exhibit in the sample actually obtained. The opportunity to do so on the basis of some specified distribution $Q(u_1, \cdots, u_T)$ of the disturbances arises precisely from the independence assumption (1.9). If the u_t are independent of the variables $\bar{z}$, holding the latter constant does not affect the distribution of the former. Of course, the properties of the estimates obtained will be found to depend on the values[13] assumed by the exogenous variables $\bar{z}$.

Finally, again following the tactics of dealing with the simpler cases first, we shall specify that successive disturbances are independent of each other,[14]

$$(1.10) \qquad Q(u_1, \cdots, u_T) = Q_1(u_1) \cdot \ldots \cdot Q_t(u_t) \cdot \ldots \cdot Q_T(u_T),$$

and further that their distribution is the same for all time periods,

$$(1.11) \qquad Q_t(u_t) = Q(u_t) \qquad (t = 1, \cdots, T).$$

These specifications will be further weakened in Chapter VII. In most of the present chapter we shall go so far as to specify that the distribution of the components u_{gt} of the vector u_t is normal, with the following parameters:[15]

$$(1.12) \qquad \mathcal{E}u_{gt} = 0, \qquad \mathcal{E}u_{gt}u_{ht} = \sigma_{gh}.$$

[13] In particular, as noted in Chapter II, footnote 7, if these values happen to satisfy linear restrictions of a certain type, they may give rise to nonidentifiability of parameters $\beta_{gi\tau}$, $\bar{\gamma}_{gk\tau}$ from repeated samples of the type described, where $\bar{z}$-values not so restrained would permit identifiability. See also Section 5 below, footnote 54.

[14] Specification (1.10) has been criticized by Cochrane and Orcutt [1949; also Orcutt and Cochrane, 1949] on grounds of insufficient realism. They have studied the estimation problem in which $Q(u_1, \cdots, u_T)$ corresponds to a simple stochastic Markoff process with known serial correlation. Preliminary studies by Chernoff and Rubin have suggested that, when this serial correlation (in the case of vectors u_t, the serial correlation matrix) is unknown, a complicated identification problem is encountered, while the derivation and computation of maximum-likelihood estimates is only made more cumbersome than in the case without serial correlation in the u_t.

[15] The symbol $\mathcal{E}$ is an operator denoting that the expected value (mathematical expectation) is to be taken of the random variable following the symbol. See, for example, Cramér [1946, Sections 15.3 and 15.4].

One of the purposes to be served by the specification of normality is to suggest a method of estimation. The properties of the estimates obtained by this method in sampling from a structure with nonnormal disturbances are studied in Chapter VII.

1.4. *The a priori restrictions.* All of the specifications introduced so far will be maintained in all versions of the model $\mathfrak{S}_T$ used in the estimation theory developed in Sections 5–7 of this chapter. Further specifications made may differ between different models used. It has been pointed out in Chapter II, Section 4, that without additional restrictions on at least some of the parameters $\beta_{gi\tau}$, γ_{g0} , $\bar{\gamma}_{gk\tau}$, σ_{gh} , none of the structural equations is identifiable. It is therefore assumed that information is available, from economic theory or other sources outside the observations, that can be put in the form of *a priori restrictions* on the parameters.

Apart from one remark at the end of Section 5.7, we shall not place any restrictions on the matrix $\Sigma \equiv [\sigma_{gh}]$ of variances and covariances of the disturbances, except that this is specified to be a symmetric, positive semidefinite matrix,[16] because otherwise it could not be the covariance matrix of a normal distribution in G latent variables. We do not throughout require Σ to be nonsingular, and hence positive definite, because we wish to admit models containing *identities*. These are structural equations without disturbances and with numerically given coefficients that arise directly from the definitions of the variables involved. Rows and columns of Σ corresponding to these equations consist of zeros only. However, in models from which the identities have been removed by the elimination of an equal number of suitably chosen variables, we do require the covariance matrix Σ of the disturbances of the remaining *behavior* equations to be nonsingular. This expresses the assumption that, while disturbances in different types of economic decisions may be statistically dependent (correlated), we do not allow the disturbance in one behavior equation to be functionally (in a joint normal distribution this can only be linearly) dependent on those in other behavior equations.[17]

We shall consider restrictions of a simple form on the coefficients $\beta_{gi\tau}$, γ_{g0} , $\bar{\gamma}_{gk\tau}$, requiring that the coefficients designated by certain combinations of subscripts, given in advance, be zero. These restrictions express information as to which variables are excluded from which behavior equations. More general restrictions, requiring that a given linear

[16] For definitions of positive semidefinite and positive definite matrices, see Appendix B.

[17] For a more detailed discussion of the nonsingularity assumption regarding Σ, see Koopmans, Rubin, and Leipnik [1950, Section 1.7].

function of the coefficients of a given equation be zero, often arise from the removal of identities by elimination of variables or may sometimes be based on technological information. Identifiability criteria and estimation theory under such restrictions are only slightly more complicated; they are discussed in Koopmans, Rubin, and Leipnik [1950, Sections 2.2.2 and 4.2]. In this chapter, we seek simplicity of exposition by admitting only restrictions that require certain specified coefficients to be zero. The computational procedures described in Chapter X admit more general linear homogeneous restrictions.

A structural equation is not essentially altered if all of its coefficients are multiplied by the same number (different from zero), provided that corresponding adjustments are made in the elements of Σ. Whenever we wish to avoid this trivial indeterminacy, we add to the a priori restrictions a normalization rule for each equation—for instance, by prescribing the value 1 or -1 for a given coefficient. Since this must be a coefficient that does not vanish in the true structure, it is a good practice to select for this purpose the coefficient of that variable with which the class of decisions described by the equation is concerned.

In order to retain flexibility in the choice of methods of estimation we shall sometimes use models $\mathfrak{S}_T$ that specify only a suitably chosen subset of the set of all a priori restrictions that might be given.

1.5. *Jointly dependent and predetermined variables*. It will be convenient to use various notations and terms for significant sets of variables and parameters. For instance, we shall, where necessary, distinguish the parameters $\beta_{gi\tau}$, γ_{g0}, $\bar{\gamma}_{gk\tau}$ from other parameters by referring to them as coefficients (i.e., of the structural equations).

With the help of coefficient matrices

$$\mathrm{B}_\tau \equiv \begin{bmatrix} \beta_{11\tau} & \cdots & \beta_{1G\tau} \\ \cdots & \cdots & \cdots \\ \beta_{G1\tau} & \cdots & \beta_{GG\tau} \end{bmatrix}, \qquad \gamma_0' \equiv \begin{bmatrix} \gamma_{10} \\ \cdots \\ \gamma_{G0} \end{bmatrix}, \tag{1.13}$$

$$\bar{\Gamma}_\tau \equiv \begin{bmatrix} \bar{\gamma}_{11\tau} & \cdots & \bar{\gamma}_{1\bar{K}\tau} \\ \cdots & \cdots & \cdots \\ \bar{\gamma}_{G1\tau} & \cdots & \bar{\gamma}_{G\bar{K}\tau} \end{bmatrix},$$

the structural equations (1.6) can be written in the matrix form

$$\begin{aligned} \mathrm{B}_0 y_t' + \mathrm{B}_1 y_{t-1}' + \cdots + \mathrm{B}_{\tau\Box} y_{t-\tau\Box}' + \gamma_0' + \bar{\Gamma}_0 \bar{z}_t' \\ + \bar{\Gamma}_1 \bar{z}_{t-1}' + \cdots + \bar{\Gamma}_{\tau\Box} \bar{z}_{t-\tau\Box}' = u_t' \quad (t = 1, \cdots, T), \end{aligned} \tag{1.14}$$

where y'_t, $\bar{z}'_t$, u'_t denote the column vectors obtained by transposing the row vectors y_t, $\bar{z}_t$, u_t, respectively.

The distinction between endogenous variables $y_{t-\tau}$ and exogenous variables $\bar{z}_{t-\tau}$ is independent of the time lag, $\tau = 0, 1, \cdots, \tau^{\square}$, with which the variable in question occurs in the equations. We arrive at another important classification, which is associated with the timing τ, if we apply Simon's analysis of causal ordering of sets of variables, described in Chapter III, to equations (1.14) for all stated values of t. In a simple case where $\tau^{\square} = 2$ and $T = 4$, the coefficient matrix of these equations can be written (if I denotes the unit matrix of order G):

(1.15)

Endogenous Variables				Exogenous Variables and Disturbances												
y_1	y_2	y_3	y_4	y_{-1}	y_0	1	$\bar{z}_{-1}$	$\bar{z}_0$	$\bar{z}_1$	$\bar{z}_2$	$\bar{z}_3$	$\bar{z}_4$	u_1	u_2	u_3	u_4
B_0				B_2	B_1	γ'	$\bar{\Gamma}_2$	$\bar{\Gamma}_1$	$\bar{\Gamma}_0$				$-I$			
B_1	B_0				B_2	γ'		$\bar{\Gamma}_2$	$\bar{\Gamma}_1$	$\bar{\Gamma}_0$				$-I$		
B_2	B_1	B_0				γ'			$\bar{\Gamma}_2$	$\bar{\Gamma}_1$	$\bar{\Gamma}_0$				$-I$	
	B_2	B_1	B_0			γ'				$\bar{\Gamma}_2$	$\bar{\Gamma}_1$	$\bar{\Gamma}_0$				$-I$

Here we have classed under the heading "exogenous variables and disturbances" all variables whose generation is not described by the equation system. In Simon's terminology, these variables constitute the zero-order set of variables in the causal ordering. It is seen directly from (1.15) that the sets of variables comprised in the vectors $y_1, y_2, \cdots, y_t, \cdots$ constitute the first order, second order, $\cdots$, tth order, $\cdots$ sets, respectively, in the causal ordering.[18]

Fixing attention now on equations (1.14) for a particular time period t, we call *jointly dependent*, or simply *dependent*, the variables[19] y_t of the highest order (tth order) causal group occurring in these equations and

[18] Of course, each set y_t may split into two or more subsets as a result of the restrictions on the elements of B_0.

[19] The reader should be warned of a subtle shift in the meaning of the term "variable" from the distinction between endogenous and exogenous variables, on the one hand, to the distinction between dependent and predetermined variables on the other. $y_{t-\tau}$ is endogenous whenever $1 \leqslant t - \tau \leqslant T$; hence the endogenous character of a y-variable depends only on the time at which it is observed. The same $y_{t-\tau}$ is dependent only if both $\tau = 0$ and $1 \leqslant t \leqslant T$; hence the dependent character of a y-variable depends on the timing both of its observation and of the equation (as read from the term u_t) in which it occurs. The expression "dependent variable" is therefore strictly defensible only if we think of a variable as a time series of T observations such that y_t ($t = 1, \cdots, T$) is a different variable from y_{t-1} ($t = 1, \cdots, T$). It is in this sense that expressions such as "moments of the predetermined variables" and "lagged endogenous variables" must be understood.

of which the generation is described by those equations. On the other hand, we call *predetermined* (as of time t) all variables[20] $y_{t-\tau}$ $(\tau = 1, \cdots, \tau^{\square})$, $\bar{z}_{t-\tau}$ $(\tau = 0, 1, \cdots, \tau^{\square})$ occurring in the same equations and belonging to lower-order causal groups. We also regard as predetermined (and, in fact, as exogenous) the dummy variable "1," which assumes the value of one for all relevant values of t.

The predetermined variables, say K in number, will be denoted by the symbols

$$\begin{aligned} z_t &\equiv [y_{t-1} \quad \cdots \quad y_{t-\tau^{\square}} \quad 1 \quad \bar{z}_t \quad \bar{z}_{t-1} \quad \cdots \quad \bar{z}_{t-\tau^{\square}}] \\ &\equiv [z_{1t} \quad z_{2t} \quad \cdots \quad z_{Kt}]. \end{aligned} \tag{1.16}$$

If we introduce corresponding symbols

$$\mathrm{B} \equiv \mathrm{B}_0, \qquad \Gamma \equiv [\mathrm{B}_1 \quad \cdots \quad \mathrm{B}_{\tau^{\square}} \quad \gamma_0' \quad \bar{\Gamma}_0 \quad \bar{\Gamma}_1 \quad \cdots \quad \bar{\Gamma}_{\tau^{\square}}] \tag{1.17}$$

for the coefficient matrices, the system (1.14) can be written in the form

$$\mathrm{B}y_t' + \Gamma z_t' = u_t' \qquad (t = 1, \cdots, T), \tag{1.18}$$

which recognizes only those distinctions between variables that will turn out to be essential for the large-sample estimation theory of the parameters B, Γ, Σ.

As will become clearer in subsequent sections, the distinction between predetermined and dependent variables derives its significance from the important fact that, for any value of t, the disturbances u_t are distributed independently of *all* predetermined variables,

$$Q(u_t \mid z_t) = Q(u_t). \tag{1.19}$$

For the exogenous variables this is implied in specification (1.9). For the lagged endogenous variables it is a consequence of their lagged character: $y_{t-1}, y_{t-2}, \cdots$ can be solved from (1.14) in terms of exogenous variables $\bar{z}_{t-1}, \bar{z}_{t-2}, \cdots$ (of which u_t is independent no matter what their timing is) and disturbances $u_{t-1}, u_{t-2}, \cdots$ [of which u_t is independent by specification (1.10) because their timing precedes that of u_t].

For certain purposes, such as the estimation of the elements of Σ, even this distinction is irrelevant. We then adopt the notation

$$x_t \equiv [y_t \quad z_t], \qquad \mathrm{A} \equiv [\mathrm{B} \quad \Gamma], \tag{1.20}$$

[20] It would be logical in this connection to include also the disturbances u_t with the predetermined variables. However, to do so would deprive us of such convenient expressions as the coefficients or the (observed) moments of predetermined variables.

to write the system (1.18) in barest outline as

$$\text{(1.21)} \qquad \mathrm{A}x'_t = u'_t \qquad (t = 1, \cdots, T).$$

Finally, we shall in Section 5 use vector symbols

$$\begin{aligned} y &\equiv [y_1 \quad \cdots \quad y_T], \\ \text{(1.22)} \qquad \bar{z} &\equiv [y_{1-\tau^{\square}} \quad \cdots \quad y_0 \quad \bar{z}_{1-\tau^{\square}} \quad \cdots \quad \bar{z}_0 \quad \bar{z}_1 \quad \cdots \quad \bar{z}_T], \\ x &\equiv [y \quad \bar{z}], \end{aligned}$$

to summarize the whole set of the observations on endogenous, exogenous, and all variables, respectively.

1.6. *The reduced form and the joint distribution of the observations.* For a given structure in the model $\mathfrak{S}_T$, that is, for a given covariance matrix Σ of the disturbances u_t and given values of the parameters B and Γ (where B must be nonsingular), the structural equations (1.18), shown in greater detail in (1.14), make it possible to determine[21] the joint distribution of all endogenous variables y_t $(t = 1, \cdots, T)$ conditional upon given values of the exogenous variables $\bar{z}$. However, knowledge of the structural equations (1.18) is not necessary for that purpose. Any set of G independent linear combinations of equations (1.18) can serve the same end (provided that the joint distribution of the disturbances is replaced by the corresponding distribution of the same linear combinations of the disturbances). It is, of course, for this very reason that in order to solve the reverse (identification) problem (i.e., the determination of B, Γ, Σ from knowledge of the distribution of the observations) one needs additional a priori restrictions on these parameters.

One particular representation of the joint (conditional) distribution of the observations is obtained by choosing those linear combinations of equations (1.18) that solve the equations for the dependent variables y_t. In matrix notation, this is done by premultiplying both members of (1.18) by the inverse B^{-1} of B, which yields

$$\text{(1.23)} \qquad y'_t = \Pi z'_t + v'_t,$$

where

$$\text{(1.24)} \qquad \Pi = -\mathrm{B}^{-1}\Gamma, \qquad v'_t = \mathrm{B}^{-1}u'_t.$$

Equations (1.23) are called the equations of the *reduced form* associated with the structure (B, Γ, Σ). The disturbances v_t of the reduced form are

[21] This task is actually carried out in Appendix C.

linearly independent combinations of the disturbances u_t in the structural equations. Hence,[22] if the u_t are normally distributed and independent for successive values of t, so are the v_t. In any case, the elements of v_t have zero means and a matrix of second moments,[23]

$$(1.25) \quad \Omega \equiv \mathcal{E}(v_t'v_t) = \mathcal{E}(\mathrm{B}^{-1}u_t'u_t\mathrm{B}'^{-1}) = \mathrm{B}^{-1}(\mathcal{E}u_t'u_t)\mathrm{B}'^{-1} = \mathrm{B}^{-1}\Sigma\mathrm{B}'^{-1},$$

which is nonsingular whenever Σ is nonsingular. Likewise, as a consequence of (1.19), they are distributed independently of the predetermined variables,

$$(1.26) \qquad \bar{Q}(v_t \mid z_t) = \bar{Q}(v_t).$$

An important property of the reduced form is that it is uniformly identifiable: only one unique set of parameters Π, Ω of the reduced form can be associated with a given distribution function of the observations. This follows from the fact that its parameters can be obtained from certain conditional expectations in the distribution of the observations. According to (1.23) the conditional expectation of y_t for a given value of z_t is

$$(1.27) \qquad \mathcal{E}(y_t' \mid z_t) = \mathcal{E}(\Pi z_t' + v_t' \mid z_t) = \Pi z_t',$$

since, by (1.26), $\mathcal{E}(v_t' \mid z_t) = \mathcal{E}v_t' = 0$.

Now whenever the distribution function of the observations is known, the conditional expectation $\mathcal{E}(y_t' \mid z_t)$ can be determined as a function of z_t, *provided* the components z_{kt} of z_t are linearly independent.[23a] Hence, in that case, Π is identifiable for every structure in the model $\mathfrak{S}_T$. By a similar argument, we find that, in the same case

$$(1.28) \quad \Omega = \mathcal{E}(v_t' v_t) = \mathcal{E}\{ [y_t' - \mathcal{E}(y_t' \mid z_t)]\,[y_t - \mathcal{E}(y_t \mid z_t)] \mid z_t\}$$

is uniformly identifiable.

It follows that the parameters Π, Ω of the reduced form constitute a unique characterization of the distribution of the observations in our model $\mathfrak{S}_T$. They are therefore a useful point of departure in establishing criteria of identifiability, and are used as such in Section 4.4. They have also been used by Anderson and Rubin [1949, 1950] as the point of departure of a method of estimating the coefficients of one identifiable structural equation in a complete structure. This method, originally called the reduced-form method for that reason, is discussed in Section 6, from a somewhat different point of departure, under the name limited-information maximum-likelihood method.

[22] See Cramér [1946, Section 24.4].

[23] $v_t'v_t$ is a matrix of rank one with typical element $v_{it}v_{jt}$. Hence $\mathcal{E}(v_t'v_t)$ denotes the matrix of variances and covariances of the v_{it}.

[23a] See Section 1, footnote 13, and Section 5, footnote 54.

2. The Purpose of Estimation

The choice of parameters to be estimated, and of methods of estimation to be used, is necessarily guided by the purpose that the estimates are to serve. As shown by examples in Chapter I, this purpose is almost always prediction, directly or ultimately, of the values of endogenous variables.

It has been stressed by Erling Sverdrup [1949, 1951] that, if a direct prediction problem of this kind can be isolated and specified, the choice of a method of estimation should be discussed in terms of desired properties of the joint distribution of the prediction(s) made and the realized value(s) of the variable(s) predicted. In particular, in a precisely defined prediction problem of this type, one may know the consequences of various possible errors of prediction and would then be able to use predictors minimizing the mathematical expectation of losses due to such errors. Abraham Wald [1939, 1945, 1950c], among others, has proposed methods of statistical decision-making designed to accomplish this.

The more classical methods of estimation applied in this volume are not as closely tailored to any one particular prediction problem. Directed to the estimation of structural parameters rather than values of endogenous variables, they yield estimates that can be regarded as raw materials, to be processed further into solutions of a wide variety of prediction problems—in particular, problems involving prediction of the effects of known changes in structure. The similarity to raw material production is close. For example, it might be economical to have a greater variety of steels produced if the quantities required in the most appropriate uses of each of them were to be large enough to sustain a level of production justifying the separate effort. However, in fact the number of qualities of steel produced is limited by the diversity and unpredictability of uses that do not individually justify the separate development of a steel-making formula. Similarly, the "knowledge" represented by estimates of structural parameters consists in the possibility of solving with limited additional effort a variety of prediction problems, although for some of these problems more satisfying solutions might have been obtained by allowing the requirements of each to guide the choice of estimates or predictors.

If this view is taken, the properties of estimates that we regard as desirable do not follow with precision from the broad class of applications envisaged. In view of the mathematical difficulties in meeting any precise requirement, this circumstance is really to be welcomed. It leaves the door open for adopting certain properties of estimates as desirable, properties which in certain circumstances we know how to attain. In the next section a number of such properties is listed.

3. Desirable Properties of Estimates

In vague terms, the requirement that we shall impose on our estimates is that their deviations from the true parameter values be, in some average sense, at least as small as those of alternative estimates, at least in large samples. The lack of preciseness in this statement may be remedied by offering definitions of a number of properties of estimates that will be regarded as desirable.[24] All of these properties relate to the sampling distribution of the estimates. In the present chapter, therefore, these properties must be interpreted with reference to the notion of (imaginary) repeated samples, described in Section 1.3, in which the values of the exogenous variables remain the same,[25] while the values of the disturbances are thought of as random drawings from the joint distribution of the disturbances.

The order in which the desirable properties are listed is primarily one of decreasing generality in the models for which we know how to obtain estimates with these properties. If the order had been chosen on grounds of mathematical simplicity of definition rather than of attainability, the small-sample properties would have been stated before the asymptotic properties.

Consistency. An estimate of a parameter is said to be consistent if, in the sampling distribution of that estimate, the probability that the absolute value of the discrepancy between the estimate and the true parameter value be less than any given arbitrarily small positive quantity approaches unity as the size of the sample approaches infinity. In symbols, if $P\{E\}$ denotes the probability of an event E, an estimate h_T of a parameter θ is consistent if, for all θ,

$$\lim_{T\to\infty} P\{|\, h_T - \theta \,| < \epsilon\} = 1, \tag{3.1}$$

where T is the sample size, and ϵ is any positive number, however small. If h_T has this property it is said to possess the probability limit θ, and this relationship of h_T to θ is also denoted

$$\operatorname*{plim}_{T\to\infty} h_T = \theta. \tag{3.2}$$

Asymptotic normality. A statistic h_T is said to be asymptotically normally distributed if there exist two sequences of numbers η_T and σ_T (where

[24] These properties of statistics are discussed in many textbooks. See, for example, Cramér [1946], Mood [1950], and Wilks [1943].

[25] In Chapter VII, Section 5, this assumption is weakened to the existence of certain probability limits for certain moments of exogenous variables.

$\sigma_T > 0$) such that the following limits exist:

$$\lim_{T\to\infty} \eta_T = \eta, \qquad \lim_{T\to\infty} \sigma_T = \sigma, \tag{3.3}$$

where $0 < \sigma < \infty$, and such that, for every λ_1 and λ_2,

$$\lim_{T\to\infty} P\left(\eta_T + \frac{\sigma_T}{\sqrt{T}}\lambda_1 \leqslant h_T \leqslant \eta_T + \frac{\sigma_T}{\sqrt{T}}\lambda_2\right) = \int_{\lambda_1}^{\lambda_2} \frac{1}{\sqrt{2\pi}} e^{-\frac{1}{2}x^2}\, dx. \tag{3.4}$$

This says that the probability distribution of h_T approaches more and more closely a normal distribution with mean η_T and standard deviation $\sigma_T/\sqrt{T}$ as T becomes larger and larger, and that the mean η_T and the quantity σ_T associated with that normal distribution approach finite limits. If h_T is asymptotically normal with $\eta = \theta$, then h_T is a consistent estimate of θ.

Asymptotic normality, while not of great importance from the point of view of the purpose of estimation, is a very convenient property in an estimate. Besides making available an asymptotically correct table of percentile points, this property has mathematical advantages, one of which is that it simplifies the definition of the important property of asymptotic efficiency. All of the estimates we shall study have the property of asymptotic normality under the assumptions of the present chapter, and they retain that property in most of the cases considered in Chapter VII.

If an estimate h_T lacks the property of consistency, this may be so because it does not possess a probability limit, or because it possesses a probability limit η that differs from the parameter θ. Only the second possibility is open if h_T is asymptotically normal. In that case we call h_T *asymptotically biased* and $\eta - \theta$ its *asymptotic bias.*

Asymptotic efficiency. We shall define this as a property possessed by a consistent and asymptotically normal estimate in comparison with all other consistent and asymptotically normal estimates.

An asymptotically normal estimate h_T (characterized by η and σ as defined above) is said to be an asymptotically efficient estimate of a parameter θ if it is consistent ($\eta = \theta$) and if, for any other asymptotically normal and consistent estimate (characterized by $\eta' = \theta$ and σ'), we have

$$\sigma' \geqslant \sigma. \tag{3.5}$$

This says that, asymptotically, no rival estimate in the category of comparison has a smaller standard deviation. This, of course, is a very desirable property for an estimate to have if the sample size is such as to give a reasonable degree of approximation to the asymptotic distribution.

In the light of the foregoing statements and distinctions we may reasonably ask why asymptotic efficiency is not the one large-sample property sought. The answer lies in the nature of the compromises which have to be made in the situations facing the statistician. Illustrations of such compromises are the following. To have asymptotically efficient estimates may sometimes require a more costly estimation procedure than is possible or desirable under the circumstances, or it may require solution of mathematical problems so far too difficult to handle. The attainment of asymptotic efficiency may also depend on information that is not available. In particular, the asymptotic efficiency of certain estimates may depend on assumptions concerning the distribution function of the population, which in some situations one is not in a position to make. Thus, some methods of estimation will be considered, particularly in Chapter VII, under circumstances where they do not yield efficient estimates even asymptotically.

We now mention two properties of estimates for samples of given finite size (of which the second is particularly desirable) which we know how to attain only under rather restrictive assumptions as to the model. These properties are

1. *Unbiasedness.* An estimate is unbiased for a sample size T (as distinct from asymptotically unbiased) if its expectation in such samples equals the true parameter value

$$\mathcal{E}h_T = \theta. \tag{3.6}$$

2. *Efficiency.* An estimate h_T is efficient in samples of size T (as distinct from asymptotically efficient) if, in such samples, the ratio of its variance about θ (mean-square difference from θ) to the variance about θ of any other estimate h_T' of the same parameter is not greater than one, i.e., if

$$\frac{\mathcal{E}(h_T - \theta)^2}{\mathcal{E}(h_T' - \theta)^2} \leqslant 1. \tag{3.7}$$

Sometimes a property analogous to efficiency can more easily be attained with reference to a more limited class of estimates. The property of best linear unbiasedness, defined in Section 4.1, is of that type.

It must be stated at the outset that disappointingly little is known about the small-sample properties of the estimates considered in this chapter apart from those simple cases where unbiasedness, or best linear unbiasedness, can be proved. Studies by Hurwicz [1950c] and Leipnik [1947] of simple one-equation models with a lagged endogenous variable create a presumption of considerable bias, in samples of moderate size, whenever lagged endogenous variables are present. Further light is thrown on this question by sampling experiments reported in Cochrane and Orcutt [1949] and Orcutt and Cochrane [1949].

4. The Extent to Which Least-Squares Methods of Estimation Are Applicable

4.0. *Introduction.* Since the method of least squares has been widely used in econometrics and is well known generally, it is perhaps useful to open the discussion of estimation methods with an investigation of those estimation problems, arising with respect to the linear models under consideration, for which this method will yield parameter estimates having desirable properties.

We consider first the properties of least-squares estimates of the parameters associated with certain classes of single-equation models, and next the properties of such estimates of the parameters of the reduced form in models $\mathfrak{S}_T$ consisting of several linear equations. It will be shown that these least-squares estimates possess one or several of the desirable properties we seek. We shall then argue that "direct" least-squares estimates of the coefficients of any structural equation (in the class of structures $\mathfrak{S}_T$) do not, in general, possess even the weakest of the desirable properties, namely consistency.

We shall also show how any identifiable coefficient of a structural equation can be determined from the coefficients of the reduced form, should the latter be known. This suggests that, when structural parameters may be presumed to be identifiable, *estimates* of them may be derived indirectly from least-squares *estimates* of the reduced-form parameters.

We shall determine in which cases such an indirect use of the least-squares method of estimation is possible. To anticipate the result here, this indirect least-squares method of estimation will be found feasible for any structural equations for which the number of coefficients that are prescribed to be zero (more generally, the number of linear restrictions on the coefficients) is just enough to produce identifiability. We shall refer to this as the case of minimum requisite information. For the case in which more restrictions are imposed (the case of extra information), we shall in Sections 5 and 6 apply the maximum-likelihood method of estimation (which again reduces to the indirect least-squares method in the case of minimum requisite information).

4.1. *Properties of least-squares estimates in single-equation models.* We shall consider first the properties of least-squares estimates of the coefficients in models involving a single equation,

$$(4.1)\qquad y_t - \pi_1 z_{1t} - \pi_2 z_{2t} - \cdots - \pi_K z_{Kt} = v_t \qquad (t = 1, \cdots, T),$$

since such models provide the simplest and most familiar setting for the application of least-squares methods. The endogenous variable y_t and the disturbance v_t are here considered as scalars; assumptions about the z_{Kt} will be formulated below. The least-squares estimates $p_1, \cdots, p_K$ of $\pi_1, \cdots, \pi_K$ are defined as those values of $\pi_1, \cdots, \pi_K$ which minimize the sum of squares

$$(4.2)\qquad \sum_{t=1}^{T} (y_t - \pi_1 z_{1t} - \cdots - \pi_K z_{Kt})^2.$$

An over-all view of the properties of least-squares estimates can perhaps be gained most readily from the following summary of a number of theorems which have been proved elsewhere.[26]

Consider the following pairs of alternative specifications:

(a) The joint distribution of the v_t is the result of independent and identical normal distributions of all v_t $(t = 1, \cdots, T)$, with mean $\mathcal{E}v_t = 0$ and variance $\mathcal{E}v_t^2 = \omega$.

(A) The joint distribution of the v_t is not specified to be normal; the v_t are independently and identically distributed random variables with mean $\mathcal{E}v_t = 0$ and finite variance $\mathcal{E}v_t^2 = \omega$ for $t = 1, \cdots, T$. (A) contains (a) as a special case.

(b) The set of variables $z_1, \cdots, z_K$ contains only exogenous variables, and hence *each* v_t is distributed independently of *all* $z_{kt'}$, with $k = 1, \cdots, K; t, t' = 1, \cdots, T$. The moment matrix m_{zz} of the z_k, with typical element $m_{z_i z_j} = \frac{1}{T}\sum_{t=1}^{T} z_{it}z_{jt}$, approaches a finite and nonsingular limit as T becomes infinite.

(B) The set of variables $z_1, \cdots, z_K$ contains predetermined (i.e., exogenous and lagged endogenous) variables and, since the v_t are independently distributed, *each* v_t is distributed independently of *all* concurrent or preceding values of $z_{kt'}$ (i.e., with $k = 1, \cdots, K; t' = 1, \cdots, t$). The expectation $\mathcal{E}m_{zz}$ of m_{zz} approaches a finite and nonsingular limit as T becomes infinite". (B) contains (b) as a special case.

It may be noted that if Condition (a) is satisfied, the least-squares estimates are also maximum-likelihood estimates; this will be shown in detail in Section 5.3. If Condition (A) is satisfied, the least squares estimates belong to a class which in Section 5.1 we will call quasi maximum-likelihood estimates.

An estimate p_k of π_k will be called "best linear unbiased" if it is un-

[26] See especially David and Neyman [1938]. For an extension of the properties formulated in this section, see Hurwicz [1950b] and Koopmans [1950a].

biased, linear in the observations y_t (but not necessarily in the z_{kt}), and of minimum variance compared with all other unbiased estimates possessing the same linearity property.

If *Conditions* (*a*) *and* (*b*) are satisfied, the least-squares estimates $p_1, \cdots, p_K$ are consistent, unbiased, efficient, and hence also best linear unbiased.

If *Conditions* (*A*) *and* (*b*) are satisfied, the least-squares estimates are consistent.[27] They are also best linear unbiased estimates since the Markoff theorem on least-squares estimates is satisfied.[28]

If *Conditions* (*a*) *and* (*B*) are satisfied, the least-squares estimates are consistent and are also asymptotically efficient.[29]

If *Conditions* (*A*) *and* (*B*) are satisfied, the least-squares estimates are consistent.[30]

4.2. *Properties of least-squares estimates of the coefficients of the reduced form.* Each equation of the reduced form of our model $\mathfrak{S}_T$ is of the form of equation (4.1) because all of the variables save one are predetermined. It follows from the propositions summarized in the preceding paragraphs that least-squares estimates of the coefficients of a reduced-form equation will be consistent, and may be best unbiased and/or asymptotically efficient,[31] depending respectively upon whether (i) the z's are exogenous and not merely predetermined and/or (ii) the distribution of the disturbances is normal.

4.3. *"Direct" least-squares estimation of the coefficients of a structural equation does not in general yield consistent estimates.* As has been stressed in Chapters I and II, and again in Section 1 of the present chapter, knowledge of the parameters of the reduced form is not sufficient to permit prediction of the effects of known structural changes. For this purpose it is necessary to have knowledge of the parameters of the structural equations. The question might then be asked "naively" whether least-squares estimates of the coefficients of a given structural equation, considered individually, might possess any of the properties we desire our estimates to have. But we are stopped already in phrasing

[27] See the discussion of properties of quasi-maximum-likelihood estimates in Section 5.2.

[28] See David and Neyman [1938].

[29] See the discussion of properties of maximum-likelihood estimates in Section 5.2.

[30] See the discussion of properties of quasi-maximum-likelihood estimates in Section 5.2.

[31] The term "efficient" must here be taken with reference to the a priori information actually used in the estimation (linearity of equations, predetermined character of the z_t's, etc.). It will be explained in Section 6.5 that the least-squares method of estimating reduced-form parameters ignores any overidentifying restrictions on the structural equations that might be given.

the question, unless it happens that this structural equation is already in reduced form. As soon as more than one intrinsically[32] dependent variable y_i occurs in the equation in question, the position of these variables in the equation as well as in the model is symmetrical and there is no valid reason, in the "naive" attempt to apply least-squares estimation, for selecting one rather than another as *the* "dependent" variable. Since, whenever the variance of the disturbance in the equation in question is positive, different choices of the "dependent" variable lead to alternative least-squares estimates possessing different probability limits, these estimates cannot all be consistent. There is, moreover, no reason to believe that any one choice of *the* "dependent" variable would produce consistent estimates. The more detailed analysis by Jean Bronfenbrenner in Chapter IX shows that this only happens by accident (unknown to the statistician) if biases from different sources cancel out; there are given several examples of, as well as a general expression for, the asymptotic bias of least-squares estimates of the coefficients of a structural equation when these estimates are based on arbitrary selection of the dependent variable. Other simple examples are given by Haavelmo in Chapter IV and by Koopmans [1945, Table, p. 458].

In the present context we shall merely show that in the simple two-equation system discussed in Chapter II [third example, equation (7)] the conditions recognized in Section 4.1 as sufficient for consistency of least-squares estimation are not met. The structural equations in this example are

$$\text{(4.3)}\quad y_{1t} + \beta_{12}y_{2t} + \gamma_{11}z_{1t} + \gamma_{10} = u_{1t} \text{ (demand)},$$

$$\text{(4.4)}\quad y_{1t} + \beta_{22}y_{2t} + \gamma_{22}z_{2t} + \gamma_{20} = u_{2t} \text{ (supply)} \quad (t = 1, \cdots, T),$$

where $\beta_{12} \neq \beta_{22}$. The equations of the reduced form are

$$\text{(4.5)}\quad y_{1t} - \pi_{11}z_{1t} - \pi_{12}z_{2t} - \pi_{10} = v_{1t},$$

$$\text{(4.6)}\quad y_{2t} - \pi_{21}z_{1t} - \pi_{22}z_{2t} - \pi_{20} = v_{2t},$$

where

$$\text{(4.7)}\quad \begin{aligned} \pi_{11} &= \frac{-\beta_{22}\gamma_{11}}{\beta_{22} - \beta_{12}}, & \pi_{12} &= \frac{\beta_{12}\gamma_{22}}{\beta_{22} - \beta_{12}}, & \pi_{10} &= \frac{\beta_{12}\gamma_{20} - \beta_{22}\gamma_{10}}{\beta_{22} - \beta_{12}}, \\ \pi_{21} &= \frac{\gamma_{11}}{\beta_{22} - \beta_{12}}, & \pi_{22} &= \frac{-\gamma_{22}}{\beta_{22} - \beta_{12}}, & \pi_{20} &= \frac{\gamma_{10} - \gamma_{20}}{\beta_{22} - \beta_{12}}, \\ v_{1t} &= \frac{\beta_{22}u_{1t} - \beta_{12}u_{2t}}{\beta_{22} - \beta_{12}}, & v_{2t} &= \frac{u_{2t} - u_{1t}}{\beta_{22} - \beta_{12}}. \end{aligned}$$

[32] A simple example of consistent least-squares estimation where the dependent character of one of the two variables y_i in an equation is only apparent is contained in Koopmans [1945, equation (14)].

Examining equation (4.6) it is seen that y_2 is in general statistically dependent upon u_1, and hence equation (4.3) does not satisfy even the weakest set of conditions sufficient for consistency of least-squares estimates given in Section 4.1. Similarly, an examination of equation (4.5) shows that y_1 is in general dependent on u_2, and hence the corresponding conditions with respect to equation (4.4) are not satisfied.

4.4 *Determination of identifiable coefficients of structural equations from the coefficients of the reduced form.* Our exploration concerning the extent to which least-squares methods of estimation are applicable to models $\mathfrak{S}_T$ has now proceeded to this point: least-squares methods when applied to an equation of the reduced form will yield estimates with at least some of the properties[33] we seek but, when applied directly to the structural equations, will not (save accidentally) yield estimates with any of these properties. In order to pursue our exploration further we now change tactics and raise the general question: Is there any *indirect* way in which least-squares methods can be utilized to yield desirable estimates of the coefficients of structural equations? Specifically, is it possible to estimate the coefficients of the reduced form by least-squares methods, and from these to derive desirable estimates of coefficients of structural equations? Before we are able to answer this question we shall have to examine the conditions under which a hypothetical exact knowledge of the coefficients of reduced-form equations (and not merely estimates of these coefficients) will yield exact knowledge of the coefficients of structural equations, and it is to this question that the present subsection is devoted.

It was pointed out in Chapter II, at the end of Section 3, that a structural equation is identifiable if and only if knowledge of its coefficients is implied by knowledge of the parameters of the distribution function of the observations. But, as has been shown in Section 1.6 of the present chapter, the parameters of the reduced form, if we again include in this term the variances and covariances of the disturbances v_t of the reduced form, constitute a complete set of parameters of this distribution function. Hence, the conditions under which the coefficients of a structural equation may be determined from the parameters of the reduced form are the conditions under which this equation is identifiable. This statement leads directly to the rank condition for identifiability stated at the end of Section 5 of Chapter II, which will now be derived.[34]

[33] The reader will notice that this application of least-squares methods does not take account of any overidentifying restrictions of the coefficients of the structural equations. See footnote 31 and Section 6.5.

[34] The equivalence of this condition (which relates to the rank of a submatrix

The structural equations of the model $\mathfrak{S}_T$ may be written in the form (1.18), which we write again here:

$$\mathrm{B}y_t' + \Gamma z_t' = u_t' \qquad (t = 1, \cdots, T). \tag{4.8}$$

We recall from Section 1.5 that y_t, z_t, and u_t are the vectors of jointly dependent variables, of predetermined variables, and of disturbances, respectively; that B is the G by G nonsingular matrix of the coefficients of the jointly dependent variables; and that Γ is the G by K coefficient matrix of the predetermined variables. Let us determine the conditions under which one particular equation in this set is identifiable. We shall consider the first structural equation, to be denoted

$$\beta y_t' + \gamma z_t' = u_{1t}' \qquad (t = 1, \cdots, T). \tag{4.9}$$

After such permutation of the elements of the vectors β and y_t and of γ and z_t as may be required, we can express the a priori information concerning the exclusion of $G^{\Delta\Delta} \equiv G - G^{\Delta}$ dependent and $K^{**} \equiv K - K^*$ predetermined variables from (4.9), specified by the model $\mathfrak{S}_T$ considered, by the restrictions[35]

$$\beta \equiv [\beta_{11} \quad \cdots \quad \beta_{1G^{\Delta}} \quad 0_{1,G^{\Delta}+1} \quad \cdots \quad 0_{1G}], \qquad \beta_{11} = -1, \tag{4.10}$$

$$\gamma \equiv [\gamma_{11} \quad \cdots \quad \gamma_{1K^*} \quad 0_{1,K^*+1} \quad \cdots \quad 0_{1K}]. \tag{4.11}$$

Corresponding to these restrictions we shall introduce the following notation for partitioned vectors:

$$\beta \equiv [\beta_{\Delta} \quad \beta_{\Delta\Delta}], \tag{4.12}$$

where $\beta_{\Delta} \equiv [\beta_{11} \quad \cdots \quad \beta_{1G^{\Delta}}]$, $\beta_{\Delta\Delta} \equiv [0_{1,G^{\Delta}+1} \quad \cdots \quad 0_{1G}]$; and

$$\gamma \equiv [\gamma_{*} \quad \gamma_{**}], \tag{4.13}$$

where $\gamma_{*} \equiv [\gamma_{11} \quad \cdots \quad \gamma_{1K^*}]$, $\gamma_{**} \equiv [0_{1,K^*+1} \quad \cdots \quad 0_{1K}]$; and, correspondingly,

$$y_t \equiv [y_{\Delta,t} \quad y_{\Delta\Delta,t}], \qquad z_t \equiv [z_{*,t} \quad z_{**,t}]. \tag{4.14}$$

The reduced form (1.23) corresponding to (4.8) is obtained by multiplying (4.8) on the left by B^{-1}, and may be written

$$y_t' - \Pi z_t' = v_t' \qquad (t = 1, \cdots, T), \tag{4.15}$$

---

of the matrix of reduced-form coefficients) to the condition given in Section 4 of Chapter II (which relates to the rank of a submatrix of the matrix of structural coefficients) is demonstrated in Appendix A.

[35] For a treatment of the identifiability problem under more general linear restrictions, see Koopmans, Rubin, and Leipnik [1950, Section 2, pp. 69–110].

where

$$\Pi = -B^{-1}\Gamma. \tag{4.16}$$

Conversely, the structural equations (4.8) are obtained from the reduced form in (4.15) by multiplying on the left by B. In particular, the first structural equation (4.9) is obtained from (4.15) by premultiplying by β, the first row of B. To write this down, let Π be partitioned by rows and by columns as follows to correspond to the partitioning (4.14) of y and z:

$$\Pi \equiv \begin{bmatrix} \Pi_{\Delta} \\ \Pi_{\Delta\Delta} \end{bmatrix} \equiv [\Pi_{*} \quad \Pi_{**}] \equiv \begin{bmatrix} \Pi_{\Delta *} & \Pi_{\Delta,**} \\ \Pi_{\Delta\Delta,*} & \Pi_{\Delta\Delta,**} \end{bmatrix}. \tag{4.17}$$

Then, the statement just made is expressed by

$$-\beta_{\Delta}\Pi_{\Delta} = \gamma, \tag{4.18}$$

which can be partitioned into the two conditions

$$-\beta_{\Delta}\Pi_{\Delta *} = \gamma_{*} \tag{4.19}$$

and

$$\beta_{\Delta}\Pi_{\Delta,**} = 0. \tag{4.20}$$

Conditions (4.19) and (4.20) express all that can be said about the coefficients $[\beta \quad \gamma]$ of the first structural equation if the parameters Π, Ω of the reduced form are known. It turns out that only the coefficient matrix Π of the reduced form is relevant.[36] It follows that the structural coefficients β_{Δ} , γ_{*} are identifiable if and only if (4.20) is satisfied by only one value of β_{Δ} , which is normalized by the second condition (4.10). If this is the case, (4.19) supplies the corresponding unique value of γ_{*} . Hence it is only necessary to study the conditions under which (4.20) has a unique solution β_{Δ} .

Since we regard as given that (4.9) is an equation of a structure which has Π as the coefficient matrix of the reduced form, (4.20) must have at least one solution, and hence

$$\rho(\Pi_{\Delta,**}) < G^{\Delta}, \tag{4.21}$$

that is, the rank of the matrix $\Pi_{\Delta,**}$ cannot be greater than $G^{\Delta} - 1$.[37]

Suppose that $\rho(\Pi_{\Delta,**}) = G^{\Delta} - 1$. Then, since (4.20) is a system of $G^{\Delta} - 1$ linear independent homogeneous equations in G^{Δ} unknowns, the ratios of the unknowns (the elements of β_{Δ}) are uniquely determined.

[36] For this reason we have in the title of this subsection spoken of the coefficients rather than the parameters of the reduced form.

[37] See, for example, MacDuffee [1943, Theorem 29, p. 60].

The adoption of the normalization rule in (4.10), whereby some element of β_Δ is set equal to -1, then permits the unique determination of all other elements of β_Δ, subject to this normalization.

If $\rho(\Pi_{\Delta,**}) < G^\Delta - 1$, an infinity of normalized solutions for β_Δ exists, and hence it is impossible to determine uniquely the coefficients of the structural equation (4.9), even though we are given full knowledge of the parameters of the reduced form.

We conclude that a necessary and sufficient condition for the identifiability of the coefficients β_Δ, γ_* in (4.9) is that

$$\rho(\Pi_{\Delta,**}) = G^\Delta - 1. \tag{4.22}$$

This condition has been called the *rank condition* for identifiability of a structural equation. It should be noted that a necessary condition for this identifiability—called the *order condition*—is implied in the rank condition. This condition is that $\Pi_{\Delta,**}$ have at least $G^\Delta - 1$ columns, which means that the number of predetermined variables specified to have zero coefficients in the equation whose identifiability is in question be at least $G^\Delta - 1$. This condition may be expressed as

$$K^{**} \geqslant G^\Delta - 1, \tag{4.23}$$

where $K^{**} \equiv K - K^*$, or, equivalently, as

$$K^{**} + G^{\Delta\Delta} \geqslant G - 1, \tag{4.24}$$

the form given to it in Chapter II, Section 4.

Condition (4.24) specifies the minimum number of pieces of information, in the form of restrictions on the coefficients, needed to give an equation a determinate position within the set of all linear combinations of the equations of the reduced form—just as a table needs at least three legs to stand up. This is a relevant fact, even though the table will still fall if its three legs are so placed that they touch the floor in three points of a straight line. The latter type of failure cannot be excluded by any prescription of the number of legs but only by a concern with their position. The analogue of this concern with respect to the identification of a structural equation is expressed by the rank condition of identifiability.

We may illustrate the application of these identifiability conditions in terms of the example given in equations (4.3) and (4.4). For each equation the value of G^Δ is 2 and of K^{**} is 1, and thus the order condition of identifiability (4.23) is satisfied. For equation (4.3) the rank condition (4.22) is

$$\rho \begin{bmatrix} \pi_{12} \\ \pi_{22} \end{bmatrix} = 1, \tag{4.25}$$

and for (4.4) the rank condition is

$$(4.26) \qquad \rho \begin{bmatrix} \pi_{11} \\ \pi_{21} \end{bmatrix} = 1.$$

It is seen from (4.7) that these conditions are satisfied whenever $\gamma_{11} \neq 0$ and $\gamma_{22} \neq 0$, respectively.

The determination of the structural coefficients, possible in this case,[38] is carried out by

$$(4.27) \qquad \begin{aligned} \beta_{12} &= -\pi_{12}/\pi_{22}, \quad \gamma_{11} = -(\pi_{11} + \beta_{12}\pi_{21}), \quad \gamma_{10} = -(\pi_{10} + \beta_{12}\pi_{20}); \\ \beta_{22} &= -\pi_{11}/\pi_{21}, \quad \gamma_{22} = -(\pi_{12} + \beta_{22}\pi_{22}), \quad \gamma_{20} = -(\pi_{10} + \beta_{22}\pi_{20}). \end{aligned}$$

4.5. *The case of minimum requisite information and the indirect least-squares method of estimation.* We may now return to the main question posed in the opening paragraph of Section 4.4: After obtaining a matrix P of least-squares estimates of the coefficient matrix Π of reduced-form equations, is it possible to determine therefrom desirable estimates of the coefficients of the structural equation (4.9)? In this section, 4.5, we show that this determination is normally possible when $K^{**} = G^{\Delta} - 1$, that is, when the number of predetermined variables in (4.9) excluded from the structural equation is exactly one less than the number of dependent variables admitted to that equation. This is the case (analogous to our three-legged table) in which at least the order condition for identifiability of the structural equation in question is satisfied. We shall refer to this as the case of *minimum requisite information* (i.e., "requisite" for identifiability, and "minimum" in *number* of restrictions needed to produce identifiability). Knowledge that the (necessary) rank condition (4.22) for identifiability is also satisfied usually cannot be obtained with certainty. However, as explained in Chapter II, Section 5, a statistical test of the hypothesis of identifiability is always possible. A test for the identifiability of a specified structural equation will be discussed in Section 8 below.

We shall show further, in Section 4.6, that the determination, from the matrix P, of estimates of structural coefficients is not possible in the same simple manner when $K^{**} > G^{\Delta} - 1$. We refer to this as the case of *extra information*, "extra" again referring merely to the number of restrictions in comparison with the number generally, but not necessarily, sufficient for identifiability. The terms *overidentification* and *overidentifying restrictions* have also been used in relation to this case, al-

[38] It should be noted from equation (4.7), which is valid whenever the model is that given by (4.3) and (4.4), that π_{21} and π_{22} cannot vanish when $\gamma_{11} \neq 0$, $\gamma_{22} \neq 0$.

though even "overidentifying" restrictions may fail to identify when by accident the rank condition for identifiability is not met.

It is, of course, clear from Section 4.4 that for an equation for which $K^{**} < G^{\Delta} - 1$ there can be no identifiability, since the necessary order condition is not met. Hence the question of estimation does not even arise.

In the remainder of this section, then, we consider the case of minimum requisite information, in which

$$K^{**} = G^{\Delta} - 1. \tag{4.28}$$

The order condition (4.23) being satisfied, there is at least this basis for the presumption that equation (4.9) is identifiable. Except for accidental samples, it will now be found also that

$$\rho(P_{\Delta,**}) = G^{\Delta} - 1, \tag{4.29}$$

and hence it will be possible to find a unique solution b_{Δ} (subject to a suitable normalization) to the equations, analogous to (4.20),

$$b_{\Delta}P_{\Delta,**} = 0. \tag{4.30}$$

This solution b_{Δ} may be taken as an estimate of β_{Δ}. Using this estimate b_{Δ}, a corresponding estimate c_* of γ_* may be obtained, by analogy with (4.19), from

$$c_* = -b_{\Delta}P_{\Delta *}. \tag{4.31}$$

This method of obtaining estimates of coefficients of the structural equations from least-squares estimates of the coefficients of the reduced-form equations is due to a suggestion by M. A. Girshick. We shall call it the *indirect least-squares method* of estimating the coefficients of the structural equations.

In the example we have been using for illustration [equations (4.3) and (4.4)] the estimates of the structural coefficients are

$$\begin{aligned} b_{12} &= -p_{12}/p_{22}, \quad c_{11} = -(p_{11} + b_{12}p_{21}), \quad c_{10} = -(p_{10} + b_{12}p_{20}); \\ b_{22} &= -p_{11}/p_{21}, \quad c_{22} = -(p_{12} + b_{22}p_{22}), c_{20} = -(p_{10} + b_{22}p_{20}). \end{aligned} \tag{4.32}$$

What may be said of the properties of the estimates of the coefficients of structural equations obtained in this way? It can be shown that all asymptotic properties, consistency, asymptotic unbiasedness, or asymptotic efficiency, as the case may be, of the estimates P will also be possessed by the estimates of the coefficients[39] β, γ of those structural

[39] The proof of this statement as it applies to consistency and asymptotic unbiasedness may be found in Cramér [1946; see the last proposition in Chapter XX, p. 255].

equations that are indeed identifiable. Small-sample properties will not necessarily carry over exactly but, if the reduced-form estimates from a finite sample are unbiased and/or efficient, the derived estimates of the structural coefficients will be approximately unbiased and/or efficient whenever the sampling standard deviations of the elements of P are sufficiently small.

The reader will have realized that determinate estimates b_Δ , c_* may be obtained by the indirect least-squares method even if the equation in question is in fact not identifiable. For, a failure of the rank condition (4.22) in terms of the parameter matrix $\Pi_{\Delta,**}$, which arises from the values of its elements rather than from the number of its columns, does not need to, and in general does not, entail a failure of the corresponding condition (4.29) in terms of the estimate $P_{\Delta,**}$. In a sufficiently large sample such a situation is likely to be detected through the test of identifiability discussed in Section 8. If this test is not applied, it still has a good chance to be revealed through high estimated sampling variances of b_Δ , c_* , the evaluation of which is discussed in Section 7.

4.6. *The case of extra information.* If for the structural equation (4.9)

$$K^{**} > G^\Delta - 1, \tag{4.33}$$

again the order condition for identifiability (4.24) is satisfied and there is at least this basis for the presumption that (4.9) is identifiable. However, in this case, except for accidental samples, it will be found that $\rho(P_{\Delta,**}) > G^\Delta - 1$, and hence, since $P_{\Delta,**}$ has G^Δ rows,

$$\rho(P_{\Delta,**}) = G^\Delta. \tag{4.34}$$

Thus, no nonvanishing solution of (4.30) exists, and hence it is not possible to derive estimates of β_Δ and γ_* from least-squares estimates of the coefficients of the reduced form in this simple way.

Two courses of action are open in this situation. One might arbitrarily choose $G^\Delta - 1$ of the columns of $P_{\Delta,**}$ to form a submatrix with rank $G^\Delta - 1$ and derive consistent estimates of the structural coefficients of identifiable equations on the basis of the least-squares estimates in this submatrix. This procedure is somewhat unsatisfactory since it neglects a priori information concerning the structural equation to be estimated and since the choice of what information to neglect is arbitrary. Another possible approach is to develop methods of estimation of the parameters of the reduced-form equations that ensure that the rank of the estimate of $\Pi_{\Delta,**}$ will be exactly $G^\Delta - 1$ even where $K^{**} > G^\Delta - 1$. Such a method has been developed by Anderson and Rubin.[40] This method will

[40] Anderson and Rubin [1949, 1950]. See also Anderson [1950].

be discussed in Section 6, where we shall adopt a somewhat different avenue of attack from that employed by Anderson and Rubin.

4.7. *Haavelmo's examples in Chapter IV and the occurrence of identities.* It may be remarked that all of the examples given by Haavelmo in Chapter IV fall in the category of minimum requisite information[41] since, as may be easily checked, in each of his equations the number of predetermined variables excluded is exactly equal to the number of dependent variables not excluded less one. It is for this reason that Haavelmo is able to accomplish the estimation of the coefficients of his structural equations by the indirect application of least-squares methods which we have outlined in this section.

It should be pointed out, however, that Haavelmo's procedure differs slightly from that outlined above in that among the structural equations of each of his three models there is an identity—that is, a structural equation with given coefficients and no disturbance. There are two equivalent ways to apply the indirect least-squares methods to the estimation of the coefficients of structural equations in a structure S_T that includes an identity. One way is to use the identity to eliminate one of its component variables and thus to remove the identity from the set of structural equations. This gives rise to a revised structure S'_T consisting of one less equation than the original structure S_T. Provided that all of the equations of the original structure are identifiable,[42] their coefficients may be derived from the coefficients of those reduced-form equations associated with the revised structure S'_T. If all the equations of the structure S_T are provided with the minimum requisite information, *estimates* of the coefficients of the original structure S_T may be derived from least-squares estimates of the coefficients of the equations of the reduced form associated with the revised structure S'_T, with the help of the given identity. This is Haavelmo's procedure.

The equivalent alternative is to proceed, without eliminating a variable and thus without removing the identity, to derive the estimates of the coefficients of S_T from the estimates of the coefficients of the reduced form associated with S_T. One of the equations in this estimated reduced form will be derivable from the other with the help of the identity.[43] There are certain disadvantages in this alternative procedure, one of the more significant of which is that one more regression equation must

[41] Haavelmo points this out in his footnote 10.

[42] The conditions for identifiability are usually most easily studied in terms of the original structure S_T.

[43] If this is overlooked, and if the observations satisfy the identity, accurately computed least-squares estimates of all equations of this reduced form will also obey the identity, and hence the same estimates are obtained.

be computed than is necessary under the first alternative. An offsetting advantage may be that the restrictions on the structural coefficients specified by the model are likely to be simpler if identities are not removed in this way.

4.8. *The application of least-squares methods to the estimation of the matrix of covariances of disturbances in the structural equations.* In Section 4 we have restricted the discussion to the application of least-squares methods to indirect estimation of the coefficients of structural equations and have not considered the estimation of the covariance matrix Σ of the disturbances. This gap will be filled in Sections 5 and 6, which are devoted to maximum-likelihood estimation of all structural parameters, where we shall also show that indirect least-squares estimation is equivalent to maximum-likelihood estimation in the case of equations provided with the minimum underpinning of a priori restrictions requisite for identifiability.

5. The Maximum-Likelihood Method of Estimation

5.0. *Introduction.* In the previous section we showed that least-squares methods of estimation may be used indirectly to obtain estimates of the coefficients of a structural equation provided that the number of a priori restrictions on the coefficients of that equation is the minimum requisite for identifiability. These estimates have desirable properties whenever the equation in question is in fact identifiable. In the event that the statistician wants to utilize a number of restrictions more than adequate for identifiability, this indirect least-squares method is not applicable. The maximum-likelihood method, to be introduced in this section, will yield estimates with similar desirable properties in this case in which the indirect least-squares method fails, and is equivalent to the latter method when only the minimum requisite number of restrictions is given.

The indirect least-squares method, when used to estimate the coefficients of any particular structural equation in a linear model, utilizes only the a priori information on restrictions which apply to that equation. Maximum-likelihood methods are more flexible in this respect in that they can be adapted either to utilize merely the a priori restrictions relating to the coefficients of the equation being estimated or to utilize information relating to other structural equations as well. Whereas the indirect least-squares method estimates separately each equation for which it can be used, the maximum-likelihood method can be used to estimate the parameters of all equations simultaneously, or the parameters of the equations of a subset simultaneously, or those of a single equation, provided of course that the equations in question are identifiable.

It was argued in Section 4 that under certain specifications indirect least-squares estimates of structural coefficients are asymptotically efficient. Of course, they only possess this property relative to that class of estimates which utilizes the same a priori information. Whenever maximum-likelihood methods are used to estimate structural parameters, and whenever they utilize more relevant a priori information than indirect least-squares estimates of the same parameters, they have a higher asymptotic efficiency than the indirect least-squares estimates.

The maximum-likelihood method is the most fully worked out estimation procedure for linear models, as here considered, which will give at least consistent estimates of identifiable structural parameters (and asymptotically efficient estimates if the disturbances are indeed normal), which will yield estimates where indirect least-squares methods will not, and which is flexible in terms of the amount of a priori information that it presupposes or utilizes.

In the present section we shall define the meaning of maximum-likelihood and quasi-maximum-likelihood estimates and summarize the results of recent work concerning their properties. We shall then, by way of introduction, apply the maximum-likelihood method to the estimation of the coefficients in a single-equation model and to the estimation of the parameters of the reduced form in the model $\mathfrak{S}_T$. We shall show that in both of these cases maximum-likelihood estimates are identical with least-squares estimates. Next we shall explain the meaning of stepwise maximization of a function and make our first application of this useful device to the estimation of the "constant terms" γ_{g0} in the structural equations [i.e., the terms which in (1.14) we treated as coefficients of the dummy variable "1"]. Finally we shall introduce the likelihood function, expressed in terms of the parameters A and Σ, that is associated with our general model $\mathfrak{S}_T$ and show how, by stepwise maximization, a concentrated likelihood function expressed in terms of A alone may be derived from it. From the latter function the maximum-likelihood estimate A of A may be obtained, in terms of which the maximum-likelihood estimate S of Σ can be expressed. Since all of the a priori information incorporated in the model $\mathfrak{S}_T$ is used in obtaining the estimates A and S, this application of the maximum-likelihood method is referred to as the full-information maximum-likelihood method.

5.1. *The definition of maximum-likelihood and quasi-maximum-likelihood estimates.* It was shown in Section 1 that, in any structure S_T of the model $\mathfrak{S}_T$, sampling variation in the disturbances $u_1, \cdots, u_T$ induces sampling variation in the jointly dependent variables $y_1, \cdots, y_T$, the values $\bar{z}_{1-\tau^\square}, \cdots, \bar{z}_T$ of (lagged and unlagged) exogenous variables and the values $y_{1-\tau^\square}, \cdots, y_0$ of the "endogenous" variables anterior to the period of observation being regarded as fixed in repeated samples and therefore hereafter all to be referred to as exogenous. In order to simplify the exposition of the maximum-likelihood method of estimation, we now assume that the normal joint density function

$$Q(u_1, \cdots, u_T) \tag{5.1}$$

of the disturbances $u_1, \cdots, u_T$ is nonsingular[44] (i.e., possesses a nonsingular covariance matrix Σ). From this distribution of the disturbances and the structural equations

$$\mathrm{A}x'_t = \mathrm{B}y'_t + \Gamma z'_t = u'_t \qquad (t = 1, \cdots, T), \tag{5.2}$$

in short from the structure S_T, the joint distribution function of the endogenous variables y_t $(t = 1, \cdots, T)$ may be derived. Let us denote the resulting joint conditional distribution[45] of the components of the vector $y \equiv [y_1 \quad \cdots \quad y_T]$ as follows:

$$F_T(y \mid \bar{z};\ \mathrm{A},\ \Sigma), \tag{5.3}$$

where y, $\bar{z}$ are the vectors summarizing the observations on endogenous and exogenous variables, respectively, introduced in (1.22). For convenience we usually work with the logarithm of (5.3) multiplied by $1/T$. We regard this new function as a function having the parameters A and Σ as arguments, after the actual observations x have been inserted:

$$(1/T) \log F_T(y \mid \bar{z};\ \mathrm{A},\ \Sigma) = L(\mathrm{A}, \Sigma; x). \tag{5.4}$$

Here we have used one vector symbol, x, for the observations of all variables because the distinction between endogenous and exogenous variables, essential for the definition of the function F_T, is superseded by the distinction between dependent and predetermined variables when it comes to the derivation and computation of maximum-likelihood estimates.[46]

The function (5.4) will be called the *logarithmic likelihood function* associated with the sample x. The method of maximum likelihood con-

[44] This implies that any identities that may have been present in the model originally have been removed by the elimination of an equal number of variables.

[45] The explicit derivation of this function is given in Section 5.4 and Appendix C. The result is given in (5.51).

[46] The reader is referred again to footnote 19.

sists in maximizing $L(\mathrm{A}, \Sigma; x)$ with respect to A and Σ and taking the maximizing values A and S as *maximum-likelihood estimates* of the true values[47] of A and Σ, respectively. These estimates are, of course, functions of the observations x and are the same as those that would be obtained by maximizing F_T with respect to A, Σ.

If the distribution function $Q_t(u_t)$ of the disturbances u_t is not required to be normal, or even the same for different values of t, it is of course still possible to form the same function (5.4) and obtain estimates of the matrices A and Σ by maximizing that function, even though this function is no longer a likelihood function. Estimates obtained in this way will therefore in this case be called *quasi-maximum-likelihood estimates.* These estimates are the same functions of the observations as the maximum-likelihood estimates for the case in which $Q_t(u_t)$ is normal and constant, but their sampling properties are different whenever the distribution $Q_t(u_t)$ is not some constant normal distribution. These sampling properties will be discussed for more general models in Chapter VII.

5.2. *Properties of maximum-likelihood and quasi-maximum-likelihood estimates.* The method of maximum likelihood yields estimates that possess some or all of the properties enumerated in Section 3, depending on the specifications of the model. A general discussion of the properties of maximum-likelihood estimates, in the classical case in which successive observations are drawn from independent identical distributions, can be found in several textbooks.[48] Much recent work has been devoted to establishing the properties of maximum-likelihood estimates of parameters of linear structures such as (1.6), which involve successively interdependent observations. A number of results have been obtained regarding the consistency of genuine and quasi-maximum-likelihood estimates. Mann and Wald [1943] have proved the consistency of such estimates in linear models in which the equation system is stable,[49] there are no exogenous variables (save a "constant term" in each equation), all parameters are identifiable, and all moments of the distribution

[47] The reader should be warned that the symbols for parameters such as A, Σ are used with two different meanings. In some contexts these symbols denote the "true" values, that is, the values of these parameters in the "true" structure, which by hypothesis has generated the observations. In other contexts these symbols denote the arguments of the likelihood function and as such are regarded as freely variable. We have refrained from complicating our notation by a distinction that will be clear to the reader from the context.

[48] Cramér [1946, Chapter XXXIII], Wilks [1943, Section 624, pp. 136–142], Wald [1949], Wolfowitz [1949].

[49] For a definition of this concept, see Koopmans, Rubin, and Leipnik [1950, Section 3.3.1].

function of the disturbances exist and are finite. Koopmans and Rubin[50] extended these results to cover cases in which exogenous variables are present, some but not necessarily all structural parameters are identifiable, and the distribution function of the disturbances is slightly less restricted. Rubin [1950] proved consistency in a special case in which the stability assumption is not met. Further results on consistency of quasi-maximum-likelihood estimates are presented by Chernoff and Rubin in Chapter VII of this volume. Some results have also been obtained on the asymptotic efficiency of genuine maximum-likelihood estimates. Wald [1948] has proved this property for a certain class of cases in which observations are serially dependent, and in which the distribution function of the observations contains one parameter only. Rubin [1948] has proved the asymptotic efficiency of maximum-likelihood estimates for a class of models containing stable linear stochastic difference equations involving several parameters and exogenous and endogenous variables.

5.3. *Maximum-likelihood estimates of the coefficients in a single-equation model are least-squares estimates.* We shall begin our study of maximum-likelihood estimation by considering two cases in which maximum-likelihood estimates are also least-squares estimates. The first case is that of a single-equation model; the second, treated in Section 5.4, is that of the reduced form of our general linear model $\mathfrak{S}_T$. The operation of the maximum-likelihood method is thus first illustrated by its application to cases already familiar to most readers.

Let us consider, then, the model containing the single equation (4.1), which we rewrite as

$$y_t - \pi z'_t = v_t , \tag{5.5}$$

where $\pi \equiv [\pi_1 \quad \cdots \quad \pi_K]$ and where y_t and v_t are scalar variables, z_t is a vector, and the coefficient of y_t is given the value 1 for normalization purposes. This model may be regarded as a special case of our general model $\mathfrak{S}_T$ in which there is only one equation, which is therefore already in reduced form. Accordingly, we now adopt specifications (a) and (B) of Section 4.1. That is, v_t has a normal distribution with mean 0 and variance ω. We write[51]

$$\bar{Q}(v_t) = \kappa_1 \cdot \omega^{-\frac{1}{2}} \cdot e^{-v_t^2/2\omega} \tag{5.6}$$

for the corresponding probability density function, where κ_1 is a numerical constant whose value is of no interest here. Successive values of v_t

[50] In Koopmans, Rubin, and Leipnik [1950, Section 3].

[51] The symbol e denotes the base of the system of natural logarithms.

are independently distributed. Furthermore, among the elements of z_t we may have lagged values $y_{t-1}, y_{t-2}, \cdots$ of the endogenous variable y_t, the remaining elements of z_t being exogenous. However, as argued more fully above in connection with (1.19), the distribution of v_t is independent of *all* elements of z_t, a fact on which the following derivation hinges.

As stated already, the distribution of v_t induces through (5.5) a distribution of the y_t conditional upon the values of the z_t. Because v_t is itself independent of z_t, this conditional distribution of y_t is again normal, with the same variance ω, but shifted to a new mean,

$$\mathcal{E}(y_t \mid z_t) = \pi z_t' + \mathcal{E}(v_t \mid z_t) = \pi z_t'. \tag{5.7}$$

We observe that this expectation depends on t since z_t is not, in general, constant through time. The probability density function associated with the conditional distribution of y_t given z_t is, by the foregoing reasoning,

$$f(y_t \mid z_t) = \kappa_1 \cdot \omega^{-\frac{1}{2}} \cdot e^{-(1/2\omega)(y_t - \pi z_t')^2}. \tag{5.8}$$

Because of the possible presence of $y_{t-1}, y_{t-2}, \cdots$ among the elements of z_t, successive values y_t ($t = 1, \cdots, T$) of the dependent variable, unlike those of v_t, need not be independently distributed. For the realized value y_{t_0-1}, drawn from the distribution (5.8) for $t = t_0 - 1$, may enter as a conditioning value among the elements of z_{t_0} in the distribution (5.8) for $t = t_0$. However, the joint distribution function of all y_t ($t = 1, \cdots, T$) can be obtained by repeated application of the rule for compounding conditional distributions.[52] With reference to the definition (1.22) of the symbols y and $\bar{z}$ (in which each y_t is now to be thought of as scalar), relation (5.8) leads to the following joint conditional probability density of the values y_t ($t = 1, \cdots, T$) of the dependent variable, for given values $\bar{z}_t$ ($t = 1, \cdots, T$) of the exogenous variables:[53]

$$F_T(y \mid \bar{z}) = \prod_{t=1}^{T} f(y_t \mid z_t) = \kappa_2 \cdot \omega^{-\frac{1}{2}T} \cdot \exp - \frac{1}{2\omega} \sum_{t=1}^{T} (y_t - \pi z_t')^2, \tag{5.9}$$

where $\kappa_2 = \kappa_1^T$.

In this function the observations enter only through their second-

[52] If $f(w_2 \mid w_1, w_0)$ is the conditional probability density function of w_2 for given w_1 and w_0 (where the w_i may be either vectors or scalars), and if $f(w_1 \mid w_0)$ is the conditional density function of w_1 for given w_0, then the joint conditional density function of w_1 and w_2 for given w_0 is $f(w_1, w_2 \mid w_0) = f(w_1 \mid w_0) \cdot f(w_2 \mid w_1, w_0)$. This is a direct consequence of the definition of a conditional distribution function (for which see, e.g., Mood [1950, Section 4.6]).

[53] The notation exp x for the exponential function is an alternative to e^x.

order moments about the origin. The (symmetric) matrix of these moments is defined as follows:

$$(5.10)\qquad M \equiv \left[\begin{array}{c|ccc} m_{yy} & m_{yz_1} & \cdots & m_{yz_K} \\ \hline m_{z_1y} & m_{z_1z_1} & \cdots & m_{z_1z_K} \\ \cdots & \cdots & \cdots & \cdots \\ m_{z_Ky} & m_{z_Kz_1} & \cdots & m_{z_Kz_K} \end{array}\right] \equiv \begin{bmatrix} m_{yy} & m_{yz} \\ m_{zy} & m_{zz} \end{bmatrix},$$

where[54] $m_{zy} = m'_{yz}$ and

$$(5.11)\qquad m_{yy} = \frac{1}{T}\sum_{t=1}^{T} y_t^2, \qquad m_{yz_i} = \frac{1}{T}\sum_{t=1}^{T} y_t z_{it}, \qquad m_{z_iz_j} = \frac{1}{T}\sum_{t=1}^{T} z_{it} z_{jt}.$$

Using equations (5.10) and (5.11), it is easily verified that

$$(5.12)\qquad \frac{1}{T}\sum_{t=1}^{T} \{y_t - \pi z'_t\}^2 = [1 \quad -\pi]M[1 \quad -\pi]',$$

and hence (5.9) may be written

$$(5.13)\qquad F_T(y \mid \bar{z}) = \kappa_2 \cdot \omega^{-\frac{1}{2}T} \cdot \exp - \frac{T}{2\omega}[1 \quad -\pi]M[1 \quad -\pi]'.$$

This function, regarded as a function of the parameters π, ω, is the likelihood function associated with the sample of observations y and z [represented in (5.13) only by M]. As noted already, it is usually more convenient to work with the logarithm of this function divided by T, which we now write in the two alternative forms

$$(5.14)\qquad \begin{aligned} \frac{1}{T}\log F_T(y \mid \bar{z}; \pi, \omega) &\equiv L(\pi, \omega; x) \\ &= \kappa_3 - \tfrac{1}{2}\log\omega - \frac{1}{2\omega}\cdot\frac{1}{T}\sum_{t=1}^{T} \{y_t - \mathcal{E}(y_t \mid z_t)\}^2 \\ &= \kappa_3 - \tfrac{1}{2}\log\omega - \frac{1}{2\omega}[1 \quad -\pi]M[1 \quad -\pi]', \end{aligned}$$

where $\kappa_3 = 1/T \log \kappa_2$. Clearly the logarithmic likelihood function (5.14) will achieve a maximum for the same values of π and ω as (5.13).

The values $p \equiv [p_1 \quad \cdots \quad p_K]$ of $\pi \equiv [\pi_1 \quad \cdots \quad \pi_K]$ at which (5.14)

[54] The moment matrix M_{zz} is specified to be nonsingular for the reasons outlined in Section 1, footnote 13.

achieves a maximum for any given ω will be the values at which the quadratic form[55]

$$\frac{1}{T}\sum_{t=1}^{T}\{y_t - \mathcal{E}(y_t \mid z_t)\}^2 = \frac{1}{T}\sum_{t=1}^{T}\{y_t - \pi z_t'\}^2 = [1 \quad -\pi]\begin{bmatrix} m_{yy} & m_{yz} \\ m_{zy} & M_{zz} \end{bmatrix}[1 \quad -\pi]' \tag{5.15}$$

achieves a minimum. Since ω does not occur in (5.15), the minimizing values p are independent of ω, and the same values must be obtained if (5.14) is maximized simultaneously with respect to π and ω. We now recall that the least-squares estimates p of π are defined to be those values p of π for which $\sum_{t=1}^{T}\{y_t - \pi z_t'\}^2$ is a minimum. Thus it may be inferred that for the model under discussion the maximum-likelihood estimates p of π are also the least-squares estimates. Consequently, the properties of these estimates may be determined from the theorems summarized in Section 4.1. The large-sample properties (consistency and asymptotic efficiency) there claimed for least-squares estimates if Conditions (a) and (b) are satisfied can indeed be seen as consequences of the fact that the least-squares estimates are, under those conditions, also maximum-likelihood estimates.

From least-squares theory[56] it is known that, by differentiating the quadratic form (5.15) partially with respect to the elements of π and setting these partial derivatives equal to zero, a set of so-called *normal equations* is obtained which may be solved simultaneously to give the least-squares estimates p of π. These normal equations may be written explicitly as follows:

$$\begin{aligned} p_1 m_{z_1 z_1} + \cdots + p_K m_{z_1 z_K} &= m_{z_1 y}\,, \\ \cdots\cdots\cdots&\cdots\cdots\cdots \\ p_1 m_{z_K z_1} + \cdots + p_K m_{z_K z_K} &= m_{z_K y}\,, \end{aligned} \tag{5.16}$$

or, in matrix form,

$$\begin{bmatrix} m_{z_1 z_1} & \cdots & m_{z_1 z_K} \\ \cdots & \cdots & \cdots \\ m_{z_K z_1} & \cdots & m_{z_K z_K} \end{bmatrix}\begin{bmatrix} p_1 \\ \cdots \\ p_K \end{bmatrix} = \begin{bmatrix} m_{z_1 y} \\ \cdots \\ m_{z_K y} \end{bmatrix} \quad \text{or} \quad M_{zz}p' = m_{zy}. \tag{5.17}$$

The solution of these equations is thus $p' = M_{zz}^{-1}m_{zy}$ or, since M_{zz} is symmetric,

$$p = m_{yz}M_{zz}^{-1}\,. \tag{5.18}$$

[55] Since (5.15) is a sum of squares, it is a positive definite quadratic form (see Appendix B) and hence possesses one and only one minimum, which is the absolute minimum.

[56] For a systematic treatment of normal regression theory the reader is referred to Wilks [1943, Chapter VII].

By inserting this maximizing value p for π in the likelihood function (5.14) and then equating to zero the partial derivative with respect to ω of the function so obtained, one easily obtains as the maximum-likelihood estimate[57] w of ω,

$$(5.19) \qquad \begin{aligned} w &= \frac{1}{T}\sum_{t=1}^{T}(y_t - pz'_t)^2 \\ &= [1 \quad -p]M[1 \quad -p]' = m_{yy} - m_{yz}M_{zz}^{-1}m_{zy}. \end{aligned}$$

This is also the estimate used in connection with the least-squares method of estimation.[58]

5.4. *Maximum-likelihood estimates of the parameters of reduced-form equations are also least-squares estimates.* We shall now consider the estimation of the parameters of the reduced-form equations (1.23) associated with a structure S_T of the general linear model $\mathfrak{S}_T$. We begin with the derivation of the likelihood function in terms of the parameters Π, Ω of the reduced form. The form of this function will allow us to draw the conclusion we seek, and will also be a useful point of departure for the derivation in Section 5.7 and Appendix C of the likelihood function in terms of structural parameters A, Σ.

We start from equations (1.23) of the reduced form, which we write here in an alternative form that will help in the understanding of the later formulae such as (5.33):

$$(5.20) \qquad y'_t - \Pi z'_t = [I \quad -\Pi]x'_t = v'_t \qquad (t = 1, \cdots, T).$$

Here I is the identity matrix of order G, y_t and v_t are now vectors of G elements, and x_t is the vector defined by (1.20). Under the specifications of $\mathfrak{S}_T$, the successive disturbance vectors $v_1, \cdots, v_T$ are independently and identically normally distributed with zero means and finite covariance matrix Ω as defined by (1.25).

The probability density function of this multivariate normal distribution is known to be[59, 60]

[57] Inspection of the second derivative shows that this procedure yields the one and only maximum, which is the absolute maximum.

[58] Since we are here concerned primarily with large-sample properties of estimates, we disregard throughout this chapter, in estimating variances and covariances of disturbances, any allowances for degrees of freedom lost in the estimation of other parameters. While, if Conditions (A) and (b) of Section 4.1 are satisfied, $(T/T - K)w$ is an unbiased estimate of ω, we do not yet know how to make a similar bias-removing correction either in single-equation models if Condition (B) replaces (b) or even in multiequation models under Conditions (A) and (b) when over-identifying restrictions are to be taken into account.

[59] See Mood [1950, Section 9.4].

[60] We use exp w as synonymous with e^w

$$(5.21)\qquad \kappa_4 \cdot \det^{-\frac{1}{2}} \Omega \cdot \exp -\tfrac{1}{2} \sum_{i,j=1}^{G} v_{it}\, \omega^{ij}\, v_{jt} = \kappa_4 \cdot \det^{-\frac{1}{2}} \Omega \cdot \exp -\tfrac{1}{2} v_t\, \Omega^{-1} v_t',$$

where κ_4 is a numerical factor, $\det^{-\frac{1}{2}} \Omega$ is the reciprocal of the square root of the determinant associated with the square and nonsingular matrix Ω, and ω^{ij} are the elements of the matrix Ω^{-1} inverse to Ω.

For every t, the distribution of the elements of v_t induces, by the first member of (5.21), a distribution of the elements of y_t conditional upon the values assumed by the elements of z_t. As before, in the case of a one-equation model, we must now use the fact stated in (1.19) or (1.26) that the disturbances u_t or v_t (whichever are in question) are distributed independently of the predetermined variables z_t. For this reason, the conditional distribution of the vector variable y_t for given z_t depends on z_t only in its means, while its covariance matrix is the same (Ω) as that of v_t. Thus, in going from v_t to y_t for given z_t, the distribution is merely shifted to a position with (conditional) means, which, to be quite explicit, we write also in indicial form,

$$(5.22)\qquad \left.\begin{aligned} \mathcal{E}(y_{1t} \mid z_t) &= \pi_{11} z_{1t} + \cdots + \pi_{1K} z_{Kt} \\ \mathcal{E}(y_{Gt} \mid z_t) &= \pi_{G1} z_{1t} + \cdots + \pi_{GK} z_{Kt} \end{aligned}\right\} \text{ or } \mathcal{E}(y_t' \mid z_t) = \Pi z_t'.$$

Hence, for any given t, the conditional joint density function of the elements of y_t is

$$(5.23)\qquad \kappa_4 \det^{-\frac{1}{2}} \Omega \cdot \exp - \tfrac{1}{2}(y_t' - \Pi z_t')' \Omega^{-1} (y_t' - \Pi z_t').$$

As before, since the elements of $y_{t-1}, y_{t-2}, \cdots$ may be found among the elements of the vector z_t, held constant in (5.23), the (observed) endogenous variables y_t may be serially interdependent, even though the (latent) disturbances u_t or v_t are specified to be serially independent. However, the conditional distribution (density) function $F_T(y \mid \bar{z})$ of the vector variable y (comprising all values of endogenous variables pertaining to the period $t = 1, \cdots, T$) for a given value of the vector variable $\bar{z}$ (comprising values of exogenous variables only) can again be obtained by compounding conditional distributions. With reference to the definitions in (1.22) of y and $\bar{z}$, we obtain, analogously to (5.9),

$$(5.24)\qquad F_T(y \mid \bar{z}) = \kappa_5 \cdot \det^{-\frac{1}{2}T} \Omega \cdot \exp -\tfrac{1}{2} \sum_{t=1}^{T} (y_t - z_t \Pi') \Omega^{-1} (y_t' - \Pi z_t'),$$

where $\kappa_5 = \kappa_4^T$ and where a transposition has been carried out under the summation sign. A further rearrangement, foreshadowed by (5.20), puts the argument of the exponential function in (5.24) in the form

$$(5.25)\qquad -\tfrac{1}{2} \sum_{t=1}^{T} x_t\, [I \quad -\Pi]' \Omega^{-1} [I \quad -\Pi] x_t'.$$

The evaluation of the sum is most conveniently[61] carried out by arraying the (row) vectors x_t ($t = 1, \cdots, T$) into a matrix

$$X \equiv \begin{bmatrix} x_1 \\ x_2 \\ \cdots \\ x_T \end{bmatrix} = \begin{bmatrix} y_1 & z_1 \\ y_2 & z_2 \\ \cdots & \cdots \\ y_T & z_T \end{bmatrix} \equiv [Y \quad Z]. \tag{5.26}$$

We also use the concept of the *trace*[62] of a square matrix R, denoted $\text{tr } R$ and defined as the sum of its diagonal elements:

$$\text{tr } R \equiv \sum_i r_{ii}. \tag{5.27}$$

It is easily seen from this definition and from the multiplication rule of matrices that, if Q has m rows and n columns, and R has n rows and m columns,

$$\text{tr } QR = \text{tr } RQ. \tag{5.28}$$

With the help of these notational devices, (5.25) can be written as

$$\begin{aligned} &-\tfrac{1}{2} \text{ tr } (X [I \quad -\Pi]'\Omega^{-1}[I \quad -\Pi]X') \\ &\qquad = -\tfrac{1}{2} \text{ tr } ([I \quad -\Pi]'\Omega^{-1}[I \quad -\Pi]X'X). \end{aligned} \tag{5.29}$$

If we now examine the matrix product $X'X$ appearing in (5.29), we find its typical element to be

$$\sum_{t=1}^{T} x_{it}x_{jt} = Tm_{x_ix_j}, \tag{5.30}$$

i.e., T times the typical element of the (symmetric) moment matrix

$$\begin{aligned} M \equiv M_{xx} &\equiv \begin{bmatrix} M_{yy} & M_{yz} \\ M_{zy} & M_{zz} \end{bmatrix} \\ &= \left[\begin{array}{ccc|ccc} m_{y_1y_1} & \cdots & m_{y_1y_G} & m_{y_1z_1} & \cdots & m_{y_1z_K} \\ \cdots & \cdots & \cdots & \cdots & \cdots & \cdots \\ m_{y_Gy_1} & \cdots & m_{y_Gy_G} & m_{y_Gz_1} & \cdots & m_{y_Gz_K} \\ \hline m_{z_1y_1} & \cdots & m_{z_1y_G} & m_{z_1z_1} & \cdots & m_{z_1z_K} \\ \cdots & \cdots & \cdots & \cdots & \cdots & \cdots \\ m_{z_Ky_1} & \cdots & m_{z_Ky_G} & m_{z_Kz_1} & \cdots & m_{z_Kz_K} \end{array}\right] \end{aligned} \tag{5.31}$$

61 The reader unfamiliar with the shorthand of matrix notation may wish to convince himself of its usefulness by writing out the indicial equivalents of the following derivation.

62 See, for example, Birkhoff and MacLane [1941, p. 309, exercise 12].

of all dependent and predetermined variables, defined by an obvious generalization of (5.10) to the case where y is a vector. Inserting the resulting expression in (5.24) we obtain

$$(5.32)\quad F_T(y \mid \bar{z}) = \kappa_5 \cdot \det^{-\frac{1}{2}T}\Omega \cdot \exp\left\{-\frac{T}{2}\operatorname{tr}\left([I \quad -\Pi]'\Omega^{-1}[I \quad -\Pi]M\right)\right\}.$$

This expression, when regarded as a function of the parameters Π and Ω, represents the likelihood function associated with the sample of observations y and $\bar{z}$. On taking the logarithm of each side of (5.32) and multiplying by $1/T$, we have for the corresponding logarithmic likelihood function, if $\kappa_6 = (1/T)\log \kappa_5$,

$$(5.33)\quad \begin{aligned} L(\Pi, \Omega) &\equiv \frac{1}{T}\log F_T(y \mid \bar{z}) \\ &= \kappa_6 - \tfrac{1}{2}\log\det\Omega - \tfrac{1}{2}\operatorname{tr}\left([I \quad -\Pi]'\Omega^{-1}[I \quad -\Pi]M\right). \end{aligned}$$

While our task is to find the values of Π and Ω that maximize this function, we first consider, as before in the maximization of (5.14), the problem of maximizing (5.33) with respect to Π for a given value of Ω. This is the problem of finding the value P of Π that minimizes the quadratic form (which we write in two ways as a reminder of its origin),

$$(5.34)\quad \begin{aligned} &\operatorname{tr}\left([I \quad -\Pi]'\Omega^{-1}[I \quad -\Pi]M\right) \\ &= \sum_{t=1}^{T}\sum_{i,j=1}^{G}\left(y_{it} - \sum_{k=1}^{K}\pi_{ik}z_{kt}\right)\omega^{ij}\left(y_{jt} - \sum_{k=1}^{K}\pi_{jk}z_{kt}\right). \end{aligned}$$

This time, the matrix Ω does occur in the function to be maximized with respect to Π. Nevertheless, the maximizing value P is even here independent of the value given to Ω. For an explicit proof of this statement, carried out by equating to zero the derivatives of (5.29) with respect to the elements of Π, we refer to Koopmans, Rubin, and Leipnik, [1950, Section 3.1.8]. Here we give only the following heuristic argument.

The form of the function (5.29) is the same whether all of the variables z_t are exogenous or whether some of them are lagged endogenous. Hence the maximizing value P must be the same function of the observations y_t, z_t $(t = 1, \cdots, T)$ in these two cases. But in the case in which all z_t are exogenous, the model, which does not place any restrictions[63] on the elements of Ω, allows us to look upon the estimation of the coefficients π_{ik} $(k = 1, \cdots, K)$ of the ith equation of the reduced form, say, as a separate one-equation problem, such as was studied in Section 5.3,

[63] Except that, as a covariance matrix of a nonsingular normal distribution, Ω must be positive definite (See Appendix B).

involving only the unknowns π_{ik} $(k = 1, \cdots, K)$ and the variance ω_{ii} of the marginal distribution of the disturbance v_i in that equation.

It follows from this reasoning, and is also proved explicitly in the article referred to, that the maximum-likelihood estimates p_{ik} of the elements π_{ik} of Π in (5.29) are the least-squares estimates, found by solving a set of "normal equations" (5.17) for each equation of the reduced form. These sets of normal equations can be written simultaneously in the form

$$(5.35)\quad \begin{bmatrix} m_{z_1z_1} & \cdots & m_{z_1z_K} \\ \cdots & \cdots & \cdots \\ m_{z_Kz_1} & \cdots & m_{z_Kz_K} \end{bmatrix} \begin{bmatrix} p_{11} & \cdots & p_{G1} \\ \cdots & \cdots & \cdots \\ p_{1K} & \cdots & p_{GK} \end{bmatrix} = \begin{bmatrix} m_{z_1y_1} & \cdots & m_{z_1y_G} \\ \cdots & \cdots & \cdots \\ m_{z_Ky_1} & \cdots & m_{z_Ky_G} \end{bmatrix},$$

or

$$(5.36)\quad M_{zz}P' = M_{zy}\,.$$

The solution is given by $P' = M_{zz}^{-1}M_{zy}$, or, since $M'_{zy} = M_{yz}$, by

$$(5.37)\quad P = M_{yz}M_{zz}^{-1}\,.$$

By substituting this expression for Π in (5.33) and then maximizing with respect to Ω, the maximum-likelihood estimate W of Ω is found to be

$$(5.38)\quad W = \frac{1}{T}\sum_{t=1}^{T} \begin{bmatrix} y_{1t} - \sum_{k=1}^{K} p_{1k}z_{kt} \\ \cdots \\ y_{Gt} - \sum_{k=1}^{K} p_{Gk}z_{kt} \end{bmatrix} \begin{bmatrix} y_{1t} - \sum_{k=1}^{K} p_{1k}z_{kt} & \cdots & y_{Gt} - \sum_{k=1}^{K} p_{Gk}z_{kt} \end{bmatrix}$$

$$= [I\ -P]M[I\ -P]' = M_{yy} - M_{yz}M_{zz}^{-1}M_{zy}\,.$$

The first expression for W shows that this estimate of Ω is formed by an obvious generalization of the corresponding "least-squares" estimate (5.19) in the case of a single equation. The elements of W are the sample covariances of the residuals[64] in the *estimated* equations of the reduced form. The estimate W will play an important role in Section 6.

[64] Throughout we use the term "residual" in a meaning different from the "disturbances" u or v. The residuals are quantities that take the place of u or v in the structural or reduced-form equation, (1.18) or (1.23), if the parameters B, Γ, or Π are replaced by their estimates. Thus, the residuals can be regarded as estimates of the disturbances.

5.5. *Stepwise maximization of a function.* We have encountered two cases in which it was convenient, in maximizing a function of two sets of parameters (ω and π in one case, Ω and Π in the other), to assign temporarily fixed values to the parameters of one set (ω or Ω) in order to carry out a provisional maximization with respect to those of the other set (π or Π). In both cases our reasoning was simplified by the fact that the maximizing values so found for the second set did not depend on the values assigned to the parameters of the first set. However, the usefulness of the "stepwise" maximization with respect to subsets of the set of parameters does not depend on such happy accidents. Furthermore, stepwise maximization is not merely a convenience, mathematically, in the maximization of complicated likelihood functions. Even more important is the fact that it adds a considerable degree of flexibility to the maximum-likelihood method of estimation by permitting one to concentrate attention and computational resources on parameters of special interest or on individual (sets of) identifiable equations. We shall therefore study this device in the present subsection and then use it repeatedly in the rest of Section 5 and throughout Section 6.

Consider a likelihood function

$$f(\eta, \theta; x) \tag{5.39}$$

to be maximized with respect to the parameters η and θ, each of which may be regarded as a vector. Let us assume that this function has one unique maximum[65] with respect to η and θ for every value of x. The logic of stepwise maximization is as follows. Let the function $f(\eta, \theta; x)$ be maximized first with respect to η. This means that, for each θ, and for the given value of x, that value

$$\hat{\eta} = \hat{\eta}\,(\theta; x) \tag{5.40}$$

of η is selected which maximizes $f(\eta, \theta; x)$ regarded as a function of η alone. Considering η and θ for a moment as scalars, this is illustrated graphically in Figure 1, where the shape of the function $f(\eta, \theta; x)$ is indicated in the two-dimensional (η, θ)-space by contour lines. For any θ, say θ^0, the maximizing value $\hat{\eta}^0$ of η is given by the η-coordinate of the point at which the perpendicular at θ^0 is tangent to a contour line.

If (5.40) is substituted in (5.39), we obtain a function

$$f\{\hat{\eta}(\theta; x), \theta; x\} \equiv g(\theta; x) \tag{5.41}$$

[65] In the event that a likelihood function has more than one local maximum, the maximum-likelihood estimate is defined as that value of the argument for which the highest maximum is attained. The argument of Section 5.5 then still applies within a region of the (η, θ)-space containing only the highest maximum. Computational problems arising from the existence of more than one local maximum are commented on by Koopmans, Rubin, and Leipnik [1950, Section 4.5.6].

of θ and x only, which we shall call a *concentrated likelihood function* because it is concentrated on the set of parameters θ. This function is illustrated for a scalar θ in Figure 2. Its definition implies the property

$$(5.42) \qquad g(\theta; x) \geqslant f(\eta, \theta; x) \text{ for all } \eta, \theta, x.$$

Now if as the second step $g(\theta; x)$ is maximized with respect to θ, we obtain a value $\hat{\theta}(x)$ of θ such that

$$(5.43) \qquad g\{\hat{\theta}(x); x\} \geqslant g(\theta; x) \text{ for all } \theta, x.$$

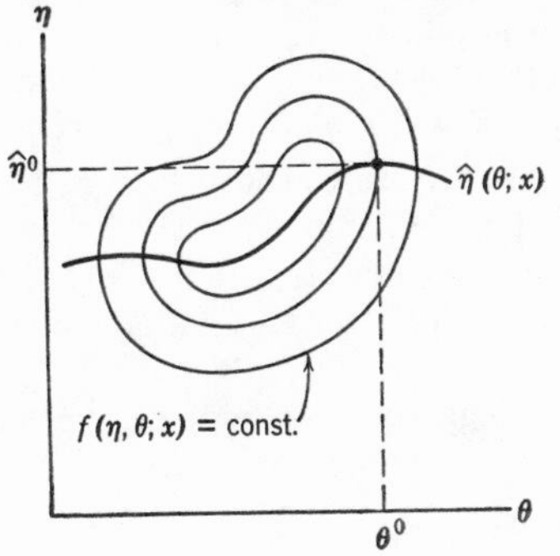

FIGURE 1

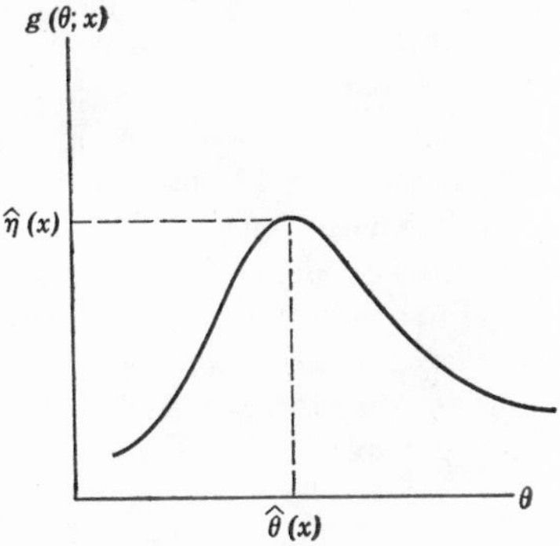

FIGURE 2

Comparison of (5.42) and (5.43) shows that, if we define

$$(5.44) \qquad \hat{\eta}(x) \equiv \hat{\eta}\{\hat{\theta}(x), x\},$$

we have

$$(5.45) \qquad f\{\hat{\eta}(x), \hat{\theta}(x); x\} \equiv g\{\hat{\theta}(x), x\} \geqslant f(\eta, \theta; x) \quad \text{for all } \eta, \theta, x.$$

Hence, the maximizing values $\hat{\theta}(x)$ and $\hat{\eta}(x)$ obtained by stepwise maximizations are the same as those that would be obtained by maximizing (5.39) simultaneously with respect to η and θ.

In problems with which we are concerned we can sometimes choose θ in such a way that we are not interested in $\hat{\eta}(x)$. In this case the variable η is effectively eliminated[66] from the function to be maximized by the substitution of $\hat{\eta}(\theta; x)$ in $f(\eta, \theta; x)$. In some such cases, if $\hat{\theta}(x)$ is all that is required, this procedure may be simplified even further by substituting for η in f a function, say $\eta = \eta(\xi)$, of a variable ξ such that the domain of ξ maps into that of η, and then proceeding as above.

[66] The use of the term "elimination," natural in itself, is further supported by the fact that, in the case of differentiable likelihood functions as here considered, the procedure in question is equivalent to an elimination, in the usual sense of that term, of the maximizing value $\hat{\eta}$ of η from the first-order conditions for a maximum of $f(\eta, \theta; x)$ in terms of both $\hat{\eta}$ and $\hat{\theta}$.

This device is particularly useful in the more general case in which η and θ are interpreted as vectors.

It may finally be remarked that stepwise maximization also simplifies the formulae and computations for the sampling variances and covariances of estimates of those parameters on which interest is concentrated. These formulae are given in Section 7.

5.6. *The estimation of constant terms in the equations and the definition of moments.* Our model $\mathfrak{S}_T$ makes provision for a constant term in each structural equation by the insertion of a dummy variable "1" in (1.6) and a corresponding column γ_0' in (1.14). If the coefficients γ_0 are eliminated from the likelihood function by a stepwise maximization, we obtain a concentrated likelihood function of the same general form as the original likelihood function, but without the dummy variable "1," provided that we redefine the moments of the observations appropriately. We shall indicate the manner of doing this for a single-equation model, though the principle is quite general.

Consider the model consisting of the single equation, with an explicit dummy variable "1,"

$$y_t - \pi_1 z_{1t} - \cdots - \pi_K z_{Kt} - \pi_0 = v_t . \tag{5.46}$$

The logarithmic likelihood function may be written

$$L(\bar{\pi}, \omega) = \kappa_3 - \tfrac{1}{2}\log\omega - \frac{1}{2\omega}\cdot\frac{1}{T}\sum_{t=1}^{T}(y_t - \bar{\pi}[z_t \quad 1]')^2, \tag{5.47}$$

where $\bar{\pi} \equiv [\pi_1 \quad \cdots \quad \pi_K \quad \pi_0]$. On setting equal to zero the partial derivative of (5.47) with respect only to π_0, we obtain as the maximizing[67] value $\hat{\pi}_0(\pi)$ of π_0

$$\hat{\pi}_0(\pi) = \frac{1}{T}\sum_{t=1}^{T}(y_t - \pi z_t'), \tag{5.48}$$

where, as in Section 5.3, $\pi \equiv [\pi_1 \quad \cdots \quad \pi_K]$.

We now define the new moments of the observations, to be referred to as moments about the mean, as follows:

$$\begin{aligned} m_{yy}^0 &= \frac{1}{T}\sum_{t=1}^{T}(y_t - y^0)^2, \quad \text{where} \quad y^0 = \frac{1}{T}\sum_{t=1}^{T} y_t, \\ m_{z_iz_j}^0 &= \frac{1}{T}\sum_{t=1}^{T}(z_{it} - z_i^0)(z_{jt} - z_j^0), \quad \text{where} \quad z_i^0 = \frac{1}{T}\sum_{t=1}^{T} z_{it} \\ &\qquad\qquad (i, j = 1, \cdots, K), \\ m_{yz_i}^0 &= \frac{1}{T}\sum_{t=1}^{T}(y_t - y^0)(z_{it} - z_i^0), \end{aligned} \tag{5.49}$$

[67] That a maximum is indeed reached for $\pi_0 = \hat{\pi}_0(\pi)$ follows from the negative-definite character of the quadratic form in (5.47); see Appendix B.

and let M^0 be the matrix of these moments, formed analogously to (5.10). Then, on substitution from (5.48) into (5.47), we obtain, using (5.49),

$$(5.50)\quad L^{(0)}(\pi, \omega) = \kappa_3 - \tfrac{1}{2}\log\omega - (1/2\omega)[1 \quad -\pi]M^0[1 \quad -\pi]',$$

which may be compared with equation (5.14). After estimates p of π are obtained from the maximization of (5.50) they may be substituted for π in equation (5.48) to obtain the estimate p_0 of π_0.

This procedure for the estimation of constant terms is applicable in all cases considered below whether we are dealing with equations of the reduced form or with structural equations. For computational purposes (see Chapter X) it is as a rule economical to perform the estimation of constant terms first, and then to estimate the other parameters from moments about the mean.[68] For the purposes of the present chapter we can allow all subsequent formulae and results to be interpreted in either of two ways. In the first interpretation a dummy variable "1" is present among the elements of $\bar{z}_t$, and M stands for the matrix of "raw" moments; in the second, no dummy variable is present, and M stands for M^0.

5.7. *The likelihood function* $L(\mathrm{A}, \Sigma)$ *associated with the general linear model* $\mathfrak{S}_T$. In Section 5.4 we derived the joint distribution function $F_T(y \mid \bar{z})$ of those values of the endogenous variables pertaining to the period of observation (comprised in the vector y) conditional upon the values of the exogenous variables (comprised in $\bar{z}$). This distribution is expressed in (5.32) in terms of the parameters Π, Ω of the reduced form. However, by (1.24) and (1.25), these parameters are functions of the structural parameters A, Σ. Therefore, all that is necessary to obtain the distribution $F_T(y \mid \bar{z})$ in terms of structural parameters is to substitute the functions indicated by (1.24) and (1.25) for Π and Ω in (5.32) and make some simplifications in the result. This task is carried out in Appendix C.

The resulting expression is[69]

$$(5.51)\quad F_T(y \mid \bar{z}) = \kappa_5 \cdot \mid \det{}^T \mathrm{B} \mid \cdot \det{}^{-\frac{1}{2}T}\Sigma \cdot \exp\{-\tfrac{1}{2}T \operatorname{tr}(\Sigma^{-1}\mathrm{A}M\mathrm{A}')\}.$$

For a given sample $(y, \bar{z})$, and regarded as a function of the structural

[68] Chernoff and Divinsky in Chapter X use a slightly different definition of moments from that given above in (5.49). As applied to the case under consideration here, they define $\bar{m}_{yy} = T^2 m^0_{yy}$, etc. With this definition of moments, the last term in (5.50) becomes $-(1/2\omega T^2)\ [1 \quad -\pi]\ \bar{M}\ [1 \quad -\pi]'$.

[69] The vertical bars in $\mid \det^T \mathrm{B} \mid$ denote the taking of the absolute value of the quantity shown between bars.

parameters A, Σ, this is the likelihood function. The corresponding logarithmic likelihood function may be written, using (5.28),

$$\text{(5.52)}\quad \begin{aligned} L(\mathrm{A}, \Sigma) &\equiv (1/T) \log F_T(y \mid \bar{z}) \\ &= \kappa_6 + \log \mid \det \mathrm{B} \mid - \tfrac{1}{2} \log \det \Sigma - \tfrac{1}{2} \operatorname{tr} (\mathrm{A}'\Sigma^{-1}\mathrm{A}M). \end{aligned}$$

As remarked in Appendix C, the form of $F_T(y \mid \bar{z})$ or of $L(\mathrm{A}, \Sigma)$ is preserved by a nonsingular linear transformation of A and the corresponding transformation of Σ. In particular, this is true for the multiplication of all coefficients α_{gh} $(h = 1, \cdots, G + K)$ of the gth equation, say, and of the related parameters σ_{gh} $(h \neq g)$ by the same nonvanishing scalar, and the multiplication of σ_{gg} by the square of this scalar. Hence a normalization rule on an equation places no restrictions on the ratios of the likelihood-maximizing values of the coefficients of that equation.

The maximization of this function under a priori restrictions on A only is most conveniently carried out stepwise. First we assign a specific value $\tilde{\mathrm{A}}$ to A (which is thus given the role of θ in Section 5.5) and maximize with respect to the elements of Σ (in the role of η). This yields, by the method illustrated in Appendix D, the conditional maximizing value

$$\text{(5.53)}\qquad \hat{\Sigma}(\tilde{\mathrm{A}}) = \tilde{\mathrm{A}}M\tilde{\mathrm{A}}'$$

of Σ for the given value $\tilde{\mathrm{A}}$ of A. This formula is similar in structure to (5.38) and allows an analogous interpretation. Let us note first that the moment matrix M may be written as follows:

$$\text{(5.54)}\qquad M = \frac{1}{T}\sum_{t=1}^{T} \begin{bmatrix} x_{1t}x_{1t} & \cdots & x_{1t}x_{G+K,t} \\ \cdots & \cdots & \cdots \\ x_{G+K,t}x_{1t} & \cdots & x_{G+K,t}x_{G+K,t} \end{bmatrix} = \frac{1}{T}\sum_{t=1}^{T} x'_t x_t .$$

Substituting this expression in (5.53) we have

$$\text{(5.55)}\qquad \hat{\Sigma}(\tilde{\mathrm{A}}) = \frac{1}{T}\sum_{t=1}^{T} \tilde{\mathrm{A}}x'_t x_t \tilde{\mathrm{A}}'.$$

Hence,

$$\text{(5.56)}\qquad \check{\Sigma}(\tilde{\mathrm{A}}) = \frac{1}{T}\sum_{t=1}^{T} u'_t(\tilde{\mathrm{A}})u_t(\tilde{\mathrm{A}}),$$

where

$$\text{(5.57)}\qquad u'_t(\tilde{\mathrm{A}}) \equiv \tilde{\mathrm{A}}x'_t \qquad (t = 1, \cdots, T)$$

represents the "sample" residuals $u_{1t}(\tilde{\mathrm{A}}), \cdots, u_{Gt}(\tilde{\mathrm{A}})$ obtained if the assigned value $\tilde{\mathrm{A}}$ is substituted for A in the structural equations (1.21). Now $\hat{\Sigma}(\tilde{\mathrm{A}})$ is the sample covariance matrix of these residuals. We emphasize again that these covariances depend on the assigned value $\tilde{\mathrm{A}}$.

If the expression (5.53) for $\hat{\Sigma}(\tilde{\mathrm{A}})$ is substituted in (5.52) one obtains[70] the concentrated logarithmic likelihood function, in which we now replace $\tilde{\mathrm{A}}$ by A,

$$(5.58) \qquad L^{(1)}(\mathrm{A}) = \kappa_7 + \log|\det \mathrm{B}| - \tfrac{1}{2}\log\det(\mathrm{A}M\mathrm{A}').$$

The value A of A that maximizes this function under the a priori restrictions imposed on A is the maximum-likelihood estimate of the true coefficient matrix A.

If, having obtained A, one now desires the maximum-likelihood estimate S of Σ, this may be obtained from (5.53) by substituting A for $\tilde{\mathrm{A}}$,

$$(5.59) \qquad S = AMA'.$$

Thus the maximum-likelihood estimate S of Σ is the covariance matrix of the residuals $u(A)$ calculated from (5.57) by taking $\tilde{\mathrm{A}} \equiv A$.

The method of estimation just described presupposes and utilizes a priori information concerning the linearity of the complete system of equations. It also permits the utilization of all a priori restrictions on the values of the coefficients of the equations, and more efficient estimates are obtained according as more (valid) restrictions are utilized. Whenever all a priori information on parameter restrictions and equation forms is utilized, this method, as indicated above, is called the full-information maximum-likelihood method.

If all of the structural equations are to be estimated, and if it has already been decided to use some overidentifying restrictions on the coefficients of each equation, then it is economical to use all information available and believed to be valid, because of the double advantage of more efficient estimates and fewer unknown elements of A to be computed. A conflict between efficiency of estimates and economy of computation arises only in deciding whether or not to utilize any overidentifying restrictions at all for certain equations. It can be shown [Koopmans, Rubin, and Leipnik, 1950, Section 3.2] that in the very special case in which each structural equation is subject to the minimum number of restrictions requisite for identifiability, the full-information maximum-likelihood estimates of A and Σ are the same functions of the observations as the indirect least squares estimates of these parameters, and hence have the same numerical values and the same sampling properties. In that case their computation by the indirect least-squares method is likely to be more economical, and some sacrifice of efficiency of estimates by disregarding a few overidentifying restrictions may sometimes be justified by these computational economies.

[70] For details, see Appendix D.

If all of the equations of a subset are subject to the minimum requisite number of restrictions, then the maximum-likelihood estimates of the coefficients α_{gh} of the subset consisting of the remaining (possibly overidentified) equations are identical with the subset estimates to be discussed in Section 6.1 and are in general more economically computed by the method described in that section. Again, it may sometimes be justified to disregard some overidentifying restrictions to achieve these computational economies.

We will not enter into further detail here concerning full-information maximum-likelihood estimation since an extended discussion is given by Koopmans, Rubin, and Leipnik [1950] and since the computation procedures related to it are discussed in Chapter X. However, it is worthwhile pointing out here that considerable computational economy would result if the model should specify that disturbances in different equations are uncorrelated (i.e., that Σ is diagonal). Since the a priori basis for such a specification is uncertain, we shall not make any such assumption in the discussion of limited-information methods in Section 6. That is, the term "a priori restrictions (or information) on a set of equations" will continue to be used in the sense of "restrictions on the *coefficients* of those equations" only.

6. Limited-Information Methods of Maximum-Likelihood Estimation

6.0. *Introduction.* In the introduction to Section 5 we stated that maximum-likelihood estimation methods are available which utilize varying amounts of the a priori information concerning the linear model $\mathfrak{S}_T$ in deriving estimates of any set of its parameters. There we described the full-information maximum-likelihood method, which uses all of the a priori information in estimating all of the parameters. In the present section we shall introduce and discuss maximum-likelihood methods that may utilize only part of the a priori information or that can be used even if that information is fragmentary. These will be called limited-information maximum-likelihood methods.

For the estimation of a given subset of the structural equations, all a priori restrictions on these equations are of course relevant, and a *minimum* requisite number of restrictions on each equation is essential. On the other hand, for the same limited purpose of estimating that subset of equations, a priori restrictions on the remaining equations of the model can be of value (in the sense of increasing efficiency of estimation) only when these restrictions are overidentifying,[71] i.e., only when

[71] This follows from the fact that only overidentifying restrictions on A imply restrictions on Π and thereby on the distribution of the observations. See the last paragraph of Section 6.5 and the next to last paragraph of Section 5.7.

they are *more* than the minimum requisite for identifiability of the equations to which they apply. If only the "minimum requisite" information (or less) is available for the remaining equations, this information may just as well be ignored for the purpose under discussion. Hence the choice is essentially that between utilizing any available set of overidentifying restrictions on the remaining equations or ignoring all restrictions on them. The methods presented in this section correspond to the second alternative. We shall show that, by the application of the principle of stepwise maximization, the coefficients of any subset of equations in $\mathfrak{S}_T$ may be estimated without the use of a priori restrictions relating to equations not in that subset. The subset may, of course, consist of only one equation

The estimates of the coefficients of a subset of equations so obtained (without the use of a priori restrictions on the remaining equations) are indeed maximum-likelihood estimates provided that the model $\mathfrak{S}_T$ is valid. For $\mathfrak{S}_T$ to be valid it is necessary, among other things, that the remaining equations be linear and that the correct classification of endogenous and exogenous variables be used. It follows from the remarks made in Section 5.2 that if $\mathfrak{S}_T$ is valid the estimates in question are consistent[72] and that they are also asymptotically efficient in comparison with all other asymptotically normal estimates using the same or less information.

There are several factors that have prompted the study of limited-information methods. While desirable properties of estimates are obtained in greater degree the larger the amount of valid and relevant a priori information utilized in their derivation, it is in general true that the difficulty, time, and expense involved in their computation increase with the number of equations for which overidentifying information is employed. For this reason, as has already been pointed out, even if estimates of the coefficients of all equations are sought, it may be preferred to sacrifice somewhat the quality of estimates for a saving in time and computational resources. Thus, one may choose to estimate the coefficients of all equations by dividing the set of equations into subsets and estimating the coefficients in each subset without the use of a priori restrictions on equations not included in it.

The incentive for disregarding a priori restrictions is even greater when the researcher is interested only in obtaining estimates of the coefficients in some equations of the model and is prepared to sacrifice the greater efficiency of the estimates that would result from utilizing "extra" restrictions on the equations he is not interested in. In that case

[72] It will appear in Chapter VII that consistency is not lost if certain specifications of the model $\mathfrak{S}_T$ are relaxed.

he can concentrate almost entirely on the subset of his interest. Finally, the econometrician may find that he does not possess the knowledge on which to base a priori restrictions on the coefficients of certain equations outside the subset of his interest. But, as long as he maintains the assumption of linearity of the complete system and correctly specifies the list of exogenous variables occurring in that system, he can still obtain maximum-likelihood estimates of the coefficients of the equations he is interested in by the adoption of limited-information methods. The information utilized is in this case limited by necessity rather than by choice.

In the remainder of Section 6 we shall discuss first the maximum-likelihood estimation of the coefficients of a subset of equations, which was developed originally by Rubin. We then consider the special case, developed earlier by Anderson and Rubin, in which the subset consists of only one equation. This maximization problem can be expressed in terms of what we shall call the *least variance ratio principle*. Following Rubin, we then show that maximum-likelihood estimation of the coefficients of any subset of equations (possibly the entire set) may be interpreted as a generalization of the least variance ratio principle. After this we develop in some detail the theory of the limited-information method applied to a single equation.

The presentation and elaboration of these methods differs from the forms chosen by their originators primarily in that we employ here the principle of stepwise maximization as a device to develop the estimation methods relating to a complete system, to a subsystem, and to a single equation from a common point of view.

Finally, a summary of some of the results reached in Sections 5 and 6 is presented in Section 6.5. It may be added that, wherever in the present subsection we have spoken of the estimation of the coefficients of a subset of equations, it is to be understood that the estimation of the other parameters associated with such a subset—the variances and covariances of the disturbances—can be performed by a further simple computation.

6.1. *Maximum-likelihood estimation of the parameters of a subset of the structural equations.* Let the set of G structural equations be divided into two subsets, denoted by subscripts I and II, containing G_{I} and G_{II} equations, respectively. We wish to apply limited-information maximum-likelihood methods to the estimation of the parameters of subset I We shall not need or wish to use information concerning the restrictions on the coefficients in the complementary subset II. We now partition the coefficient matrix A according to the partitioning of the equations, as follows:

$$\text{(6.1)} \qquad \mathrm{A} \equiv \begin{bmatrix} \mathrm{A_I} \\ \mathrm{A_{II}} \end{bmatrix}.$$

The corresponding partitioning of the covariance matrix of the disturbances may be written in the form

$$\text{(6.2)} \qquad \Sigma \equiv \begin{bmatrix} \Sigma_{\mathrm{I\,I}} & \Sigma_{\mathrm{I\,II}} \\ \Sigma_{\mathrm{II\,I}} & \Sigma_{\mathrm{II\,II}} \end{bmatrix}.$$

In Appendix E we apply the method of stepwise maximization to remove from the likelihood function (5.52) all parameters $\mathrm{A_{II}}$, $\Sigma_{\mathrm{II\,II}}$, $\Sigma_{\mathrm{I\,II}}$ associated wholly or partly with subset II. If we were to attempt to take into account "extra" restrictions on equations II in that partial maximization, the resulting concentrated likelihood function in terms of the coefficient matrix $\mathrm{A_I}$ would be complicated indeed. However, as a consequence of our decision to disregard such overidentifying information, we obtain in Appendix E the following relatively simple function:[73]

$$\text{(6.3)} \qquad \begin{aligned} L^{(2)}(\mathrm{A_I}) = \kappa_9 &+ \tfrac{1}{2} \log \det (\mathrm{B_I} W \mathrm{B_I'}) \\ &- \tfrac{1}{2} \log \det W - \tfrac{1}{2} \log \det (\mathrm{A_I} M \mathrm{A_I'}), \end{aligned}$$

where $\mathrm{B_I}$ is the part of $\mathrm{A_I} = [\mathrm{B_I} \;\; \Gamma_{\mathrm{I}}]$ containing the coefficients of dependent variables y_i. The function (6.3) was first obtained by Rubin [1948] by a somewhat different method of derivation.

Estimates A_{I} of $\mathrm{A_I}$ obtained through maximization of this function subject to the a priori restrictions on $\mathrm{A_I}$ are limited-information maximum-likelihood estimates that disregard any knowledge of the restrictions on the elements of $\mathrm{A_{II}}$. However, their derivation presupposes that the complete system is linear, and, because of the manner in which M and W appear in (6.3), it is necessary for their computation to know the predetermined variables that appear in the equations of the entire system.[74]

[73] When $G_{\mathrm{I}} \equiv G$, $\det \mathrm{B_I} W \mathrm{B_I'} = \det^2 \mathrm{B} \cdot \det W$. Thus it is readily seen that the function (6.3) becomes that in (5.58) if the subset of equations being estimated is the entire set.

[74] Careful scrutiny of the matrix products in (6.3) will reveal that moments involving those dependent variables y_i excluded from subset I by the model occur in (6.3) only in the parameter-free term $-\frac{1}{2} \log \det W$, and therefore affect only the value of the maximum, but not the value A_{I} of the argument $\mathrm{A_I}$ for which it is reached

It is implied in (5.59), since stepwise and simultaneous maximization yield the same result, that the limited-information maximum-likelihood estimate $S_{I\,I}$ of $\Sigma_{I\,I}$ is given by

$$S_{I\,I} = A_I M A_I' . \tag{6.4}$$

6.2. *Maximum-likelihood estimation of the coefficients of a single structural equation: The least variance ratio principle.* Anderson and Rubin [1949, 1950; Anderson, 1950], as noted in Section 4.6, originated a method for deriving maximum-likelihood estimates of the parameters of a single equation that is part of a complete set of structural equations. This problem is, of course, a special form of the one discussed above in Section 6.1 in that the subset of equations whose parameters are to be estimated contains only one equation.

Let us suppose that we wish to estimate the coefficients of the first equation (4.9) of the complete set of structural equations (4.8). Again the vectors β and γ [in (4.9)] are partitioned as in (4.12) and (4.13) so as to separate in each vector the elements prescribed to be zero from the remaining elements, and the vectors y_t and z_t are correspondingly partitioned as in (4.14). The equation to be estimated is then written

$$\beta_{\Delta} y'_{\Delta,t} + \gamma_{*} z'_{*,t} = u_{1t} \qquad (t = 1, \cdots, T). \tag{6.5}$$

We shall assume that the rank condition for the identifiability of (6.5) is satisfied.

In the present case the concentrated likelihood function (6.3) becomes, but for an additive quantity independent[75] of the coefficients α,

$$L^{(3)}(\alpha) = \tfrac{1}{2} \log \beta W \beta' - \tfrac{1}{2} \log \alpha M \alpha', \tag{6.6}$$

where

$$\alpha \equiv [\beta \quad \gamma]. \tag{6.7}$$

In order to express this function only in terms of the unrestricted coefficients β_{Δ} and γ_{*}, W may be partitioned as follows:[76]

$$W \equiv \begin{bmatrix} W_{\Delta\Delta} & W_{\Delta,\Delta\Delta} \\ W_{\Delta\Delta,\Delta} & W_{\Delta\Delta,\Delta\Delta} \end{bmatrix}, \tag{6.8}$$

[75] For convenience the constant and the term $-\tfrac{1}{2} \log \det W$, which includes only functions of the observations and not structural parameters, have been dropped from the expression.

[76] We write the symbols Δ and $*$ as subscripts to moment matrices as abbreviations for the fuller subscripts such as y_{Δ}, $y_{\Delta\Delta}$, z_{*}, z_{**}, which we shall only need in one instance, in equation (6.19) below. Where only two subscripts, Δ or $*$, occur, the separating comma is superfluous and has been omitted.

and M may be partitioned as follows:

$$(6.9)\qquad M \equiv \begin{bmatrix} M_{\Delta\Delta} & M_{\Delta,\Delta\Delta} & M_{\Delta *} & M_{\Delta,**} \\ M_{\Delta\Delta,\Delta} & M_{\Delta\Delta,\Delta\Delta} & M_{\Delta\Delta,*} & M_{\Delta\Delta,**} \\ M_{*\Delta} & M_{*,\Delta\Delta} & M_{**} & M_{*,**} \\ M_{**,\Delta} & M_{**,\Delta\Delta} & M_{**,*} & M_{**,**} \end{bmatrix},$$

corresponding to the partitionings (4.12) and (4.13) of α. We may now write (6.6) as

$$(6.10)\qquad L^{(3)}(\alpha_{(\Delta *)}) = \tfrac{1}{2}\log \beta_\Delta W_{\Delta\Delta}\beta'_\Delta - \tfrac{1}{2}\log \alpha_{(\Delta *)}M_{(\Delta *)}\alpha'_{(\Delta *)},$$

where

$$(6.11)\qquad \alpha_{(\Delta *)} = [\beta_\Delta \quad \gamma_*]$$

and $M_{(\Delta *)}$ is the moment matrix M with the matrices in the second and fourth sets of rows and columns of the partitioning in (6.9) deleted.

We shall perform one more partial maximization of the function (6.10). In this step we regard γ_* as the "η-variable" and β_Δ as the "θ-variable," by analogy with Section 5.5. To eliminate γ_* by maximization it is necessary to find that value $\hat{\gamma}_*(\beta_\Delta)$ of γ_* which for given β_Δ minimizes $\alpha_{(\Delta *)} \cdot M_{(\Delta *)}\alpha'_{(\Delta *)}$. Now it is readily seen that

$$(6.12)\qquad \begin{aligned} \alpha_{(\Delta *)}M_{(\Delta *)}\alpha'_{(\Delta *)} &= \beta_\Delta M_{\Delta\Delta}\beta'_\Delta + 2\beta_\Delta M_{\Delta *}\gamma'_* + \gamma_* M_{**}\gamma'_* \\ &= \frac{1}{T}\sum_{t=1}^{T}(\beta_\Delta y'_{\Delta,t} + \gamma_* z'_{*,t})^2. \end{aligned}$$

Let us form, with the given β_Δ, a scalar "composite" dependent variable $\tilde{y}_{1t}$ that is a linear combination

$$(6.13)\qquad \tilde{y}_{1t} = \beta_\Delta y'_{\Delta,t}$$

of the dependent variables $y_{\Delta,t}$ occurring in the equation to be estimated. Writing

$$(6.14)\qquad \alpha_{(\Delta *)}M_{(\Delta *)}\alpha'_{(\Delta *)} = \frac{1}{T}\sum_{t=1}^{T}(\tilde{y}_{1t} + \gamma_* z'_{*,t})^2,$$

we see that the values $\hat{\gamma}_*(\beta_\Delta)$ that, for given β_Δ, minimize $\alpha_{(\Delta *)}M_{(\Delta *)} \cdot \alpha'_{(\Delta *)}$ are but for sign equal to the least-squares estimates of the coefficients in the regression of the composite dependent variable $\tilde{y}_{1t}$ on $z_{*,t}$ (i.e., on the predetermined variables whose coefficients in the equation being estimated are not specified to be zero). But, from least-squares theory [cf. equation (5.18)],

$$(6.15)\qquad \hat{\gamma}_*(\beta_\Delta) = -\, m_{\tilde{y}_1 *}M_{**}^{-1} = -\, \beta_\Delta M_{\Delta *}M_{**}^{-1} \equiv -\, \beta_\Delta P^*_{\Delta *}.$$

Hence, from (6.12), using (6.15), we may write the minimum of $\alpha_{(\Delta *)} M_{(\Delta *)} \alpha'_{(\Delta *)}$ with respect to γ_* for given β_Δ as follows:

$$\min_{\gamma_*} \frac{1}{T} \sum_{t=1}^{T} (\beta_\Delta y'_{\Delta t} + \gamma_* z'_{*,t})^2 = \beta_\Delta (M_{\Delta\Delta} - M_{\Delta *} M_{**}^{-1} M_{*\Delta}) \beta'_\Delta = \beta_\Delta W^*_{\Delta\Delta} \beta'_\Delta, \tag{6.16}$$

if we define

$$W^*_{\Delta\Delta} \equiv M_{\Delta\Delta} - M_{\Delta *} M_{**}^{-1} M_{*\Delta} . \tag{6.17}$$

By comparison with the interpretation of W given at the end of Section 5.4, we see that $\beta_\Delta W^*_{\Delta\Delta} \beta'_\Delta$ is the "sample" variance, for given β_Δ, of the residual in a regression of the composite variable $\tilde{y}_{1t}$ on $z_{*,t}$ (i.e., on the predetermined variables not excluded from the equation being estimated).

Similarly, $\beta_\Delta W_{\Delta\Delta} \beta'_\Delta$ can be interpreted as the "sample" variance (for given β_Δ) of the residual in a regression of $\tilde{y}_{1t}$ on *all* the predetermined variables z_t (including those whose coefficients in the first equation are specified to be zero). We may write this, using an unrestricted vector $\gamma^\dagger = [\gamma_1^\dagger \quad \cdots \quad \gamma_K^\dagger]$, as follows:

$$\min_{\gamma^\dagger} \frac{1}{T} \sum_{t=1}^{T} (\beta_\Delta y'_{\Delta,t} + \gamma^\dagger z'_t)^2 = \beta_\Delta W_{\Delta\Delta} \beta'_\Delta, \tag{6.18}$$

where[77]

$$W_{\Delta\Delta} \equiv W_{y_\Delta y_\Delta} \equiv M_{y_\Delta y_\Delta} - M_{y_\Delta z} M_{zz}^{-1} M_{z y_\Delta} . \tag{6.19}$$

We shall assume that both $W^*_{\Delta\Delta}$ and $W_{\Delta\Delta}$ are nonsingular.[78]

Using (6.16) and (6.18), we may write the concentrated likelihood function that has only the elements of the vector β_Δ as its arguments, as follows:

$$L^{(4)}(\beta_\Delta) = -\tfrac{1}{2} \log \frac{\min_{\gamma_*} \sum_{t=1}^{T} (\beta_\Delta y'_{\Delta,t} + \gamma_* z'_{*,t})^2}{\min_{\gamma^\dagger} \sum_{t=1}^{T} (\beta_\Delta y'_{\Delta,t} + \gamma^\dagger z'_t)^2} = -\tfrac{1}{2} \log \frac{\beta_\Delta W^*_{\Delta\Delta} \beta'_\Delta}{\beta_\Delta W_{\Delta\Delta} \beta'_\Delta} \equiv -\tfrac{1}{2} \log l(\beta_\Delta), \tag{6.20}$$

say, where $l(\beta_\Delta)$ is termed the *variance ratio*.

[77] See footnote 76.

[78] In view of the nonsingularity of Σ and hence of Ω, specified by the model, this assumption excludes only samples whose probability of occurrence is zero.

The maximization of $L^{(4)}(\beta_\Delta)$ will yield limited-information maximum-likelihood estimates b_Δ of β_Δ. These may be substituted for β_Δ in equation (6.15) to obtain the limited-information maximum-likelihood estimates

$$c_* \equiv \hat{\gamma}_*(b_\Delta) = -b_\Delta M_{\Delta *} M_{**}^{-1} = -b_\Delta P_{\Delta *}^* \tag{6.21}$$

of γ_*. But the maximization of $L^{(4)}(\beta_\Delta)$ involves the minimization of the variance ratio $l(\beta_\Delta)$ with respect to β_Δ. It is for this reason that this procedure for obtaining estimates of the coefficients of a single equation is also called the *least variance ratio principle.*

The least variance ratio principle for the estimation of the coefficients of a single equation has an intuitive appeal, independent of the fact that it yields maximum-likelihood estimates in the present linear model with normal disturbances. The principle explicitly divides the variables of the complete system into four classes, arising from the dichotomies "dependent" versus "predetermined," and "excluded from" versus "admitted to" the equation to be estimated. Within each class variables are treated symmetrically. The excluded dependent variables are ignored.

We note further that the regression of $\tilde{y}_{1t}$ $(= \beta_\Delta y_{\Delta,t})$ on all predetermined variables z_t, taken in the *distribution* (5.8) of y_t for given z_t, is of the form

$$\mathcal{E}(\tilde{y}_{1t} \mid z_t) = \gamma_* z'_{*,t} . \tag{6.22}$$

This follows from the form of (6.5), where $\gamma_{**} = 0$, and from the fact, noted in (1.19), that the disturbance u_t is independent of all predetermined variables $z_t = [z_{*,t} \quad z_{**,t}]$. Thus, in the "true" regression (6.22), the excluded predetermined variables $z_{**,t}$ do not occur. Now the least variance ratio principle attempts to come as close as possible to such a situation in the sample. It estimates the unknown coefficient vector β_Δ by such a vector b_Δ that, if b_Δ is substituted for β_Δ in the definition (6.13) of the composite variable $\tilde{y}_{1t}$, the relative increase in the residual variance in a *sample* regression of $\tilde{y}_{1t}$ on the predetermined variables, which results from the exclusion of the variables $z_{**,t}$, shall be as small as possible. In this way the identifying restrictions and, as the case may be, any extra (overidentifying) restrictions on the equation to be estimated are properly used, while restrictions on any other equations are ignored.

Because of these intuitive merits, it is not surprising to find in Chapter VII that the least variance ratio estimates of the coefficients of a single equation, or the generalized least variance ratio estimates for a subset of equations, discussed below, have good properties even in certain partially nonlinear models with nonnormal disturbances. When the model $\mathfrak{S}_T$ is valid, however, their chief recommendation lies in the fact that they are maximum-likelihood estimates, with the properties of consistency and asymptotic efficiency (within the class of estimates using the same a priori information).

6.3. *Interpretation of the maximum-likelihood estimation of the coefficients of a subset of the structural equations as an application of a generalized least variance ratio principle.* It was first shown by Rubin [1948] that the maximum-likelihood method of estimation of the coefficients of any subset of the structural equations may be regarded as a generalization of the least variance ratio method. For readers interested in this generalization, we state it without proof in this subsection because the expression for the concentrated likelihood function involved is a direct analogue of the expression (6.20) just derived. Thereafter we shall, in Section 6.4, continue our discussion of the special case of a single equation.

Let us rewrite equation (6.3) in the following form (omitting the constant and the term that does not involve parameters):

$$L^{(5)}(\mathrm{A_I}) = -\tfrac{1}{2}\log\left(\frac{\det(\mathrm{A_I}M\mathrm{A_I'})}{\det(\mathrm{B_I}W\mathrm{B_I'})}\right). \tag{6.23}$$

The interpretation we shall give to this expression involves the use of a concept known as *generalized variance*, which is used in multivariate statistical analysis. The generalized variance of a multivariate probability distribution is defined[79] as the determinant value of the covariance matrix of the variables in question.

As in the case of the variance, the term can also be applied to a sample instead of a distribution. Let us again assign to $\mathrm{B_I}$ the role of θ in Section 5.5. In the given value of $\mathrm{B_I}$ a number of elements must be zero to meet the a priori restrictions. We now define a vector $\tilde{y}_t'$ of as many (G_{I}) composite dependent variables as there are equations in subset I,

$$\tilde{y}_t' = [\tilde{y}_{1t} \quad \cdots \quad \tilde{y}_{G_{\mathrm{I}}t}]' \equiv \mathrm{B_I}y_t'. \tag{6.24}$$

Thus the element in the ith row of this column vector is the sum of products of the jointly dependent variables and their coefficients in the ith equation of the subset being estimated. It is not difficult to show that $\det(\mathrm{B_I}W\mathrm{B_I'})$ is the generalized "sample" variance of the residuals in the least-squares regressions of each element of $\tilde{y}_t$ on all the predetermined variables in the complete model. Writing for a moment $\mathrm{A}^\dagger \equiv$

[79] Cf., for example, Cramér [1946, pp. 301, 406].

$[\mathrm{B} \quad \Gamma^\dagger]$, it can be shown further that the (unrestricted) coefficients $\Gamma_\mathrm{I}^\dagger(\mathrm{B}_\mathrm{I})$ of these regressions can be obtained by minimizing

$$\text{(6.25)} \qquad \det\,(\mathrm{A}_\mathrm{I}^\dagger M \mathrm{A}_\mathrm{I}^{\dagger\prime}) = \det\left\{\frac{1}{T}\sum_{t=1}^{T}(\mathrm{B}_\mathrm{I} y_t' + \Gamma_\mathrm{I}^\dagger z_t')(\mathrm{B}_\mathrm{I} y_t' + \Gamma_\mathrm{I}^\dagger z_t')'\right\}$$

with respect to the unrestricted matrix[80] $\Gamma_\mathrm{I}^\dagger$ as well as, in direct accordance with the least-squares principle, by minimizing separately each diagonal element of $\mathrm{A}_\mathrm{I}^\dagger M \mathrm{A}_\mathrm{I}^{\dagger\prime}$. Hence, applying stepwise maximization to the function (6.23), the limited-information maximum-likelihood estimates B_I of the coefficients B_I of a subset I of a complete set of equations can be obtained by maximizing with respect to B_I, subject to the a priori restrictions given, the concentrated likelihood function

$$\text{(6.26)} \qquad L^{(6)}(\mathrm{B}_\mathrm{I}) = -\tfrac{1}{2}\log\frac{\displaystyle\min_{\Gamma_\mathrm{I}\,(\text{restr.})}\det\,([\mathrm{B}_\mathrm{I} \quad \Gamma_\mathrm{I}]M[\mathrm{B}_\mathrm{I} \quad \Gamma_\mathrm{I}]')}{\displaystyle\min_{\Gamma_\mathrm{I}^\dagger(\text{unrestr.})}\det\,([\mathrm{B}_\mathrm{I} \quad \Gamma_\mathrm{I}^\dagger]M[\mathrm{B}_\mathrm{I} \quad \Gamma_\mathrm{I}^\dagger]')}$$

$$= -\tfrac{1}{2}\log l(\mathrm{B}_\mathrm{I}),$$

say, which is, in view of (6.25), an expression entirely analogous to (6.20). Corresponding estimates C_I of Γ_I are obtained as those values of Γ_I that perform the minimization in the numerator in the second member of (6.26) when B_I is substituted for B_I. Finally, estimates $S_{\mathrm{I\,I}}$ of the variances and covariances of the disturbances in the equations of subset I are obtained from the proper submatrix of (5.59).

The function $l(\mathrm{B}_\mathrm{I})$ is termed the *generalized variance ratio*. In view of (6.24) the limited-information maximum-likelihood estimates B_I of B_I are obtained by minimizing the generalized variance ratio $l(\mathrm{B}_\mathrm{I})$, subject to the a priori restrictions on B_I.

6.4. *Maximum-likelihood estimation of the parameters of a single structural equation, concluded.* We have found that to maximize the concentrated likelihood function $L^{(4)}(\beta_\Delta)$ of the coefficients of a single equation, given by (6.20), it is necessary to minimize the expression

$$\text{(6.27)} \qquad l(\beta_\Delta) \equiv \frac{\beta_\Delta W_{\Delta\Delta}^* \beta_\Delta'}{\beta_\Delta W_{\Delta\Delta}\beta_\Delta'} = \frac{\displaystyle\min_{\gamma_*}\sum_{t=1}^{T}(\beta_\Delta y_{\Delta,t}' + \gamma_* z_{*,t}')^2}{\displaystyle\min_{\gamma^\dagger}\sum_{t=1}^{T}(\beta_\Delta y_{\Delta,t}' + \gamma^\dagger z_t')^2}$$

with respect to β_Δ. The value of this function is unchanged if β_Δ is multiplied by a nonvanishing scalar constant[81] μ. It follows that, if a mini-

[80] No similar equivalence holds, in general, for minimization with respect to a restricted matrix Γ_I.

[81] See the comment in Section 5.7 immediately following equation (5.52).

mum of (6.27) is reached for $\beta_\Delta = b_\Delta$, it is also reached for $\beta_\Delta = \mu b_\Delta$. Therefore, since the effect of imposing a particular rule of normalization on β_Δ in minimizing (6.27) is only to choose a particular value of μ, the ratios of the elements of b_Δ remain unaffected thereby. We can therefore proceed without normalization for the present. If we differentiate the logarithm of the second member in (6.27) with respect to the elements of $\beta_\Delta \equiv [\beta_{11} \quad \cdots \quad \beta_{1G^\Delta}]$, and set the derivatives equal to zero, we obtain the following necessary conditions for a minimum,

$$(6.28) \qquad \frac{(\beta_\Delta W^*_{\Delta\Delta})_i}{\beta_\Delta W^*_{\Delta\Delta}\beta'_\Delta} = \frac{(\beta_\Delta W_{\Delta\Delta})_i}{\beta_\Delta W_{\Delta\Delta}\beta'_\Delta} \qquad (i = 1, \cdots, G^\Delta),$$

where $(\beta_\Delta W^*_{\Delta\Delta})_i$ denotes the ith element of the vector $\beta_\Delta W^*_{\Delta\Delta}$, and $(\beta_\Delta W_{\Delta\Delta})_i$ is similarly defined. In view of (6.27) the conditions (6.28) may be written as

$$(6.29) \qquad (\beta_\Delta W^*_{\Delta\Delta})_i = l\cdot(\beta_\Delta W_{\Delta\Delta})_i \qquad (i = 1, \cdots, G^\Delta)'$$

or where l stands for $l\ (\beta_\Delta)$, as

$$(6.30) \qquad \beta_\Delta(W^*_{\Delta\Delta} - lW_{\Delta\Delta}) = 0.$$

For a given value of l (6.30) may be regarded as a system of G^Δ homogeneous linear equations. For this system to have a nonvanishing solution β_Δ at all, it is necessary[82] that

$$(6.31) \qquad \rho(W^*_{\Delta\Delta} - lW_{\Delta\Delta}) \leqslant G^\Delta - 1,$$

and hence that

$$(6.32) \qquad \det\,(W^*_{\Delta\Delta} - lW_{\Delta\Delta}) = 0.$$

The left-hand member of (6.32) is a polynomial in l of degree[83] G^Δ.

We have now reached the conclusion that, if the function $l(\beta'_\Delta)$ defined by (6.27) possesses a minimum, the ratios of the elements of a vector $\beta_\Delta = b_\Delta$ for which this minimum is reached must be obtainable by finding a root l_i of the polynomial equation (6.32), substituting its value for l in (6.30), and solving for β_Δ. Let $b^{(i)}_\Delta$ denote a normalized solution. Postmultiplication of (6.30) by $b^{(i)\prime}_\Delta$ then shows that the value reached by $l(\beta_\Delta)$ in the point $b^{(i)}_\Delta$ is in fact equal to the root l_i.[84] It fol-

[82] See, for example, MacDuffee [1943, Theorem 29, p. 60].

[83] See footnote 78 and the assumption to which it is attached.

[84] The possibility that $b^{(i)}_\Delta W_{\Delta\Delta} b^{(i)\prime}_\Delta$ might vanish is excluded by the positive definiteness of $W_{\Delta\Delta}$. That $W^*_{\Delta\Delta}$ and $W_{\Delta\Delta}$ are symmetric positive semidefinite follows from the fact that $W^*_{\Delta\Delta}$ and $W_{\Delta\Delta}$ are moment matrices. For discussion of these assertions and definition of the term "positive definite," see Appendix B. $W_{\Delta\Delta}$ will be positive definite with probability one whenever, as we have assumed, Σ, and hence Ω, is nonsingular.

lows that only the smallest root l_1 of (6.32) can possibly lead to an absolute minimum $l(b_{\Delta}^{(1)})$ of $l(\beta_{\Delta})$, if an absolute minimum exists. That the smallest root does lead to an absolute minimum can be proved on the basis of the continuity[85] of the function (6.27). However, it can in the present context also be proved with more elementary means, and this is done in the last paragraph of Appendix F.

Since $b_{\Delta}^{(1)}$ is now our maximum-likelihood estimate of β_{Δ}, we shall denote it simply by b_{Δ}. It is defined by the condition

$$(6.33) \qquad b_{\Delta}(W_{\Delta\Delta}^{*} - l_1 W_{\Delta\Delta}) = 0, \qquad l_1 \leqslant l_i \qquad (i = 2, \cdots, G^{\Delta})$$

plus such a normalization rule as may be imposed.

A procedure for computing l_1 and b_{Δ} is described in Section 3 of Chapter X. It may be noted here that in computation it is convenient to put (6.32) and (6.33) in slightly different forms, described in detail by Chernoff and Divinsky.

We must for a moment discuss the possibility that

$$(6.34) \qquad \rho(W_{\Delta\Delta}^{*} - l_1 W_{\Delta\Delta}) < G^{\Delta} - 1.$$

Should this eventuality arise, it would be possible to obtain an infinite set of (normalized) values of b_{Δ} as solutions of (6.33). It is shown in Appendix F that if $W_{\Delta\Delta}$ is nonsingular (as we have assumed above), $\rho(W_{\Delta\Delta}^{*} - l_i W_{\Delta\Delta}) = G^{\Delta} - 1$ whenever l_i is a single root, and $\rho(W_{\Delta\Delta}^{*} - l_i W_{\Delta\Delta}) < G^{\Delta} - 1$ when l_i is a multiple root. In particular, this assertion relates to the smallest root l_1 with which we are concerned. It follows from this that if l_1 is single, a solution $\beta_{\Delta} = b_{\Delta}$ may be obtained to equation (6.33) that will be unique after normalization. It may be shown that if the order condition of identifiability of the equation in question is satisfied, the smallest root l_1 of (6.32) will be single save for exceptional samples, which occur with probability zero.

It will be recalled from Section 4 that indirect least-squares estimates of the coefficients of the first equation of the model $\mathfrak{S}_T$ may be obtained if the order condition of identifiability is just satisfied, $K^{**} = G^{\Delta} - 1$, but that this method fails when $K^{**} > G^{\Delta} - 1$. We shall now show that when the order condition for identifiability is just met (the case of minimum requisite information), the limited-information single-equation estimates obtained by the procedure just outlined are identical with the indirect least-squares estimates. To do this we must further discuss the smallest root l_1 of (6.32), which is at the same time the minimum of $l(\beta_{\Delta})$.

It is easily shown that the value of the smallest root l_1 of (6.32) can never be less than unity. This follows from the fact that $l(\beta_{\Delta})$ is, by

[85] On the compact set $\beta_{\Delta}\beta_{\Delta}' = 1$.

(6.27), a ratio of two residual variances, the denominator of which can never exceed the numerator. The numerator is the variance of the residual from a regression of $\tilde{y}_{\Delta,t}$ on $z_{*,t}$ whereas the denominator is the variance of the residual from a regression of $\tilde{y}_{\Delta,t}$ on $z_t \equiv [z_{*,t} \quad z_{**,t}]$. Since the regression coefficients in question are estimated by the minimization of residual variances, the narrower choice of dependent variables in the regression associated with the numerator has the effect of making the residual variance in the numerator greater than or equal to (but never less than) the residual variance in the denominator.

The condition under which $l_1 = 1$ follows from an extension of the same reasoning. Since l_1 is the minimum of $l(\beta_\Delta)$ as defined in the last member of (6.27), $l_1 = 1$ if and only if there exists a value b_Δ of β_Δ for which the minimizing value $\hat{\gamma}^\dagger(b_\Delta)$ of the unrestricted vector in the denominator of $l(b_\Delta)$,

$$(6.35) \quad \hat{\gamma}^\dagger(b_\Delta) = -b_\Delta M_{\Delta z} M_{zz}^{-1} = -b_\Delta P_{\Delta z} = -b_\Delta [P_{\Delta *} \quad P_{\Delta,**}],$$

has the property

$$(6.36) \qquad \hat{\gamma}^\dagger_{**}(b_\Delta) = -b_\Delta P_{\Delta,**} = 0.$$

For, if no such value b_Δ exists, the minimum residual variance in the numerator of (6.27) must exceed that in the denominator, and $l_1 > 1$. On the other hand, if such a value b_Δ exists, the minimum residual variances in numerator and denominator must be equal for that value b_Δ of β_Δ, and the minimum value $l_1 = 1$ of $l(\beta_\Delta)$ is reached there. Thus, $l_1 = 1$ if and only if (6.36) has a solution b_Δ, that is, if and only if

$$(6.37) \qquad \rho(P_{\Delta,**}) \leqslant G^\Delta - 1,$$

and, in that case, any solution b_Δ of (6.36) maximizes the likelihood function or, equivalently, minimizes the variance ratio (6.27).

Condition (6.37) is satisfied whenever the order condition of identifiability is just met ($K^{**} = G^\Delta - 1$). We recognize in (6.36) the condition (4.30) defining the indirect least-squares estimates b_Δ of β_Δ, while the corresponding estimates c_* of γ_* given by (4.31) are read from (6.35). Thus the least variance ratio principle derived by applying the limited-information maximum-likelihood method to a single equation coincides with the indirect least-squares estimation of that equation whenever the latter method is applicable. Of course, unique estimates b_Δ (but for normalization) are obtained only if

$$(6.38) \qquad \rho(P_{\Delta,**}) = G^\Delta - 1,$$

an event occurring with probability one whenever the order condition for identifiability is just met.

If $K^{**} > G^{\Delta} - 1$, we have with probability one $\rho(P_{\Delta,**}) = G^{\Delta}$ and hence $l_1 > 1$. In this case the indirect least-squares method fails, but the least variance ratio principle produces limited-information maximum-likelihood estimates. These estimates b_{Δ} and c_* may be derived from equations (6.33) and (6.21), and are unique if l_1 is a single root, an event occurring with probability one.

The reader will have noticed that, if the order condition of identifiability is met, the method described will produce unique estimates with probability one even if the true structure is such that the rank condition for identifiability is not met. What warning does the researcher receive that this is the case? This question arose also at the end of Section 4.5, and the answers given there may be restated here in somewhat more general terms.

There are two useful warning signals that have a high probability of being operative in the case under consideration. The sampling variance of the maximum-likelihood estimate of an identifiable parameter θ_1 tends to infinity whenever some other parameter θ_2 tends to a value θ_2^0 that would destroy the identifiability of θ_1. It is therefore probable that the estimated sampling variances of a coefficient, of which the evaluation is discussed in Section 7, will be high whenever that coefficient is not identifiable, or is nearly so.

The second warning signal is computationally less expensive to observe. It has already been mentioned, in Chapter II, Section 5, that the hypothesis of identifiability of a parameter or a set of parameters is always subject to statistical test. In Section 8.2 we shall describe a statistical test of the simultaneous identifiability of all coefficients of a structural equation by a given set of a priori restrictions on that equation.

For the sake of completeness, we recall that the leading element s_{11} in (5.59) gives us the maximum-likelihood estimate

$$s_{11} = [b_{\Delta} \quad c_*] \begin{bmatrix} M_{\Delta\Delta} & M_{*\Delta} \\ M_{\Delta *} & M_{**} \end{bmatrix} \begin{bmatrix} b'_{\Delta} \\ c'_* \end{bmatrix} \tag{6.39}$$

of the variance σ_{11} of the disturbances in the first structural equation.

The present derivation of limited-information maximum-likelihood estimates of the parameters of a single equation conceals an interesting property which was central in the original presentation of the method by Anderson and Rubin. In their treatment [Anderson and Rubin, 1949, Section 5], the coefficients Π of the reduced-form equations are estimated by maximizing the likelihood function (expressed in terms of the reduced-form parameters) subject to the restriction that $\rho(\Pi_{\Delta,**}) \leqslant$

$G^{\Delta} - 1$. This restriction ensures that unique estimates $[b_{\Delta} \quad c_{*}]$ can be derived with probability one from the estimates $\hat{\Pi}$ so obtained. The estimates $[b_{\Delta} \quad c_{*}]$ obtained by Anderson and Rubin are, of course, the same functions of the observations as those obtained by the derivation we have given.

6.5. *Conclusion.* Let us now summarize some of the results reached in Sections 5 and 6. We have shown the relation between a priori restrictions on structural coefficients and the identifiability of these parameters and have argued that meaningful estimation presupposes identifiability. On the basis of the (necessary) order condition for the identifiability of a given structural equation we have considered two possible situations. In the first, the restrictions on the coefficients of that equation are just adequate to satisfy this condition (the "minimum requisite information" case). In the second, more than the minimum requisite number of restrictions exist.

Maximum-likelihood methods of estimation have been discussed that yield consistent estimates of structural parameters and that vary in the amount of a priori information utilized with regard to the restrictions on the coefficients of other equations of a model than those being estimated. If the model $\mathfrak{S}_T$ is valid, these estimates are in each case asymptotically efficient as compared with other estimates using the same or less information. If just the minimum requisite number of restrictions is available for each equation of the structure, the maximum-likelihood estimates of the structural parameters will be the same functions of the observations whether each equation is estimated by the indirect least-squares method, by the limited-information single-equation method, by the limited-information method applied to any other subset of the equations, or by the full-information method. In the more general case, in which some equations are provided with "extra" (overidentifying) restrictions, indirect least-squares methods are not applicable to those equations without neglecting restrictions on them, and the maximum-likelihood estimates vary according to the amount utilized of overidentifying information that pertains to other equations. In general, the more (valid) overidentifying information is used in deriving maximum-likelihood estimates, the more efficient the estimates will be, at least asymptotically and presumably also for finite samples.

Let us also review the connections between the identifiability and estimation of the parameters A, Σ, of the structure and the parameters Π, Ω of the reduced form. The parameters Π, Ω are always identifiable in linear models $\mathfrak{S}_T$ of the type here considered, whereas A, Σ may or may not be. While we have only made explicit the a priori restrictions imposed on the coefficients A, restrictions on the coefficients Π are implied by those on A whenever at least one equation of the structure is subject to "overidentifying" (i.e., more than the minimum requisite number of) restrictions. Parameters Σ, and therefore also Ω, have been left unrestricted except for the requirement of positive definiteness of these matrices. Maximum-likelihood estimates of Π, Ω may be obtained using all, some, or none of the "overidentifying" restrictions on the structural parameters, but only unrestricted estimates have been considered in this chapter. Maximum-likelihood estimates of identifiable parameters A, Σ may be obtained indirectly from corresponding estimates of Π, Ω, in which case their properties will depend on the extent to which overidentifying restrictions were utilized in the derivation of the estimates of Π, Ω (as is done by Anderson and Rubin). Alternatively and equivalently, as discussed in Sections 5 and 6 of this chapter, maximum-likelihood estimates of A, Σ may be obtained directly by maximizing the likelihood function expressed in terms of these parameters. Again, in estimating any row of A (and the corresponding elements of Σ) a choice is required as to what amount of overidentifying information that may be available concerning the rest of the equations will actually be utilized. This choice is guided by balancing computational economy against possible loss of efficiency in estimation.

7. Asymptotic Sampling Variances and Covariances of the Maximum-Likelihood Estimates

Within a wide range of models, including the model $\mathfrak{S}_T$ considered in this chapter, maximum-likelihood estimates of identifiable parameters have the property of asymptotic normality, and a general formula is available for the asymptotic sampling variances and covariances of such estimates. For models involving independence of successive observations, proofs of this statement and of the formula can be found in several textbooks.[86] Extensions of these results relevant to the model $\mathfrak{S}_T$ have been given by Mann and Wald [1943] and by Koopmans, Rubin, and Leipnik [1950, Section 3].

As before, let

$$L(\theta, x) \equiv (1/T) \log F_T(\theta, x) \tag{7.1}$$

represent the logarithmic likelihood function associated with the model $\mathfrak{S}_T$, expressed in terms of an identifiable parameter vector θ and a sample vector x. Define a matrix $L \equiv [l_{ij}]$ with typical element

$$l_{ij} \equiv \mathcal{E} \frac{\partial^2 L(\theta, x)}{\partial\theta_i \, \partial\theta_j} \equiv \int \frac{\partial^2 L(\theta, x)}{\partial\theta_i \, \partial\theta_j} F_T(\theta, x) \, dy_1(1) \cdots dy_G(T), \tag{7.2}$$

[86] For instance, Cramér [1946, p. 500].

the expectation being taken over the distribution of the endogenous variables y. Then, if $\hat{\theta}$ denotes the vector of maximum-likelihood estimates $\hat{\theta}_i$ of the components θ_i of θ, the sampling distribution of the statistics

$$\sqrt{T}\cdot(\hat{\theta}_i - \theta_i) \tag{7.3}$$

in sampling from a structure of the model $\mathfrak{S}_T$ tends, as T becomes infinitely large, to a multivariate normal distribution with means zero and covariance matrix

$$\operatorname*{plim}_{T\to\infty} T\,\mathcal{E}(\hat{\theta}' - \theta')(\hat{\theta} - \theta) = -L^{-1}, \tag{7.4}$$

the negative inverse of L.

The same formula (7.4) remains applicable [Koopmans, Rubin, and Leipnik, 1950, Section 3.3.10] if θ comprises only a subset of the parameters of the model $\mathfrak{S}_T$ while $L(\theta, x)$ represents the corresponding concentrated logarithmic likelihood function, obtained by prior maximization with respect to the remaining parameters. Thus, we can evaluate sampling variances and covariances of the estimates A of A from the likelihood function (5.58), of the estimates A_{I} of the coefficients A_{I} of a subset of the structural equations from the likelihood function (6.3), and of the estimates a of the coefficients α of a single equation from the likelihood function (6.10).

Of course, the matrix L^{-1} in (7.4) is a function of the unknown parameters θ. It can be estimated by inserting for θ the maximum-likelihood estimates $\hat{\theta}$.

Computational procedures for the evaluation of L^{-1} are described for a number of different choices of θ in Chapter X.

8. Statistical Tests of the Validity and of the Identifying Character of the A Priori Restrictions on a Single Structural Equation

8.1. *A test of the restrictions on one structural equation.* So far we have formally treated the a priori restrictions on any structural equation as a matter beyond doubt. This is a defensible tactic in that it helps us to construct pieces of a formal theory that serve specifically defined tasks, such as the estimation of parameters within the framework of a given model. At the same time, it should not preclude us from considering that the choice of the model itself is subject to uncertainty. We shall now discuss a test, developed by Anderson and Rubin [1949, Section 6], of a certain part of the specifications that enter into our model $\mathfrak{S}_T$, viz., the a priori restrictions on the coefficients of one particular structural equation (say the first). The test ignores any restrictions relating to equations other than the first.

We choose as the "maintained hypothesis" a complete model $\mathfrak{S}_T$ which specifies the lists of dependent and predetermined variables, the linearity of the structural equations, and the normality and serial independence of the disturbances. It is convenient also to specify in $\mathfrak{S}_T$ that the exogenous variables $\bar{z}_t$ are linearly independent. However, $\mathfrak{S}_T$ implies no restrictions whatever on the values of the structural coefficients. Hence, $\mathfrak{S}_T$ is not sufficiently restricted to identify any of the structural equations.

We choose as the "null hypothesis" the model $\mathfrak{S}_T^0$ obtained from $\mathfrak{S}_T$ by imposing on the coefficients of the first structural equation only restrictions of the form

$$(8.1) \qquad \alpha \equiv [\beta_\Delta \quad 0_{\Delta\Delta} \quad \gamma_* \quad 0_{**}]$$

used also in Sections 4.4 and 6.2. The "alternative hypothesis" is thus the model $\mathfrak{S}_T^1 = \mathfrak{S}_T - \mathfrak{S}_T^0$ consisting of all structures of $\mathfrak{S}_T$ not satisfying the null hypothesis.

While we have expressed the maintained, null, and alternative hypotheses in the form of *models* (i.e., sets $\mathfrak{S}$ of *structures*), the theory of the testing of hypotheses can now be applied on the basis of the corresponding sets $\mathfrak{F}$ of *distributions* of the observations. Corresponding to $\mathfrak{S}_T$ we have the class $\mathfrak{F}_T$ of distribution functions (5.24) of the observations, represented by all possible values of the parameters Π, Ω of the reduced form. Corresponding to $\mathfrak{S}_T^0$ we have the subclass of $\mathfrak{F}_T^0$ containing those distributions for which

$$(8.2) \qquad \rho(\Pi_{\Delta,**}) \leqslant G^\Delta - 1,$$

because for each such distribution there is a linear combination of the first G^Δ equations of the reduced form, with coefficients β_Δ satisfying (4.20), that meets the restrictions expressed by (8.1). Finally, corresponding to $\mathfrak{S}_T^1$ we have the subclass $\mathfrak{F}_T^1$ containing those distributions for which

$$(8.3) \qquad \rho(\Pi_{\Delta,**}) = G^\Delta.$$

These correspondences permit the straightforward application of the theory of testing hypotheses, in which the likelihood ratio criterion[87] provides a useful test. This criterion is defined as the ratio of the maximum of the likelihood function $F_T(\Pi, \Omega, x)$ with respect to Π and Ω as restricted in $\mathfrak{F}_T^0$ [i.e., by (8.2)] to the maximum of that function within $\mathfrak{F}_T$ [with Π unrestricted]. Application of this criterion as carried out by Anderson and Rubin leads to the smallest root l_1 of equation (6.32) as

[87] See, for instance, Mood [1950, Section 12.5].

the appropriate test statistic. In Appendix G we show that the likelihood ratio criterion is a monotonic function of l_1.

In order to aid in the intuitive understanding of this test, we shall here motivate the use of the criterion in question by a different reasoning. For expository simplicity we shall limit our discussion to the case in which no lagged endogenous variables occur in the model $\mathfrak{S}_T$, so that all variables z_t are exogenous and can be thought of as constant in repeated samples.[88] Since then the symbols z_t and $\bar{z}_t$ have identical meaning, we shall also use z to denote the vector $\bar{z}$ defined in (1.22) [in which the "prehistoric" elements y_t $(t \leqslant 0)$ now do not enter].

We shall make use of parameters $\Omega_{\Delta\Delta}$, $\Omega^*_{\Delta\Delta}$ (to be defined), which in some sense are structural counterparts of the sample quantities $W_{\Delta\Delta}$, $W^*_{\Delta\Delta}$. In this way we can define the smallest root λ_1 of

$$\det(\Omega^*_{\Delta\Delta} - \lambda\Omega_{\Delta\Delta}) = 0, \tag{8.4}$$

the "structural" counterpart of l_1, and study its properties. The quantities $\Omega_{\Delta\Delta}$, $\Omega^*_{\Delta\Delta}$ are to be defined as functions of "structural" moments M_{xx} constructed analogously to the functions of sample moments M_{xx} defining $W_{\Delta\Delta}$ and $W^*_{\Delta\Delta}$. The structural moments M_{xx} will in turn be defined as expectations of the corresponding sample moments, which are conditional upon given values of the exogenous variables z_t for all relevant values of t.

From the reduced form

$$y'_t = \Pi z'_t + v'_t \tag{8.5}$$

and the independence of v_t from z_t, discussed in Section 1.6, we have

$$\mathcal{E}(y'_t \mid z_t) = \Pi z'_t. \tag{8.6}$$

Similarly, we now define

$$\mathrm{M}_{xx} \equiv \mathcal{E}(M_{xx} \mid z) = \frac{1}{T}\sum_{t=1}^{T} \mathcal{E}(x'_t x_t \mid z_t), \tag{8.7}$$

where $x_t = [y_t \quad z_t]$, as the matrix of "structural" moments. These are, by virtue of their definition, functions of the parameters Π, Ω of the distribution of the observations and of the moments M_{zz} of the exogenous variables (which are likewise free of sampling fluctuations). In particular, of course, $\mathrm{M}_{zz} = M_{zz}$.

The submatrices M_{yy} and M_{yz} of M_{xx} can be evaluated from (8.5), using the definition (1.25) of Ω, as follows:

$$\begin{aligned} \mathrm{M}_{yy} &= \frac{1}{T}\sum_{t=1}^{T} \Pi z'_t z_t \Pi' + 0 + 0 + \frac{1}{T}\sum_{t=1}^{T} \mathcal{E}(v'_t v_t \mid z_t) \\ &= \Pi \mathrm{M}_{zz} \Pi' + \Omega, \end{aligned} \tag{8.8}$$

[88] See Section 1.3.

$$\text{(8.9)} \quad \mathrm{M}_{yz} = \frac{1}{T}\sum_{t=1}^{T} \Pi z_t' z_t = \Pi M_{zz} .$$

We are now ready to define the structural counterpart $\Omega^*_{\Delta\Delta}$ of $W^*_{\Delta\Delta}$, by analogy with (6.17), by

$$\text{(8.10)} \qquad \Omega^*_{\Delta\Delta} \equiv \mathrm{M}_{\Delta\Delta} - \mathrm{M}_{\Delta *} M^{-1}_{**} \mathrm{M}_{*\Delta} .$$

In order to relate it to $\Omega_{\Delta\Delta}$ we partition Π according to

$$\text{(8.11)} \qquad \Pi = \begin{bmatrix} \Pi_\Delta \\ \Pi_{\Delta\Delta} \end{bmatrix}, \qquad \Pi_\Delta = [\Pi_{\Delta *} \quad \Pi_{\Delta,**}]$$

and use (8.8) and (8.9) to obtain

$$\begin{aligned} \Omega^*_{\Delta\Delta} - \Omega_{\Delta\Delta} &= \Pi_\Delta (M_{zz} - M_{z*} M^{-1}_{**} M_{*z}) \Pi'_\Delta \\ \text{(8.12)} \quad &= [\Pi_{\Delta *} \quad \Pi_{\Delta,**}] \begin{bmatrix} 0_{**} & 0_{*,**} \\ 0_{**,*} & M_{**,**} - M_{**,*} M^{-1}_{**} M_{*,**} \end{bmatrix} \begin{bmatrix} \Pi'_{\Delta *} \\ \Pi'_{\Delta,**} \end{bmatrix} \\ &= \Pi_{\Delta,**} {}^*M_{**,**} \Pi'_{\Delta,**} , \end{aligned}$$

where

$$\text{(8.13)} \qquad {}^*M_{**,**} \equiv M_{**,**} - M_{**,*} M^{-1}_{**} M_{*,**}$$

is the moment matrix of the residuals from regressions of the $z_{**,t}$ on the $z_{*,t}$.

Armed with this expression for $\Omega^*_{\Delta\Delta} - \Omega_{\Delta\Delta}$, let us now return to the polynomial equation (8.4) and write it as

$$\text{(8.14)} \qquad \begin{aligned} &\det(\Omega^*_{\Delta\Delta} - \lambda\Omega_{\Delta\Delta}) \\ &\qquad = \det\{\Pi_{\Delta,**} {}^*M_{**,**} \Pi'_{\Delta,**} - (\lambda - 1)\Omega_{\Delta\Delta}\} = 0. \end{aligned}$$

In order to explore the situation both under the null hypothesis and under the alternative, we recall the specification that the exogenous variables z_t be linearly independent. This implies that the matrix ${}^*M_{**,**}$ is nonsingular, because if it were singular there would exist a nonvanishing linear combination of the variables $z_{**,t}$ which would be a linear function of the variables $z_{*,t}$ contrary to the specification stated. Finally, since ${}^*M_{**,**}$ is also, as already noted, a moment matrix, it is positive definite. As observed in Appendix B, this implies that $\Pi_{\Delta,**} {}^*M_{**,**} \Pi'_{\Delta,**}$ is positive semidefinite.

It follows from this and the positive definiteness of Ω (and hence of $\Omega_{\Delta\Delta}$), by Theorem 1 of Appendix B, that the smallest root λ_1 of (8.14) satisfies

$$\text{(8.15)} \qquad \lambda_1 - 1 \geqslant 0, \qquad \text{or} \quad \lambda_1 \geqslant 1.$$

It follows further, from Theorem 4 of Appendix B, that under the null hypothesis [under which (8.2) applies]

$$\rho(\Pi_{\Delta,**}{}^{*}M_{**,**}\Pi'_{\Delta,**}) \leqslant G^{\Delta} - 1, \tag{8.16}$$

and under the alternative hypothesis [under which (8.3) applies]

$$\rho(\Pi_{\Delta,**}{}^{*}M_{**,**}\Pi'_{\Delta,**}) = G^{\Delta}. \tag{8.17}$$

In the light of Theorem 1 of Appendix B, this implies that under the null hypothesis

$$\lambda_1 = 1, \tag{8.18}$$

and under the alternative hypothesis

$$\lambda_1 > 1. \tag{8.19}$$

We can therefore regard our problem as that of testing the hypothesis that $\lambda_1 = 1$ against the alternative that $\lambda_1 > 1$. Accordingly, it seems natural to choose as the test statistic the corresponding sample root l_1. In traditional language, we are then testing the significance of the excess of l_1 over 1.

We have already seen, in Section 6.4, that $l_1 = 1$ if (8.1) represents no more than the "minimum requisite" information.[89] This corresponds to the fact that, if $K^{**} + G^{\Delta\Delta} \leqslant G - 1$, the restrictions on the first equation do not in any way restrict the distribution of the observations. The alternative hypothesis is then empty, because (8.3) cannot hold if $K^{**} \leqslant G^{\Delta} - 1$ $(= G - G^{\Delta\Delta} - 1)$. Therefore a test is unnecessary, and this is borne out by the inevitable outcome $l_1 = 1$, which fails to reject the null hypothesis $\lambda_1 = 1$.

However, if (8.1) corresponds to the case of "extra" information,[90] even if the null hypothesis (8.2) is satisfied, we will with probability one have

$$\rho(P_{\Delta,**}) = G^{\Delta}. \tag{8.20}$$

Hence, by an argument similar to that leading to (8.19), we shall have

$$l_1 > 1 \tag{8.21}$$

with probability one even if the null hypothesis is true.

An asymptotic distribution of a suitable function of l_1 can be derived from the fact, demonstrated in Appendix G, that l_1 is obtained as a likelihood ratio. Under the null hypothesis the statistic

$$T \log l_1 \tag{8.22}$$

[89] See Section 4.5.

[90] See Section 4.6.

is distributed asymptotically as χ^2 with $K^{**} - G^{\Delta} + 1$ degrees of freedom.[91] It has already been noted that the test is unnecessary whenever this number of degrees of freedom is zero or negative.

Neither the fact that the test statistic l_1 can be derived from the likelihood ratio principle nor the fact that l_1 has the asymptotic distribution indicated depends on the assumption, made here for expository purposes, that there are no lagged endogenous variables among the predetermined variables z_t.[92] Anderson and Rubin [1950, p. 581] go on to show that the asymptotic distribution of l_1 indicated is valid in a much wider class of models $\mathfrak{S}_T$ in which, for instance, normality of disturbances is not specified (and hence l_1 is no longer obtainable from a likelihood ratio).

8.2. *A test of the identifiability of a structural equation.* Most of the analysis of Section 8.1 can also serve for the discussion of a test to determine whether the a priori restrictions (8.1) on a structural equation are sufficient to identify that equation. In this case the maintained hypothesis is the model, previously denoted $\mathfrak{S}_T^0$, in which the restrictions (8.1) are satisfied. These restrictions are now supposed to be sufficient in number to meet the order condition (4.23) of identifiability. In order to obtain a test of the (necessary and sufficient) rank condition of identifiability it is convenient[93] to choose as the null hypothesis the restriction

$$\rho(\Pi_{\Delta,**}) \leqslant G^{\Delta} - 2 \tag{8.23}$$

on Π, and hence as the alternative hypothesis

$$\rho(\Pi_{\Delta,**}) = G^{\Delta} - 1, \tag{8.24}$$

because (8.2) holds in the maintained model $\mathfrak{S}_T^0$. Taken literally, this gives us a test of nonidentifiability rather than of identifiability.

Now, if the null hypothesis is satisfied, the value $\lambda = 1$ will decrease the rank of the matrix

$$\Omega^*_{\Delta\Delta} - \lambda\Omega_{\Delta\Delta} \tag{8.25}$$

[91] For example, suppose that in a particular case in which $K^{**} - G^{\Delta} + 1 = 1$ and $T = 30$ we found $l_1 = 1.5$. Then $T \log l_1 = \chi^2 = 5.283$, and we would reject the null hypothesis at the 0.025 significance level but not at the 0.01 level.

[92] Our argument can be extended to the case in which lagged endogenous variables are present if we define the "structural" moments by the third member of (8.7), which then no longer equals the second member. These moments reflect the sampling fluctuations of the lagged endogenous variables, and the same is true for l_1 if the alternative hypothesis is true; but this does not destroy the intuitive appeal of the argument.

[93] In order to follow the general practice of reserving the term null hypothesis for the lower-dimensional subset of the parameter space.

by at least 2, to a value at most $G^{\Delta} - 2$. It is shown in Appendix F that in this case $\lambda = 1$ is at least a double root of (8.4), whence the second smallest root $\lambda_2 = 1$. If the alternative hypothesis is satisfied, β_{Δ} is uniquely determined by

$$(\Omega^*_{\Delta\Delta} - \Omega_{\Delta\Delta})\beta'_{\Delta} = 0, \tag{8.26}$$

which can only be the case if $\lambda = 1$ is a single root, whence $\lambda_2 > 1$. We conclude that a test of nonidentifiability is obtained if we test the null hypothesis that $\lambda_2 = 1$ against the alternative hypothesis that $\lambda_2 > 1$.

This, of course, suggests the use of the second smallest "sample" root of equation (6.32) as the test criterion. In Appendix G we show that this is indeed equivalent to the use of the likelihood ratio criterion. However, the asymptotic distribution $T \log l_2$ is not a χ^2 distribution under the null hypothesis because of the multiplicity $(\lambda_1 = \lambda_2)$ of the corresponding "structural" root λ_2 in that case. Instead, we may use the statistic

$$T \log (l_1 l_2), \tag{8.27}$$

or its asymptotic equivalent $T(l_1 + l_2 - 2)$, both of which are distributed asymptotically[94] as χ^2 with $K^{**} - G^{\Delta} + 2$ degrees of freedom under the null hypothesis (provided that $\lambda_3 > \lambda_2$). The test is unnecessary if this number of degrees of freedom is zero or negative because in that case the order condition for identifiability is not satisfied.

8.3. *Use of these tests as a preliminary to the estimation of parameters.* It is natural to use the test of the set of restrictions on a given equation before proceeding to estimate its coefficients, which is a subsequent step in computational procedure. It is likewise natural to abandon without further computation a set of restrictions strongly rejected by the test. Similarly, it is natural to apply a test of identifiability before proceeding with the calculation of sampling variances of estimates, which require greater computational effort, and to abandon the latter computation, and forego any use of the estimates, if the indication of nonidentifiability is strong. But, since the models that are not rejected form a selection based on the observations, it must be remembered that probability statements associated with the sampling variances of the estimates, valid for any preconceived model, are only approximately true for this class of unrejected models.

A similar difficulty arises if the test of the set of all restrictions, or some other likelihood ratio test of one set of restrictions against another,

[94] See Hsu [1941, Theorem on p. 193] and Anderson [1951, Theorem 5, p. 122]. We are indebted to M. A. Girshick and J. Gurland for clarifying this point.

less stringent set, is used repeatedly to guide the choice of model. It was pointed out in Chapter II, Section 7, that these difficulties can only be overcome in a theory of simultaneous choice of model and estimates. The problems of the foundations of statistical inference, here touched upon, fall outside the scope of this volume.

Appendix A

THE NECESSARY AND SUFFICIENT CONDITION FOR THE IDENTIFIABILITY OF A STRUCTURAL EQUATION

We consider the identifiability of a structural equation (say the first)

$$\beta_\Delta y'_{\Delta.t} + 0_{\Delta\Delta} y'_{\Delta\Delta.t} + \gamma_* z'_{*.t} + 0_{**} z'_{**.t} = u_{1t} \tag{A.1}$$

in the complete set of structural equations

$$\mathrm{B} y'_t + \Gamma z'_t = u'_t \tag{A.2}$$

belonging to the model $\mathfrak{S}_T$, as defined in Section 1.

In Section 4.4 it was shown that a necessary and sufficient condition for the identifiability of this equation is that

$$\rho[\Pi_{\Delta.**}] = G^\Delta - 1. \tag{A.3}$$

Another rank condition of identifiability, stated in terms of a submatrix of

$$\mathrm{A} \equiv [\mathrm{B} \quad \Gamma] \equiv \begin{bmatrix} \beta_\Delta & 0_{\Delta\Delta} & \gamma_* & 0_{**} \\ \mathrm{A}_\Delta & \mathrm{A}_{\Delta\Delta} & \mathrm{A}_* & \mathrm{A}_{**} \end{bmatrix}, \tag{A.4}$$

was mentioned in Chapter II, Section 4, and proved elsewhere [Koopmans, Rubin, and Leipnik, 1950, Section 2.2]. Since both criteria are necessary and sufficient for the identifiability of the equation in question, they must be logically equivalent. It may be worth while to give here an explicit proof of that fact. Accordingly, we use the criterion (A.3) to prove the following

Theorem: *A necessary and sufficient condition for the identifiability of the structural equation (A.1) is that*

$$\rho[\mathrm{A}_{\Delta\Delta} \quad \mathrm{A}_{**}] = G - 1. \tag{A.5}$$

Proof: From the definition (1.23) of the reduced form we have

$$[I \quad -\Pi] = \mathrm{B}^{-1}\mathrm{A}, \tag{A.6}$$

from which it follows that

$$\begin{bmatrix} 0_{\Delta.\Delta\Delta} & -\Pi_{\Delta.**} \\ I_{\Delta\Delta.\Delta\Delta} & -\Pi_{\Delta\Delta.**} \end{bmatrix} = \mathrm{B}^{-1}\mathrm{A}_\S, \tag{A.7}$$

where

$$\mathrm{A}_\S \equiv \begin{bmatrix} 0_{\Delta\Delta} & 0_{**} \\ \mathrm{A}_{\Delta\Delta} & \mathrm{A}_{**} \end{bmatrix} \tag{A.8}$$

Multiplying both sides of (A.7) on the right by the nonsingular matrix

$$\bar{\Pi} \equiv \begin{bmatrix} I_{\Delta\Delta,\Delta\Delta} & -\Pi_{\Delta\Delta,**} \\ 0_{**,\Delta\Delta} & -I_{**,**} \end{bmatrix}, \tag{A.9}$$

we obtain

$$\bar{\bar{\Pi}} \equiv \begin{bmatrix} 0_{\Delta,\Delta\Delta} & \Pi_{\Delta,**} \\ I_{\Delta\Delta,\Delta\Delta} & 0_{\Delta\Delta,**} \end{bmatrix} = \mathrm{B}^{-1}\mathrm{A}_{\S}\bar{\Pi}, \tag{A.10}$$

from which it follows[95] that $\bar{\bar{\Pi}}$ and $\mathrm{A}_{\S}$ have equal rank. But, from the definition of $\bar{\bar{\Pi}}$ in (A.10), we see that[96]

$$\rho[\bar{\bar{\Pi}}] = \rho[\Pi_{\Delta,**}] + (G - G^{\Delta}) \tag{A.11}$$

and hence, since by (A.8) $\mathrm{A}_{\S}$ and $[\mathrm{A}_{\Delta\Delta} \quad \mathrm{A}_{**}]$ also have equal rank, we have

$$\rho[\mathrm{A}_{\Delta\Delta} \quad \mathrm{A}_{**}] = \rho[\Pi_{\Delta,**}] + (G - G^{\Delta}). \tag{A.12}$$

Thus, if (A.1) is identifiable [i.e., if (A.3) holds], (A.5) holds, and conversely.

Appendix B

POSITIVE DEFINITE AND POSITIVE SEMIDEFINITE MATRICES

Definition: *Let A be the symmetric real matrix of a quadratic form*

$$xAx' \equiv [x_1 \cdots x_n] \begin{bmatrix} a_{11} & \cdots & a_{1n} \\ \cdots & \cdots & \cdots \\ a_{n1} & \cdots & a_{nn} \end{bmatrix} \begin{bmatrix} x_1 \\ \cdots \\ x_n \end{bmatrix} \equiv \sum_{i,j=1}^{n} a_{ij}x_ix_j. \tag{B.1}$$

If

$$xAx' \geqslant 0 \tag{B.2}$$

for all real vectors x, the quadratic form xAx' and the matrix A are defined to be *positive semidefinite*. If

$$xAx' > 0 \text{ for all } x \neq 0, \tag{B.3}$$

xAx' and A are defined to be positive definite. Hence, in particular, a positive definite form is positive semidefinite.

A positive definite matrix is nonsingular, for, if A were singular, there would be a nonvanishing x such that $xA = 0$; so $xAx' = 0$, contradicting the definition of positive definiteness.

If xAx' is a real and positive definite quadratic form and we substitute $x = yP$ for x, where P may be rectangular but has a rank equal to the number of its rows, then the resulting form yBy', where $B = PAP'$, is positive definite. For, if for

[95] Because the multiplication of a matrix by a nonsingular matrix does not change its rank. See MacDuffee [1943, Chapter II, especially Theorems 17 and 22 and Corollary 23].

[96] This follows readily as a generalization of property (h) of the direct sum of two square matrices given in MacDuffee [1943, p. 114].

some nonvanishing value $\bar{y}$ of y, $\bar{y}B\bar{y}' \leqslant 0$, then for $\bar{x} \equiv \bar{y}P$ (which does not vanish because of the assumptions about the rank of P) we should have $\bar{x}A\bar{x}' \leqslant 0$, contrary to assumption. It is proved similarly that if A is positive semidefinite, then B is positive semidefinite (irrespective of the rank of P).

These statements are frequently used with a square, nonsingular, choice of P.

By choosing P rectangular and so as to have only one nonvanishing element, equal to one, in each row, it follows that any principal minor of a positive (semi-) definite matrix is positive (semi-) definite.

We now prove an important theorem concerning the characteristic roots of positive definite matrices.

THEOREM 1: *The roots of the polynomial equation*

$$\det (A - \lambda B) = 0, \tag{B.4}$$

in which B is a real positive definite matrix, are real if A is a real symmetric matrix, positive if A is also positive definite, and nonnegative if A is positive semidefinite. Zero is a root if A is positive semidefinite but not definite.

PROOF: Let λ_n be any root, real or complex, of equation (B.4). Then there exists a vector $z \neq 0$, possibly complex, such that

$$(A - \lambda_n B)z' = 0. \tag{B.5}$$

We write $z = x + iy$, where x and y are real vectors and i is the imaginary unit $\sqrt{-1}$. It follows that

$$\bar{z}(A - \lambda_n B)z' = 0, \tag{B.6}$$

where $\bar{z}$ is the vector of complex conjugates of the elements of z. Hence $\bar{z}Az' = \lambda_n \bar{z}Bz'$, or $(x - iy)A(x + iy)' = \lambda_n(x - iy)B(x + iy)'$, or, after some cancellation of terms,

$$xAx' + yAy' = \lambda_n(xBx' + yBy'). \tag{B.7}$$

Since B is positive definite and $xAx' + yAy'$ is real, λ_n must be real. In addition, if A is positive definite, $\lambda_n > 0$ for all n, and, if A is positive semidefinite, $\lambda_n \geqslant 0$ for all n. If A is positive definite but not definite, the smallest root must be zero.

An important special case of this theorem arises when B is the identity matrix I. In this case the roots λ_n of equation (B.4), now written as

$$\det (A - \lambda I) = 0, \tag{B.8}$$

are called the *characteristic roots of A*. We thus have the

COROLLARY: *The characteristic roots of a real symmetric matrix A are real, positive if A is positive definite, and nonnegative if A is positive semidefinite.*

An important special case of a real symmetric matrix is the diagonal matrix

$$\Lambda = \begin{bmatrix} \lambda_1 & 0 & \cdots & 0 \\ 0 & \lambda_2 & \cdots & 0 \\ \cdots & \cdots & \cdots & \cdots \\ 0 & 0 & \cdots & \lambda_n \end{bmatrix}. \tag{B.9}$$

It is seen immediately from (B.8) that for such a matrix the elements on the leading diagonal are at the same time the characteristic roots of Λ. In order to indicate, in the next theorem, a reason for the importance of diagonal matrices we introduce the concept of an orthogonal matrix. This is a matrix R such that

$$RR' = I. \tag{B.10}$$

Since I is nonsingular, so is every orthogonal matrix. A transformation $x = yR$ with an orthogonal matrix R is called an orthogonal transformation.

THEOREM 2: *Any real quadratic form xAx', where A has characteristic roots $\lambda_1, \cdots, \lambda_n$, may be reduced to the diagonal form $y\Lambda y'$ by an orthogonal transformation $x = yR$. Thus,*

$$xAx' = yRAR'y' = y\Lambda y', \qquad RAR' = \Lambda \quad \text{or} \quad A = R'\Lambda R. \tag{B.11}$$

We cannot give the proof of this theorem here,[97] but we may remark on its geometric significance. Any quadratic equation of the form $xAx' = 1$ is the analytic expression for a second-degree surface in n-space. The orthogonal transformation $x = yR$ may be regarded as having the effect of rotating the axes to which the points x are referred to new positions, to which the points y are referred, and which are coincident with the principal axes of the second-degree surface in question.

If A is positive semidefinite, we can define the diagonal matrix $\Lambda^{\frac{1}{2}}$ of which each diagonal element is the nonnegative square root of the corresponding element of Λ. Then, defining

$$\Lambda^{\frac{1}{2}}R \equiv Q, \tag{B.12}$$

we obtain from the last equality in (B.11),

THEOREM 3: *A positive semidefinite matrix A can be represented by*

$$A = R'\Lambda'^{\frac{1}{2}}\Lambda^{\frac{1}{2}}R = Q'Q, \tag{B.13}$$

where the square matrix Q is real and is nonsingular if A is positive definite, singular if A is semidefinite but not definite.

An immediate consequence of Theorem 3 is

THEOREM 4: *If A is positive definite and P is any matrix with the same number of rows, then P and $P'AP$ have the same rank.*

To prove this theorem we use the fact that the rank of any matrix C is the maximum number of linearly independent solutions of the equation $Cx = 0$. Now any solution x of $Px = 0$ obviously also solves $P'APx = 0$. Conversely, any solution of $P'APx = 0$ obviously also solves

$$x'P'APx = x'P'Q'QPx = (QPx)'(QPx) = 0, \tag{B.14}$$

which is possible only if $QPx = 0$, or, since Q is nonsingular, if $Px = 0$. Hence the sets of solutions of $Px = 0$ and $P'APx = 0$, respectively, are identical, and the maximum number of linearly independent solutions x that can be selected in each case is necessarily the same.[98]

---

[97] See Birkhoff and MacLane [1941, Theorem 19, p. 249, and Theorem 32, p. 305].

[98] This theorem and its converse are proved as Theorem 18 in Chapter IX, p. 249, of Birkhoff and MacLane [1941].

We now prove a theorem which links moment matrices to the concepts of positive definiteness and semidefiniteness.

THEOREM 5: *A moment matrix M is positive semidefinite, and is positive definite if and only if the variables whose moments are included in it are not linearly dependent.*

PROOF: Using the definition of moments given in equation (5.54) we have

(B.15) $$M = \frac{1}{T} \sum_{t=1}^{T} x_t' x_t .$$

The quadratic form

(B.16) $$\xi M \xi' = \frac{1}{T} \sum_{t=1}^{T} \xi x_t' x_t \xi' \geqslant 0$$

because, apart from the positive factor $1/T$, it is the sum of the squares of the vector products $\xi x_t'$. This form equals zero if and only if $\xi x_t' = 0$ for all t. This is the case for some ξ if and only if the elements of x are linearly dependent. On the other hand, if and only if $\xi x_t' \neq 0$ for all $\xi \neq 0$, we also have $\xi M \xi' > 0$ for all $\xi \neq 0$, and hence M is positive definite.

The following theorem finds frequent application to moment matrices in the sample or in the structure.

THEOREM 7: *If the symmetric matrix*

(B.17) $$A = \begin{bmatrix} B & C \\ C' & D \end{bmatrix}$$

is positive definite, then

(B.18) $$E \equiv B - CD^{-1}C'$$

is also positive definite.

PROOF: Since $xAx' > 0$ for all $x \neq 0$, we substitute $x = y[I \quad -CD^{-1}]$, where $x \neq 0$ whenever $y \neq 0$, to obtain

(B.19) $$\begin{aligned} y[I \quad -CD^{-1}] &\begin{bmatrix} B & C \\ C' & D \end{bmatrix} \begin{bmatrix} I \\ -D^{-1}C' \end{bmatrix} y' \\ &= yBy' - yCD^{-1}C'y' - yCD^{-1}C'y' + yCD^{-1}DD^{-1}C'y' \\ &= y(B - CD^{-1}C')y' = yEy' > 0. \end{aligned}$$

Since this is true for any $y \neq 0$, E is positive definite.

If (B.17) represents the partitioning of a moment matrix according to two subsets of the variables involved, then E is the moment matrix of the residuals of the least-squares regressions of each variable of the first subset on all variables of the second subset.

Appendix C

DERIVATION OF THE LIKELIHOOD FUNCTION ASSOCIATED WITH A SAMPLE IN THE MODEL $\mathfrak{S}_T$

In this appendix we complete the derivation, begun in Section 5.4, of the joint distribution of the observations (or, regarded as a function of the parameters, the likelihood function associated with the sample) from the specification of the general linear model $\mathfrak{S}_T$, given in Section 1.3.

In Section 5.4 we reached the conclusion that, in terms of the parameters Π, Ω of the reduced form, this function is

$$F_T(y \mid \bar{z}) = \kappa_5 \cdot \det^{-\frac{1}{2}T} \Omega \cdot \exp \{-\tfrac{1}{2}T \operatorname{tr} ([I \quad -\Pi]'\Omega^{-1}[I \quad -\Pi]M)\}. \tag{C.1}$$

In order to express this function in terms of the structural parameters A, Σ instead, we must, as indicated in Section 5.7, insert for $[I \quad -\Pi]$ and Ω the expressions

$$\begin{aligned} [I \quad -\Pi] &= [I \quad \mathrm{B}^{-1}\Gamma] = \mathrm{B}^{-1}[\mathrm{B} \quad \Gamma] = \mathrm{B}^{-1}\mathrm{A}, \\ \Omega &= \mathrm{B}^{-1}\Sigma\mathrm{B}'^{-1}. \end{aligned} \tag{C.2}$$

These expressions are based on relations (1.24) and (1.25), which in turn follow immediately from the definition of the reduced form.

Since the determinant associated with a product of square matrices equals the product of the determinants associated with the matrices,

$$\det \Omega = \det^2 (\mathrm{B}^{-1}) \cdot \det \Sigma = \det^{-2} \mathrm{B} \cdot \det \Sigma, \tag{C.3}$$

and hence

$$\det^{-\frac{1}{2}T} \Omega = |\det^T \mathrm{B}| \cdot \det^{-\frac{1}{2}T} \Sigma, \tag{C.4}$$

where the vertical bars denote taking the absolute value of the quantity appearing between them.

The matrix product under the trace sign becomes, by the rules for taking inverses and transposes of matrix products,[99]

$$(\mathrm{B}^{-1}\mathrm{A})'(\mathrm{B}^{-1}\Sigma\mathrm{B}'^{-1})^{-1}(\mathrm{B}^{-1}\mathrm{A})M = \mathrm{A}'\mathrm{B}'^{-1}\mathrm{B}'\Sigma^{-1}\mathrm{B}\mathrm{B}^{-1}\mathrm{A}M = \mathrm{A}'\Sigma^{-1}\mathrm{A}M. \tag{C.5}$$

Using (C.4) and (C.5), the resulting expression for the likelihood function is

$$F_T(y \mid \bar{z}) = \kappa_5 \cdot |\det^T \mathrm{B}| \cdot \det^{-\frac{1}{2}T} \Sigma \cdot \exp \{- \tfrac{1}{2}T \operatorname{tr} (\Sigma^{-1}\mathrm{A}M\mathrm{A}')\}, \tag{C.6}$$

where we have used the identity (5.28) to interchange A′ and $\Sigma^{-1}\mathrm{A}M$ under the trace sign. The corresponding logarithmic likelihood function is

$$\begin{aligned} \mathrm{L}(\mathrm{A}, \Sigma) &\equiv 1/T \log F_T(y \mid \bar{z}) \\ &= \kappa_6 + \log |\det \mathrm{B}| - \tfrac{1}{2} \log \det \Sigma - \tfrac{1}{2} \operatorname{tr} (\Sigma^{-1}\mathrm{A}M\mathrm{A}'). \end{aligned} \tag{C.7}$$

As might be expected, the form of L is preserved under any nonsingular linear transformation of A with the corresponding transformation of Σ,

$$\begin{aligned} \overset{\oplus}{\mathrm{A}} &= \Upsilon\mathrm{A}, \\ \overset{\oplus}{\Sigma} &= \Upsilon\Sigma\Upsilon'. \end{aligned} \tag{C.8}$$

---

[99] See, for instance, Birkhoff and MacLane [1941, Chapter VIII, Sections 3 and 4].

To check this, write (C.7) in terms of the parameters $\text{A}^{\oplus}$, $\Sigma^{\oplus}$, substitute the right-hand members of (C.8) for these parameters, and show that the function so obtained is identical with (C.7).

APPENDIX D

DERIVATION OF THE EQUATION $\hat{\Sigma}(\text{A}) = \text{A}M\text{A}'$ IN THE PROCESS OF STEPWISE MAXIMIZATION OF THE LIKELIHOOD FUNCTION (C.7)

In Appendix C the following logarithmic likelihood function was derived:

$$\text{(D.1)} \qquad L(\text{A}, \Sigma) = \kappa_6 + \log |\det \text{B}| - \tfrac{1}{2} \log \det \Sigma - \tfrac{1}{2} \operatorname{tr} (\Sigma^{-1}\text{A}M\text{A}').$$

We wish to find the value $\hat{\Sigma}(\text{A})$ that maximizes this function for some given value of A. If we let $\Psi = \Sigma^{-1}$ and $U = \text{A}M\text{A}'$, both Ψ and U will be symmetric matrices. Ψ is nonsingular and, because of specification (1.7), U is also nonsingular whenever M is positive definite (see Appendix B), as we shall assume. (D.1) may now be written

$$\text{(D.2)} \quad L(\text{A}, \Sigma) \equiv \bar{L}(\text{A}, \Psi) = \kappa_6 + \log |\det \text{B}| + \tfrac{1}{2} \log \det \Psi - \tfrac{1}{2} \operatorname{tr} (\Psi U).$$

Maximization of this expression with respect to Ψ gives the same result as maximizing (D.1) with respect to Σ. If we differentiate (D.2) with respect to each element ψ_{ij} of Ψ (writing $\psi^{ij} = \sigma_{ij}$ for the element in the ith row and jth column of Ψ^{-1} Σ) we have,[100] taking into account the symmetry of Ψ and U,

$$\text{(D.3)} \quad \text{if} \quad i \neq j, \qquad \frac{\partial \bar{L}}{\partial \psi_{ij}} = \tfrac{1}{2}(\psi^{ij} + \psi^{ji}) - \tfrac{1}{2}(u_{ij} + u_{ji}) = \psi^{ij} - u_{ij} = \sigma_{ij} - u_{ij}$$

and

$$\text{(D.4)} \qquad \text{if} \quad i = j, \qquad \frac{\partial \bar{L}}{\partial \psi_{ij}} = \tfrac{1}{2}(\sigma_{ii} - u_{ii}),$$

where $i, j = 1, \cdots, G$. If we now determine a value $\hat{\Sigma}(\text{A})$ of Σ such that $\partial \bar{L}/\partial \psi_{ij} = 0$ $(i, j = 1, \cdots, G)$, we obtain from (D.3) and (D.4)

$$\text{(D.5)} \qquad \hat{\Sigma}(\text{A}) = U = \text{A}M\text{A}'.$$

As remarked already, this matrix meets the requirement that Σ be restricted to be positive definite. The proof that (D.5) indeed indicates a unique and absolute maximum of $L(\text{A}, \Sigma)$ with respect to Σ is entirely analogous to that given by Koopmans, Rubin, and Leipnik [1950, Section 3.1.9] for the case of maximization with respect to Ω.

If we substitute in (D.1) the maximizing value (D.5) for Σ, we obtain as the last term the constant $-\tfrac{1}{2} \operatorname{tr} \{(\text{A}M\text{A}')^{-1}\text{A}M\text{A}'\} = -\tfrac{1}{2}T$. Hence, if $\kappa_7 = \kappa_6 - \tfrac{1}{2}T$,

$$\text{(D.6)} \quad L(\text{A}) \equiv L\{\text{A}, \hat{\Sigma}(\text{A})\} = \kappa_7 + \log |\det \text{B}| - \tfrac{1}{2} \log \det (\text{A}M\text{A}').$$

This is the concentrated likelihood function from which maximum-likelihood estimates A of A can be obtained by further maximization under identifying restrictions.

---

[100] See Koopmans, Rubin, and Leipnik [1950, Section 3.1.7] for a discussion of the rules for differentiating certain functions of matrices.

APPENDIX E

THE CONCENTRATED LIKELIHOOD FUNCTION RELEVANT TO THE ESTIMATION OF SUBSETS OF STRUCTURAL EQUATIONS BY THE LIMITED-INFORMATION MAXIMUM-LIKELIHOOD METHOD

The derivation to be given in this appendix starts from the logarithmic likelihood function (C.7) associated with the general linear model $\mathfrak{S}_T$, which we write again here:

$$L(\mathrm{A}, \Sigma) = \kappa_6 + \log |\det \mathrm{B}| - \tfrac{1}{2} \log \det \Sigma - \tfrac{1}{2} \operatorname{tr} (\Sigma^{-1}\mathrm{A}M\mathrm{A}'). \tag{E.1}$$

Let A be partitioned as follows:

$$\mathrm{A} \equiv \begin{bmatrix} \mathrm{A}_{\mathrm{I}} \\ \mathrm{A}_{\mathrm{II}} \end{bmatrix} \equiv \begin{bmatrix} \mathrm{B}_{\mathrm{I}} & \Gamma_{\mathrm{I}} \\ \mathrm{B}_{\mathrm{II}} & \Gamma_{\mathrm{II}} \end{bmatrix}, \tag{E.2}$$

where A_{I} is the G_{I} by $G + K$ matrix of the coefficients of subset I, consisting of the first G_{I} equations of the structure (i.e., the equations that we wish to estimate), and A_{II} is the G_{II} by $G + K$ matrix of the coefficients of subset II, the last G_{II} equations of the structure, in which we are not interested. Of course, $G_{\mathrm{I}} + G_{\mathrm{II}} = G$. The corresponding partitioning of Σ can be written

$$\Sigma \equiv \begin{bmatrix} \Sigma_{\mathrm{I\,I}} & \Sigma_{\mathrm{I\,II}} \\ \Sigma_{\mathrm{II\,I}} & \Sigma_{\mathrm{II\,II}} \end{bmatrix}. \tag{E.3}$$

With reference to the description of stepwise maximization in Section 5.5, we shall regard the parameters A_{I} , $\Sigma_{\mathrm{I\,I}}$ as parameters "θ" to be retained, and A_{II} , $\Sigma_{\mathrm{I\,II}} = \Sigma'_{\mathrm{II\,I}}$, $\Sigma_{\mathrm{II\,II}}$ as parameters "η" to be eliminated by partial maximization. In doing so we do not attempt to use any overidentifying restrictions on the matrix A_{II} of the second subset of equations. In fact, we have no interest in the identification of these equations, and feel free to replace them by suitable linear combinations of themselves and to add to them linear combinations of the equations of subset I, if that helps in carrying out the elimination of these parameters. We shall therefore make use of the transformation (C.8) with a nonsingular matrix Υ.

In order for this transformation not to affect the equations of subset I, we must choose Υ such that it partitions as follows:

$$\Upsilon \equiv \begin{bmatrix} I_{\mathrm{I\,I}} & 0_{\mathrm{I\,II}} \\ \Upsilon_{\mathrm{II\,I}} & \Upsilon_{\mathrm{II\,II}} \end{bmatrix}, \qquad \Upsilon_{\mathrm{II\,II}} \text{ nonsingular.} \tag{E.4}$$

This gives to the submatrices of

$$\Sigma^{\oplus} \equiv \begin{bmatrix} \Sigma^{\oplus}_{\mathrm{I\,I}} & \Sigma^{\oplus}_{\mathrm{I\,II}} \\ \Sigma^{\oplus}_{\mathrm{II\,I}} & \Sigma^{\oplus}_{\mathrm{II\,II}} \end{bmatrix}, \tag{E.5}$$

as defined in (C.8), the forms

$$\Sigma^{\oplus}_{\mathrm{I\,I}} = \Sigma_{\mathrm{I\,I}}, \tag{E.6}$$

$$\Sigma^{\oplus}_{\mathrm{I\,II}} = \Sigma^{\oplus\prime}_{\mathrm{II\,I}} = \Sigma_{\mathrm{I\,I}}\Upsilon'_{\mathrm{II\,I}} + \Sigma_{\mathrm{I\,II}}\Upsilon'_{\mathrm{II\,II}}, \tag{E.7}$$

$$\begin{aligned} \Sigma^{\oplus}_{\mathrm{II\,II}} = {} & \Upsilon_{\mathrm{II\,I}}\Sigma_{\mathrm{I\,I}}\Upsilon'_{\mathrm{II\,I}} + \Upsilon_{\mathrm{II\,I}}\Sigma_{\mathrm{I\,II}}\Upsilon'_{\mathrm{II\,II}} \\ & + \Upsilon_{\mathrm{II\,II}}\Sigma_{\mathrm{II\,I}}\Upsilon'_{\mathrm{II\,I}} + \Upsilon_{\mathrm{II\,II}}\Sigma_{\mathrm{II\,II}}\Upsilon'_{\mathrm{II\,II}}. \end{aligned} \tag{E.8}$$

Since Σ is positive definite,[101] $\Sigma_{I\,I}$ is likewise positive definite, and hence nonsingular. We shall use our freedom of choice of $\Upsilon_{II\,I}$ so as to make $\Sigma^{\circledast}_{I\,II} = 0$. This means that we replace subset II by such linear combinations of all structural equations that the disturbances of the new subset $II^{\circledast}$, say, are independent of those of subset I. According to (E.7), this is achieved by taking

$$\Upsilon'_{II\,I} = -\Sigma^{-1}_{I\,I}\,\Sigma_{I\,II}\,\Upsilon'_{II\,II} \tag{E.9}$$

for whatever choice of $\Upsilon_{II\,II}$ we shall decide to make below. Substituting expression (E.9) for $\Upsilon_{II\,I}$ in (E.8) we obtain

$$\Sigma^{\circledast}_{II\,II} = \Upsilon_{II\,II}\,{}^{I}\Sigma_{II\,II}\,\Upsilon'_{II\,II}, \tag{E.10}$$

where

$${}^{I}\Sigma_{II\,II} = \Sigma_{II\,II} - \Sigma_{II\,I}\,\Sigma^{-1}_{I\,I}\,\Sigma_{I\,II} \tag{E.11}$$

is again positive definite, because it is a moment matrix of the residuals of the regressions of the components of u_{II} on those of u_I, these regressions being taken in the nonsingular normal distribution of all components of $u = [u_I \quad u_{II}]$. It follows from Theorem 3 of Appendix B (with ${}^{I}\Sigma_{II\,II}$ for A and $\Upsilon'_{II\,II}$ for Q^{-1}) that we can use our freedom of choice of $\Upsilon_{II\,II}$ so as to make

$$\Sigma^{\circledast}_{II\,II} = \Upsilon_{II\,II}\,{}^{I}\Sigma_{II\,II}\,\Upsilon'_{II\,II} = I_{II\,II}. \tag{E.12}$$

In addition to making the disturbances $u^{\circledast}_{II}$ of $II^{\circledast}$ independent of those of I, we have now also made them independent of each other and set the variance of each equal to one. Since this has been possible without placing any restrictions on A_{II}, $\Sigma_{II\,I}$, or $\Sigma_{II\,II}$, we have not used any overidentifying information regarding the equations of II.

As remarked at the end of Appendix C, the likelihood function (E.1) expressed in the new parameters $A^{\circledast}$, $\Sigma^{\circledast}$ is of the same form as (E.1) itself. In writing it down we now make use of the simplifications achieved by a special choice of Υ. The matrix product under the trace in the likelihood function (E.1), written in terms of the new parameters $\Sigma^{\circledast}$ and

$$A^{\circledast} \equiv \begin{bmatrix} A_I \\ A^{\circledast}_{II} \end{bmatrix}, \tag{E.13}$$

becomes

$$\begin{bmatrix} \Sigma^{-1}_{I\,I} & 0_{I\,II} \\ 0_{II\,I} & I_{II\,II} \end{bmatrix} \begin{bmatrix} A_I \\ A^{\circledast}_{II} \end{bmatrix} M[A'_I \quad A^{\circledast\prime}_{II}] = \Sigma^{-1}_{I\,I}\,A_I M A'_I + A^{\circledast}_{II} M A^{\circledast\prime}_{II}, \tag{E.14}$$

and the new likelihood function takes the simplified form

$$\begin{aligned} L^{\circledast}(A^{\circledast}, \Sigma^{\circledast}) = \kappa_8 + \log|\det B^{\circledast}| - \tfrac{1}{2}\log\det\Sigma_{I\,I} \\ - \tfrac{1}{2}\operatorname{tr}(\Sigma^{-1}_{I\,I}\,A_I M A'_I) - \tfrac{1}{2}\operatorname{tr}(A^{\circledast}_{II} M A^{\circledast\prime}_{II}). \end{aligned} \tag{E.15}$$

Instead of determining explicitly[102] a maximizing value $\hat{A}^{\circledast}_{II}(A_I)$ of $A^{\circledast}_{II}$ for given

[101] For a discussion of positive definite matrices, see Appendix B.

[102] This could not even be done without placing further restrictions on $A^{\circledast}_{II}$, which is not identifiable as it stands because (E.12) and hence (E.15) permit a further orthogonal transformation $A^{\dagger}_{II} = \Lambda A^{\circledast}_{II}$, $\Lambda\Lambda' = I$.

A_I and substituting the result in (E.15), we shall merely write the (necessary) first-order conditions

$$\text{(E.16)} \qquad \frac{\partial L^{\oplus}}{\partial \alpha^{\oplus}_{gk}} = 0 \qquad (g = G_I + 1, \cdots, G; \quad k = 1, \cdots, G + K)$$

for a maximum of (E.15) with respect to $A^{\oplus}_{II}$, and then eliminate $A^{\oplus}_{II}$ from (E.15) and (E.16) to obtain the same result.

Contributions to (E.16) come only from the second and fifth terms in the right-hand member of (E.15). To evaluate the contribution of the second term, denote by $\beta^{\oplus,ig}$ the element in the ith column and the gth row of the inverse $B^{\oplus-1}$ of $B^{\oplus}$. Then[103]

$$\text{(E.17)} \qquad \frac{\partial}{\partial \beta^{\oplus}_{gi}} \log |\det B^{\oplus}| = \beta^{\oplus,ig}, \qquad \frac{\partial}{\partial \gamma^{\oplus}_{gl}} \log |\det B^{\oplus}| = 0.$$

The contribution of the fifth term is

$$\text{(E.18)} \qquad -\tfrac{1}{2}\frac{\partial}{\partial \alpha^{\oplus}_{gk}} \operatorname{tr}(A^{\oplus}_{II} M A^{\oplus\prime}_{II}) = -\tfrac{1}{2}(A^{\oplus}_{II} M)_{gk} - \tfrac{1}{2}(M A^{\oplus\prime}_{II})_{kg} = -(A^{\oplus}_{II} M)_{gk}$$

$$(g = G_I + 1, \cdots, G; \quad k = 1, \cdots, G + K).$$

Hence the first-order conditions (E.16) can be written symbolically

$$\text{(E.19)} \qquad \frac{\partial L^{\oplus}}{\partial A^{\oplus}_{II}} = \{(B^{\oplus\prime})^{-1}\}_{II}[I \quad 0] - A^{\oplus}_{II} M = 0,$$

where the numbers of rows and columns of the matrices I and 0 can be inferred from the other matrices in the equation.

The fifth term in (E.15) can be evaluated immediately from (E.19) by

$$\text{(E.20)} \qquad A^{\oplus}_{II} M A^{\oplus\prime}_{II} = \{(B^{\oplus\prime})^{-1}\}_{II}[I \quad 0][B^{\oplus}_{II} \quad \Gamma^{\oplus}_{II}]' = \{(B^{\oplus\prime})^{-1}\}_{II} B^{\oplus\prime}_{II} = I_{II\ II}$$

and is found to be the constant G_{II}. To evaluate the second term in (E.15), we partition the last term in (E.19),

$$\text{(E.21)} \qquad A^{\oplus}_{II} M = [B^{\oplus}_{II} \quad \Gamma^{\oplus}_{II}] \begin{bmatrix} M_{yy} & M_{yz} \\ M_{zy} & M_{zz} \end{bmatrix},$$

in order to write (E.19) in the form of the two conditions

$$\text{(E.22}y\text{)} \qquad \{(B^{\oplus\prime})^{-1}\}_{II} = B^{\oplus}_{II} M_{yy} + \Gamma^{\oplus}_{II} M_{zy},$$

$$\text{(E.22}z\text{)} \qquad 0 = B^{\oplus}_{II} M_{yz} + \Gamma^{\oplus}_{II} M_{zz}.$$

We assume as before[104] that the matrix M, and hence M_{zz}, is nonsingular. Then (E.22z) implies

$$\text{(E.23)} \qquad \Gamma^{\oplus}_{II} = -B^{\oplus}_{II} M_{yz} M_{zz}^{-1},$$

which, if substituted into (E.22y), implies

$$\text{(E.24)} \qquad \{(B^{\oplus\prime})^{-1}\}_{II} = B^{\oplus}_{II} W,$$

---

[103] See Koopmans, Rubin, and Leipnik [1950, Section 3.1.7] for a discussion of the rules for differentiating certain functions of matrices.

[104] See Appendix D.

where W is the nonsingular matrix defined by (5.38). Now, writing for the second term[105] in (E.15)

$$\log |\det \mathrm{B}^{\oplus}| = \tfrac{1}{2} \log \det (\mathrm{B}^{\oplus} W \mathrm{B}^{\oplus\prime}) - \tfrac{1}{2} \log \det W, \tag{E.25}$$

we can evaluate the first term on the right in (E.25) from (E.24) by

$$\mathrm{B}^{\oplus} W \mathrm{B}^{\oplus\prime} = \begin{bmatrix} \mathrm{B}_{\mathrm{I}}^{\oplus} W \mathrm{B}^{\oplus\prime} \\ \mathrm{B}_{\mathrm{II}}^{\oplus} W \mathrm{B}^{\oplus\prime} \end{bmatrix} = \begin{bmatrix} \mathrm{B}_{\mathrm{I}}^{\oplus} W \mathrm{B}^{\oplus\prime} \\ \{(\mathrm{B}^{\oplus\prime})^{-1}\}_{\mathrm{II}} \mathrm{B}^{\oplus\prime} \end{bmatrix} = \begin{bmatrix} \mathrm{B}_{\mathrm{I}}^{\oplus} W \mathrm{B}_{\mathrm{I}}^{\oplus\prime} & \mathrm{B}_{\mathrm{I}}^{\oplus} W \mathrm{B}_{\mathrm{II}}^{\oplus\prime} \\ 0_{\mathrm{II\,I}} & I_{\mathrm{II\,II}} \end{bmatrix}, \tag{E.26}$$

so that, since $\mathrm{B}_{\mathrm{I}}^{\oplus} = \mathrm{B}_{\mathrm{I}}$,

$$\log \det (\mathrm{B}^{\oplus} W \mathrm{B}^{\oplus\prime}) = \log \det (\mathrm{B}_{\mathrm{I}} W \mathrm{B}_{\mathrm{I}}'). \tag{E.27}$$

Taking together (E.27), (E.25), (E.20), and (E.15), the concentrated likelihood function in terms of A_{I} and $\Sigma_{\mathrm{I\,I}}$ is found to be[106]

$$\begin{aligned} L(\mathrm{A}_{\mathrm{I}}, \Sigma_{\mathrm{I\,I}}) &= \kappa_8 + \tfrac{1}{2} \log \det (\mathrm{B}_{\mathrm{I}} W \mathrm{B}_{\mathrm{I}}') \\ &\quad - \tfrac{1}{2} \log \det W - \tfrac{1}{2} \log \det \Sigma_{\mathrm{I\,I}} - \tfrac{1}{2} \operatorname{tr} (\Sigma_{\mathrm{II}}^{-1} \mathrm{A}_{\mathrm{I}} M \mathrm{A}_{\mathrm{I}}'). \end{aligned} \tag{E.28}$$

By further partial maximization with respect to $\Sigma_{\mathrm{I\,I}}$, analogous to that carried out in Appendix D, it can be further concentrated to the form

$$L(\mathrm{A}_{\mathrm{I}}) = \kappa_9 + \tfrac{1}{2} \log \det (\mathrm{B}_{\mathrm{I}} W \mathrm{B}_{\mathrm{I}}') - \tfrac{1}{2} \log \det W - \tfrac{1}{2} \log \det (\mathrm{A}_{\mathrm{I}} M \mathrm{A}_{\mathrm{I}}') \tag{E.29}$$

depending on A_{I} only.

Appendix F

SOME PROPERTIES OF THE ROOTS OF det $(W^*_{\Delta\Delta} - lW_{\Delta\Delta}) = 0$

With respect to the matrix $(W^*_{\Delta\Delta} - lW_{\Delta\Delta})$ it was asserted in Section 6 that if $W^*_{\Delta\Delta}$ and $W_{\Delta\Delta}$ are nonsingular and symmetric, and if $W_{\Delta\Delta}$ is positive definite, then $\rho(W^*_{\Delta\Delta} - lW_{\Delta\Delta}) = G^{\Delta} - 1$ if l is a single root of the equation

$$\det (W^*_{\Delta\Delta} - lW_{\Delta\Delta}) = 0, \tag{F.1}$$

and $\rho(W_{\Delta\Delta} - lW_{\Delta\Delta}) < G^{\Delta} - 1$ if l is a multiple root.

Since $W_{\Delta\Delta}$ is real, symmetric, and positive definite, there exists a real nonsingular matrix Q such that[107]

$$W_{\Delta\Delta} = QQ'. \tag{F.2}$$

Defining further

$$\overline{W} \equiv Q^{-1} W^*_{\Delta\Delta} Q'^{-1}, \tag{F.3}$$

---

105 Using the proposition that, if A and B are square matrices of the same order, det (AB) = (det A)(det B).

106 Since a unique expression (E.28) is obtained without inquiring into the uniqueness of a solution of (E.16), it is not necessary to go into second-order conditions to determine whether a maximum, rather than another type of stationary point with respect to $\mathrm{A}_{\mathrm{I\,I}}^{\oplus}$, has been used—provided that we know that at least one maximum exists and that the highest maximum is reached at a point where (E.1) is differentiable. It has been shown elsewhere [Koopmans, Rubin, and Leipnik, 1950, Section 4.5.6] that this is indeed the case.

107 See Appendix B, Theorem 3.

there exists a real orthogonal matrix R such that[108]

(F.4) $$R'\overline{W}R \equiv V, \qquad R'R = I,$$

where V is a diagonal matrix. Because of the nonsingularity of Q and R, (F.1) is equivalent to[109]

(F.5) $$\det \{R'Q^{-1}(W^*_{\Delta\Delta} - lW_{\Delta\Delta})Q'^{-1}R\} = \det (V - lI) = 0,$$

and also for any l the rank of $(W^*_{\Delta\Delta} - lW_{\Delta\Delta})$ is the same as that of $(V - lI)$. Since V is diagonal, its diagonal elements are the roots l_i ($i = 1, \cdots, G$) of (F.1), and the statement in the first sentence of this appendix follows directly.

With the help of the transformation used in (F.5) it is easy to show that the smallest root l_1 is indeed the absolute minimum of the function (6.27), which we write again here:

(F.6) $$l(\beta_\Delta) = \frac{\beta_\Delta W^*_{\Delta\Delta}\beta'_\Delta}{\beta_\Delta W_{\Delta\Delta}\beta'_\Delta}.$$

Since Q and R are nonsingular, the transformation

(F.7) $$\beta_\Delta = \xi R'Q^{-1}$$

establishes a one-to-one relationship between the vector spaces of β and ξ. Through this transformation the function (F.6) can be expressed in ξ as follows:

(F.8) $$l(\beta_\Delta) \equiv l(\xi) = \frac{\xi V\xi'}{\xi\xi'} = \frac{\sum_{i=1}^{G^\Delta} l_i\xi_i^2}{\sum_{i=1}^{G^\Delta} \xi_i^2} \geqslant l_1$$

since $l_i \geqslant l_1$ for all i. The lower bound l_1 is, indeed, attained if all elements of ξ are zero except that corresponding to l_1. The transformed vector β_Δ corresponding to this ξ is a solution of the equation (6.33) defining the maximum-likelihood estimate b_Δ.

Appendix G

DERIVATION OF THE TEST CRITERIA USED IN SECTION 8 FROM THE LIKELIHOOD RATIO PRINCIPLE

We consider first the test on the set of restrictions

(G.1) $$\alpha = [\beta_\Delta \quad 0_{\Delta\Delta} \quad \gamma_* \quad 0_{**}]$$

on the first equation in a model $\mathfrak{S}_T$, discussed in Section 8.1. In the concentrated likelihood function

(G.2) $$F_T(\beta_\Delta) = \left(\frac{\beta_\Delta W^*_{\Delta\Delta}\beta'_\Delta}{\beta_\Delta W_{\Delta\Delta}\beta'_\Delta}\right)^{-\frac{1}{2}T}$$

[108] Appendix B, Theorem 2.

[109] Because the multiplication of a matrix by a nonsingular matrix does not change its rank. See MacDuffee [1943, Chapter II, especially Theorems 17 and 22 and Corollary 23].

corresponding to (6.20), maximization has already been carried out with respect to all parameters Σ and all rows of A other than the first, without placing any (overidentifying) restrictions on these parameters. Maximization has also been carried out with respect to γ subject to (G.1). The maximum of the likelihood function over all structures of the model $\mathfrak{S}_T$ satisfying the null hypothesis (G.1) (to be tested) is therefore, in the light of Appendix F,

$$\max_{\beta_\Delta} F_T(\beta_\Delta) = l_1^{-\frac{1}{2}T}. \tag{G.3}$$

Under the maintained hypothesis, no overidentifying restrictions at all are placed on α. In that case, as shown in Section 6.4, $l_1 = 1$, so

$$\max_{\beta_\Delta} F_T(\beta_\Delta) = 1. \tag{G.4}$$

The likelihood ratio for testing the restrictions (G.1) is therefore the ratio $l_1^{-\frac{1}{2}T}$ of (G.3) to (G.4), and its logarithm is $-\frac{1}{2}T \log l_1$.

Consider next the test, discussed in Section (8.2), whether the restrictions (G.1) produce identifiability of the first equation. In this case (G.1) represents the maintained hypothesis, and (G.3) the maximum of the likelihood function under that hypothesis. As the null hypothesis (to be tested) we choose the hypothesis of nonidentifiability of the first equation through the restrictions (G.1). We can make this explicit by stipulating as the null hypothesis that the structure contains two equations with a coefficient matrix of two rows,[110]

$$\mathrm{A_I} = [\mathrm{B_{I,\Delta}} \quad 0_{\mathrm{I},\Delta\Delta} \quad \Gamma_{\mathrm{I},*} \quad 0_{\mathrm{I},**}]. \tag{G.5}$$

Since B is specified to be nonsingular, this can only be true for a structure of the model $\mathfrak{S}_T$ if

$$\rho(\mathrm{B_{I,\Delta}}) = 2. \tag{G.6}$$

According to Section 6.3, the maximum of the likelihood function over all structures of the model $\mathfrak{S}_T$ satisfying the null hypothesis (G.5) is

$$\max_{\mathrm{B_{I,\Delta}}} \left(\frac{\min\limits_{\Gamma_{\mathrm{I},**}=0} \det \mathrm{A_I} M \mathrm{A_I'}}{\min\limits_{\Gamma_{\mathrm{I}(\text{unrestr.})}} \det \mathrm{A_I} M \mathrm{A_I'}} \right)^{-\frac{1}{2}T} = \max_{\mathrm{B_{I,\Delta}}} \left(\frac{\det \mathrm{B_{I,\Delta}} W^*_{\Delta\Delta} \mathrm{B'_{I,\Delta}}}{\det \mathrm{B_{I,\Delta}} W_{\Delta\Delta} \mathrm{B'_{I,\Delta}}} \right)^{-\frac{1}{2}T} \tag{G.7}$$

To evaluate this quantity, let

$$\mathrm{B_{I,\Delta}} \equiv KR'Q^{-1}, \qquad \rho(K) = 2, \tag{G.8}$$

where Q and R are defined by (F.2), (F.3), and (F.4). Since Q and R are nonsingular, the maximization (G.2) with respect to $\mathrm{B_{I,\Delta}}$ gives the same result as maximization with respect to K of

$$\left(\frac{\det KR'Q^{-1}W^*_{\Delta\Delta}Q'^{-1}RK'}{\det KR'Q^{-1}W_{\Delta\Delta}Q'^{-1}RK'} \right)^{-\frac{1}{2}T} = \left(\frac{\det KVK'}{\det KK'} \right)^{-\frac{1}{2}T} \tag{G.9}$$

Let R be so chosen that the diagonal matrix V shows the roots l of (F.5) in increasing order,

$$1 \leqslant l_1 \leqslant l_2 \leqslant \cdots \leqslant l_{G^\Delta}. \tag{G.10}$$

[110] The symbols $0_{\mathrm{I},\Delta\Delta}$ and $0_{\mathrm{I},**}$ stand here for two-row matrices of $G^{\Delta\Delta}$ and K^{**} columns, respectively, all of their elements being zero.

Writing

$$K = \bar{K} \cdot \begin{bmatrix} 1 & 0 & k_{13} & \cdots & k_{1G^\Delta} \\ 0 & 1 & k_{23} & \cdots & k_{2G^\Delta} \end{bmatrix}, \tag{G.11}$$

we see[111] that the value of (G.9) is independent of the nonsingular matrix $\bar{K}$ of order 2, which we therefore take as $\bar{K} = I$. Let Σ_i'' denote summation over all values $i = 3, \cdots, G$. Then the partial derivative of

$$\det KVK' = \det \begin{bmatrix} l_1 + \sum_i'' l_i k_{1i}^2 & \sum_i'' l_i k_{1i} k_{2i} \\ \sum_i'' l_i k_{1i} k_{2i} & l_2 + \sum_i'' l_i k_{2i}^2 \end{bmatrix} \tag{G.12}$$

with respect to any l_j $(j = 3, \cdots, G^\Delta)$ is

$$\begin{aligned} k_{1j}^2(l_2 + \textstyle\sum_i'' l_i k_{2i}^2) + k_{2j}^2(l_1 + \sum_i'' l_i k_{1i}^2) - 2k_{1j}k_{2j} \sum_i'' l_i k_{1i} k_{2i} \\ = l_2 k_{1j}^2 + l_1 k_{2j}^2 + \textstyle\sum_i'' l_i (k_{1j}k_{2i} - k_{2j}k_{1i})^2 \geqslant 0 \end{aligned} \tag{G.13}$$

because of (G.10). It follows that

$$\det KVK' \geqslant \det \begin{bmatrix} l_1 + l_3 \sum_i'' k_{1i}^2 & l_3 \sum_i'' k_{1i} k_{2i} \\ l_3 \sum_i'' k_{1i} k_{2i} & l_2 + l_3 \sum_i'' k_{2i}^2 \end{bmatrix}. \tag{G.14}$$

If we define

$$h_{11} = \sum_i'' k_{1i}^2, \qquad h_{12} = \sum_i'' k_{1i} k_{2i}, \qquad h_{22} = \sum_i'' k_{2i}^2, \tag{G.15}$$

these quantities can be freely chosen subject to[112]

$$h_{11} \geqslant 0, \qquad h_{22} \geqslant 0, \qquad h_{11}h_{22} - h_{12}^2 \geqslant 0. \tag{G.16}$$

Then, since

$$\det KK' = \det \begin{bmatrix} 1 + h_{11} & h_{12} \\ h_{12} & 1 + h_{22} \end{bmatrix} = 1 + h_{11} + h_{22} + h_{11}h_{22} - h_{12}^2 > 0, \tag{G.17}$$

we have

$$\begin{aligned} \frac{\det KVK'}{\det KK'} &\geqslant \frac{l_1 l_2 + l_1 l_3 h_{22} + l_2 l_3 h_{11} + l_3^2(h_{11}h_{22} - h_{12}^2)}{1 + h_{11} + h_{22} + h_{11}h_{22} - h_{12}^2} \\ &= l_1 l_2 \frac{1 + (l_3/l_2)h_{22} + (l_3/l_1)h_{11} + (l_3^2/l_1 l_2)(h_{11}h_{22} - h_{12}^2)}{1 + h_{22} + h_{11} + (h_{11}h_{22} - h_{12}^2)}. \end{aligned} \tag{G.18}$$

---

[111] See footnote 105. The possibility that (G.9) may be maximized by a matrix K such that $\begin{bmatrix} k_{11} & k_{12} \\ k_{21} & k_{22} \end{bmatrix}$ is singular is ruled out by the results of the analysis below.

[112] $\sqrt{h_{11}}$ and $\sqrt{h_{22}}$ are the lengths of, and $h_{12}/\sqrt{h_{11}h_{22}}$ is the cosine of the angle formed by, the two vectors $[k_{13} \cdots k_{1G^\Delta}]$ and $[k_{23} \cdots k_{2G^\Delta}]$.

In the fraction in the last member of (G.18), because of (G.10), each of the non-negative quantities 1, h_{11}, h_{22}, and $h_{11}h_{22} - h_{12}^2$ has a (positive) coefficient in the numerator which is at least as large as its (positive) coefficient in the denominator. It follows that the last member of (G.18) is minimized if $h_{11} = h_{22} = h_{12} = 0$. We also note from (G.15) that in that case the inequality sign in (G.14), and hence also that in (G.18), becomes an equality sign. Therefore (G.9) is maximized by

$$K = \begin{bmatrix} 1 & 0 & 0 & \cdots & 0 \\ 0 & 1 & 0 & \cdots & 0 \end{bmatrix}, \tag{G.19}$$

the maximum being

$$\max_K \left(\frac{\det KVK'}{\det KK'} \right)^{-\frac{1}{2}T} = (l_1 l_2)^{-\frac{1}{2}T}. \tag{G.20}$$

The ratio of this maximum of the likelihood function under the hypothesis to be tested to the maximum (G.3) under the maintained hypothesis is $l_2^{-\frac{1}{2}T}$, its logarithm $-\frac{1}{2} T \log l_2$.

Chapter VII

ASYMPTOTIC PROPERTIES OF LIMITED-INFORMATION ESTIMATES UNDER GENERALIZED CONDITIONS

By H. Chernoff and H. Rubin[1]

1. Introduction

In Chapter VI a method was presented for obtaining maximum-likelihood estimates of the coefficients of a subsystem of a complete linear system of stochastic equations.[2] This method was derived on the assumption that the disturbances of the system have a joint normal distribution with mean zero and are serially uncorrelated. (It was also assumed that at a given time the disturbances are distributed independently of all variables predetermined[3] at that time.) If a scientist wishes to estimate the coefficients of the subsystem and/or the covariances of the estimates, either he must be sure on a priori grounds or he must verify that the above assumptions are satisfied for his system. This is sometimes difficult or impossible to do since the assumptions are rather stringent. The question then arises as to whether and how relaxed conditions may be obtained so that the statistician, after having verified that these conditions are satisfied for his system, may blithely proceed with the computational method already developed and still obtain "good" estimates. It is to be understood that any relaxation in the conditions is an asset to the scientist. On the other hand, he may find himself in the position where he has to pay for this asset by specifying conditions which, while considerably weaker, are more complicated to work with. Indeed, the conditions to be presented in this paper are already a compromise in that still weaker ones do exist but they are much more complex.

[1] The authors wish to express their gratitude to Benjamin Lefkowitz for his assistance in clarifying many of the problems they encountered.

[2] See, in particular, Sections 6.1 and 6.3 of Chapter VI. The subsystem can, of course, be the complete system or even only one equation of a complete system.

[3] For a definition of predetermined variables and jointly dependent variables see Chapter VI, Section 1.5.

2. Review of the Original Case

In this section we shall summarize the results given in Chapter VI that relate to estimating (i) the coefficients of a linear system, (ii) the covariance matrix of the estimates of these coefficients, and (iii) the covariance matrix of the disturbances.

Suppose that we have a structure represented by a complete system of stochastic equations,

$$\text{B}y_t' + \Gamma z_t' = u_t' . \tag{1}$$

At time t the elements of y_t and z_t are variables presumed observable without error, those of y_t being jointly dependent and those of z_t being predetermined. The elements of u_t are nonobservable disturbances that have a joint normal distribution with mean zero and an unknown nonsingular covariance matrix Σ. The elements of u_t are distributed independently of those of z_t. The disturbances are serially independent, that is, the disturbances at time t are distributed independently of those at time τ ($t \neq \tau$). Since the system is complete, u_t is a vector with as many components as y_t, and thus B is a square matrix that is assumed to be nonsingular. We decompose u into two subvectors $u = [q \quad r]$. Then (1) may be written

$$\text{B}_\text{I}y_t' + \Gamma_\text{I}z_t' = q_t' , \tag{2a}$$

$$\text{B}_\text{II}y_t' + \Gamma_\text{II}z_t' = r_t' . \tag{2b}$$

Correspondingly, Σ is decomposed into $\begin{bmatrix} \Sigma_\text{I I} & \Sigma_\text{I II} \\ \Sigma_\text{II I} & \Sigma_\text{II II} \end{bmatrix}$. Suppose that we are interested in estimating $\text{A}_\text{I} = [\text{B}_\text{I} \quad \Gamma_\text{I}]$. We assume now that the elements of A_I are subject to certain a priori known restrictions in the form of polynomial equations which are sufficient for the identifiability of A_I almost everywhere.[4]

As discussed in Chapter VI, Section 6.3, the maximum-likelihood estimate of A_I is that value A_I of A_I which, subject to the above restrictions, minimizes

$$V = \frac{\det(\text{A}_\text{I}M_{xx}\text{A}_\text{I}')}{\det(\text{A}_\text{I}W_{xx}\text{A}_\text{I}')}, \tag{3}$$

where $x = [y \quad z]$ and where $M = M_{xx}$ is the moment matrix of the variables x formed according to

$$M_{ab} = \frac{1}{T}\sum_{t=1}^{T} a_t'b_t , \tag{4a}$$

[4] For a discussion of identifiability, see Chapter II of this volume and Koopmans, Rubin, and Leipnik [1950, Section 2], Wald [1950a], and Hurwicz [1950a].

where a and b stand for x, y, z, or any other vector function of t and where[5]

$$W_{xx} = M_{xx} - M_{xz}M_{zz}^{-1}M_{zx} = \begin{bmatrix} W_{yy} & 0 \\ 0 & 0 \end{bmatrix}, \tag{4b}$$

so that, in particular,

$$W_{yy} = M_{yy} - M_{yz}M_{zz}^{-1}M_{zy} . \tag{4c}$$

Indeed, $V^{T/2}$ is the reciprocal of the likelihood function except for a constant factor.

An estimate of the covariance matrix of the maximum-likelihood estimate A_{I} of A_{I} may be obtained as follows. Since A_{I} is subject to restrictions, the elements of A_{I} may be represented as functions of a smaller number of unrestricted parameters. The maximum-likelihood estimate of the covariance matrix of the estimates of the unrestricted parameters is given by $(1/T)(-L)^{-1}$, where $-L$ is the expectation of the matrix of second-order partial derivatives of $\frac{1}{2}\log V$ with respect to the unrestricted parameters evaluated at the maximum-likelihood estimates of these parameters.[6]

Finally, the maximum-likelihood estimate of the covariance matrix $\Sigma_{\mathrm{I\,I}}$ of the disturbances q_t of the subsystem (2a) is given by $A_{\mathrm{I}}M_{xx}A'_{\mathrm{I}}$.

Under the assumptions stated at the beginning of this section and the additional assumption that M_{zz} approaches a nonsingular limit in probability,[7] the estimates described above have been shown to be consistent, asymptotically efficient, and asymptotically normal almost everywhere in the parameter space.[8]

If one were to calculate the estimates by using V in (3) when these assumptions are not valid, the estimates so obtained are no longer maximum-likelihood estimates but are what we shall call quasi-maxi-

[5] W_{yy} has meaning even if M_{zz}^{-1} does not exist. W_{yy} is, in any case, the observed covariance of the residuals from the least-squares regression of the components of y_t on those of z_t.

[6] See Chapter VI, Section 7. For computational convenience L is frequently replaced by the matrix of second-order partial derivatives without expectations being taken. It can be shown that the estimate obtained by this replacement is, everywhere in this chapter, consistent and efficient when the original estimate has these properties.

[7] If $X_1, X_2, \cdots, X_T, \cdots$ is a sequence of chance variables, we say that $X_T \to c$ in probability if $\lim_{T\to\infty} \text{prob}\,\{|X_T - c| > \epsilon\} = 0$ for every $\epsilon > 0$. When we talk of M_{zz} approaching a nonsingular limit we must note (i) that each element of M_{zz} is a chance variable that depends on T and (ii) that each element of M_{zz} must converge to the corresponding element of a nonsingular matrix.

[8] References to proofs are given in Chapter VI, Section 5.2. See Chapter VI, Section 3, for definitions of consistency, asymptotic efficiency, and asymptotic normality.

mum-likelihood estimates. We shall investigate various conditions under which quasi-maximum-likelihood estimates are consistent and/or asymptotically normal.

3. Omission of Variables

We assume that all of the conditions mentioned in Section 2 are valid for the system except that the statistician does not have data on all of the variables. Suppose that data are unavailable for some of the variables that are present in the complete system but not in the subsystem to be estimated. In other words, the a priori restrictions state that, in the subsystem $B_I y'_t + \Gamma_I z'_t = q'_t$, the coefficients of the unavailable variables are all zero. Then the statistician may act as though these variables do not appear at all in the complete system. That is, he may replace the system by a modified one obtained from the original by assuming that throughout the complete system the coefficients of the unavailable variables are all zero. If the subsystem is identifiable in this modified system, the statistician may go through the motions of obtaining maximum-likelihood estimates with respect to the new system. For the original system, these estimates will be quasi-maximum-likelihood estimates. The quasi-maximum-likelihood estimates of (i) the coefficients, (ii) the covariances of the estimates of the coefficients, and (iii) $\Sigma_{I\,I}$ are all consistent almost everywhere.[9]

First we note that the likelihood expression does not actually involve the jointly dependent variables that are not present in the subsystem. Hence, the omission of these variables has no effect on the estimates.

When the missing data concern predetermined variables (which are, of course, not present in the subsystem) there is a loss of efficiency.[10] It is this loss of efficiency that restrains the statistician from arbitrarily ignoring all the predetermined variables (not in the subsystem) that can be dropped without the loss of identifiability. On the other hand, in large systems it is a great computational aid to be able to neglect some of these variables.[11] It may be noted here that if the subsystem con-

[9] See Rubin [1948] for proof. For the case of a single equation a proof has been given by Anderson and Rubin [1950].

[10] The reader is referred to Chapter VIII for an evaluation of this loss of efficiency in a simple model.

[11] In problems in which there are few observations on the variables it has been noted that the use of many predetermined variables may cause a loss of estimability. The reason for this is that the denominator in (3) becomes zero when there are too few observations compared with the number of coordinates of z. In such cases the procedure of "forgetting" predetermined variables becomes indispensable. At the same time, the need for a study of the allowances for "degrees of freedom lost" in the estimation of $\Sigma_{I\,I}$, referred to in Chapter VI, footnote 58, becomes great.

tains only one equation, and if this equation has G^{Δ} jointly dependent variables in it, then at least $G^{\Delta} - 1$ predetermined variables not in the equation must be used for the purpose of identification. However, if our subsystem contains more than one equation, it may well be that we do not need (for identifiability) any of the predetermined variables that do not occur in the subsystem. *Thus it is often possible to compute consistent estimates for a subsystem while very little is known about the rest of the system.*

If the statistician has a choice of variables to neglect he should choose the ones to neglect in such a way as to make W_{yy} as small as possible. As thus stated, the above criterion is rather vague, for no method has been mentioned of measuring the size of matrices. Suppose that A and B are two symmetric matrices. If $yAy' \geqslant yBy'$ for all vectors y, then we can say that A is at least as large as B. (In general, such a comparison cannot be made since, for many pairs of matrices A and B, there are two vectors y_1 and y_2 such that $y_1Ay_1' > y_1By_1'$ and $y_2Ay_2' < y_2By_2'$.)

Every additional z used does decrease W_{yy} in the sense just indicated. If there is a question of which of two z's to use, and one z gives rise to a smaller W_{yy} than the other, then we should use that z. However, one will often find that, asymptotically, if one z is used, certain parameters will be more efficiently estimated while other parameters will be less efficiently estimated than would be the case if the other z were used. It is well to note[12] that W_{yy} represents the unexplained covariance of the residuals from the least-squares regression

$$y_t' = \Pi z_t' + v_t' . \tag{5}$$

Here Π represents the matrix of coefficients of the regressions of each element of y on the elements of z. To reduce W_{yy} it is desirable to use those z's which help explain most of the variance of the y's in the above regression.

It has been stated that the jointly dependent variables that are not present in the subsystem are not involved in the likelihood expression. This fact helps to remove some of the difficulty in selecting appropriate z's by indicating certain elements of W_{yy} that are simultaneously unnecessary for computations and not indicative of the efficiency of estimation of the parameters involved.

4. Errors in Observation

In this section we shall indicate how to treat some cases in which the variables are subject to observational errors. (These errors will be

[12] See footnote 5.

assumed to be distributed independently of all variables of the system and of each other.) We shall often distinguish between the *latent* variable (exact values of the variable) and the *virtual* (observed) variable (the latent variable plus the random error of observation). *When a variable is subject to error, data will be available on the virtual variable but not on the latent variable.*

The general problem of estimation when all variables are subject to errors of observation is quite complex.[13] There are, however, several cases often arising in practice which may be appropriately treated here by considering specific examples. Frequently one finds that, if the latent variable is predetermined in the subsystem to be estimated, one should act as though the latent variable were replaced by the virtual variable and that this virtual variable should be treated as jointly dependent; in other cases (predetermined variables not in the subsystem or jointly dependent variables) the latent variables may be replaced by the virtual variables while the predetermined or jointly dependent character of the variables should not be changed. Considerable use will be made of the results of the preceding section.

Suppose, for example, that one were estimating the coefficients β_{12} and γ_{11} of the first equation of the following system of two equations:[14]

$$\text{(6a)} \qquad B_{I}y' + \Gamma_{I}z' \equiv y_1 + \beta_{12}y_2 + \gamma_{11}z_1 \equiv q',$$

$$\text{(6b)} \qquad B_{II}y' + \Gamma_{II}z' \equiv y_2 + \gamma_{22}z_2 + \gamma_{23}z_3 \equiv r'.$$

If in the observation of z_1 there is a random error ϵ_1, which is normal with zero mean and independent of the predetermined variables, then what we observe is the virtual variable $y_3 = z_1 + \epsilon_1$ instead of z_1.

Elaborating our original system we now have

$$\text{(7a)} \quad B_{I}^{*}y^{*\prime} + \Gamma_{I}^{*}z^{*\prime} \equiv y_1 + \beta_{12}y_2 + \gamma_{11}y_3 = q' + \gamma_{11}\epsilon_1 \equiv q^{*\prime},$$

$$\text{(7b)} \quad B_{II}^{*}y^{*\prime} + \Gamma_{II}^{*}z^{*\prime} \equiv \begin{bmatrix} y_2 + \gamma_{22}z_2 + \gamma_{23}z_3 \\ y_3 - z_1 \end{bmatrix} = \begin{bmatrix} r \\ \epsilon_1 \end{bmatrix} \equiv r^{*\prime}.$$

Our problem is equivalent to that of estimating the coefficients of the first equation of this new system when the variable z_1 (a predetermined variable not present in the subsystem) is unobserved. This new system satisfies all the conditions of Section 2 except the observability of z_1. We should note here that it was necessary to call the virtual variable of z_1 jointly dependent because this variable, y_3, is correlated with q^*. The results mentioned in Section 3 give us consistency for the quasi-

[13] A more complete discussion of shock-error models has been given by Anderson and Hurwicz [1947].

[14] Subscripts t are omitted when there is no ambiguity.

maximum-likelihood estimates for (7a) obtained by ignoring the presence of z_1. These estimates may be regarded as having been obtained by applying the computational technique of Section 2 after replacing in equation (6a) the latent predetermined variable z_1 by its virtual variable y_3, to be treated as jointly dependent. This procedure also yields a consistent estimate of the covariance matrix of the estimates of β_{12} and γ_{11}. However, the technique discussed in Section 2 of estimating $\Sigma_{\mathrm{I\,I}}$ fails. For if this technique is applied, it will yield an estimate of the variance of q^* and not of q. In fact, $\Sigma_{\mathrm{I\,I}}$ is not identifiable under the assumptions made.

The argument we have used applies just as long as the subsystem (7a) remains identifiable when the coefficient of z_1 in (7b) is replaced by zero.

A similar argument may be applied to the case of possible errors in the jointly dependent variables in the subsystem to be estimated. The case of errors in the jointly dependent variables not in the subsystem is trivial since, as has been previously pointed out, observations on these are not required for our estimates.

The remaining case of importance is that in which the predetermined variables not appearing in the subsystem to be estimated are subject to errors of observation. As a special case, suppose z_2 and z_3 in equations (6) are such variables. The virtual variables are $z_4 = z_2 + \epsilon_2$ and $z_5 = z_3 + \epsilon_3$; we also let $\epsilon_2 = z_6$ and $\epsilon_3 = z_7$. Elaborating our original system (6) once more, we now have

$$\text{(8a)} \quad \mathrm{B}_{\mathrm{I}}^{**} y^{**\prime} + \Gamma_{\mathrm{I}}^{**} z^{**\prime} \equiv y_1 + \beta_{12} y_2 + \gamma_{11} y_3 = q' + \gamma_{11}\epsilon_1 \equiv q^{**\prime},$$

$$\text{(8b)} \quad \mathrm{B}_{\mathrm{II}}^{**} y^{**\prime} + \Gamma_{\mathrm{II}}^{**} z^{**\prime} \equiv \begin{bmatrix} y_2 + \gamma_{22} z_4 + \gamma_{23} z_5 - \gamma_{22} z_6 - \gamma_{23} z_7 \\ y_3 - z_1 \end{bmatrix} = \begin{bmatrix} r \\ \epsilon_1 \end{bmatrix} \equiv r^{**\prime}.$$

Our problem is equivalent to that of estimating the coefficients of (8a) when this system satisfies all the conditions of Section 2 except the observability of z_1, z_6, and z_7. Once more we apply the results of Section 3, which give us the consistency of the quasi-maximum-likelihood estimates of (8a) obtained by ignoring the presence of z_1, z_6, and z_7. Again, these estimates may be regarded as having been obtained by applying the computational technique of Section 2 after replacing in equations (6) the latent variables by their virtual variables. The virtual variables for the predetermined latent variables should be considered jointly dependent (predetermined) when the latent variables are present (are not present) in the original subsystem.

5. Distribution of Disturbances

The conditions on the disturbances noted in Section 2 are quite strong and not often satisfied. They require (i) that u_t be distributed independently of the predetermined variables, (ii) that the distribution of u_t be the same for all t, (iii) that the distribution of u_t be normal with zero mean, (iv) that u_t be distributed independently of u_τ for $t \neq \tau$, and (v) that $\Sigma = \mathcal{E}(u'_t u_t)$ be nonsingular. In this section a set of eight conditions will be examined with reference to the system (2). These will then be used to relax the original conditions.

Condition I: *There is a nonsingular matrix* $\Sigma_{\text{I I}}$ *such that*[15]

$$M_{qq} \rightarrow \Sigma_{\text{I I}} \qquad \textit{in probability.} \tag{9}$$

Condition I is, of course, much weaker than the specification that the distribution of $u_t = [q_t \quad r_t]$ be fixed for all t and Σ be nonsingular. Here all that is required is that the distribution of q_t not fluctuate too wildly with time.

Condition II: *There is a nonsingular matrix N such that*

$$M_{zz} \rightarrow N \qquad \textit{in probability.} \tag{10}$$

Apropos of the considerations of Section 3, we may note that this specification is applied only to those predetermined variables that are not omitted in the computation of quasi-maximum-likelihood estimates.

Condition III:

$$M_{qz} \rightarrow 0 \qquad \textit{in probability.} \tag{11}$$

Given Conditions I and II, Condition III is weaker than the independence required in Section 2. It applies only to q_t (as distinguished from u_t). In conjunction with Conditions I and II it states that the sample correlation between z_t and q_t is "small" in large samples.

Condition IV: *There is a matrix* M *such that*

$$\text{M}_{xz} \rightarrow \text{M} \qquad \textit{in probability,} \tag{12}$$

where

$$\text{M}_{xz} = \frac{1}{T} \sum_{t=1}^{T} \mathcal{E}_t(x'_t) z_t \tag{13a}$$

[15] See (4a) for a definition of M_{qq}.

and $\mathcal{E}_t(x'_t)$ *is defined as the conditional expectation of* x'_t *given all (observed and unobserved) variables predetermined at time* t.

It should be noted that M_{xz} is a random variable. If Condition II holds, Condition IV is no stronger than

CONDITION IVa: *There is a matrix* M_1 *such that*

(13b) $$\mathrm{M}_{yz} \to \mathrm{M}_1 \qquad \textit{in probability.}$$

We derive this implication as follows: Partitioning M_{xz} according to $\mathrm{M}_{xz} = [\mathrm{M}_{yz} \quad \mathrm{M}_{zz}]$, we note that $\mathcal{E}_t(z'_t) = z'_t$ and hence $\mathrm{M}_{zz} = M_{zz}$. Finally, $M_{zz} \to N$ in probability by Condition II. Hence the convergence of M_{yz} implies (together with Condition II) the convergence of M_{xz}. Another alternative to Condition IV may be obtained as follows: Assuming that Condition II applies to all predetermined variables in the complete system, we premultiply equations (2) by B^{-1}, obtaining

(14a) $$y'_t = -\mathrm{B}^{-1}\Gamma z'_t + \mathrm{B}^{-1}u'_t$$

and thus

(14b) $$\mathrm{M}_{yz} = -\mathrm{B}^{-1}\Gamma M_{zz} + \mathrm{B}^{-1}\left[\frac{1}{T}\sum_{t=1}^{T} \mathcal{E}_t(u'_t)z_t\right],$$

and, after taking the limit in probability, we see that Condition IVa is equivalent to

CONDITION IVb: *There is a matrix* M_2 *such that*

(14c) $$\frac{1}{T}\sum_{t=1}^{T} \mathcal{E}_t(u'_t)z_t \to \mathrm{M}_2 \qquad \textit{in probability.}$$

Condition IVb then would certainly be satisfied if $\mathcal{E}_t(u'_t) = 0$. Hence, Condition IV would be satisfied if Condition II held (where z is interpreted as the vector of all predetermined variables in the complete system). It would also be satisfied in less restrictive cases, and use can be made of any of the three forms depending upon convenience in the problem at hand.

CONDITION V:

(15a) $$M_{xz} - \mathrm{M}_{xz} \to 0 \qquad \textit{in probability.}$$

This condition can similarly be considered in alternative forms:

CONDITION Va:

(15b) $$M_{yz} - \mathrm{M}_{yz} \to 0 \qquad \textit{in probability.}$$

CONDITION Vb:

$$\frac{1}{T}\sum_{t=1}^{T}\left[u_t' - \mathcal{E}_t(u_t')\right]z_t \to 0 \qquad \textit{in probability.} \tag{15c}$$

Conditions IV and V represent rather mild restrictions on the behavior of u_t and z_t.

Let us call M^* an admissible matrix if there is at least one matrix A_{I} subject to the a priori restrictions on A_{I} such that $A_{\mathrm{I}}\mathrm{M}^* = 0$.

CONDITION VI: *The equation* $A_{\mathrm{I}}\mathrm{M}^* = 0$ *(where* A_{I} *is subject to the restrictions on* A_{I}*) defines* A_{I} *as a* single valued, *differentiable function of* M^* *on the admissible matrices in some neighborhood of* M.

Condition VI is introduced to insure identifiability and consistency. We indicate here only how identifiability is established. Since

$$M_{qz} = \frac{1}{T}\sum_{t=1}^{T} q_t' z_t = \frac{1}{T}\sum_{t=1}^{T} \mathrm{A}_{\mathrm{I}} x_t' z_t = \mathrm{A}_{\mathrm{I}} M_{xz},$$

$$M_{qz} - \mathrm{A}_{\mathrm{I}}\mathrm{M} = \mathrm{A}_{\mathrm{I}}(M_{xz} - \mathrm{M}_{xz}) + \mathrm{A}_{\mathrm{I}}(\mathrm{M}_{xz} - \mathrm{M}). \tag{16}$$

By Condition V, $M_{xz} - \mathrm{M}_{xz} \to 0$ in probability; by Condition IV, $\mathrm{M}_{xz} - \mathrm{M} \to 0$ in probability; and by Condition III, $M_{qz} \to 0$ in probability. Hence $\mathrm{A}_{\mathrm{I}}\mathrm{M} = 0$. Since the solution of $A_{\mathrm{I}}\mathrm{M} = 0$ (subject to the restrictions on A_{I}) is unique, we can assert that A_{I} is identifiable if Conditions III, IV, V, and VI are satisfied.

The condition in Section 2 that corresponds to Condition VI is the one imposing polynomial restrictions on A_{I} that are sufficient for identifiability.

At this point we add the remark that the condition in Section 2 imposing nonsingularity of Σ has been relaxed to imposing merely the nonsingularity of $\Sigma_{\mathrm{I\,I}}$ (see Condition I). Thus it is possible for some equations not in the subsystem (2a) to be identities. Hence, if the variables y_1, y_2, and $y_3 = y_1 + y_2$ occur in the subsystem, the obvious functional relationship between them may be disregarded: $y_3 - y_1 - y_2 = 0$ is considered an equation *not* in the subsystem with disturbance identically zero. Then Σ is singular but, by the above-mentioned relaxation, this fact leads to no difficulty. The privilege of disregarding this relationship is computationally advantageous when the coefficients of the subsystem are subject to linear restrictions.[16]

Under Conditions I, II, III, IV, V, and VI the quasi-maximum-likelihood estimates of A_{I} and $\Sigma_{\mathrm{I\,I}}$ are consistent.[17]

[16] See Chapter X.

[17] See Rubin [1948, Section 5].

CONDITION VII: *The elements of* $\sqrt{T}M_{qz}$ *are asymptotically normally distributed.*

In view of the central limit theorem,[18] this condition constitutes a relatively weak restriction on q and z.

CONDITION VIII: *If* $N_{ik,jn}$ *represents the asymptotic covariance of*[19] $\sqrt{T}m_{q_iz_k}$ *with* $\sqrt{T}m_{q_jz_n}$, *then* $N_{ik,jn} - m_{q_iq_j}m_{z_kz_n} \to 0$ *in probability for all* $i, j, k,$ *and* n.

If Conditions I to VII are satisfied, then the quasi-maximum-likelihood estimates of A_I are asymptotically normally distributed.[20] If Condition VIII is also satisfied, then the quasi-maximum-likelihood estimates of the unrestricted parameters of A_I are asymptotically normally distributed with a covariance matrix that is consistently estimated[21] by $(1/T)(-L)^{-1}$.

6. Nonlinear Equations

We shall indicate how a large class of systems of nonlinear equations may be treated as though they were systems of linear equations, this treatment yielding quasi-maximum-likelihood estimates that are consistent under suitable hypotheses. We shall state a general result and then illustrate by a special example how this result may be applied.

We assume the existence of a serially independent set of vector random variables $\cdots, u_t, u_{t-1}, \cdots$, which will be called *basic* disturbances, and an exogenous[22] vector variable $\bar{z}$ and a set of vector relations,

$$y_t = f_t(u_t, u_{t-1}, \cdots, \bar{z}), \tag{17a}$$

$$z_t = g_t(u_{t-1}, u_{t-2}, \cdots, \bar{z}), \tag{17b}$$

$$q_t = h_t(u_t, u_{t-1}, \cdots, \bar{z}), \tag{17c}$$

such that

$$A_I x'_t \equiv B_I y'_t + \Gamma_I z'_t = q'_t . \tag{18}$$

[18] See Cramér [1937].

[19] The symbol $m_{q_iz_k}$ denotes the element in the ith row and kth column of M_{qz}, etc.

[20] The proof is an extension of one used by Anderson and Rubin [1950].

[21] It should be emphasized here that L is computed from V in the same way as in Section 2.

[22] An exogenous variable is a variable distributed independently of the basic disturbances.

We assume that y_t and z_t are observable so that the quasi-maximum-likelihood estimation of A_I *in* (18) *may be carried out.* We need not assume any knowledge about the nature of f_t, g_t, and h_t as long as Conditions I, II, III, IV, V, and VI are known or assumed to be satisfied. Then the quasi-maximum-likelihood estimates are consistent estimates of A_I and $\Sigma_{I\,I}$.[23] If Condition VII is also satisfied, these estimates of A_I are asymptotically normal and, if Condition VIII is satisfied, the covariance matrix of the unrestricted parameters is consistently estimated[24] by $(1/T)(-L)^{-1}$.

Example: We wish to estimate the parameters α, β, γ, δ, ϵ, ζ of the following system of equations:

$$\tilde{y}_{t1} + \alpha\tilde{z}_{t1}\tilde{y}_{t2} + \beta\tilde{y}_{t-1,3} + \gamma = u_{t1}\tilde{y}_{t-1,1}, \tag{19a}$$

$$\tilde{y}_{t3} + \delta\tilde{y}_{t1}\tilde{y}_{t3} + \epsilon\tilde{z}_{t2} \quad + \zeta = u_{t2}\tilde{z}_{t1}\tilde{z}_{t2}, \tag{19b}$$

$$h(\tilde{y}_{t1}, \tilde{y}_{t2}, \tilde{y}_{t3}, \tilde{y}_{t-1,2}, \tilde{z}_{t1}, u_{t3}, u_{t4}, u_{t5}) = 0, \tag{19c}$$

where u_{t1}, u_{t2}, u_{t3}, u_{t4}, and u_{t5} are the serially independent basic disturbances and $\tilde{z}_{t1}$, $\tilde{z}_{t2}$ are exogenous variables. It is assumed that $\tilde{y}_{t1}$, $\tilde{y}_{t2}$, $\tilde{y}_{t3}$, $\tilde{z}_{t1}$, and $\tilde{z}_{t2}$ are observed variables. It is given that the function h is such that the equations (19) can be solved for $\tilde{y}_{t1}$, $\tilde{y}_{t2}$, and $\tilde{y}_{t3}$ as functions of the other variables and parameters in these equations, that is,

$$\tilde{y}_{ti} = k_{ti}(\tilde{y}_{t-1,1}, \tilde{y}_{t-1,2}, \tilde{y}_{t-1,3}, u_{t1}, u_{t2}, \cdots, u_{t5}, \tilde{z}_{t1}, \tilde{z}_{t2}) \qquad (i = 1, 2, 3; \text{ all } t). \tag{20}$$

Equation (20) is the analogue of the familiar reduced form. As in the case of the reduced form, it is frequently possible to apply equation (20) for $t - 1$, $t - 2$, $\cdots$ to obtain

$$\tilde{y}_{ti} = f_{ti}(u_{t1}, \cdots, u_{t5}, u_{t-1,1}, \cdots, \tilde{z}_{t1}, \tilde{z}_{t2}, \tilde{z}_{t-1,1}, \cdots) \qquad (i = 1, 2, 3; \text{ all } t). \tag{21}$$

At this point we remark that equations (19a) and (19b) would be linear if $\tilde{z}_{t1}\tilde{y}_{t2}$, $\tilde{y}_{t1}\tilde{y}_{t3}$, $u_{t1}\tilde{y}_{t-1,1}$, and $u_{t2}\tilde{z}_{t1}\tilde{z}_{t2}$ were replaced by "simpler" variables. In effect, we shall perform exactly this replacement by suitably defining vectors $x_t = [y_t \;\; z_t]$ and q_t. Let

$$\tilde{z} = [\cdots \;\; \tilde{z}_{t-1,1} \;\; \tilde{z}_{t-1,2} \;\; \tilde{z}_{t1} \;\; \tilde{z}_{t2} \;\; \cdots], \tag{22a}$$

$$u_t = [u_{t1} \;\; u_{t2} \;\; u_{t3} \;\; u_{t4} \;\; u_{t5}], \tag{22b}$$

[23] See Rubin [1948].
[24] See Cramér [1937].

(22c) $$y_t = [\tilde{y}_{t1} \quad \tilde{y}_{t2} \quad \tilde{y}_{t3} \quad \tilde{z}_{t1}\tilde{y}_{t2} \quad \tilde{y}_{t1}\tilde{y}_{t3}],$$

(22d) $$z_t = [\tilde{y}_{t-1,1} \quad \tilde{y}_{t-1,2} \quad \tilde{y}_{t-1,3} \quad \tilde{z}_{t1} \quad \tilde{z}_{t2} \quad \tilde{z}_{t1}\tilde{z}_{t2} \quad 1],$$

(22e) $$q_t = [u_{t1}\tilde{y}_{t-1,1} \quad u_{t2}\tilde{z}_{t1}\tilde{z}_{t2}].$$

From equation (21) it is evident that y_t, z_t, and q_t satisfy relations of the type (17a), (17b), and (17c). Substituting in equations (19a) and (19b) we see that a vector equation of the form (18) is obtained. In this equation the elements of A_I are subject to restrictions which in this case happen to be linear. It is now possible to compute quasi-maximum-likelihood estimates of the unrestricted parameters α, β, γ, δ, ϵ, ζ, of A_I. If enough information is available concerning the variables u_{ti}, z_{tj} and the relationship (19c), it may be possible to discover which of the Conditions I to VIII are satisfied, and thus to check whether our estimates are consistent and/or asymptotically normal.

In our selection of y_t and z_t [see equations (22c) and (22d)] there was a certain amount of arbitrariness. It would have been possible to find other vectors y_t and z_t that would have fulfilled the requirements necessary to obtain (18). For example, the element $\tilde{y}_{t2}$ might have been omitted from y_t. As was noted in Section 3, this omission would not have affected our estimates. Also, we might have chosen other elements to be included in z_t. [In fact, the only elements of z_t that had to be included were 1, $\tilde{y}_{t-1,3}$, and $\tilde{z}_{t2}$, for they are the only predetermined terms appearing in equations (19a) and (19b) with coefficients not known to be zero.] The remarks in Section 3 concerning the effects on asymptotic efficiency of the omission or inclusion of certain z's are applicable here. Hence, if there were a large number of observations, it would be profitable to expand z_t so that z_t would contain elements such as $y_{t-1,1}^2$, $y_{t-1,1}^3$, $y_{t-1,1}y_{t-1,2}$, etc.

An additional remark appropriate here is that Conditions I to VIII are frequently more readily satisfied when an element is withdrawn from z_t and inserted in y_t, provided that identifiability is not thereby lost.

Chapter VIII

AN EXAMPLE OF LOSS OF EFFICIENCY IN STRUCTURAL ESTIMATION

By S. G. Allen, Jr.

1. Introduction

In Section 3 of the preceding chapter conditions were stated under which consistent estimates of coefficients of a subsystem of equations in a complete system can be obtained. In particular, as long as the identifiability of the subsystem is preserved, we can obtain consistent estimates of coefficients in the subsystem by the method of maximum likelihood even if we ignore the presence in the rest of the system of one or more predetermined variables known to be absent from the subsystem. This procedure, in effect, ignores certain of the overidentifying restrictions on the coefficients being estimated. The consistency of estimates so obtained is an important practical result: the use of overidentifying restrictions makes computation costly, and frequently time series for all of the predetermined variables excluded from the subsystem are not available. However, these estimates cannot in general be as efficient, at least in large samples, as estimates that make use of all valid identifying restrictions. Therefore, it is important that the statistician know the effect on the efficiency of estimates when he reduces the amount of information used.

Unfortunately for these purposes, the exact sampling distribution of estimates of coefficients in multiequation systems is unknown. Since their asymptotic behavior is known, knowledge of their asymptotic properties will furnish some guidance in the case of estimates obtained from large samples.

The problem then is that set forth in Section 3 of the preceding chapter. There it was suggested that if predetermined variables must be ignored and if there is a choice as to which of these variables is ignored, then, in the interest of the efficiency of the estimates, the choice should lead to the "smallest" W_{yy}. The purpose of the present chapter is to justify this remark for one simple model by study of the relative asymptotic variances of two different estimates of a coefficient.

2. The Model

Let

$$y_{1t} + \beta y_{2t} \qquad\qquad + \delta_1 = u_t\,, \tag{1a}$$

$$y_{2t} + \gamma_1 z_{1t} + \gamma_2 z_{2t} + \delta_2 = r_t \tag{1b}$$

be a complete system of two stochastic equations, where u_t and r_t have a nonsingular bivariate normal distribution, independent of time t and of the predetermined variables z_{1t} and z_{2t}, and where they have zero means and covariance matrix Σ. It is further assumed that

$$[\mathcal{E} z_{it} z_{jt}] = [\mu_{ij}] = \mathrm{M} \qquad (i, j = 1, 2). \tag{2}$$

In what follows we shall treat z_{1t} and z_{2t} as random variables, with a distribution independent of t, independent also for different values of t, and possessing finite first- and second-order moments. The reader will have no difficulty in rephrasing the reasoning in a form suited to the assumption that z_{1t} and z_{2t} are given time series.

3. Asymptotic Properties of Alternative Estimates of β

Suppose that we are interested only in an estimate of the coefficient β. It will be observed that the model specifies two restrictions on equation (1a), namely, that the coefficients of both z_{1t} and z_{2t} are restricted to zero. From the latter restrictions it is possible to derive explicit restrictions on β so that the identifiability of that coefficient is clear. If we take expectations on both sides of (1a), we see that the constant term δ_1 satisfies

$$\delta_1 = -\mathcal{E} y_{1t} - \beta \mathcal{E} y_{2t}\,. \tag{3}$$

If we denote by $\dot{x}_{it}$ the deviation of a random variable x_{it} from its expected value, then, in view of (3), equation (1a) may be rewritten as

$$\dot{y}_{1t} + \beta \dot{y}_{2t} = u_t\,. \tag{4}$$

Multiplying both sides of (4) through by $\dot{z}_{1t}$ and taking expectations, we obtain

$$\mathcal{E} \dot{y}_{1t} \dot{z}_{1t} + \beta \mathcal{E} \dot{y}_{2t} \dot{z}_{1t} = 0, \tag{5}$$

and, similarly, we may obtain

$$\mathcal{E} \dot{y}_{1t} \dot{z}_{2t} + \beta \mathcal{E} \dot{y}_{2t} \dot{z}_{2t} = 0. \tag{6}$$

The restrictions (5) and (6) immediately suggest a very simple procedure for estimating β: in place of the population moments $\mathcal{E} \dot{y}_{1t} \dot{z}_{1t}$, $\mathcal{E} \dot{y}_{2t} \dot{z}_{1t}$, etc., substitute sample moments in *either* (5) or (6) and solve for β. In fact, either estimate will be obtained by the method of maximum likelihood if use is made only of the presence of the corresponding variable z_i in equation (1b). However, in finite samples an estimate obtained from one of the two equations (5) and (6) (with sample moments substituted for population moments) will rarely satisfy the other equation. The estimate of β is overdetermined, so to speak, when overidentifying restrictions are present. Essentially, this is the reason why the method of maximum likelihood yields estimates that are more difficult to compute when overidentifying restrictions are employed.

To study the effect of ignoring predetermined variables on the asymptotic efficiency of estimates, we shall compare the estimate obtained by the method of maximum likelihood when one of the predetermined variables, say z_2, is ignored with another estimate obtained by the same method but making use of both predetermined variables. Let these estimates be denoted by $b^\dagger$ and b, respectively. To simplify this task we shall derive these estimates through the minimization of variance ratios depending on the single parameter β. These variance ratios have themselves been obtained[1] by maximizing the corresponding likelihood functions with respect to the other parameters, γ_1, γ_2, δ_1, δ_2, and Σ, associated with the model (1). The "likelihood function" from which we derive the estimate $b^\dagger$ is obtained from the likelihood function associated with the model (1) by arbitrarily (and, in general, incorrectly) specifying $\gamma_2 = 0$.

Let

$$M_{pq} = \frac{1}{T} \sum_{t=1}^{T} p_t' q_t , \tag{7}$$

where p_t and q_t are any row vectors, and let

$$\bar{x}_i = \frac{1}{T} \sum_{t=1}^{T} x_{it} , \tag{8}$$

where x_{it} is any of the variables y_{it}, z_{it}. We define the row vectors with two elements each,

$$y_t = [y_{1t} - \bar{y}_1 \quad y_{2t} - \bar{y}_2], \qquad z_t = [z_{1t} - \bar{z}_1 \quad z_{2t} - \bar{z}_2], \tag{9}$$

$$\underline{\beta} = [1 \quad \beta], \qquad \underline{\gamma} = [\gamma_1 \quad \gamma_2], \tag{10}$$

$$\underline{b} = [1 \quad b], \qquad \underline{b}^\dagger = [1 \quad b^\dagger], \tag{11}$$

and the "vector" with one element

$$z_t^\dagger = [z_{1t} - \bar{z}_1]. \tag{12}$$

[1] The procedure for doing this has been indicated in some detail in Sections 6.1 and 6.2 of Chapter VI.

Then b is obtained by minimizing

$$V = \frac{\underline{\beta} M \underline{\beta}'}{\underline{\beta} W \underline{\beta}'} = \frac{m_{11} + 2m_{12}\beta + m_{22}\beta^2}{w_{11} + 2w_{12}\beta + w_{22}\beta^2}, \tag{13}$$

where

$$M = M_{yy}, \qquad W = M_{yy} - M_{yz}M_{zz}^{-1}M_{zy} \tag{14}$$

and where a_{ij} denotes the jth element in the ith row of a matrix A. The quantity $V^{-T/2}$, multiplied by a constant, is the concentrated likelihood function[2] in terms of β. Since b maximizes the likelihood function, it is consistent.[3]

The estimate $b^\dagger$ is obtained by minimizing

$$V^\dagger = \frac{\underline{\beta} M \underline{\beta}'}{\underline{\beta} W^\dagger \underline{\beta}'} = \frac{m_{11} + 2m_{12}\beta + m_{22}\beta^2}{w_{11}^\dagger + 2w_{12}^\dagger\beta + w_{22}^\dagger\beta^2}, \tag{15}$$

where

$$W^\dagger = M - M_{yz\dagger}M_{z\dagger z\dagger}^{-1}M_{z\dagger y}. \tag{16}$$

Now, in general, $b^\dagger$ does not maximize the concentrated likelihood function[4] of β. Nevertheless, it is consistent. The computed value of this estimate is

$$b^\dagger = -\frac{\frac{1}{T}\sum_{t=1}^{T}(y_{1t} - \bar{y}_1)(z_{1t} - \bar{z}_1)}{\frac{1}{T}\sum_{t=1}^{T}(y_{2t} - \bar{y}_2)(z_{1t} - \bar{z}_1)}, \tag{17}$$

which, as $T \to \infty$, converges in probability to the value of β specified in restriction (5),[5] i.e.,

$$\beta = -\frac{\mathcal{E}\dot{y}_{1t}\dot{z}_{1t}}{\mathcal{E}\dot{y}_{2t}\dot{z}_{1t}}. \tag{18}$$

Since b is a consistent estimate, its asymptotic variance is zero. However, we know that $\sqrt{T}(b - \beta)$ is asymptotically normal[6] with mean zero and variance

$$\operatorname*{plim}_{T\to\infty} T\mathcal{E}(b - \beta)^2 = -L^{-1}, \tag{19}$$

[2] See Chapter VI, Section 6.2, and Chapter VII, Section 2.

[3] See Chapter VI, Section 5.2.

[4] For a special case in which $b^\dagger$ is a maximum-likelihood estimate, see footnote 10 below.

[5] We make use here and in the remainder of this chapter of an important theorem on the probability limits of rational functions of random variables. See Cramér [1946, p. 255].

[6] See Chapter VI, Section 7.

where

$$L = -\mathcal{E}\frac{d^2(\frac{1}{2}\log V)}{d\beta^2}. \tag{20}$$

With the knowledge of (19) and an analogous expression referring to $\sqrt{T}(b^\dagger - \beta)$, we can discuss the efficiency of b and $b^\dagger$ for large T.

L itself is not easily evaluated, but a consistent estimate of L is[7]

$$\hat{L} = -\left.\frac{d^2(\frac{1}{2}\log V)}{d\beta^2}\right|_{\beta=b}. \tag{21}$$

It follows that

$$\operatorname*{plim}_{T\to\infty} T\mathcal{E}(b-\beta)^2 = \operatorname*{plim}_{T\to\infty} -\hat{L}^{-1}. \tag{22}$$

To evaluate the right-hand member we remark that, since b minimizes (13), the expression

$$\frac{d(\frac{1}{2}\log V)}{d\beta} = \frac{m_{12}+m_{22}\beta}{\underline{\beta}M\underline{\beta}'} - \frac{w_{12}+w_{22}\beta}{\underline{\beta}W\underline{\beta}'} \tag{23}$$

vanishes for $\beta = b$. Hence the second derivative,

$$\frac{d^2(\frac{1}{2}\log V)}{d\beta^2} = -\left(\frac{m_{12}+m_{22}\beta}{\underline{\beta}M\underline{\beta}'}\right)^2 + \frac{m_{22}}{\underline{\beta}M\underline{\beta}'} + \left(\frac{w_{12}+w_{22}\beta}{\underline{\beta}W\underline{\beta}'}\right)^2 - \frac{w_{22}}{\underline{\beta}W\underline{\beta}'}, \tag{24}$$

when evaluated at $\beta = b$, reduces to

$$\left.\frac{d^2(\frac{1}{2}\log V)}{d\beta^2}\right|_{\beta=b} = \frac{m_{22}}{\underline{b}M\underline{b}'} - \frac{w_{22}}{\underline{b}W\underline{b}'}. \tag{25}$$

Thus we may write (22) as

$$\operatorname*{plim}_{T\to\infty} T\mathcal{E}(b-\beta)^2 = \operatorname*{plim}_{T\to\infty}\left(\frac{m_{22}}{\underline{b}M\underline{b}'} - \frac{w_{22}}{\underline{b}W\underline{b}'}\right)^{-1}. \tag{26}$$

Since formula (19) remains valid if b and L are replaced by $b^\dagger$ and $L^\dagger$, respectively,[8] we obtain in a similar manner

$$\operatorname*{plim}_{T\to\infty} T\mathcal{E}(b^\dagger-\beta)^2 = \operatorname*{plim}_{T\to\infty}\left(\frac{m_{22}}{\underline{b}^\dagger M\underline{b}^{\dagger\prime}} - \frac{w^\dagger_{22}}{\underline{b}^\dagger W^\dagger\underline{b}^{\dagger\prime}}\right)^{-1}. \tag{27}$$

For an evaluation of (26) and (27) we shall make use of some of the

[7] See Chapter VII, Section 2, especially footnote 6.

[8] $L^\dagger$ is defined in terms of $V^\dagger$ analogously to (20). The statement made in the text follows from Chapter VII, last sentence of Section 5.

asymptotic properties of the various statistics involved in these expressions. We first observe that

(28) $$\operatorname*{plim}_{T\to\infty} m_{22} = \text{var}\ (y_{2t}),$$

which by (1b) is

(29) $$\text{var}\ (y_{2t}) = \sigma_{rr} + \gamma M \gamma'.$$

Secondly, we recall from Chapter VI, Section 6.2, "that $\beta_\Delta W^*_{\Delta\Delta}\beta'_\Delta$ is the 'sample' variance, for given β_Δ, of the residual in a regression of the composite variable $\tilde{y}_{1t}$ on $z_{*,t}$ (i.e., on the predetermined variables whose coefficients in the equation being estimated are not specified to be zero)." In our model, $\underline{\beta}$ assumes the role of β_Δ, $\underline{\beta}y'_t$ that of $\tilde{y}_{1t}$. Furthermore, the only variable in $z_{*,t}$ (in the sense of the foregoing quotation) appearing in equation (1a) is identically equal to one. This means that $W^*_{\Delta\Delta}$ in the present case degenerates to the matrix M given in (14), a matrix of moments in the form appearing in (5.49) of Chapter VI, Section 5.6. Our model has specified that $\underline{\beta}y'_t$ $(= u_t)$ is independent of predetermined variables and that the variance of $\underline{\beta}y'_t$ is σ_{uu}. Hence, $\underline{\beta}M\underline{\beta}'$ is, for given β, a consistent estimate of this variance. And since both b and $b^\dagger$ are consistent, it follows that

(30) $$\operatorname*{plim}_{T\to\infty} \underline{b}M\underline{b}' = \operatorname*{plim}_{T\to\infty} \underline{b}^\dagger M\underline{b}^{\dagger\prime} = \operatorname*{plim}_{T\to\infty} \underline{\beta}M\underline{\beta}' = \sigma_{uu}.$$

Elsewhere it has been shown[9] that W is a consistent estimate of the covariance matrix of disturbances in the reduced form of (1a) and (1b), i.e., of

(31) $$\Omega = \begin{bmatrix} 1 & \beta \\ 0 & 1 \end{bmatrix}^{-1} \begin{bmatrix} \sigma_{uu} & \sigma_{ur} \\ \sigma_{ur} & \sigma_{rr} \end{bmatrix} \begin{bmatrix} 1 & 0 \\ \beta & 1 \end{bmatrix}^{-1}.$$

$W^\dagger$, however, is not a consistent estimate of Ω. In particular, consider $w^\dagger_{22}$ as the estimate of the variance of the residual in a regression of y_2 on z_1. This variance must be larger than σ_{rr} if $\gamma_2 \neq 0$ and z_1 and z_2 are not perfectly correlated. In the terminology of linear regression theory, part of the "explainable" variation of y_2 due to the variation of z_2 is included in the "unexplainable" or residual variation when we ignore z_2. To be more precise, the residual from the linear regression of z_2 on z_1, taken in the joint distribution of z_1 and z_2, is defined as

(32) $$s_t = \dot{z}_{2t} - \rho\sqrt{\mu_{22}/\mu_{11}}\ \dot{z}_{1t},$$

where ρ is the coefficient of correlation of z_1 and z_2. Furthermore, if we define

(33) $$r^\dagger_t = r_t - \gamma_2 s_t,$$

[9] See Chapter VI, Section 5.4.

(34) $$\gamma_1^\dagger = \gamma_1 + \gamma_2\rho\sqrt{\mu_{22}/\mu_{11}}\,,$$

then $W^\dagger$ is a consistent estimate of the covariance matrix of disturbances in the reduced form of the system,[10]

(35a) $$\dot{y}_{1t} + \beta\dot{y}_{2t} \qquad = u_t\,,$$

(35b) $$\dot{y}_{2t} + \gamma_1^\dagger\dot{z}_{1t} = r_t^\dagger\,,$$

derived from (1a), (1b) in the manner indicated by (4). The distributional assumptions of Section 2 imply that

(36) $$\mathcal{E}u_ts_t = \mathcal{E}r_ts_t = 0.$$

Therefore, the covariance matrix of the reduced form of (35a) and (35b) is

(37) $$\Omega^\dagger = \begin{bmatrix} 1 & \beta \\ 0 & 1 \end{bmatrix}^{-1} \begin{bmatrix} \sigma_{uu} & \sigma_{ur} \\ \sigma_{ur} & \sigma_{r^\dagger r^\dagger} \end{bmatrix} \begin{bmatrix} 1 & 0 \\ \beta & 1 \end{bmatrix}^{-1},$$

where

(38) $$\sigma_{r^\dagger r^\dagger} = \sigma_{rr} + \gamma_2^2\sigma_{ss} = \sigma_{rr} + \gamma_2^2\mu_{22}(1 - \rho^2).$$

From the expressions for Ω and $\Omega^\dagger$ and from the consistency properties of b, $b^\dagger$, W, and $W^\dagger$, we conclude that

(39) $$\operatorname*{plim}_{T\to\infty} \underline{b}W\underline{b}' = \underline{\beta}\Omega\underline{\beta}' = \sigma_{uu}\,,$$

(40) $$\operatorname*{plim}_{T\to\infty} \underline{b}^\dagger W^\dagger \underline{b}^{\dagger\prime} = \underline{\beta}\Omega^\dagger\underline{\beta}' = \sigma_{uu}\,,$$

(41) $$\operatorname*{plim}_{T\to\infty} w_{22} = \sigma_{rr}\,,$$

(42) $$\operatorname*{plim}_{T\to\infty} w_{22}^\dagger = \sigma_{rr} + \gamma_2^2\mu_{22}(1 - \rho^2).$$

In particular, we note from (42) that $w_{22}^\dagger$ is a positively biased estimate of σ_{rr}.

Finally, with the substitutions available from (28)–(30) and (39)–(42), we may rewrite (26) as

(43) $$\operatorname*{plim}_{T\to\infty} T\mathcal{E}(b - \beta)^2 = \frac{\sigma_{uu}}{\gamma M \gamma'},$$

[10] L. Hurwicz has pointed out that if, in addition to the other assumptions made, z_{1t} and z_{2t} have a bivariate normal distribution, $b^\dagger$ is in fact a maximum-likelihood estimate. For then all assumptions made with respect to the random variables u_t and r_t apply to u_t and $r_t^\dagger$, and therefore the likelihood function may be written in the form $(V^\dagger)^{-T/2}\cdot$constant. If the variables z_i are not so distributed, then $V^\dagger$ need bear no relation to the likelihood function of β. For this reason we have been careful not to call $b^\dagger$ a maximum-likelihood estimate but rather an estimate obtained by the method of maximum likelihood.

and (27) as

$$\text{(44)} \qquad \underset{T\to\infty}{\text{plim}}\; T\mathcal{E}(b^{\dagger} - \beta)^2 = \frac{\sigma_{uu}}{\gamma M \gamma' - \gamma_2^2 \mu_{22}(1 - \rho^2)}.$$

For large T the right-hand members of (43) and (44), multiplied by $1/T$, give approximations to the sampling variances of b and $b^{\dagger}$, respectively.

Since the probability limit of T times the sampling variance, shown for the estimate b in (43), is smaller than the corresponding limit for any alternative (asymptotically normal) estimate (i.e., since b is asymptotically efficient), we conclude that as $T \to \infty$ the efficiency[11] $e(b)$ of b tends to one and the efficiency of $b^{\dagger}$ tends to the limit

$$\text{(45)} \qquad e_0(b^{\dagger}) = \frac{\sigma_{uu}}{\gamma M \gamma'} \bigg/ \frac{\sigma_{uu}}{\gamma M \gamma' - \gamma_2^2 \mu_{22}(1 - \rho^2)}.$$

This expression simplifies to

$$\text{(46)} \qquad e_0(b^{\dagger}) = 1 - \frac{\gamma_2^2 \mu_{22}(1 - \rho^2)}{\gamma M \gamma'}.$$

If we define $b^{\dagger\dagger}$ as the estimate obtained when the variable z_1 instead of z_2 is ignored, then, analogously to (46), we have

$$\text{(47)} \qquad e_0(b^{\dagger\dagger}) = 1 - \frac{\gamma_1^2 \mu_{11}(1 - \rho^2)}{\gamma M \gamma'}.$$

In linear regression terminology, the asymptotic efficiency of $b^{\dagger}$ (of $b^{\dagger\dagger}$) is the ratio of the variance of y_2 "explained" by the regression of that variable on z_1 (on z_2) alone to the variance of y_2 "explained" by the regression on both z_1 and z_2. Clearly, such a ratio must always be less than or equal to one. And it is evident from (46) and (47) that the efficiency of $b^{\dagger}$ (of $b^{\dagger\dagger}$) is a decreasing function of the bias in $w_{22}^{\dagger}$ (in $w_{22}^{\dagger\dagger}$, the analogue of $w_{22}^{\dagger}$ in computing $b^{\dagger\dagger}$) as an estimate of σ_{rr}. Therefore, if either $w_{22}^{\dagger}$ is smaller than $w_{22}^{\dagger\dagger}$, or $w_{22}^{\dagger\dagger}$ is smaller than $w_{22}^{\dagger}$, our choice between computing $b^{\dagger}$ and $b^{\dagger\dagger}$ is indicated. For, in this event, the likelihood is greater that the smaller statistic has the smaller bias (relative, say, to the total explained variance of y_2).

Intuitively we should expect that little harm results from ignoring a predetermined variable if its "explaining value" in the equation system is small. The terms $\gamma_1^2\mu_{11}/\gamma M\gamma'$ and $\gamma_2^2\mu_{22}/\gamma M\gamma'$ might be thought of as indications of the explaining value of z_1 and z_2, respectively. On the other hand, we should not expect an estimate based on the inclusion of two highly correlated predetermined variables to be significantly more efficient than one that ignores one of them. Expressions (46) and (47) show that all the estimates considered differ little in their asymptotic efficiency if the correlation coefficient of z_1 and z_2 is almost equal to one in absolute value.

[11] As defined by Cramér [1946, p. 489].

Chapter IX

SOURCES AND SIZE OF LEAST-SQUARES BIAS IN A TWO-EQUATION MODEL

By Jean Bronfenbrenner

The method of least squares has been widely used for the estimation of economic relationships, and it is therefore of some interest to investigate the properties of least-squares estimates in this application. The properties depend, of course, on the nature of the model defining the relationships to be estimated.

It is frequently useful in economic analysis to postulate stochastic relations, in which a random disturbance is inserted to indicate that the associated undisturbed relation is satisfied, not exactly, but to a given degree of approximation with a given probability. More specifically, we may wish to consider a model in which the current values of a number of economic variables (hereafter called endogenous variables) are simultaneously determined by a system of stochastic relations.[1] The current values of these endogenous variables will be referred to as jointly dependent variables.[2] In a model of this sort the assumptions under which least-squares procedures are known to yield asymptotically unbiased estimates are not fulfilled. Haavelmo [1943], Koopmans [1945], and others have shown that, in fact, large-sample bias will ordinarily result if such procedures are used under these circumstances.

The purpose of this paper is to examine, for a simple two-equation linear model, the sources and the magnitude of the bias in least-squares estimates noted by Haavelmo. A more general linear model is briefly discussed in the appendix to this chapter. It should be emphasized that we are concerned here with the properties of least-squares estimates for very large or, to be precise, infinite samples. The bias under discussion is asymptotic bias—i.e., the difference between the parameters and the probability limits[3] of the estimates in question as the sample becomes infinitely large.

Suppose that the parameters of the following equation,

$$y_1 + \beta_{12}y_2 + \gamma_1 z_1 + \epsilon_1 = u_1 , \tag{1}$$

are to be estimated from the observed points $(y_{1t}, \; y_{2t}, \; z_{1t})$

[1] A detailed description of a linear version of such a model is given in Chapter VI, Section 1.3.

[2] For further discussion of this distinction, see Chapter VI, Section 1.5.

[3] For the definitions of probability limit and asymptotic bias, see Chapter VI, Section 3.

$(t = 1, 2, 3, \cdots)$; and suppose that y_1 and y_2 are also constrained by a second relation,

$$\beta_{21}y_1 + y_2 + \gamma_2 z_2 + \epsilon_2 = u_2 . \tag{2}$$

The variables y_1, y_2, z_1, and z_2 are observable, while u_1 and u_2 are non-observable random disturbances. Throughout this chapter the variables denoted by the letter y are assumed to be endogenous. The variables denoted by z, which will be called exogenous, are assumed to be determined outside of the system of equations under consideration. Thus they influence, but are not influenced by, the endogenous variables. They may be either random variables or fixed functions of time. For the purposes of this chapter we need merely assume that they are determined independently of the disturbances, u_i, that their second moments approach either a finite limit or a finite probability limit as the sample size increases indefinitely, and that the matrix of these moments is non-singular in the limit. The random disturbances u_i represent, not errors in measurement, from which we abstract here, but the aggregate effect of many omitted variables, each exercising small influence. The models with which we deal are therefore pure "shock" models. It is further assumed that u_1 and u_2 have a joint normal distribution, which is constant over time and independent of the exogenous variables, and that they have expected values equal to zero, variances equal to σ_1^2 and σ_2^2, respectively, and covariance equal to σ_{12}.

We note that, in the model consisting of equations (1) and (2), almost all structures meet the conditions for identifiability;[4] consistent and asymptotically unbiased estimation[5] of the parameters of these equations is therefore possible.

For concreteness, let (1) and (2) be supply and demand relations for an individual commodity, with y_1 the quantity of the commodity, y_2 its price, z_1 the wage rate in the industry producing the commodity, and z_2 income.[6]

We may think of the plane

$$y_1 + \beta_{12}y_2 + \gamma_1 z_1 + \epsilon_1 = 0 \tag{3}$$

as representing the "true" or "undisturbed" relationship that would exist between y_1, y_2, and z_1 if we could abstract from the disturbance u_1.[7]

[4] See Chapter II. Only if $\gamma_1 = 0$ or $\gamma_2 = 0$ would equation (1) or (2), respectively, lose identifiability.

[5] For definitions of consistency and asymptotic unbiasedness, see Chapter VI, Section 3.

[6] This requires some possibly unrealistic assumptions about the exogenous character of income and the wage rate.

[7] Since we are dealing with a linear relationship, (3) may also be thought of as a relationship between expected values and, in this sense, an "average" relationship.

Furthermore, each observed point (y_{1t}, y_{2t}, z_{1t}) may be considered as an approximation to some "true" point $(\bar{y}_{1t}, \bar{y}_{2t}, z_{1t})$ on the plane (3). By the "true point" we shall mean the point which would be observed if u_{1t} and u_{2t} in (1) and (2) were both equal to zero, given the observed values of z_{1t} and z_{2t}. The reason for assigning the same values to z_{1t} and z_{2t} in this definition of the "true point" as these variables have in the "observed point" is that, under our assumptions, z_1 and z_2 are determined in some way entirely independent of u_1 and u_2. We may now say that the observed point (y_{1t}, y_{2t}, z_{1t}) is a composite of three things: the "true" point, the effect of u_{1t}, and the effect of u_{2t}.

We wish to examine in particular the effect of u_{1t}, which must, of course, be distributed among the several coordinates of the observed point in a manner compatible with (1). When the values of the variables and the disturbance at a particular time t are substituted in (1), the term $\gamma_1 z_{1t}$ on the left-hand side remains exactly what it would have been if the coordinates of the "true" point had been substituted, and the whole effect of the disturbance u_{1t} must be distributed among the other terms, reflecting itself in deviations from the values these terms would have had for $u_{1t} = u_{2t} = 0$. This is equivalent to saying that if repeated samples could be taken for each t (each involving a different drawing u_{1t}), then y_{1t} and y_{2t} would absorb all of the sampling fluctuation in u_{1t}.[8]

Except under very special circumstances, we are now prohibited from assuming that y_2, like z_1, remains unaffected by sampling fluctuations in u_1. More precisely, we are prohibited from assuming that in repeated samples, with different drawings of u_{1t}, both z_{1t} and y_{2t} would be independent of u_{1t}, while y_{1t} absorbed the full effect of the sampling fluctuations in u_{1t}. For y_1 and y_2 are constrained by relation (2) as well as relation (1); and, for any particular z_{2t}, different values of y_{1t} (reflecting different values of u_{1t}) would require correspondingly different values of y_{2t} in order that (2) might be satisfied. An exception to this could occur only in the unlikely case of a singular distribution of u_1 and u_2 such that $u_2 = \beta_{21} u_1$, with the result that u_2 is required always to move in such a way as to cancel out the changes in y_1 due to variation in u_1.

Thus, in general, the effect of sampling fluctuation in u_1 is not confined to either y_1 or y_2 but must be present in both of these variables. The failure of the tth observed point to lie on the plane (3) is due to deviations of both y_{1t} and y_{2t} from the values $\bar{y}_{1t}$ and $\bar{y}_{2t}$ they would have had for $u_{1t} = u_{2t} = 0$. In view of this, we could hardly expect to obtain an unbiased estimate of (3)—even from an infinite sample—by minimizing

[8] It is, of course, impossible to draw repeated samples when the observations consist of historical time series; but the concept of such samples is used in assessing the probable accuracy of estimates derived from one sample. See also Chapter VI, Section 3, first paragraph.

the sum-square residual in the y_1-direction while disregarding the size of the residuals in the y_2-direction. We would, of course, do no better by minimizing residuals in the y_2-direction. This is the basic objection to using least-squares methods to estimate the parameters of a stochastic equation that is part of a system of simultaneous equations.

In order to isolate the several factors which affect the size of the asymptotic bias in least-squares estimation of (1), let us examine certain still simpler models. In the figures that follow, solid lines represent "true" or "undisturbed" relationships. Dotted lines represent relationships that hold for specific nonzero values of the disturbance. We may think of such a nonzero value as causing the relationship to shift from

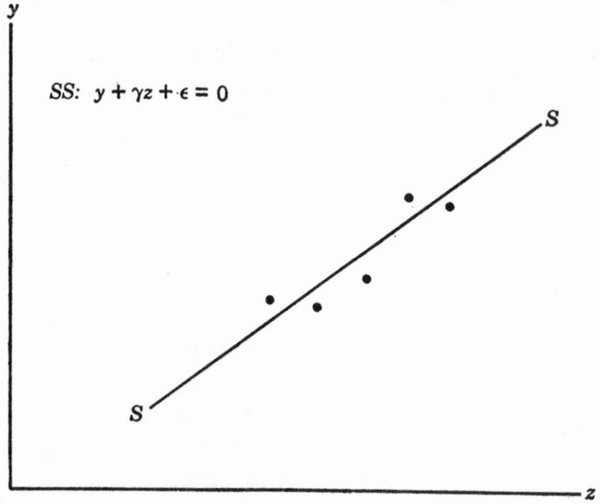

FIGURE 1—Case I.

its solid-line position to a dotted-line position. The number of points (observations) shown in each figure is necessarily finite, but the reader should understand that we are concerned with what happens when the number of observations increases indefinitely.

CASE I: $$y + \gamma z + \epsilon = u.$$

This is a situation in which the least-squares procedure is entirely appropriate for the estimation of γ. Under our assumptions, the value of z is obtained from its own independent law of behavior, and the value of y corresponding to this z is then determined from the above relation. For example, z might be a price set by a governmental authority and y the quantity supplied. Thus we may think of z as capable of free variation along its axis, and for different values of z we observe a number of different points which, except for the effect of sampling fluctuations in u, trace out the line

$$y + \gamma z + \epsilon = 0.$$

Furthermore, we know that the failure of an observed point to lie on this line is due exclusively to the influence of sampling fluctuations in u upon the y-coordinate of the point. In this situation minimizing the sum-square residual in the y-direction can be shown to yield unbiased estimates of γ in samples of any size.[9]

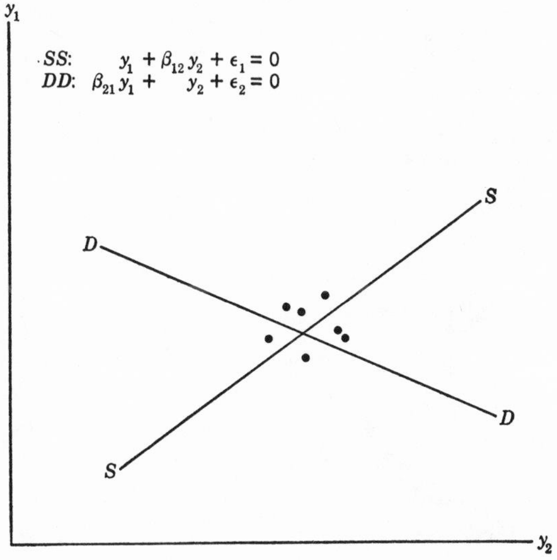

FIGURE 2—Case II.

In all subsequent cases we consider a model specifying two equations and study the asymptotic bias incurred if the first equation were to be estimated by the least-squares method with y_1 selected as the so-called "dependent" variable.

CASE II:

$$y_1 + \beta_{12} y_2 + \epsilon_1 = u_1 ,$$
$$\beta_{21} y_1 + y_2 + \epsilon_2 = u_2 .$$

This is a case of lack of identifiability.[10] Here y_1 and y_2 are constrained by two relationships, which are sufficient to determine uniquely the

[9] See Chapter VI, Section 4.1.
[10] See Chapter II.

point $(\bar{y}_{1t}, \bar{y}_{2t}) = (\bar{y}_1, \bar{y}_2)$ that satisfies both "undisturbed" relationships for all t. Observed points stray from the intersection of DD and SS only to the extent prescribed by u_1 and u_2. Thus, all we can observe is a scatter of points (y_{1t}, y_{2t}) about $(\bar{y}_1, \bar{y}_2)$, and no tracing out of either line can be obtained. Estimation of β_{12}, or of any of the parameters β_{21}, σ_1^2, σ_{12}, σ_2^2, is therefore impossible,[11] either by least squares[12] or by any other method.

CASE III:

$$\begin{aligned} y_1 + \beta_{12}y_2 \qquad\qquad + \epsilon_1 &= u_1, \\ \beta_{21}y_1 + \quad y_2 + \gamma z + \epsilon_2 &= u_2, \\ \sigma_{12} &= 0. \end{aligned}$$

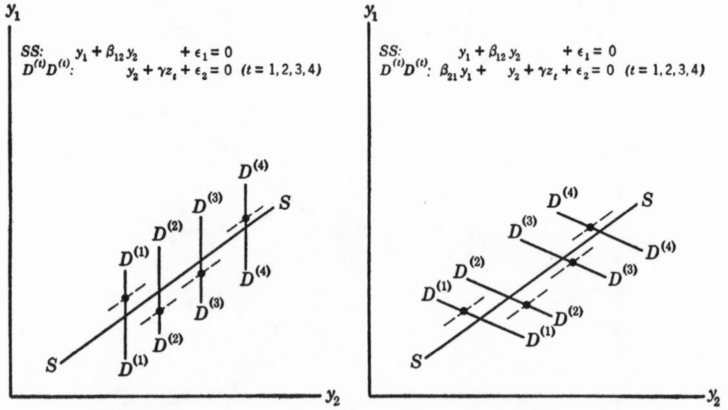

Case IIIa: $\beta_{21} = 0$ Case IIIb: $\beta_{21} \neq 0$

FIGURE 3

In Case III an exogenous variable z appears in the second equation only. For a fixed value of z this equation can again be reduced to a two-dimensional relationship between y_1 and y_2. We may represent the "undisturbed" relationship, conditional on this value of z, by a line in the y_1y_2-plane. For different levels of z we obtain a family of parallel lines (see Figure 3). The "undisturbed" point $(\bar{y}_{1t}, \bar{y}_{2t})$ corresponding to any observed point (y_{1t}, y_{2t}) is determined as the intersection of the

[11] In the absence of additional, very specific restrictions on the joint distribution of the u_i.

[12] For the reader of Chapter VI, Section 1, we may add that if a least-squares statistic "estimating" β_{12} with y_1 selected as "dependent variable" is determined nevertheless, its probability limit is the regression coefficient ω_{12}/ω_{22} of v_1 on v_2 in the distribution of the disturbances of the reduced form; see Chapter VI, equations (1.23)–(1.25).

line SS with the line of the above family that corresponds to $z = z_t$. Thus it is again possible to observe points that differ as to the "undisturbed" point which they approximate, so that we have a scatter about the entire line SS rather than about a single point of this line. The presence of z in the second equation gives us identifiability of the first by permitting y_2 to behave in a manner that resembles the free variation of z in Case I.

Note that the equation not containing z is the one whose graph is traced out. If both equations contained z, both lines would shift with variations in z. Then the observed points would approximate intersec-

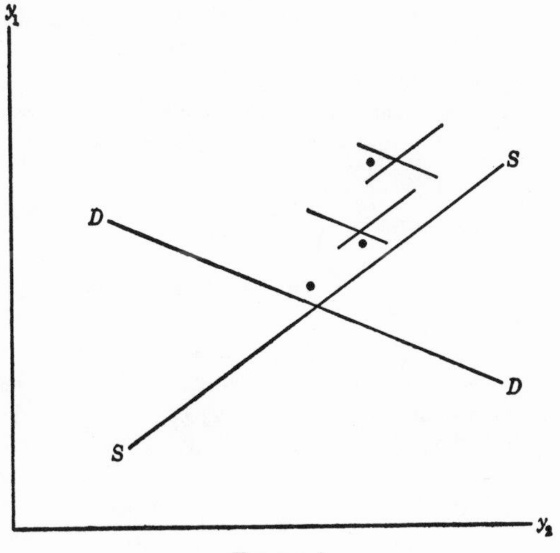

FIGURE 4

tions of the sort shown in Figure 4 and would trace out a line corresponding to a linear combination of the two equations.[13]

Now we come to the important distinction between Case IIIa, in which $\beta_{21} = 0$, and Case IIIb, in which β_{21} is different from zero. Let us consider an observed point (y_{1t}, y_{2t}, z_{1t}) with which is associated some specific value of u_1, say u_{1t}. If $u_{1t} \neq 0$, its effect is to shift SS in a parallel fashion—i.e., the slope β_{12} remains the same, while the intercept becomes $u_{1t} - \epsilon_1$ instead of $-\epsilon_1$. If we assume for the moment that $u_2 = 0$, the observed point will be determined as the intersection of the

[13] If z actually entered into the first equation we should not attempt to estimate this relation from observations on y_1 and y_2 only. Proceeding to three dimensions we would find that identifiability was lacking and that the situation was analogous to Case II.

shifted line SS (represented in Figure 3 by a dotted line) with the line DD corresponding to $z = z_t$. We see that in Case IIIa the y_2-coordinate of the observed point remains what it would have been for $u_{1t} = 0$, while u_{1t} is added to the y_1-coordinate. Minimizing the sum-square residual in the y_1-direction therefore seems entirely appropriate. In Case IIIb, however, the effect of sampling fluctuations in u_{1t} is present in both y_{1t} and y_{2t}, and neither coordinate is the same as for the point determined by the intersection of the "undisturbed" relationships. Thus, in Case IIIb there seems to be no reason to suppose that minimizing residuals in the y_1-direction is in any way preferable to minimizing in the y_2-direction or that either process should result in an unbiased estimate of β_{12}. This case represents a third situation, intermediate between Cases I and II, since estimation of the first equation is now possible (i.e., identifiability is present) but the least-squares estimates contain asymptotic bias. This bias may be found explicitly if we solve for y_1 and y_2 in terms of z, u_1, and u_2 to obtain the reduced form:

$$y_1 = \frac{1}{1 - \beta_{12}\beta_{21}} (\beta_{12}\gamma z + \beta_{12}\epsilon_2 - \epsilon_1 + u_1 - \beta_{12}u_2), \tag{4}$$

$$y_2 = \frac{1}{1 - \beta_{12}\beta_{21}} (-\gamma z + \beta_{21}\epsilon_1 - \epsilon_2 - \beta_{21}u_1 + u_2). \tag{5}$$

If the variance of z approaches a finite limit or a finite probability limit, μ_{zz}, as the sample size increases indefinitely, then the least-squares "estimate" $b_{12}^{(1)}$ of β_{12}, obtained by selecting y_1 as the dependent variable in (1), approaches the finite probability limit

$$\beta_{12}^{(1)} = \operatorname*{plim}_{T\to\infty} b_{12}^{(1)} = \operatorname*{plim}_{T\to\infty} - \frac{\overset{0}{m}_{y_1y_2}}{\overset{0}{m}_{y_2y_2}}, \tag{6}$$

where

$$\overset{0}{m}_{y_iy_j} = \frac{1}{T}\sum_{t=1}^{T} y_{it}y_{jt} - \frac{1}{T^2}\sum_{t=1}^{T} y_{it} \sum_{t=1}^{T} y_{jt} \tag{7}$$

is the second moment of y_i with y_j. Under the assumptions of Case III, the second moments of u_1 with u_2, u_1 with z, and u_2 with z all have probability limits equal to zero, while the variances of u_1, u_2, and z have the probability limits σ_1^2, σ_2^2, and μ_{zz}, respectively. Thus, when we substitute (4) and (5) in (6), we obtain

$$\beta_{12}^{(1)} = \frac{\beta_{21}\sigma_1^2 + \beta_{12}\sigma_2^2 + \beta_{12}\gamma^2\mu_{zz}}{\beta_{21}^2\sigma_1^2 + \sigma_2^2 + \gamma^2\mu_{zz}}. \tag{8}$$

Since the sample moments are consistent and asymptotically unbiased estimates of the population moments and since we are dealing with a rational function of the moments, we may regard the probability limit $\beta_{12}^{(1)}$ of $b_{12}^{(1)}$ as the regression coefficient of y_1 on y_2 in a sample of infinite size. The asymptotic bias that is present when the least-squares regression coefficient $b_{12}^{(1)}$ is used as an "estimate" of β_{12} is therefore given by the difference $\beta_{12}^{(1)} - \beta_{12}$.

From (8) it is clear that $\beta_{12}^{(1)} = \beta_{12}$ when $\beta_{21} = 0$, as in Case IIIa. This is what we should expect, both from the graphical argument and from the fact that y_2 is independent of u_1 if y_1 does not appear in the second relation and if u_1 and u_2 are independently distributed. This case then reduces to Case I.

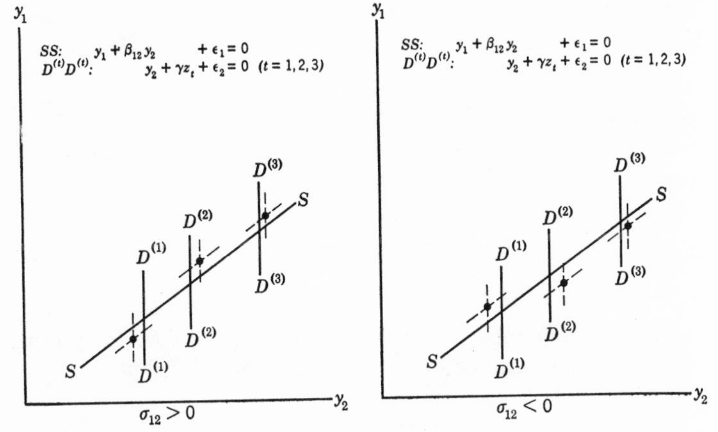

FIGURE 5—Case IV.

For $\beta_{21} \neq 0$, the asymptotic least-squares bias in the estimation of β_{12} is

$$\beta_{12}^{(1)} - \beta_{12} = \frac{(1 - \beta_{12}\beta_{21})\beta_{21}\sigma_1^2}{\beta_{21}^2\sigma_1^2 + \sigma_2^2 + \gamma^2\mu_{zz}}. \tag{9}$$

This is a special case of a more general formula, which will be developed later.

CASE IV:

$$y_1 + \beta_{12}y_2 \qquad + \epsilon_1 = u_1,$$
$$y_2 + \gamma z + \epsilon_2 = u_2,$$
$$\sigma_{12} \neq 0.$$

We have not yet discussed the effect of correlation between u_1 and u_2. In order to distinguish this effect from that of β_{21}, we now assume

$\beta_{21} = 0$. Suppose that we have a positive correlation between the u_i ($\sigma_{12} > 0$) and suppose that SS shifts upward because of a positive value of u_{1t}. Then the line DD that corresponds to $z = z_t$ will be shifted to the right by a positive value of u_{2t} more frequently than it is shifted to the left by a negative u_{2t}. Similarly, downward shifts in SS will tend to be accompanied more often by leftward shifts of DD. This gives us the same kind of pattern of observed points as in Case IIIb, where the lines DD were diagonal rather than vertical (reflecting the presence of β_{21}) but where σ_{12} was assumed to be zero. (Compare the figure for $\sigma_{12} < 0$ with Case IIIb in Figure 3.) In particular, the observed points lie in a similar position relative to the corresponding "undisturbed" points. Again the effect of sampling fluctuations in u_1 is present in both y_1 and y_2. Neither coordinate remains unaffected by the occurrence of a nonzero value of u_1 and there is no reason to suppose that minimizing residuals in the y_1-direction will lead to an unbiased estimate of β_{12}. Again assuming that the variance of z approaches the finite limit or probability limit μ_{zz}, we may obtain an explicit expression for the bias that occurs in this case. Solving for y_1 and y_2, we have for the reduced form

$$(10) \qquad y_1 = \beta_{12}\gamma z + \beta_{12}\epsilon_2 - \epsilon_1 + u_1 - \beta_{12}u_2 ,$$

$$(11) \qquad y_2 = -\gamma z - \epsilon_2 + u_2 .$$

By a calculation similar to that used in Case III we then find that the least-squares estimate of β_{12} approaches the probability limit

$$\beta_{12}^{(1)} = \frac{\beta_{12}\sigma_2^2 + \beta_{12}\gamma^2\mu_{zz} - \sigma_{12}}{\sigma_2^2 + \gamma^2\mu_{zz}}.$$

The asymptotic least-squares bias in the estimation of β_{12} is therefore

$$(12) \qquad \beta_{12}^{(1)} - \beta_{12} = \frac{-\sigma_{12}}{\sigma_2^2 + \gamma^2\mu_{zz}}.$$

The correlation ρ_{12} between u_1 and u_2 is, of course, contained in the term σ_{12}, since $\sigma_{12} = \rho_{12}\sigma_1\sigma_2$, and (12) may be written so that ρ_{12} appears explicitly in the expression for bias.

CASE V:

$$\begin{aligned} y_1 + \beta_{12}y_2 \qquad\quad + \epsilon_1 &= u_1 , \\ \beta_{21}y_1 + \quad y_2 + \gamma z + \epsilon_2 &= u_2 , \\ \sigma_{12} &\neq 0. \end{aligned}$$

More generally, we may consider cases in which both β_{21} and σ_{12} are different from zero. Our two equations then have the same form as in

Case III, omitting the restriction $\sigma_{12} = 0$. Such a situation is shown in Figure 6. Clearly the two sources of bias may conceivably cancel each other in this case, if, for example, a situation like the one on the right in Figure 3 is combined with precisely the right amount of positive correlation between the disturbances. This situation is closely connected with the condition discussed earlier,

$$u_2 = \beta_{21}u_1 , \tag{13}$$

under which the y_2-coordinate will remain unaffected by sampling fluctuations in u_1. However, to avoid bias in large samples it is not neces-

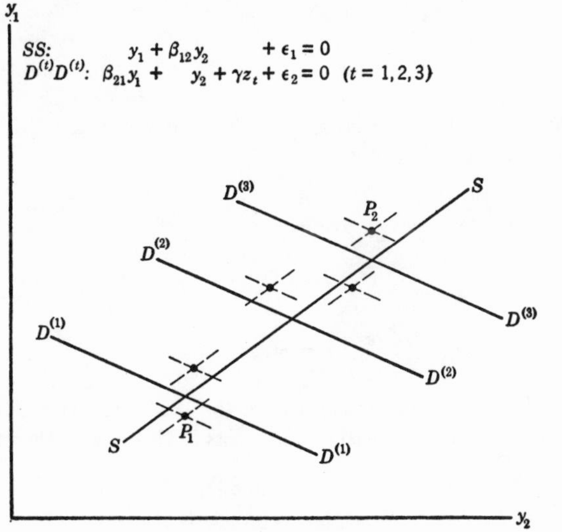

FIGURE 6—Case V.

sary that each y_{2t} assume the "true" value $\bar{y}_{2t}$ that would occur for $u_{1t} = u_{2t} = 0$. It is sufficient that the conditional expectation of y_{2t} for given values of z_{1t}, z_{2t}, and u_{1t} be $\bar{y}_{2t}$. Thus, it is sufficient for the absence of bias that

$$\mathcal{E}(u_2 \mid u_1) = \beta_{21}u_1 , \tag{14}$$

and this is precisely the situation under which the two sources of bias cancel each other.

In Figure 6 the dotted lines, as usual, represent the shifts caused by the occurrence of particular nonzero values of u_1 and u_2. Note that for points like P_1 and P_2 the y_2-coordinate is what it would be for $u_1 = u_2 = 0$.

If the correlation between u_1 and u_2 is such as to make these points typical (in the sense that the value of u_2 is its expected value, given u_1), then the two sources of bias cancel each other.

General two-equation linear case. Let us now return to the model consisting of equations (1) and (2). This is still more general because both of the equations contain exogenous variables. The expression for bias in this case is obtained as follows. Solving for y_1 and y_2, we have

$$y_1 = \frac{1}{1 - \beta_{12}\beta_{21}} (-\gamma_1 z_1 + \beta_{12}\gamma_2 z_2 - \epsilon_1 + \beta_{12}\epsilon_2 + u_1 - \beta_{12}u_2), \tag{15}$$

$$y_2 = \frac{1}{1 - \beta_{12}\beta_{21}} (\beta_{21}\gamma_1 z_1 - \gamma_2 z_2 + \beta_{21}\epsilon_1 - \epsilon_2 - \beta_{21}u_1 + u_2). \tag{16}$$

If we assume that the second moments of the joint probability distribution of z_1 and z_2 approach the finite limits or probability limits $\mu_{z_1z_1}$, $\mu_{z_1z_2}$, and $\mu_{z_2z_2}$, then we obtain for the probability limit of the least-squares estimate of β_{12}

$$\beta_{12}^{(1)} = \frac{\beta_{21}\sigma_1^2 - (1 + \beta_{12}\beta_{21})\sigma_{12} + \beta_{12}\sigma_2^2 + \beta_{12}\gamma_2^2\mu_{z_2^0z_2^0}}{\beta_{21}^2\sigma_1^2 - 2\beta_{21}\sigma_{12} + \sigma_2^2 + \gamma_2^2\mu_{z_2^0z_2^0}}, \tag{17}$$

where

$$\mu_{z_2^0z_2^0} = \mu_{z_2z_2} - \frac{\mu_{z_1z_2}^2}{\mu_{z_1z_1}}$$

is the variance of the residual z_2^0 from the least-squares regression of z_2 on z_1.[14] The asymptotic least-squares bias in this case is therefore

$$\beta_{12}^{(1)} - \beta_{12} = \frac{(1 - \beta_{12}\beta_{21})(\beta_{21}\sigma_1^2 - \sigma_{12})}{\beta_{21}^2\sigma_1^2 - 2\beta_{21}\sigma_{12} + \sigma_2^2 + \gamma_2^2\mu_{z_2^0z_2^0}}. \tag{18}$$

This is the most general case to be discussed in this chapter, and it will be of interest to analyze and interpret the expression for bias that has been obtained. First we give a numerical example to indicate how large the bias (18) may sometimes be.[15] Suppose the equations of our model are in fact

$$y_1 + 0.1\, y_2 + z_1 = u_1,$$

$$-0.2\, y_1 + y_2 + 0.1\, z_2 = u_2,$$

[14] See Chapter VI, equation (5.19).

[15] An example based on actual data is given by Haavelmo in Chapter IV, Section 5. For another constructed example, see Koopmans [1945].

and suppose that $\sigma_1 = 1$, $\sigma_2 = 0.01$, $\mu_{z_2^0 z_2^0} = 2$, and $\sigma_{12} = 0.005$. Then, from (18),

$$\beta_{12}^{(1)} - \beta_{12} = -\frac{1.02(0.2 + 0.005)}{0.04 + 0.002 + 0.0001 + 0.02} = -3.367.$$

This is a very large relative error.

Proceeding to the analysis of (18) we find that y_2 plays a crucial role, as we might have expected since this is the variable wrongly treated as independent of u_1 when residuals are minimized in the y_1-direction. It is possible to interpret both the numerator and the denominator of (18) as quantities which describe certain aspects of the behavior of y_2 in relation to other variables of the system. To demonstrate this we rewrite (16), substituting for z_2 its value in terms of z_1 and z_2^0, to obtain

$$(19)\quad \begin{aligned} y_2 &= \frac{1}{1 - \beta_{12}\beta_{21}}\left[\left(\beta_{21}\gamma_1 - \gamma_2\frac{\mu_{z_1 z_2}}{\mu_{z_1 z_1}}\right) z_1 - \gamma_2 z_2^0 - (\beta_{21}u_1 - u_2)\right] + \eta \\ &= y_2^{(z_1)} + y_2^{(z_2^0)} + y_2^{(u)} + \eta, \end{aligned}$$

say, where η is a constant. This may be regarded as a decomposition of y_2 according to the sources of its variation. The second and third terms,

$$(20)\quad -\frac{\gamma_2}{1 - \beta_{12}\beta_{21}} z_2^0 - \frac{\beta_{21}u_1 - u_2}{1 - \beta_{12}\beta_{21}} = y_2^{(z_2^0)} + y_2^{(u)},$$

give us the component of y_2 that is uncorrelated with z_1. The component of y_2 that is independent of both z_1 and z_2 is the third term,

$$(21)\quad -\frac{\beta_{21}u_1 - u_2}{1 - \beta_{12}\beta_{21}} = y_2^{(u)}.$$

If we divide both numerator and denominator of (18) by $(1 - \beta_{12}\beta_{21})^2$, the numerator becomes the negative of the covariance of the disturbance u_1 with (21), the "unexplained" component $y_2^{(u)}$ of y_2. Thus the bias is proportional to cov $(u_1, y_2^{(u)})$, i.e., the covariance between u_1 and that component of y_2 which depends on u_1 and u_2. (There can, of course, be no covariance between u_1 and those components of y_2 which depend on the z_i.) Since u_1 enters into the expression (21) for $y_2^{(u)}$ with the coefficient $\beta_{21}/(1 - \beta_{12}\beta_{21})$, there will be a contribution from this source to the covariance in question only if $\beta_{21} \neq 0$, as we saw in Case IIIb. Similarly, there will be a contribution arising from the presence of u_2 in the expression $y_2^{(u)}$ only if $\sigma_{12} \neq 0$, as we saw in Case IV. We observe from (18) that these two sources of bias cancel each other if and only if

$$(22)\quad \sigma_{12} = \beta_{21}\sigma_1^2,$$

as we should have expected from the condition (14) mentioned in the discussion of Case V.

The variance of y_2 is built up from the variances of its components in (19) by

$$\text{(23)} \qquad \operatorname{var}(y_2) = \operatorname{var}(y_2^{(z_1)}) + \operatorname{var}(y_2^{(z_2^0)}) + \operatorname{var}(y_2^{(u)}).$$

In particular, the denominator of (18) after we have divided by $(1 - \beta_{12}\beta_{21})^2$ is seen to be the variance of (20). Thus the bias (18) is found to vary inversely with the variance $\operatorname{var}(y_2^{(z_2^0)} + y_2^{(u)})$ of that component $y_2^{(z_2^0)} + y_2^{(u)}$ of y_2 which is uncorrelated with z_1.

The analysis just given can be summarized in the formula

$$\text{(24)} \qquad \beta_{12}^{(1)} - \beta_{12} = \frac{-\operatorname{cov}(u_1, y_2^{(u)})}{\operatorname{var}(y_2^{(z_2^0)} + y_2^{(u)})} = \frac{-\operatorname{cov}(u_1, y_2^{(u)})}{\operatorname{var}(y_2^{(z_2^0)}) + \operatorname{var}(y_2^{(u)})}.$$

In explanation of the denominator in (24), we recall that in Case III the introduction of z into the second equation had the effect of lending to y_2 the free variation of which z itself was capable. Thus we were able to observe points which, except for the effect of sampling fluctuations in u_1, traced out SS. We recall further that this effect depended on the absence of z from the first equation. Therefore, it is not surprising that in the more general case only that part of y_2's variance

$$\text{(25)} \qquad \operatorname{var}(y_2^{(z_2^0)}) = \gamma_2^2 \mu_{z_2^0 z_2^0}$$

which is explained by z_2^0 (i.e., by the net effect of z_2, after having allowed already for the effect of z_1) contributes to identification. We shall call this the identification term in (18). If this term is zero, z_1 and z_2 are in fact the same variable and identifiability is absent.[16] However, (18) tells us something more than this, which perhaps we had no reason to suspect a priori. Whenever the identification term is not zero, the size of the least-squares bias is a decreasing function of this term. Furthermore, the identification term plays exactly the same role in decreasing bias as does the part of y_2's variance that depends on the disturbances.

[16] The reader may be surprised that in this case the expression (18) for the asymptotic bias does not take the indefinite form 0/0, because now β_{12} is actually indeterminate in terms of observable characteristics. However, (18) was never intended as a means of determining β_{12} from $\beta_{12}^{(1)}$, or from an estimate thereof, and would need supplementation by other relationships involving additional observable characteristics if it were to be so used (instead of the more straightforward estimation methods of Chapter VI) in the case where identifiability is present. In case identifiability were absent, only insufficient supplementation could be found, although (18) would remain a valid statement connecting structural parameters, not all identifiable.

Appendix

AN EXPRESSION FOR ASYMPTOTIC LEAST-SQUARES BIAS IN A MORE GENERAL LINEAR MODEL

Let y be a row vector of endogenous variables; z, a row vector of exogenous variables whose moment matrix approaches a finite nonsingular limit or probability limit; and u, a row vector of normally distributed, serially independent disturbances with zero mean and constant variance. For any matrix or vector A, let A' denote the transpose of A and let ${}_1A$ denote the matrix A with the first row deleted. Let

$$\beta_\Delta y_\Delta' + \gamma_* z_*' = u_1$$

be a single equation (say the first) in a complete system of G stochastic equations,

$$\mathrm{B}y' + \Gamma z' = u'.$$

If $\Pi = -\mathrm{B}^{-1}\Gamma$ and $v' = \mathrm{B}^{-1}u'$, then this system has the reduced form

$$y' = \Pi z' + v'.$$

Let $y_{\Delta\Delta}$ and z_{**} be row vectors which contain, respectively, the elements of y and of z not appearing in the first equation. Then $[y_\Delta \quad y_{\Delta\Delta}]$ is a partitioning of y and $[z_* \quad z_{**}]$ is a partitioning of z. If G^Δ is the number of elements in y_Δ, let $[\Pi_{\Delta.*} \quad \Pi_{\Delta.**}]$ be a partitioning of the first G^Δ rows of Π such that $\Pi_{\Delta.**}$ contains as many columns as z_{**}. Let $(\mathrm{B}^{-1})_\Delta$ be the first G^Δ rows of B^{-1}. Let σ_1 be the vector given by the first row of the population covariance matrix Σ of the elements of u. Let v_Δ be a row vector containing the first G^Δ elements of v, and let ${}_{11}\Omega_\Delta$ be the population covariance matrix of the last $G^\Delta - 1$ elements of v_Δ. Finally let $\mathrm{M}_{z^0z^0}$ be the limit or probability limit of the covariance matrix of the residuals from the regressions of the elements of z_{**} on the elements of z_*.

If the first element of y_Δ is treated as the dependent variable, then the asymptotic bias in the least-squares estimation of the last $G^\Delta - 1$ elements of the vector β_Δ is given by

$$\Psi^{-1} \cdot {}_1(\mathrm{B}^{-1})_\Delta \cdot \sigma_1' ,$$

where

$$\Psi = {}_1\Pi_{\Delta.**} \cdot \mathrm{M}_{z^0z^0} \cdot {}_1\Pi_{\Delta.**}' + {}_{11}\Omega_\Delta$$

is the probability limit of that part of the covariance matrix of the elements of y_Δ which is independent of the elements of z_*. Furthermore, if $\mathrm{M}_{z_*z_*}$ and M_{z_*z} denote, respectively, the limits or probability limits of the covariance matrices of the elements of z_* with themselves and with all the elements of z, the asymptotic least-squares bias in estimating γ_* is

$$\mathrm{M}_{z_*z_*}^{-1} \cdot \mathrm{M}_{z_*z} \cdot {}_1\Pi_{\Delta.**}' \cdot \Psi^{-1} \cdot {}_1(\mathrm{B}^{-1})_\Delta \cdot \sigma_1^1 .$$

These expressions for bias remain valid in cases where lagged endogenous variables are present if certain further conditions are met which insure that the second moments of the endogenous variables still approach finite probability limits under these circumstances.

Chapter X

THE COMPUTATION OF MAXIMUM-LIKELIHOOD ESTIMATES OF LINEAR STRUCTURAL EQUATIONS

By Herman Chernoff and Nathan Divinsky

1. Introduction

The purpose of this chapter is to explain the methods used to calculate estimates of the parameters of systems of simultaneous stochastic difference equations. Four methods will be explained in detail and will be illustrated with the work done on the variants of a model of three equations proposed by Klein.[1] All four methods are maximum-likelihood methods[2] if the distribution of disturbances is in fact normal. These methods are: the full-information method with no restrictions on the covariance matrix of the disturbances, the full-information method with diagonal covariance matrix of disturbances, the limited-information

[1] This model is Klein's Model I. See Klein [1950, Chapter III, especially pp. 58–80]. The authors are indebted to J. G. C. Templeton and D. Waterman for supervising the completion of the tables and for carrying out adjustments in the notation, and to D. Waterman and E. Goldstein for assistance in reading proof.

[2] The theory of these methods is discussed in Chapter VI, especially Sections 5 and 6.

single-equation method, and the limited-information subsystem-of-equations method. These are abbreviated F.I.N.D., F.I.D., L.I.S.E., L.I.S. All of these methods apply only to the case in which the disturbances are assumed to be serially uncorrelated, although extensions can be made to the case in which they are serially correlated.

The F.I.N.D. and F.I.D. methods make use of all the information (or assumptions) concerning the restrictions on the parameters. The L.I.S.E. and L.I.S. methods make use only of the information concerning the restrictions on the parameters of the single equation or of the subsystem of equations to be estimated, as the case may be.

Two models, to be designated (*a*) and (*b*), will be used to illustrate these methods. These models involve the following variables: C_t, consumption; π_t, net profits; W_{1t}, private wage bill; W_{2t}, government wage bill; I_t, net investment; Z_t, capital at end of year t; Y_t, net income; τ_t, business taxes; G_t, government spending; F_t, net foreign balance. The subscript t serves to date the variables; t is measured in years and equals time from 1931. All variables apart from t are measured in the real value unit: billions of 1934 dollars. The equations of both models are

$$\text{(1.i)} \quad C_t = \alpha_0 + \alpha_1\pi_t + \alpha_2(W_{1t} + W_{2t}) + \alpha_3\pi_{t-1} + u_{1t},$$

$$\text{(1.ii)} \quad I_t = \alpha_4 + \alpha_5\pi_t + \alpha_6\pi_{t-1} + \alpha_7 Z_{t-1} + u_{2t},$$

$$\text{(1.iii)} \quad W_{1t} = \alpha_8 + \alpha_9(Y_t + \tau_t - W_{2t}) + \alpha_{10}t + \alpha_{11}(Y_{t-1} + \tau_{t-1} - W_{2,t-1}) + u_{3t},$$

subject to the following three identities:

$$\text{(2)} \quad \begin{aligned} I_t &= Z_t - Z_{t-1}, \\ Y_t + \tau_t &= C_t + I_t + G_t + F_t, \\ Y_t &= W_{1t} + W_{2t} + \pi_t. \end{aligned}$$

In Model (*a*), C_t, I_t, W_{1t}, Z_t, π_t, Y_t are assumed to be jointly dependent. In Model (*b*), C_t, I_t, W_{1t}, Z_t, π_t, Y_t, $(G_t + F_t)$, τ_t are assumed to be jointly dependent. In the following we shall drop the subscripts t whenever possible without ambiguity, and variables lagged by one time unit will be denoted by a minus one subscript (e.g., π_{t-1} will be denoted by π_{-1}). Now the three identities can be used to eliminate three jointly dependent variables, leaving three stochastic linear equations in which only three jointly dependent variables are involved for Model (*a*). For Model (*b*) five jointly dependent variables are left. This implies that for Model (*a*) the three equations form a complete system while for Model (*b*) they only form a subsystem of a complete system, but the two additional equations that would make the model complete are not stated. In Model (*b*) nothing is assumed about the restrictions on the parameters of the remaining equations. Thus the F.I.N.D. and F.I.D. methods cannot be applied to estimate the coefficients in this model. Instead, one may use either L.I.S.E. or L.I.S. For Model (*a*) one may use F.I.N.D. or F.I.D., depending on the assumptions concerning the covariance matrix Σ of the disturbances u_{1t}, u_{2t}, u_{3t}. One may also use L.I.S.E. for each individual equation or use L.I.S.E. on one of the equations and L.I.S. for the subsystem consisting of the other two.

It should be noted that L.I.S.E. is the only method for which an initial approximation to the estimates is not required. It is also a comparatively cheap method of obtaining consistent estimates. Thus, if the other methods are to be applied, it is a logical step to obtain L.I.S.E. estimates first and to use them as an initial approximation in the other methods where more information concerning the nature of the parameters is used.

This chapter assumes a knowledge of the abbreviated Doolittle method for matrix inversion.[3]

2. Notation and General Procedure

In the computations that are performed for the various estimation processes certain special notations have been found very useful. Some of the notations will be explained here before developing the L.I.S.E. technique.

The symbol y_t represents a vector or a matrix of one row whose elements are the jointly dependent variables. The symbol z_t represents a vector of predetermined variables. In Model (*a*), omitting subscripts t, $y_1 = C$, $y_2 = \pi$, $y_3 = W_1 + W_2$, $y_4 = I$, $y_5 = W_1$, $y_6 = Y + \tau - W_2$, $z_1 = t$, $z_2 = \pi_{-1}$, $z_3 = Z_{-1}$, $z_4 = (Y + \tau - W_2)_{-1}$. Let x_t be the vector consisting of the elements of z_t adjoined to those of y_t; thus

$$x_t = [y_t \quad z_t] = [y_{t1} \quad y_{t2} \quad \cdots \quad z_{t1} \quad z_{t2} \quad \cdots].$$

The symbol A_{yx} denotes a matrix with as many rows as there are elements of y and as many columns as there are elements of x. The matrix product $y_t A_{yx}$ is a row vector with as many elements as x has.

The symbol A'_{yx} denotes the transpose of the matrix A_{yx}, and x'_t denotes a one-column matrix. The product $A_{yx}x'_t$ is a one-column matrix with as many elements as there are elements of y_t. The product $y_tA_{yx}x'_t$ is a one by one matrix (scalar), while y'_tx_t is a matrix with as many rows as there are elements of y and with as many columns as there are elements of x. The subscripts yx are sometimes omitted from A_{yx} in cases where no misunderstanding can arise.

Just as x_t may be partitioned into $[y_t \quad z_t]$, so A_{yx} can be partitioned

[3] The Doolittle method is discussed by Dwyer [1951].

into $[B \quad C]$, so that $A_{yx}x'_t = By'_t + Cz'_t$. Finally, there will occur situations in which the first element of y_t will not be needed. In this instance we write ${}_1y_t = [y_{t2} \quad y_{t3} \quad \cdots]$. The symbol ${}_{10}A$ represents the matrix A with the first row deleted, ${}_{01}A$ is the matrix A with the first column deleted, and ${}_{11}A$ is the matrix A with the first row and the first column deleted.

Considerable use is made of the moment matrix[4]

$$\bar{M}_{xx}^{(0)} = T \sum_t x'_t x_t - \sum_t x'_t \cdot \sum_t x_t, \tag{3}$$

where T represents the number of observations on x_t. Since we have twenty-one years of observation, $T = 21$ in our problem. It is of great convenience in calculating to deal with a moment matrix in which the elements on the main diagonal are close to one. If the variables x_{ti} were replaced by $k_i x_{ti} = x_{ti}^{(a)}$, then the ijth element $\bar{m}_{ij}^{(0)}$ of $\bar{M}_{xx}^{(0)}$ is replaced by $k_i k_j \bar{m}_{ij}^{(0)} = \bar{m}_{ij}^{(a)}$. In particular, the diagonal elements of $\bar{M}_{xx}^{(a)}$ can be made close to one by selecting the k_i properly. An equation which originally read $\alpha_1 x_{t1} + \alpha_2 x_{t2} + \cdots = u_t$ can be transformed to $(\alpha_1/k_1)x_{t1}^{(a)} + (\alpha_2/k_2)x_{t2}^{(a)} + \cdots = u_t$ or $\alpha_1^{(a)}x_{t1}^{(a)} + \alpha_2^{(a)}x_{t2}^{(a)} \cdots = u_t$, where $\alpha_i = \alpha_i^{(a)}k_i$. It is then necessary to readjust the results after the computations are completed.[5] Hereafter the expressions in terms of the original variables and coefficients will always have superscripts (0), e.g., $x^{(0)}$. Where necessary for clarity, the adjusted variables will have superscripts (a), but otherwise their superscripts will be omitted. Finally, it will usually be convenient to let k_i be that power of 10 which makes $\bar{m}_{ii}^{(a)}$ lie between 10 and 0.1.

Since the computations are such that mistakes occur easily, a good deal of effort should be devoted to independent checks of the results. One of the most useful tools in this endeavor is the check sum. Thus, when a series of numbers is copied from one source to another, the sum of the original numbers and the sum of the copied numbers are obtained and compared. If the two sums are equal, it is reasonable to assume, although it is not absolutely certain, that the copying has been correctly carried out. Check sums are applicable to most matrix operations. For example, if one is obtaining $C = A \cdot B$, where $A = \| a_{ij} \|$, $B = \| b_{jk} \|$, $C = \| c_{ik} \|$, then $c_{ik} = \sum_j a_{ij}b_{jk}$. If one constructs the sum column $b_{j\Sigma} = \sum_k b_{jk}$, then $\sum_j a_{ij}b_{j\Sigma} = \sum_j a_{ij} \sum_k b_{jk} = \sum_k \sum_j a_{ij}b_{jk} = \sum_k c_{ik} = c_{i\Sigma}$. Thus, by computing $b_{j\Sigma}$, multiplying it on the left by A, and comparing this result with the sum column of the product (i.e., $c_{i\Sigma}$),

[4] For computational convenience we use a definition of the moment matrix differing from that used in Chapter VI, equation (5.54).

[5] For computational convenience no normalization is introduced until the very end of the computations.

we have an adequate check on the work. This method also applies to the inversion of matrices. Check sums in the computations reproduced at the end of this chapter are set in italics.

In complicated computations there arises an accumulation of rounding-off errors. In order to avoid the effect of these it pays to carry out the computations to a great many significant figures. Indeed, from six to nine figures are usually carried to avoid the effects of rounding-off errors[6] even though the data are such that the fourth figures of the results have little meaning.

3. Limited-Information Single-Equation Method

Consider a single equation of a system, which we shall write

$$\beta_1 y_1 + \beta_2 y_2 \cdots + \beta_{G^\Delta} y_{G^\Delta} + \gamma_1 z_1 + \cdots + \gamma_{K^*} z_{K^*} + \epsilon = u. \tag{4}$$

We shall denote by y_Δ the vector of the G^Δ jointly dependent variables appearing in the single equation; z_* is the vector of predetermined variables appearing in the equation, and z_{**} is the vector of predetermined variables appearing in the complete model but not appearing in the equation under consideration, so that $z = [z_* \quad z_{**}]$. Let G^Δ, K^*, K^{**}, K represent the number of elements of y_Δ, z_*, z_{**}, z, respectively, with $K = K^* + K^{**}$.

In particular, let us deal with each of the equations of Model (*b*) by the L.I.S.E. method. Then C, I, W_1, Z, π, Y, $G + F$, τ are assumed to be jointly dependent. The remaining variables, W_2, π_{-1}, Z_{-1}, $(Y + \tau - W_2)_{-1}$, and t, are regarded as predetermined.

For the first equation we have

$$\begin{aligned}
&\beta_1^1 C + \beta_2^1 \pi + \beta_3^1 (W_1 + W_2) + \gamma_1^1 \pi_{-1} + \epsilon_1 = u_1, \\
&y_\Delta = [C \quad \pi \quad (W_1 + W_2)], \qquad z_* = [\pi_{-1}], \\
&z_{**} = [W_2 \quad Z_{-1} \quad (Y + \tau - W_2)_{-1} \quad t], \\
&G^\Delta = 3, \qquad K^* = 1, \qquad K^{**} = 4, \qquad K = 5.
\end{aligned} \tag{5.i}$$

For the second equation we have

$$\begin{aligned}
&\beta_1^2 I + \beta_2^2 \pi + \gamma_1^2 \pi_{-1} + \gamma_2^2 Z_{-1} + \epsilon_2 = u_2, \\
&y_\Delta = [I \quad \pi], \qquad z_* = [\pi_{-1} \quad Z_{-1}], \\
&z_{**} = [W_2 \quad (Y + \tau - W_2)_{-1} \quad t], \\
&G^\Delta = 2, \qquad K^* = 2, \qquad K^{**} = 3, \qquad K = 5.
\end{aligned} \tag{5.ii}$$

[6] Nine figures are usually carried because to do so costs little more than to carry six figures. On the other hand, carrying more than nine (on the ten-bank desk calculators used) is considerably more expensive than carrying nine.

For the third equation we have

$$\beta_1^3 W + \beta_2^3(Y + \tau - W_2) + \gamma_1^3 t + \gamma_2^3(Y + \tau - W_2)_{-1} + \epsilon_3 = u_3 ,$$

$$\text{(5.iii)} \quad \begin{aligned} y_\Delta &= [W_1 \quad (Y + \tau - W_2)], \qquad z_* = [t \quad (Y + \tau - W_2)_{-1}], \\ z_{**} &= [W_2 \quad \pi_{-1} \quad Z_{-1}], \end{aligned}$$

$$G^\Delta = 2, \qquad K^* = 2, \qquad K^{**} = 3, \qquad K = 5.$$

It should be noted here that if Model (*a*) were being treated in this way, this would require as the only difference from Model (*b*) that the z_{**}'s would include in addition τ and $G + F$.

We shall concentrate most of our explanations on the second equation. Hence we shall omit the superscripts from $\beta_1^2 , \cdots , \gamma_1^2 , \cdots$ and the subscripts from u_2 and ϵ_2 in what follows. However, some of the work can be most efficiently done for all the equations simultaneously. In the L.I.S.E. case the logarithmic likelihood function is given by

$$\text{(6)} \qquad L^{(4)}(\beta_\Delta) = \text{const.} - \tfrac{1}{2} \log \frac{\beta_\Delta \overline{W}^*_{\Delta\Delta} \beta'_\Delta}{\beta_\Delta \overline{W}_{\Delta\Delta} \beta'_\Delta} ,$$

where β_Δ is the vector of coefficients of y_Δ , and $\overline{W}_{\Delta\Delta}$ and $\overline{W}^*_{\Delta\Delta}$ are as defined below in (7) and (12). Note that this expression for $L^{(4)}$ is obtained from that given in Chapter VI, formula (6.20), by substituting $\overline{W}_{\Delta\Delta}$ and $\overline{W}^*_{\Delta\Delta}$ (based on $\bar{M}$) for $W_{\Delta\Delta}$ and $W^*_{\Delta\Delta}$ (based on M), respectively.

First the time series for the variables $x^{(0)}$ are prepared[7] in Table 1.1,[8] and a sum column is formed. Below the series the sum of each column is obtained over the 21-year period 1921–1941. This computation is checked against the check sum. Then the means are computed and checked, $m^{(0)} = (1/T) \sum_t x_t^{(0)}$, where $T = 21$. In Table 1.2 part of the calculation of $\bar{M}^{(0)}_{xx} = T \sum_t x_t^{(0)\prime} x_t^{(0)} - \sum_t x_t^{(0)\prime} \cdot \sum_t x_t^{(0)}$ is illustrated. Note that the page is broken up into small blocks consisting of four lines each. For example, in the block corresponding to $y_2^{(0)}$ and $z_5^{(0)}$ we have on the first line $\sum_t y_{t2}^{(0)} \cdot z_{t5}^{(0)}$; on the second line $T \cdot \sum_t y_{t2}^{(0)} \cdot z_{t5}^{(0)}$; on the third line $\sum_t y_{t2}^{(0)} \cdot \sum_t z_{t5}^{(0)}$; and on the fourth line $T \cdot \sum_t y_{t2}^{(0)} \cdot z_{t5}^{(0)} - \sum_t y_{t2}^{(0)} \cdot \sum_t z_{t5}^{(0)}$, which is the corresponding element of $\bar{M}^{(0)}_{xx}$. Because of the sym-

[7] While several of the following tables have been omitted to conserve space, we shall refer to them by number as though they were included. Furthermore, in these tables only one sum column appears—let the reader keep in mind that in actual practice two sum columns are always used, which are identical if no error is present.

The computations were performed with nine digits, of which only six are reproduced, without rounding the sixth digit off upward if the seventh is 5 or more. Because of the cutting-off of the printed tables after the sixth place, some of the check sums may appear to be slightly in error.

[8] Not reproduced. The time series omitted here may be found in Klein [1950, p. 135].

metry of $\bar{M}_{xx}^{(0)}$, the blocks below the main diagonal need not be filled in. Finally, the check sums are carried out as usual and the sum must include the terms that were not filled in.

At this point the adjustment factors are determined. Since the moment corresponding to $y_1^{(0)}$ is 19770.02, the appropriate adjustment factor is $k_1 = 0.01$. It is a peculiarity of this particular set of time series that all the adjustment factors are 0.01. Although this permits short cuts and simplifications, we shall proceed in the general fashion. In Table 2.1 is given the translation page, which is very useful for reference throughout the work. The variables are listed and given labels and the adjustments noted and the adjusted means listed. In Table 2.2 the adjusted moment matrix $\bar{M}_{xx}^{(a)}$ is copied and a sum column formed. In general, when the adjustments vary, the check-sum method of checking the adjustments does not apply. In that case one cannot overemphasize the need to check and double check the copying. In this particular case all elements of $\bar{M}_{xx}^{(0)}$ are multiplied by $0.01 \times 0.01 = 10^{-4}$ and the check sum applies. A great many of the numbers copied for $\bar{M}_{xx}^{(a)}$ are used again on the next page and it is usually a good policy for saving time and avoiding copying errors to use a carbon paper to reproduce $\bar{M}_{zz}^{(a)}$ and $\bar{M}_{zy}^{(a)}$ on the next computation page for use in Table 3. For this reason it is recommended that the z's precede the y's in Table 2, contrary to the usual notation.

We are now working with adjusted matrices, suppressing the superscript in $\bar{M}^{(a)}$. In Table 3 the main computation is that of $\bar{M}_{yz}\bar{M}_{zz}^{-1}\bar{M}_{zy}$. This involves a useful variation of the abbreviated Doolittle method. First $\bar{M}_{zz}$ and $\bar{M}_{zy}$ are copied at the top of the page, and then the forward solution of the Doolittle method is carried out immediately below. Then the ijth element of $\bar{M}_{yz}\bar{M}_{zz}^{-1}\bar{M}_{zy}$ can be computed by cumulating the product of the terms in the odd rows of the ith column with the terms in the even rows of the jth column. For example, the term in $\bar{M}_{yz}\bar{M}_{zz}^{-1}\bar{M}_{zy}$ corresponding to 0.728666 is obtained as (1.213170) · (0.024545) + (0.775604)(0.807153) + (−0.352785)(−0.198699) + (0.052376)(0.019086) + (−0.000917)(−1.917294). Since $\bar{M}_{yz}\bar{M}_{zz}^{-1}\bar{M}_{zy}$ is symmetric, the terms below the main diagonal are omitted.

In the meantime, $\bar{M}_{yy}$ has been carbon copied in a convenient place, and

$$\bar{W}_{yy} = \bar{M}_{yy} - \bar{M}_{yz}\bar{M}_{zz}^{-1}\bar{M}_{zy} \tag{7}$$

is computed.

The work done up to now is applicable to all of the equations. Now let us proceed to compute the estimates of the coefficients of the second equation, where $y_\Delta = [I \quad \pi]$, $z_* = [\pi_{-1} \quad Z_{-1}]$.

In Table 4.1, $\bar{M}_{**} = \bar{M}_{z_*z_*}$, which is a submatrix of $\bar{M}_{zz}$, is copied from $\bar{M}_{xx}$ and then inverted. In Table 4.2, $\bar{M}_{*\Delta}$ is copied from $\bar{M}_{xx}$, and we compute

$$P^{*\prime}_{\Delta *} = \bar{M}^{-1}_{**}\bar{M}_{*\Delta}, \tag{8}$$

$$\bar{M}_{\Delta *}P^{*\prime}_{\Delta *} = \bar{M}_{\Delta *}\bar{M}^{-1}_{**}\bar{M}_{*\Delta}, \tag{9}$$

where $\bar{M}_{\Delta *}$ is the transpose of $\bar{M}_{*\Delta}$. In Table 4.3 we compute

$$R_{\Delta\Delta} = \bar{M}_{\Delta z}\bar{M}^{-1}_{zz}\bar{M}_{z\Delta} - \bar{M}_{\Delta *}P^{*\prime}_{\Delta *}. \tag{10}$$

(Note that $\bar{M}_{\Delta z}\bar{M}^{-1}_{zz}\bar{M}_{z\Delta}$ is a submatrix of $\bar{M}_{yz}\bar{M}^{-1}_{zz}\bar{M}_{zy}$.) Then $\bar{W}_{\Delta\Delta}$ is copied from $\bar{W}_{yy}$ in Table 3 and

$$Q_{\Delta\Delta} = R^{-1}_{\Delta\Delta}\bar{W}_{\Delta\Delta} \tag{11}$$

is computed.[9]

We are now in a position to obtain the adjusted estimates of the coefficients of the jointly dependent variables as that value b_Δ of the vector β_Δ which minimizes the variance ratio $\beta_\Delta\bar{W}^*_{\Delta\Delta}\beta'_\Delta/\beta_\Delta\bar{W}_{\Delta\Delta}\beta'_\Delta$, where

$$\bar{W}^*_{\Delta\Delta} = R_{\Delta\Delta} + \bar{W}_{\Delta\Delta}. \tag{12}$$

Thus we must choose $\beta_\Delta = b_\Delta$ so as to minimize

$$\frac{\beta_\Delta(R_{\Delta\Delta} + \bar{W}_{\Delta\Delta})\beta'_\Delta}{\beta_\Delta\bar{W}_{\Delta\Delta}\beta'_\Delta} = 1 + \frac{\beta_\Delta R_{\Delta\Delta}\beta'_\Delta}{\beta_\Delta\bar{W}_{\Delta\Delta}\beta'_\Delta}.$$

This is achieved if we take b_Δ so as to minimize $\beta_\Delta R_{\Delta\Delta}\beta'_\Delta/\beta_\Delta\bar{W}_{\Delta\Delta}\beta'_\Delta$. Taking partial derivatives with respect to the ith element β_i of β_Δ $(i = 1, \cdots, G^\Delta)$ and setting them equal to zero (noting that $R_{\Delta\Delta}$ and $\bar{W}_{\Delta\Delta}$ are symmetric matrices), we obtain

$$(\beta_\Delta\bar{W}_{\Delta\Delta}\beta'_\Delta)(\sum_m \beta_m r_{mi}) = (\beta_\Delta R_{\Delta\Delta}\beta'_\Delta)(\sum_n \beta_n w_{ni}) \quad (i = 1, \cdots, G_\Delta).$$

That is,

$$\frac{\beta_\Delta R_{\Delta\Delta}\beta'_\Delta}{\beta_\Delta\bar{W}_{\Delta\Delta}\beta'_\Delta} = \frac{\Sigma_m\beta_m r_{mi}}{\Sigma_n\beta_n w_{ni}} = \frac{i\text{th element of } (R_{\Delta\Delta}\beta'_\Delta)}{i\text{th element of } (\bar{W}_{\Delta\Delta}\beta'_\Delta)}$$

for each i. Therefore $R_{\Delta\Delta}\beta'_\Delta = l^\dagger\bar{W}_{\Delta\Delta}\beta'_\Delta$ or $(R_{\Delta\Delta} - l^\dagger\bar{W}_{\Delta\Delta})\beta'_\Delta = 0$, where $l^\dagger$ is a minimum. Thus we must choose the vector b_Δ to correspond to the smallest root $l^\dagger = l^\dagger_1$ of $| R_{\Delta\Delta} - l^\dagger\bar{W}_{\Delta\Delta} | = 0$ or to the largest root $k^\dagger = k^\dagger_1 = 1/l^\dagger_1$ of $| \bar{W}_{\Delta\Delta} - k^\dagger R_{\Delta\Delta} | = 0$. Note that, since any constant multiple

[9] In the case where $K^{**} = H - 1$, $R_{\Delta\Delta}$ can be shown to be singular and this computation cannot be done. To solve this case, see Appendix 1. Another special case is that in which $K^* = 0$ (i.e., where no z's appear in the equation). Appendix 2 treats this case.

of b_Δ will serve just as well as b_Δ itself, normalization does not affect this procedure.

In Table 4.4 we find the characteristic vector corresponding to the largest root $k_1^\dagger$ of $| \overline{W}_{\Delta\Delta} - k^\dagger R_{\Delta\Delta} | = 0$. We take an arbitrary column vector[10,11] $q'_{(0)}$. Then we compute $q'_{(1)} = Q_{\Delta\Delta} q'_{(0)}$ and $k^\dagger_{(1)}$ equal to a column vector whose elements are the quotients of corresponding elements of $q'_{(1)}$ and $q'_{(0)}$. That is, if $q'_{(0)} = \begin{pmatrix} 4.09 \\ 0.26 \end{pmatrix}$, $q'_{(1)} = \begin{pmatrix} 59.2 \\ 2.1 \end{pmatrix}$, then $k^\dagger_{(1)} = \begin{pmatrix} 14.5 \\ 8.2 \end{pmatrix}$. Next we compute $q'_{(2)} = Q_{\Delta\Delta} q'_{(1)} = Q^2_{\Delta\Delta} q'_{(0)}$ and $k^\dagger_{(2)}$ as the column vector whose elements are the quotients of corresponding elements of $q'_{(2)}$ and $q'_{(1)}$. We continue in this fashion until all elements of $k^\dagger_{(n)}$ converge to the same limit, which is the largest root $k_1^\dagger$. Then the last column vector $q'_{(n)}$, or any multiple of it, is the characteristic vector we want. This vector equals b'_Δ up to the desired degree of approximation.

To prove that each element of $k^\dagger_{(n)}$ converges to $k_1^\dagger$, and that $q'_{(n)}$ converges to the corresponding characteristic vector b'_Δ, we consider the G^Δ characteristic roots $k_1^\dagger \geqslant k_2^\dagger \geqslant \cdots \geqslant k^\dagger_{G^\Delta} > 0$ of $| k^\dagger I - Q_{\Delta\Delta} | = 0$. These are the same as the roots of $| \overline{W}_{\Delta\Delta} - k^\dagger R_{\Delta\Delta} | = 0$. We also consider the corresponding characteristic vectors $b'_1, \cdots, b'_{G^\Delta}$. Since these b_g $(g = 1, \cdots, G^\Delta)$ span the G^Δ-dimensional space, our arbitrary vector $q'_{(0)}$ can be written $q'_{(0)} = \lambda_1 b'_1 + \cdots + \lambda_{G^\Delta} b'_{G^\Delta}$, and since $Q_{\Delta\Delta}\, b'_i = k_i^\dagger\, b'_i$ we have

$$q'_{(n)} = Q^n_{\Delta\Delta} q'_{(0)} = \lambda_1 k_1^{\dagger n} b'_1 + \cdots + \lambda_{G^\Delta} k^{\dagger n}_{G^\Delta} b'_{G^\Delta}.$$

The ith component $q'_{i(n)} =$

$$\lambda_1 k_1^{\dagger n} (b'_1)_i \left\{ 1 + \frac{\lambda_2}{\lambda_1} \left(\frac{k_2^\dagger}{k_1^\dagger} \right)^n \frac{(b'_2)_i}{(b'_1)_i} + \cdots + \frac{\lambda_{G^\Delta}}{\lambda_1} \left(\frac{k^\dagger_{G^\Delta}}{k_1^\dagger} \right)^n \frac{(b'_{G^\Delta})_i}{(b'_1)_i} \right\}.$$

As n increases, the quantity in braces approaches one. (Since $k_2^\dagger / k_1^\dagger$, $\cdots$, $k^\dagger_{G^\Delta}/k_1^\dagger$ all lie between zero and one, their nth powers approach zero.) Thus $q'_{(n)}$ is approximately equal to $\lambda_1 k_1^{\dagger n} b'_1$, and each element of $k^\dagger_{(n)}$ is approximately equal to $\lambda_1 k_1^{\dagger n} (b_1)_i / \lambda_1 k_1^{\dagger n-1} (b_1)_i = k_1^\dagger$, of b'_1, the largest root. Since $q'_{(n)}$ is approximately equal to a scalar multiple $\lambda_1 k_1^{\dagger n} b'_1$ of b'_1, we see that $q'_{(n)}$ is approximately a characteristic vector corresponding to $k_1^\dagger$.

An error in the later stages of this iterative process will probably show up; and at any stage, if it does not show up, it can at worst only delay convergence. At times convergence is slow. To treat this situation see Appendix 3.

Now we compute $c'_* = -P^{*\prime}_{\Delta *} b'_\Delta$. Finally, in Table 4.5, we list the

[10] The $q'_{(0)}$ in the Table is really $q'_{(10)}$; i.e., our $q'_{(0)}$ is the result of ten preliminary iterations which are omitted to conserve space.

[11] See Knopp [1928].

variables $[b_\Delta \quad c_*]'$, the adjusted means m' taken from the translation page (Table 2.1), and the adjustments. Then $e = -[b_\Delta \quad c_*]m'$ is computed. In this case $e = -2.877828$. Then $[b_\Delta \quad c_* \quad e]$ is deadjusted to $[b_\Delta^{(0)} \quad c_*^{(0)} \quad e^{(0)}]$ and finally is normalized by dividing through by the leading coefficient to get $[b_\Delta^{(0)} \quad c_*^{(0)} \quad e^{(0)}]^{(\text{norm})}$. Hence cur estimate is $[b_\Delta^{(0)} \quad c_*^{(0)} \quad e^{(0)}]^{(\text{norm})} = [1.0 \quad 0.022994 \quad -0.746704 \quad 0.181972 \quad -25.780463]$, that is, the estimated equation is

$$I + 0.022994\,\pi - 0.764704\,\pi_{-1} + 0.181972\,Z_{-1} - 25.780463 = u. \tag{13}$$

Now that the estimates have been obtained it may be desirable to compute estimates of their sampling variances and covariances. This is done in Table 5. In Table 5.1, b_Δ' and $\overline{W}_{\Delta\Delta}$ are copied from Table 4. Then $b_\Delta \overline{W}_{\Delta\Delta}$ and $b_\Delta \overline{W}_{\Delta\Delta} b_\Delta'$ are computed, the latter being a scalar. Finally ${}_{11}\{(b_\Delta \overline{W}_{\Delta\Delta})'(b_\Delta \overline{W}_{\Delta\Delta})\}$ is calculated. Note that $(b_\Delta \overline{W}_{\Delta\Delta})'$ is a column vector and $b_\Delta \overline{W}_{\Delta\Delta}$ is a row vector; $(b_\Delta \overline{W}_{\Delta\Delta})'(b_\Delta \overline{W}_{\Delta\Delta})$ is therefore a matrix of rank one whose ijth element is the product of the ith element of $b_\Delta \overline{W}_{\Delta\Delta}$ by the jth element of $b_\Delta \overline{W}_{\Delta\Delta}$. From this matrix ${}_{11}\{(b_\Delta \overline{W}_{\Delta\Delta})'(b_\Delta \overline{W}_{\Delta\Delta})\}$ is obtained by deleting the first row and first column. In this particular case ${}_{11}\{(b_\Delta \overline{W}_{\Delta\Delta})'(b_\Delta \overline{W}_{\Delta\Delta})\}$ is a one by one matrix. In Table 5.2 we compute $l_1^\dagger = 1/k_1^\dagger$, $1 + l_1^\dagger$, $l_1^\dagger / b_\Delta \overline{W}_{\Delta\Delta} b_\Delta'$, $C = (1 + l_1^\dagger) b_\Delta \overline{W}_{\Delta\Delta} b_\Delta$, and $C^* = C/(T - F)(b_1 k_1)^2$, where[12] k_1 is the adjustment factor for the first element of y_Δ, $F = G^\Delta + K^*$, and $T = 21$. In Table 5.3 we take ${}_{11}R_{\Delta\Delta}$ and $\{l_1^\dagger / b_\Delta \overline{W}_{\Delta\Delta} b_\Delta'\} \cdot {}_{11}\{(b_\Delta \overline{W}_{\Delta\Delta})'(b_\Delta \overline{W}_{\Delta\Delta})\}$ and compute

$${}_{11}H = {}_{11}R_{\Delta\Delta} - \frac{l_1^\dagger}{b_\Delta \overline{W}_{\Delta\Delta} b_\Delta'} \cdot {}_{11}\{(b_\Delta \overline{W}_{\Delta\Delta})'(b_\Delta \overline{W}_{\Delta\Delta})\}.$$

Then we compute $({}_{11}H)^{-1}$, which in this particular case is the inverse of a one by one matrix. This is called $F_{\beta\beta}$. One might define $F_{\beta\beta}$ to have G^Δ rows and columns, as many as there are elements of y_Δ, but, since the row and column corresponding to y_1 have zero elements throughout, only $G^\Delta - 1$ rows and columns are shown. We shall use the subscript β only for vectors and matrices of order $G^\Delta - 1$. We next write down $({}_{10}P_{\Delta *}^*)'$, which is $P_{\Delta *}^{*\prime}$ with the column corresponding to the first element of y_Δ deleted. Then we compute[13] $F_{\beta\gamma} = F_{\beta\beta} \cdot {}_{10}P_{\Delta *}^*$, and then $F_{\gamma\gamma}^\dagger = ({}_{10}P_{\Delta *}^*)' F_{\beta\gamma}$. Finally $\overline{M}_{**}^{-1}$ is copied from Table 4.1 and $F_{\gamma\gamma} = F_{\gamma\gamma}^\dagger + \overline{M}_{**}^{-1}$ is computed. In Table 5.4 we compute

$$C^* \begin{bmatrix} F_{\beta\beta} & -F_{\beta\gamma} \\ -F_{\gamma\beta} & F_{\gamma\gamma} \end{bmatrix} = \frac{1}{(b_1^{(0)})^2} V^*(b_\Delta, c_*) = V^*(b_\Delta, c_*)^{(\text{norm})}, \tag{14}$$

[12] $T - F$ is used, rather than T, partly as an analogy to classical regression and partly heuristically. See Chapter VI, footnote 58.

[13] The subscript γ will serve the same purpose as $*$.

the estimate of the covariance matrix of the estimates of $[\beta_\Delta \quad \gamma_*]$ subject to the normalization $\beta_1 = 1$. In order to consider the covariances involving e, we write down ${}_1m'$, which is the column vector of adjusted means of the elements of y_Δ and z_* with the exception of the adjusted mean of y_1^Δ. We compute $V^*(b_\Delta, c_*)\cdot{}_1m'/(b_1^{(0)})^2$. This is a column which gives $-1/(b_1^{(0)})^2$ times the estimates of the covariances of the elements of b_Δ and c_* with e. Finally, to get $1/(b_1^{(0)})^2$ times the variance of e, we compute ${}_1m\cdot V^*(b_\Delta, c_*)\cdot{}_1m'/(b_{1*}^{(0)})^2$ and C^*/T^2 and add them together to obtain $V^*(e)/(b_1^{(0)})^2$. Then we write down $[k \quad 1]'$, the vector of adjustment factors of $[y_\Delta \quad z_* \quad 1]$. We use this to deadjust the matrix $V^*(b_\Delta, c_*, e)$, multiplying the general (i, j) term by the k_i corresponding to the row and by the k_j corresponding to the column, and we finally obtain $V^*(b_\Delta^{(0)}, c_*^{(0)}, e^{(0)})^{(\text{norm})}$.

At this point we may add that if we had used a different definition for the moment matrix our calculation would be changed slightly. If our moment matrix had been

$$\bar{M}/T = \sum x_t'\cdot x_t - (1/T)(\sum x_t')(\sum x_t), \tag{15}$$

the difference would arise only in C^*/T^2, which would be replaced by C^*/T. In both cases this result is equal to $1/T\cdot\sum u_t^{*2}/(T - F)$, where u_t^* is the computed residual in $b_1^{(0)}y_1^{(0)} + \cdots + e^{(0)} = u^*$. If our moment matrix had been

$$\bar{M}/T^2 = (1/T)\sum x_t'\cdot x_t - (1/T^2)(\sum x_t')(\sum x_t), \tag{16}$$

then C^*/T^2 would be replaced by C^*. Otherwise all calculations would be formally the same.

4. Gradient Methods of Maximization[14, 15]

To compute the F.I.D., F.I.N.D., and L.I.S. estimates of the parameters of a set of stochastic difference equations it is necessary to maximize a function of many variables. Suppose that one is given a continuous function $f(\alpha_1, \alpha_2, \cdots, \alpha_n)$ that achieves a maximum at the unknown point $\alpha_1 = a_1, \alpha_2 = a_2, \cdots, \alpha_n = a_n$. Consider the problem of finding this point. One way is to set the partial derivatives of f equal to zero and solve the resulting equations,

$$\frac{\partial f(\alpha_1, \cdots, \alpha_n)}{\partial \alpha_i} = 0 \qquad (i = 1, 2, \cdots, n). \tag{17}$$

However, if f is a function of any complexity, the above equations may be quite difficult to solve. An alternative procedure would be the following iterative technique. It is known[16] that, in a space with rectangular co-

[14] See Koopmans, Rubin, and Leipnik [1950, Section 4].

[15] This section may be omitted at the first reading if it is found to be too difficult.

[16] See, e.g., Courant [1936, p. 89].

ordinates $\alpha_1, \cdots, \alpha_n$ in which the units of scale are the same along all axes (with respect to some metric which will be discussed later), a function increases most rapidly from a point α_0 in the direction given by the vector $[\partial f/\partial \alpha_1 \quad \partial f/\partial \alpha_2 \quad \cdots \quad \partial f/\partial \alpha_n]$ evaluated at α_0. This vector is sometimes called the gradient, or direction of steepest ascent. Thus, if one has an initial approximation $[\alpha_{(0)1} \quad \alpha_{(0)2} \quad \cdots \quad \alpha_{(0)n}]$ to the point $[a_1 \; a_2 \; \cdots \; a_n]$, one may compute $d_i = \partial f/\partial \alpha_i \mid_{\alpha_j = \alpha_{(0)j}}$ and then take

$$\alpha_{(1)i} = \alpha_{(0)i} + h_1 d_i, \tag{18}$$

where h_1 is a positive number. Compared to the initial point, this new point is in the direction of steepest ascent and at a distance depending on h_1. Thus the function has assumed a greater value at the new point than at the original point, if h_1 is small enough and if not all $d_i = 0$. This procedure may be repeated to give $[\alpha_{(2)1} \quad \cdots \quad \alpha_{(2)n}]$, $[\alpha_{(3)1} \quad \cdots \quad \alpha_{(3)n}]$, etc. Under reasonable assumptions, there are numbers h_j for which the sequence of successive points $[\alpha_{(j)1} \quad \cdots \quad \alpha_{(j)n}]$ will converge to $[a_1 \quad \cdots \quad a_n]$. From Figure 1 below, where contours corresponding to several constant values of the function are given, it is clear that if too large a value of h_1 is taken the value of the function will be decreased (i.e., the step in the direction of the gradient will have been so large that the top of the hill is overshot too much). Thus, it becomes evident that one must exercise care in the choice of the h_i. More details on the choice of h_i will follow later.

Let us investigate the concept of steepest ascent a little more carefully. Consider the two-dimensional case depicted in Figures 1 and 2. By the direction of steepest ascent from a point $\alpha_{(0)}$ one would ordinarily mean the direction from $\alpha_{(0)}$ to that point on the circumference of a small circle about $\alpha_{(0)}$ at which the function reaches its highest value (see Figure 2). Now in n-dimensional space, the equivalent of a circle (called a hypersphere) is the locus of all points having a certain fixed distance from a given point. One may define the distance between two points $[\alpha_{(0)1} \quad \cdots \quad \alpha_{(0)n}]$, $[\alpha_{(0)1} + \epsilon_1 \quad \cdots \quad \alpha_{(0)n} + \epsilon_n]$ by $\left(\sum_{i=1}^n \epsilon_i^2\right)^{\frac{1}{2}}$. This distance formula defines the Euclidean metric. However, one may weigh the values of ϵ_2 more heavily than the values of other ϵ_i, and $\sqrt{\epsilon_1^2 + 2\epsilon_2^2 + \epsilon_3^2 + \cdots + \epsilon_n^2}$ may be used as the measure of distance. Indeed, for any positive definite symmetric matrix $U = \| u_{ij} \|$, one may consider

$$\sqrt{\sum_{i,j} \epsilon_i u_{ij} \epsilon_j}$$

as the measure of "distance." Then one may consider a small "hypersphere," that is, the locus of points at a fixed small "distance" from $\alpha_{(0)}$ in that metric (an ellipsoid in the Euclidean metric) and take the point on the "hypersphere" where the function takes on its largest value.

(For the case of two dimensions, see Figure 2. The dotted arrow represents the direction of steepest ascent with respect to a metric corresponding to the ellipse about the initial point.) It can be shown that if the metric is such that the ellipsoid about $\alpha_{(0)}$ is similar to the approximately ellipsoidal contours about $[a_1 \quad a_2 \quad \cdots \quad a_n]$ on which the function is constant, then the ensuing direction is very close to that of the line joining $\alpha_{(0)}$ to $[a_1 \quad \cdots \quad a_n]$. In general, if the metric associated with U is used, the corresponding direction of steepest ascent is given by

$$d_i = \sum_{j=1}^{n} u^{ij} \frac{\partial f}{\partial \alpha_j}\bigg|_{\alpha=\alpha_{(0)}}, \tag{19}$$

where $[u^{ij}] = U^{-1}$.

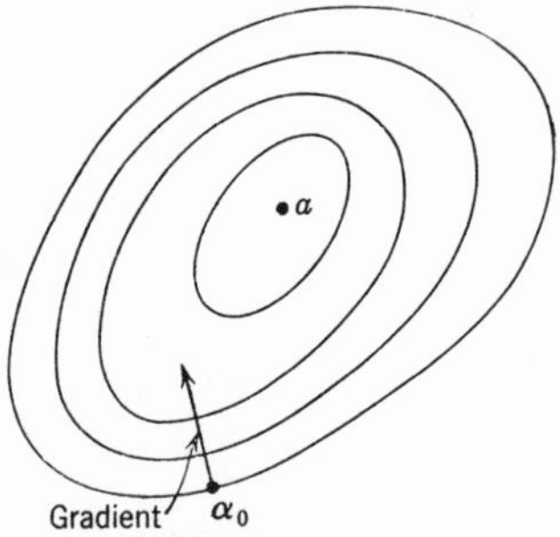

FIGURE 1

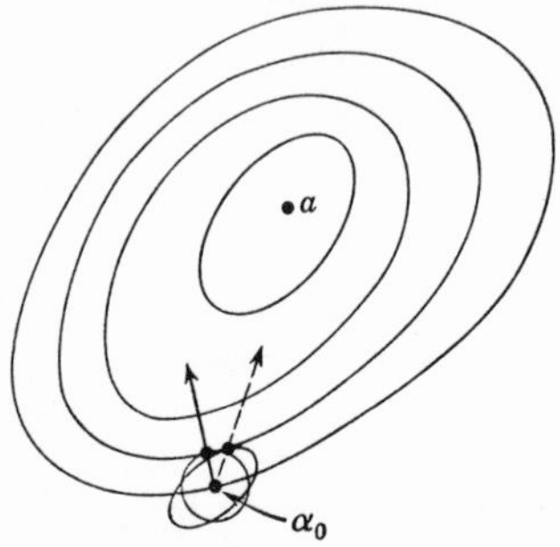

FIGURE 2

Suppose that the point $[\alpha_1 \quad \alpha_2 \quad \cdots \quad \alpha_n]$ is represented by the vector α and that the mth approximation is $\alpha_{(m)} = [\alpha_{(m)1} \quad \alpha_{(m)2} \quad \cdots \quad \alpha_{(m)n}]$. The error of the mth approximation is defined by

$$e_{(m)} = \alpha_{(m)} - a. \tag{20}$$

It can be shown[17] that there are n vectors $v^1, v^2, \cdots, v^n$ associated with n positive numbers $\lambda_1, \lambda_2, \cdots, \lambda_n$ such that

$$\begin{aligned} e_{(0)} &= v^1 + v^2 + \cdots + v^n, \\ e_{(1)} &= (1 - h_1\lambda_1)v^1 + (1 - h_1\lambda_2)v^2 + \cdots + (1 - h_1\lambda_n)v^n \\ &\qquad + \text{higher-order terms}, \\ e_{(2)} &= (1 - h_2\lambda_1)(1 - h_1\lambda_1)v^1 + (1 - h_2\lambda_2)(1 - h_1\lambda_2)v^2 \\ &\qquad + \cdots + (1 - h_2\lambda_n)(1 - h_1\lambda_n)v^n + \text{higher-order terms}, \end{aligned} \tag{21}$$

[17] See Koopmans, Rubin, and Leipnik [1950, Sections 4.3.3 and 4.4.6].

where h_1, h_2, $\cdots$, as before, are the values h_j associated with the first, second, $\cdots$ iterations. Since the object of the method is to reduce the errors, one should try to get values h_j which make the $(1 - h_1\lambda_i) \cdot (1 - h_2\lambda_i) \cdots (1 - h_m\lambda_i)$, $i = 1, \cdots, n$, small. If $\lambda_1, \lambda_2, \cdots$ were known it would be wise to take an occasional $h = 1/\lambda_1$, an occasional $h = 1/\lambda_2$, etc. The values of the λ_i depend on the matrix U. If U is redefined by $u_{ij} = -\partial^2 f/\partial\alpha_i\partial\alpha_j$ evaluated at $\alpha = \alpha_{(m)}$ after each iteration, then the λ_i are all approximately 1. In this case $h = 1$ is a very good value to take. Then the errors are all small terms owing to the fact that third-order terms have been omitted from the above formulae. When one is not close to the point a, the third-order terms may be important, the approximations in those formulae may be poor, and hence it may not be wise to go through all the labor of computing $[\partial^2 f/\partial\alpha_i\partial\alpha_j]$ at $\alpha = \alpha_{(m)}$ and inverting this matrix. One may instead take for U another matrix which is not very different from the one above (i.e., the λ_i are still very close to 1), but easier to compute. Furthermore, one need not revise the matrix U at each iteration.

5. Variables Subject to Linear Restrictions

In the F.I.D., F.I.N.D., and L.I.S. methods the likelihood function is a function of the unknown coefficients of all equations estimated. Since frequently there are linear restrictions on those coefficients (e.g., some of them are zero, and the differences of some of them are zero), a notation was developed to permit easy transition from a function of many parameters that are subject to linear restrictions to a function of a smaller number of "free" independent parameters that are subject to no restrictions. This method will be illustrated with the particular problem with which we are dealing.

In equations (1) and (2) of Model (a) we may use the three identities to eliminate the three jointly dependent variables I, Y, and C as follows:

$$C_t = Y_t + \tau_t - I_t - (G_t + F_t)$$

$$C_t = W_{1t} + W_{2t} + \pi_t + \tau_t - Z_t + Z_{t-1} - (G_t + F_t),$$

$$Y_t + \tau_t - W_{2t} = W_{1t} + \pi_t + \tau_t.$$

Substituting the expressions for I_t, Y_t, C_t, and $Y_t + \tau_t - W_{2t}$ in the first three equations we obtain

$$\text{(22.i)} \quad \begin{aligned} &W_{1t} + W_{2t} + \pi_t + \tau_t - Z_t + Z_{t-1} - (G_t + F_t) \\ &\qquad = \alpha_0 + \alpha_1\pi_t + \alpha_2(W_{1t} + W_{2t}) + \alpha_3\pi_{t-1} + u_{1t}, \end{aligned}$$

$$\text{(22.ii)} \quad Z_t - Z_{t-1} = \alpha_4 + \alpha_5\pi_t + \alpha_6\pi_{t-1} + \alpha_7 Z_{t-1} + u_{2t},$$

$$\text{(22.iii)} \quad W_{1t} = \alpha_8 + \alpha_9(W_{1t} + \pi_t + \tau_t) + \alpha_{10}t + \alpha_{11}(Y_{t-1} + \tau_{t-1} - W_{2,t-1}) + u_{3t}\,.$$

Let $\pi_t = y_{1t}$, $W_{1t} = y_{2t}$, $Z_t = y_{3t}$, $W_{2t} = z_{1t}$, $\pi_{t-1} = z_{2t}$, $Z_{t-1} = z_{3t}$, $t = z_{4t}$, $\tau_t = z_{5t}$, $G_t + F_t = z_{6t}$, $(Y_{t-1} + \tau_{t-1} - W_{2,t-1}) = z_{7t}$. Then our equations become

$$\text{(23.i)} \quad (\alpha_1 - 1)y_{1t} + (\alpha_2 - 1)y_{2t} + y_{3t} + (\alpha_2 - 1)z_{1t} + \alpha_3 z_{2t} - z_{3t} - z_{5t} + z_{6t} + \alpha_0 + u_{1t} = 0,$$

$$\text{(23.ii)} \quad \alpha_5 y_{1t} - y_{3t} + \alpha_6 z_{2t} + (\alpha_7 + 1)z_{3t} + \alpha_4 + u_{2t} = 0,$$

$$\text{(23.iii)} \quad \alpha_9 y_{1t} + (\alpha_9 - 1)y_{2t} + \alpha_{10} z_{4t} + \alpha_9 z_{5t} + \alpha_{11} z_{7t} + \alpha_8 + u_{3t} = 0.$$

In matrix form we may write

$$\mathrm{A}x'_t + \gamma'_0 + u'_t = 0,$$

where

$$\text{(24)} \quad \mathrm{A} = \begin{array}{c} \\ \end{array}\begin{array}{cccccccccc} y_1 & y_2 & y_3 & z_1 & z_2 & z_3 & z_4 & z_5 & z_6 & z_7 \end{array}$$

$$\mathrm{A} = \left[\begin{array}{cccccccccc} \alpha_1-1 & \alpha_2-1 & 1 & \alpha_2-1 & \alpha_3 & -1 & 0 & -1 & 1 & 0 \\ \alpha_5 & 0 & -1 & 0 & \alpha_6 & \alpha_7+1 & 0 & 0 & 0 & 0 \\ \alpha_9 & \alpha_9-1 & 0 & 0 & 0 & 0 & \alpha_{10} & 9 & 0 & \alpha_{11} \end{array}\right] \begin{array}{c} y_1 \\ y_2 \\ y_3 \end{array}$$

$$\gamma_0 = [\alpha_0 \quad \alpha_4 \quad \alpha_8], \qquad u_t = [u_{1t} \quad u_{2t} \quad u_{3t}].$$

Let α = vec A be defined as the row vector obtained by adjoining the second row of A to the first and to this vector again adjoining the third row:[18]

$$\text{(25)} \quad \alpha = [(\alpha_1 - 1) \quad (\alpha_2 - 1) \quad 1 \quad (\alpha_2 - 1) \quad \alpha_3 \quad -1 \quad 0 \quad -1 \quad 1 \quad 0 \quad \alpha_5 \quad 0 \quad -1 \quad 0 \quad \alpha_6 \quad (\alpha_7 + 1) \quad 0 \quad 0 \quad 0 \quad 0 \quad \alpha_9 \quad (\alpha_9 - 1) \quad 0 \quad 0 \quad 0 \quad 0 \quad \alpha_{10} \quad \alpha_9 \quad 0 \quad \alpha_{11}].$$

The elements of this vector are linear combinations of the much smaller number of components of a vector $\alpha^\star$, and thus we may write $\alpha = \alpha^\star \Phi^\star$. There is some arbitrariness in the choice[19] of $\alpha^\star$ and $\Phi^\star$. However, a convenient choice can easily be made, especially in this case where the elements of each row of A are independent of those in the other rows.

[18] This notation will be used in the remainder of this chapter. Thus vec A, where A is a matrix, will denote the vector obtained by adjoining the second row of A to the first row, etc.; vec A = $[a_{11} \;\cdots\; a_{1n} \;\; a_{21} \;\cdots\; a_{2n} \;\cdots\cdots\; a_{n1} \;\cdots\; a_{nn}]$.

[19] $\Phi^\star$ is the basic matrix discussed in Koopmans, Rubin, and Leipnik [1950, pp. 160–166; especially p. 164].

Let $\alpha_1^1 = \alpha_1 - 1$, $\alpha_2^1 = \alpha_2 - 1$, $\alpha_3^1 = 1$, $\alpha_4^1 = \alpha_3$, and $\alpha_1 = [\alpha_1^1 \ \ \alpha_2^1 \ \ \alpha_3^1 \ \ \alpha_4^1]$. Then the first row of A is given by

$$\text{(26.i)} \quad \begin{aligned} &[(\alpha_1 - 1) \quad (\alpha_2 - 1) \quad 1 \quad (\alpha_2 - 1) \quad \alpha_3 \quad -1 \quad 0 \quad -1 \quad 1 \quad 0] \\ &\qquad = [\alpha_1^1 \quad \alpha_2^1 \quad \alpha_3^1 \quad \alpha_4^1]\, \Phi_x^1, \end{aligned}$$

where Φ_x^1 is illustrated in Table 7.1

Let $\alpha_1^2 = \alpha_5$, $\alpha_2^2 = -1$, $\alpha_3^2 = \alpha_6$, $\alpha_4^2 = \alpha_7 + 1$, and $\alpha^2 = [\alpha_1^2 \ \ \alpha_2^2 \ \ \alpha_3^2 \ \ \alpha_4^2]$. Then the second row of A is given by

$$\text{(26.ii)} \quad \begin{aligned} &[\alpha_5 \quad 0 \quad -1 \quad 0 \quad \alpha_6 \quad (\alpha_7 + 1) \quad 0 \quad 0 \quad 0 \quad 0] \\ &\qquad = [\alpha_1^2 \quad \alpha_2^2 \quad \alpha_3^2 \quad \alpha_4^2]\, \Phi_x^2, \end{aligned}$$

where Φ_x^2 is as in Table 7.1.

Let $\alpha_1^3 = \alpha_9$, $\alpha_2^3 = 1$, $\alpha_3^3 = \alpha_{10}$, $\alpha_4^3 = \alpha_{11}$, and $\alpha^3 = [\alpha_1^3 \ \ \alpha_2^3 \ \ \alpha_3^3 \ \ \alpha_4^3]$. Then the third row of A is given by

$$\text{(26.iii)} \quad \begin{aligned} &[\alpha_9 \quad (\alpha_9 - 1) \quad 0 \quad 0 \quad 0 \quad 0 \quad \alpha_{10} \quad \alpha_9 \quad 0 \quad \alpha_{11}] \\ &\qquad = [\alpha_1^3 \quad \alpha_2^3 \quad \alpha_3^3 \quad \alpha_4^3]\, \Phi_x^3, \end{aligned}$$

where again Φ_x^3 is as in Table 7.1. Finally, let

$$\text{(27)} \qquad \alpha^\star = [\alpha^1 \quad \alpha^2 \quad \alpha^3],$$

$$\text{(28)} \qquad \Phi^\star = \begin{bmatrix} \Phi_x^1 & 0 & 0 \\ 0 & \Phi_x^2 & 0 \\ 0 & 0 & \Phi_x^3 \end{bmatrix}.$$

Then $\alpha = \alpha^\star \Phi^\star$.

The guiding principle of selecting the elements of α^1, α^2, and α^3 is to take elements that are independent. Thus the first row had originally the three independent coefficients, α_1, α_2, α_3, and 1. If it had not been slightly more convenient to do otherwise, we might have let $\alpha_1^1 = \alpha_1$, $\alpha_2^1 = \alpha_2$, $\alpha_3^1 = \alpha_3$, and $\alpha_4^1 = 1$. Once α^1 is given, Φ_x^1 is thereby determined. The reader is invited to check this by constructing Φ_x^1 for the alternative choice of α^1 just mentioned.

Each of the Φ_x^i ($i = 1, 2, 3$) has 4 rows. This is due to the special circumstance that for this particular system of equations each row of A depended on exactly three α's and the constant 1. It is not necessary for the development which follows that all the Φ_x^i have the same number of rows.

At times it will be important to consider the vectors α^1, α^2, α^3, and $\alpha^\star$ without the elements α_3^1, α_2^2, and α_2^3, for these may be considered as fixed and not variable. (They are sometimes called normalizing elements.) To this end we can use the notation

(29)
$$
\begin{aligned}
{}_{\oplus}\alpha^{1} &= [\alpha_1^1 \quad \alpha_2^1 \quad \alpha_4^1],\\
{}_{\oplus}\alpha^{2} &= [\alpha_1^2 \quad \alpha_3^2 \quad \alpha_4^2],\\
{}_{\oplus}\alpha^{3} &= [\alpha_1^3 \quad \alpha_3^3 \quad \alpha_4^3],\\
{}_{\oplus}\alpha^{\star} &= [{}_{\oplus}\alpha^{1} \quad {}_{\oplus}\alpha^{2} \quad {}_{\oplus}\alpha^{3}],
\end{aligned}
$$

where the left subscript $_{\oplus}$ denotes that the normalized elements are omitted.

Similarly, ${}_{\oplus}\Phi^{\star}$ will denote the matrix $\Phi^{\star}$ with the rows corresponding to the normalized elements omitted. These are the third, sixth, and tenth rows. If $a_{(1)}$ and $a_{(2)}$ are two estimates of the vector α, their elements are subject to the same linear restrictions. Thus $a_{(1)} = a^{\star}_{(1)}\Phi^{\star}$, $a_{(2)} = a^{\star}_{(2)}\Phi^{\star}$, so

(30)
$$d = a_{(1)} - a_{(2)} = (a^{\star}_{(1)} - a^{\star}_{(2)})\Phi^{\star} = d^{\star}\Phi^{\star}.$$

Now $d^{\star} = a^{\star}_{(1)} - a^{\star}_{(2)}$ has zeros in the positions corresponding to the normalized elements, so that $d = {}_{\oplus}d^{\star} \cdot {}_{\oplus}\Phi^{\star}$. In other words, the difference of two estimates of A can be expressed without the use of the normalized elements, because only nine of the twelve elements of $a^{\star}$ are variables.

6. Mathematical Considerations Concerning the Full-Information Method in the Nondiagonal Case[20]

In the F.I.N.D. method (where no restrictions are imposed on the covariance matrix) the logarithmic likelihood function is given by

(31)
$$L^{(1)}(\mathrm{A}) = \text{const.} + \log|\det \mathrm{B}| - \tfrac{1}{2}\log\det \bar{S}(\mathrm{A}),$$

where $\bar{S}(\mathrm{A}) \equiv \mathrm{A}\bar{M}_{xx}\mathrm{A}'$ and where $\mathrm{A} = [\mathrm{B} \quad \Gamma]$ is the matrix of coefficients to be estimated, while the likelihood function has already been maximized with respect to the matrix of the covariances of the disturbances, Σ. This function may be compared with that represented in (5.58) of Chapter VI, from which it differs only with respect to the definition of moments used. For this reason, the maximum-likelihood estimate of Σ computed from the maximum-likelihood estimate A of A is not $\bar{S}(A)$, but is given by $(1/T^2)\bar{S}(A) = S$ as defined in Chapter VI, equation (5.59).

To maximize $L^{(1)}(\mathrm{A})$ with respect to variations in the elements of A

[20] This section may be omitted at the first reading if it is found to be too difficult.

(subject to restrictions) we consider the Taylor expansion of $L^{(1)}(\mathrm{A})$, which has been derived elsewhere,[21] as follows:[22,23]

$$
\begin{aligned}
L^{(1)}(A_0 + h\Delta A_0) = {} & \log|\det B_0| - \tfrac{1}{2}\log\det \bar{S}_0 \\
& + h\,\{\mathrm{tr}\,(B_0'^{-1}\Delta B_0') - \mathrm{tr}\,(\bar{S}_0^{-1}A_0\bar{M}_{xx}\Delta A_0')\} \\
& + \tfrac{1}{2}h^2\,\mathrm{tr}\,\{-(B_0'^{-1}\Delta B_0')^2 \\
& + \bar{S}_0^{-1}(A_0\bar{M}_{xx}\Delta A_0' + (\Delta A_0)\bar{M}_{xx}A_0')\bar{S}_0^{-1}A_0\bar{M}_{xx}\Delta A_0' \\
& - \bar{S}_0^{-1}(\Delta A_0)\bar{M}_{xx}\Delta A_0'\} + 0(h^3).
\end{aligned} \tag{32}
$$

The symbol A_0 represents an initial approximation to the adjusted parameter matrix A, and $\bar{S}_0 = A_0\bar{M}_{xx}A_0'$. The direct product $C \otimes E$ of C and E (right direct product as defined in MacDuffee [1933, p. 81]), which are square matrices of order m and n, respectively, is a square matrix of order mn, with one block for each element of C. The ijth block is the ijth element of C times E; i.e.,

$$
C \otimes E = \begin{bmatrix} c_{11}E & c_{12}E & \cdots & c_{1m}E \\ c_{21}E & c_{22}E & \cdots & c_{2m}E \\ \cdots & \cdots & \cdots & \cdots \\ c_{m1}E & c_{m2}E & \cdots & c_{mm}E \end{bmatrix}
$$

$$
= \left[\begin{array}{ccc|c|ccc}
c_{11}e_{11} & \cdots & c_{11}e_{1n} & & c_{1m}e_{11} & \cdots & c_{1m}e_{1n} \\
c_{11}e_{21} & \cdots & c_{11}e_{2n} & \cdots & c_{1m}e_{12} & \cdots & c_{1m}e_{2n} \\
\cdots & \cdots & \cdots & & \cdots & \cdots & \cdots \\
c_{11}e_{n1} & \cdots & c_{11}e_{nn} & & c_{1m}e_{n1} & \cdots & c_{1m}e_{nn} \\
\hline
& \cdots & & \cdots & & \cdots & \\
\hline
c_{m1}e_{11} & \cdots & c_{m1}e_{1n} & & c_{mm}e_{11} & \cdots & c_{mm}e_{1n} \\
\cdots & \cdots & \cdots & \cdots & \cdots & \cdots & \cdots \\
c_{m1}e_{n1} & \cdots & c_{m1}e_{nn} & & c_{mm}e_{n1} & \cdots & c_{mm}e_{nn}
\end{array}\right]
$$

[21] See Koopmans, Rubin, and Leipnik [1950, equation (4.207)].

[22] For the definition of the trace tr C of a square matrix C, see Chapter VI, Section 5.4, equation (5.27).

[23] We use the subscript zero to denote the arbitrary values A_0, B_0, $\bar{S}_0$, of the parameters A, B, $\bar{\Sigma} = T^2\Sigma$ on which this expansion is based. Depending on the context, these values may stand either for initial or subsequent trial values in

Expression (32) can also be written as

$$L^{(1)}(A_0 + h\Delta A_0) = \log |\det B_0| - \tfrac{1}{2}\log\det \bar{S}_0$$

$$+ h\,\{\text{vec}\,[B_0'^{-1} \quad 0_{yz}]({}_{\oplus}\Phi^{\star})' - a_0^{\star}\Phi^{\star}(\bar{S}_0^{-1}\otimes \bar{M}_{zz})({}_{\oplus}\Phi^{\star})'\}({}_{\oplus}d^{\star})' \tag{33}$$

$$+ \tfrac{1}{2}h^2\,\{{}_{\oplus}d^{\star}\cdot {}_{\oplus\oplus}L_0^{\star\star}\cdot({}_{\oplus}d^{\star})'\} + 0(h^3),$$

where $L_0^{\star\star}$ is the matrix $L^{\star\star}$ of the second partial derivatives of the logarithmic likelihood function,[24] evaluated at the point $\mathrm{A} = A_0$, and where $d^{\star}$ corresponds to ΔA_0 in the same way that $a_0^{\star}$ corresponds to A_0. The computation of this matrix for any given value of A will be examined later. It has also been shown that the ijth element of $\bar{S}_0$ is given by[25] $(a_0^i)V^{(i,j)}(a_0^j)'$, where

$$V^{(i,j)} = (\Phi_z^i)\bar{M}_{zz}(\Phi_z^j)'. \tag{34}$$

The direction of steepest ascent is given by ${}_{\oplus}d^{\star} = {}_{\oplus}n^{\star}({}_{\oplus\oplus}U^{\star\star})^{-1}$, where[26]

$${}_{\oplus}n^{\star} = \text{vec}\;[(B_0')^{-1} \quad 0_{yz}]({}_{\oplus}\Phi^{\star})' - a_0^{\star}\Phi^{\star}(\bar{S}_0^{-1}\otimes \bar{M}_{zz})({}_{\oplus}\Phi^{\star})' \tag{35}$$

and where ${}_{\oplus\oplus}U^{\star\star}$ is determined by the concept of distance adopted. There are three very useful definitions of $U^{\star\star}$ that were developed for this problem. One is $U^{\star\star} = P^{\star\star}$ where $P^{\star\star} = \Phi^{\star}(\bar{S}_0^{-1}\otimes\bar{M}_{zz})\Phi^{\star\prime}$; the gradient method associated with $P^{\star\star}$ is called the $\mathcal{P}_h$ method. Another method is the $\mathcal{R}_h$ method, where $U^{\star\star} = R^{\star\star}$ with $R^{\star\star}$ made up of blocks $R^{(i,j)} = \bar{S}_0^{ij}\,N^{(i,j)}$ and

$$N^{(i,j)} = \Phi_z^i\bar{M}_{zz}\bar{M}_{zz}^{-1}\bar{M}_{zz}(\Phi_z^j)'. \tag{36}$$

The third is the $\mathcal{L}_h$ or Newton method, where $U^{\star\star} = -L^{\star\star}$.

---

iterative approximations to the maximum-likelihood estimates A, B, $\bar{S}$, or for those estimates themselves, or (in general reasoning) for an arbitrary set of parameter values. (See also footnote 29 below.)

The notation $0(h^3)$ indicates that the remainder in the expansion is of third order in h (i.e., that there is a constant K such that the remainder is $\leqslant Kh^3$ for h sufficiently small. For the definition of "vec," see footnote 18.

[24] The matrix $L^{\star\star} = [\partial^2 L^{(1)}(\mathrm{A})/\partial(\text{vec}\,\mathrm{A})^2]$ should not be confused with the likelihood function itself, which will always be written with its argument A attached.

[25] The elements of the inverse of a matrix are denoted by superscripts with a lower case letter. A block corresponding to a_0^i and a_0^j is denoted by a capital letter with superscripts (i, j).

[26] The matrix 0_{yz} is simply a matrix of G rows and K columns, each of whose elements is zero.

7. Computations in the Full-Information Method in the Nondiagonal Case[27]

A number of computations must be carried out once and for all in order to be used for the successive iterations. As in L.I.S.E., we must construct the time series for the moment matrix $\bar{M}_{xx}^{(0)}$ and the adjusted moment matrix $\bar{M}_{xx}^{(a)}$ or $\bar{M}_{xx}$. Slight differences may arise in that some variables that are convenient in L.I.S.E. are not needed in F.I.N.D. For example, C is used in L.I.S.E. but was eliminated in setting up F.I.N.D. Specifying

$$x = [y_1 \quad y_2 \quad y_3 \quad z_1 \quad z_2 \quad \cdots \quad z_7]$$
$$= [\pi \quad W_1 \quad Z \quad W_2 \quad \pi_{-1} \quad Z_{-1} \quad t \quad \tau \quad (G + F) \quad (Y + \tau - W_2)_{-1}]$$

we proceed as in the L.I.S.E. method to obtain the adjusted moment matrix $\bar{M}_{xx}^{(a)}$ (Tables 1 and 2). Also, as in the L.I.S.E. method, $\bar{M}_{yz}\bar{M}_{zz}^{-1}\bar{M}_{zy}$ is computed. Use is made of $\bar{M}_{xz}\bar{M}_{zz}^{-1}\bar{M}_{zx} = \begin{bmatrix} \bar{M}_{yz}\bar{M}_{zz}^{-1}\bar{M}_{zy} & \bar{M}_{yz} \\ \bar{M}_{zy} & \bar{M}_{zz} \end{bmatrix}$. Table 6 contains $\bar{M}_{xx}$ and $\bar{M}_{xz}\bar{M}_{zz}^{-1}\bar{M}_{zx}$, although in computing they would usually end up on different pages.

Table 7 illustrates the Φ_x^i and the computation of $\Phi_x^i\bar{M}_{xx}$ and $\Phi_x^i\bar{M}_{xz}\bar{M}_{zz}^{-1}\bar{M}_{zx}$. This computation is quite simple and consists mostly of copying elements of $\bar{M}_{xx}$ and $\bar{M}_{xz}\bar{M}_{zz}^{-1}\bar{M}_{zx}$ because most of the rows of the Φ's contain a single 1, all other elements being zero.

In Tables 8.1 and 8.2

$$V^{(i,j)} = \Phi_x^i\bar{M}_{xx}(\Phi_x^j)' \tag{37}$$

and

$$N^{(i,j)} = \Phi_x^i\bar{M}_{xz}\bar{M}_{zz}^{-1}\bar{M}_{zx}(\Phi_x^j)' \tag{38}$$

are computed.[28] This again is as simple as the above calculations, and the sum row of Φ is used as the sum column of Φ' in checking. The matrices $V^{(i,j)}$ and $N^{(i,j)}$ are described as "reduced" (by the basic matrices

[27] Sections 3, 7, 9, and 11 of this chapter give computations on two related models. These computations were not carried out independently, but are connected as follows: Two separate estimates by the L.I.S.E. method are given—a very crude one given as $A_{(0)}$ in Table 28, and a more refined one using ten iterations, given on p. 258. The former was used as an initial approximation for the F.I.D. computations summarized in Table 28. The latter was used as an initial approximation for the L.I.S. computations summarized in Table 21. Finally, the F.I.D. estimate B of Table 27 ($B_{(13)}$ of Table 28) was used as an initial approximation for the F.I.N.D. computations summarized in Table 11.

[28] One must keep in mind that superscripts in parentheses on capital letters designate blocks and not elements of the inverse.

Φ_x^i); the matrices $\Phi_x^i \bar{M}_{xz}$ and $\Phi_x^i \bar{M}_{xz} \bar{M}_{zz}^{-1} \bar{M}_{zx}$ are called "semireduced." It should be noted that, since $V^{(2,1)} = (V^{(1,2)})'$, it is necessary only to compute $V^{(1,1)}$, $V^{(1,2)}$, $V^{(1,3)}$, $V^{(2,2)}$, $V^{(2,3)}$, and $V^{(3,3)}$. For sum checking the computation of these V's, the sum of each column of each V is useful. However, for later work one can make good use of the sum of each row. (For $V^{(1,1)}$, $V^{(2,2)}$, $V^{(3,3)}$ the sum of the rows is equal to the sum of the columns by symmetry.) Also, for many calculations ${}_{\oplus\oplus}V^{(i,j)}$ is needed instead of $V^{(i,j)}$. We observe here that the sum of all the elements in this submatrix is formed and will be found useful. $N^{(i,j)}$ is obtained and treated in the same fashion. It should be pointed out once more that all these blocks are 4 by 4 blocks only by accident. In general, the (i, j)th block has as many rows as there are parameters in the ith equation and as many columns as there are parameters in the jth equation.

We may now proceed with the iterations. The process of obtaining ${}_{\oplus}n^{\star}$ is the same for all of the methods. In Table 9 we illustrate the computation of ${}_{\oplus}n^{\star}$ in the first iteration. The initial approximation would normally be derived from the L.I.S.E. estimates. In this case, however, F.I.D. estimates had already been obtained (see Table 28), and these were used as the initial approximation. Thus the components of $B_{(13)}$ of Table 28 are the components of $a^{\star}_{(0)}$ of Table 11. First[29]

$$p_i^j = a^i V^{(i,j)} \tag{39}$$

is computed with check sums. It will soon be found useful to obtain the sum row $p_\Sigma^j = p_1^j + p_2^j + p_3^j$. In this computation $p_2^1 = a^2 V^{(2,1)}$ is computed by cumulating products of elements of a^2 with those of the *rows* of $V^{(1,2)}$, for the columns of $V^{(2,1)}$ are the rows of $V^{(1,2)}$.

Next the matrix $\bar{S} = [\bar{s}_{ij}]$ is computed, where

$$\bar{s}_{ij} = a^i V^{(i,j)} (a^j)' = p_i^j (a^j)'. \tag{40}$$

Since $\bar{S}$ is symmetric it is not necessary to obtain the terms below the main diagonal. This computation is checked by $p_\Sigma^j (a^j)' = \bar{s}_{11} + \bar{s}_{21} + \bar{s}_{31} = \bar{s}_{11} + \bar{s}_{12} + \bar{s}_{13}$. Adding 1 to this we obtain a quantity which checks with the sum of the first row of the Doolittle work done on $\bar{S}$ in Table 9. We then invert $\bar{S}$ to get $\bar{S}^{-1} = [\bar{s}^{ij}]$. Incidentally, we compute det $\bar{S}$ by multiplying the top terms on the main diagonal of the forward solution; that is, $10^3 \cdot \det \bar{S} = (0.463675)(0.453154)(0.108059) = 0.022705$. The next step is to construct B, which is the first square part of $A = [B \quad C]$, which in turn is completely characterized by $a = \operatorname{vec} A = a^{\star}\Phi^{\star}$. The first row of A is $a^1\Phi_x^1$. Thus the first row of B is $a^1\Phi_y^1$. The second row of B is $a^2\Phi_y^2$, etc. Thus

[29] For simplicity we have omitted in equations (39)–(44) subscripts (0) indicating the iterations to which the quantities a^i, $\bar{s}_{ij}$, B, etc., refer.

$$B' = [(a^1\Phi_y^1)' \quad (a^2\Phi_y^2)' \quad (a^3\Phi_y^3)']. \tag{41}$$

Having constructed B, we obtain (see footnote 3) the inverse $B^{-1} = [b^{ij}]$ and check it. While the inversion may be performed by the Doolittle procedure, in this particular case B is so simple that it is convenient to find the determinant and adjoint of B and thence find the inverse.

Now we compute

$$\begin{aligned} m^1 &= \bar{s}^{11}p_1^1 + \bar{s}^{12}p_2^1 + \bar{s}^{13}p_3^1, \\ m^2 &= \bar{s}^{21}p_1^2 + \bar{s}^{22}p_2^2 + \bar{s}^{23}p_3^2, \\ m^3 &= \bar{s}^{31}p_1^3 + \bar{s}^{32}p_2^3 + \bar{s}^{33}p_3^3. \end{aligned} \tag{42}$$

Actually only ${}_{\oplus}m^{\star} = [{}_{\oplus}m^1 \quad {}_{\oplus}m^2 \quad {}_{\oplus}m^3]$ is required. Then we compute

$$l^i = \{\Phi_y^i(B^{-1})_i\}' \qquad (i = 1, 2, 3). \tag{43}$$

That is, l^1, for example, is the transpose of the vector obtained by multiplying Φ_y^1 into the first column of B^{-1}. Here again only $[{}_{\oplus}l^1 \quad {}_{\oplus}l^2 \quad {}_{\oplus}l^3]$ is required. Finally, ${}_{\oplus}n^{\star} = {}_{\oplus}l^{\star} - {}_{\oplus}m^{\star}$.

It now remains to compute $P^{\star\star}$, $R^{\star\star}$, or $L^{\star\star}$, as the case may be. Since the only difference between $P^{\star\star}$ and $R^{\star\star}$ lies in the use of $V^{\star\star}$ or $N^{\star\star}$, respectively, we shall use $R^{\star\star}$ as the illustration in Table 10. We compute $R^{\star\star}$ by

$$R^{(i,j)} = \bar{s}^{ij}N^{(i,j)},$$

multiplying the blocks of $N^{\star\star}$ by the corresponding element of $\bar{S}^{-1}$. Again we omit the rows and columns corresponding to the normalized parameters. We write $({}_{\oplus}n^{\star})'$ next to ${}_{\oplus\oplus}R^{\star\star}$ in preparing the inversion. The sum column is written out and it should check in this fashion, where "(sum of $N^{(i,j)}$)" stands for the sum of all elements in the matrix $N^{(i,j)}$: $10^{-1}\bar{s}^{11}\cdot$(sum of $N^{(1,1)}$) + $10^{-1}\bar{s}^{12}\cdot$(sum of $N^{(1,2)}$) + $10^{-1}\bar{s}^{13}\cdot$(sum of $N^{(1,3)}$) + the sum of the elements of ${}_{\oplus}n^1$ [which is equal to (4.314815)(7.716584) + (−2.153116)(4.859279) + (4.211728)(11.805756) + 2.375189] must be equal to ten times the sum of the first three rows, 10(1.700770 + 4.158856 + 1.633460). Similarly $10^{-1}\cdot\bar{s}^{21}$ (sum of $N^{(2,1)}$) + $10^{-1}\cdot\bar{s}^{22}\cdot$(sum of $N^{(2,2)}$) + $10^{-1}\bar{s}^{23}\cdot$(sum of $N^{(2,3)}$) + the sum of the elements of ${}_{\oplus}n^2$ [which is equal to (−2.153116)(4.859279) + (3.263736)(6.337798) + (−3.127532)(8.615121) + (−2.286249)] must be equal to ten times the sum of the fourth, fifth, and sixth rows, 10(−0.971591 − 0.757835 − 0.171373). The final three rows are checked in the same fashion, and then the Doolittle method is applied to get

$$({}_{\oplus}d^{\star})' = ({}_{\oplus\oplus}R^{\star\star})^{-1}({}_{\oplus}n^{\star})'. \tag{44}$$

This ${}_{\oplus}d^{\star}$ gives the direction of steepest ascent with respect to the measure of distance given by ${}_{\oplus\oplus}R^{\star\star}$ in the nine-dimensional space of unrestricted parameters.[30] Since the computation and inversion of ${}_{\oplus\oplus}R^{\star\star}$ consumes much time, we may modify the $\mathcal{R}_h$ method by using the same ${}_{\oplus\oplus}R^{\star\star}$ for several iterations instead of recomputing it with the new estimate of A after each iteration. (A similar remark applies to the $\mathcal{L}_h$ and $\mathcal{P}_h$ methods.)

Table 11 gives sections of the summary page of the iterations. The initial approximation $a^{\star}_{(0)}$ is listed. Then det B, det $\bar{S}$, and $(\det B)^2/\det \bar{S}$, respectively, are listed and calculated. Since $L^{(1)}(\mathrm{A}) = $ constant $+\frac{1}{2}\log\{(\det \mathrm{B})^2/\det \mathrm{A}\bar{M}_{xx}\mathrm{A}'\}$, $L^{(1)}(\mathrm{A})$ will attain a maximum when the function in braces does so. Then $d^{\star}_{(0)}$ is listed, and finally a value of $h = h_1$ is obtained to determine the length of the step in the appropriate direction. Thus, $a^{\star}_{(1)} = a^{\star}_{(0)} + h_1 d^{\star}_{(0)}$. It will be noted that iterations 1, 2, and 3 make use of the same $R^{\star\star}$ that was computed in Table 10. The last few (except the very last) iterations use the same $L^{\star\star}$.

The problem of choosing the h_i may be clarified by the following considerations. For the $\mathcal{R}_h$ and $\mathcal{L}_h$ methods, if we have a large sample and a model which is "good" in that the restrictions imposed by it are actually satisfied by the "true" structure, then $h_i = 1$ can be shown to have very good properties. For the $\mathcal{P}_h$ method, $h_i = 1$ in conjunction with h's greater than one are to be used (again assuming we have a large sample). Because we seldom have a large sample it is well to start with an $h < 1$ (undershooting). Then several iterations with h increasing may be taken. Note that in the fifth iteration, where the second $R^{\star\star}$ is used, the ratio of the elements of $d^{\star}_{(4)}$ to those of $d^{\star}_{(3)}$ is very roughly about $\frac{1}{5}$. This indicates that the last value of h (i.e., h_4) was only about $\frac{4}{5}$ as large as it should be. Thus $h_5 = \frac{5}{4}$ was used next. The h_i's were not all chosen in this fashion. After a large h is used it is best to use small h's again, for a large h will tend to overshoot considerably in several directions while a subsequent small h will diminish the errors (i.e., the differences between the approximation and the maximizing value) in these directions.

The $\mathcal{L}_h$ method is peculiar in that the closer one is to the maximum, the better effect values of h close to one have. Indeed, convergence is quite rapid if the remaining distance from the maximum is small. On the other hand, if that distance is large, the $\mathcal{L}_h$ method has a certain amount of instability and is, in view of its expensiveness, not desirable. Thus a recommended method would be to start with the relatively stable $\mathcal{P}_h$ method for several iterations, then to switch to the $\mathcal{R}_h$ method for more iterations, and finally to use the $\mathcal{L}_h$ method. In all of these cases it usually

[30] If the $\mathcal{P}_h$ method were used, we would compute $P^{\star\star}$ by $P^{(i,j)} = \bar{s}^{ij}V^{(i,j)}$ and then $({}_{\oplus}d^{\star})' = ({}_{\oplus\oplus}P^{\star\star})^{-1}({}_{\oplus}n^{\star})'$. This ${}_{\oplus}d^{\star}$ would give the direction of steepest ascent with respect to another measure of distance, namely, ${}_{\oplus\oplus}P^{\star\star}$.

pays to use a given $P^{\star\star}$, $R^{\star\star}$, or $L^{\star\star}$ for several iterations without recalculation. Finally if the $d^{\star}$ for an iteration is approximately in the same direction as for the preceding iteration, one may use the method described in the last paragraph to select a good value of h.

When the final approximation to A is obtained, it is deadjusted just as in the L.I.S.E. method.

The computation of $L^{\star\star}$ is relatively complicated, but necessary, at the end of the iterative process, for the estimates of the variances and covariances of the estimates of the parameters are given by $(1/T)(-_{\oplus\oplus}L^{\star\star})^{-1}$ evaluated at the final approximation to A. Tables 12 and 13 illustrate the computation of $L^{\star\star}$ evaluated at the initial approximation. Then, using this $L^{\star\star}$, we compute in Table 14.1, for use in the $\mathfrak{L}_h$ method,

$$({}_{\oplus}d^{\star})' = (-{}_{\oplus\oplus}L^{\star\star})^{-1}({}_{\oplus}n^{\star})'.$$

To get the estimates of the covariances we evaluate $L^{\star\star}$ at the final approximation and then take $(1/T)(-_{\oplus\oplus}L^{\star\star})^{-1}$. This is done in Table 14.2.

It can be shown that the needed positive-definite symmetric matrix $-L^{\star\star}$ can be decomposed into a sum of four symmetric matrices, $-L^{\star\star} = {}^{1}L^{\star\star} - {}^{2}L^{\star\star} - {}^{3}L^{\star\star} + {}^{4}L^{\star\star}$. Let

$$(45)\qquad C_y^i = \Phi_y^i B^{-1}, \qquad f_i^j = \sum_n \bar{s}^{in} p_n^j, \qquad G^{(i,j)} = \sum_n (p_n^i)' f_n^j.$$

Then

$$(46)\qquad \begin{aligned} {}^{1}L^{(i,j)} &= (c_j^i)' c_i^j, \\ {}^{2}L^{(i,j)} &= (f_j^i)'(f_i^j), \\ {}^{3}L^{(i,j)} &= \bar{s}^{ij} G^{(i,j)}, \\ {}^{4}L^{(i,j)} &= \bar{s}^{ij} V^{(i,j)}, \end{aligned}$$

where $(c_j^i)'$ is the jth column of C_y^i; and finally $-L^{\star\star}$ is computed. In the tables we actually computed ${}_{\oplus}C_y^i$, ${}_{\oplus\oplus}G^{(i,j)}$, ${}_{\oplus\oplus}{}^{1}L^{(i,j)}$, ${}_{\oplus\oplus}{}^{2}L^{(i,j)}$, ${}_{\oplus\oplus}{}^{3}L^{(i,j)}$, and ${}_{\oplus\oplus}{}^{4}L^{(i,j)}$, and so computed $-{}_{\oplus\oplus}L^{\star\star}$, but presubscripts ${}_{\oplus}$ have been omitted from the tables where no misunderstanding can arise. The covariances are now deadjusted as in the L.I.S.E. method.

8. Mathematical Considerations Concerning the Limited-Information Subsystem Method

In the L.I.S. method the logarithmic likelihood function is given by[31]

$$(47)\qquad L^{(2)}(\mathrm{A_I}) = \text{const.} - \tfrac{1}{2}\log\frac{\det \mathrm{A_I}\,\overline{M}_{xx}\,\mathrm{A_I}'}{\det \mathrm{B_I}\,\overline{W}_{xx}\,\mathrm{B_I}'},$$

[31] The likelihood function (47) is obtained from that given in Chapter VI, Section 6.1, equation (6.3), by substituting $\overline{M}_{xx}$ for M and $\overline{W}_{xx}$ for W, and absorbing in the constant all terms not dependent on parameters.

where

$$\overline{W}_{xx} = \begin{bmatrix} \overline{W}_{yy} & 0 \\ 0 & 0 \end{bmatrix}, \qquad \overline{W}_{yy} = \bar{M}_{yy} - \bar{M}_{yz}\bar{M}_{zz}^{-1}\bar{M}_{zy}.$$

$\mathrm{A_I} = [\mathrm{B_I} \quad \Gamma_\mathrm{I}]$ is the matrix of coefficients in the subsystem, and we have

$$\mathrm{A} = \begin{bmatrix} \mathrm{A_I} \\ \\ \mathrm{A_{II}} \end{bmatrix} = \begin{bmatrix} \mathrm{B_I} & \Gamma_\mathrm{I} \\ \\ \mathrm{B_{II}} & \Gamma_\mathrm{II} \end{bmatrix}.$$

For a complete system, $\mathrm{A_I} = \mathrm{A}, \mathrm{B_I} = \mathrm{B}$ is square and hence $\det(\mathrm{B_I}\overline{W}_{yy}\mathrm{B_I'}) = (\det \mathrm{B})^2 \det \overline{W}_{yy}$, and $\overline{W}_{yy}$ is constant with respect to the parameters. Thus, for a complete system,

$$L^{(2)}(\mathrm{A_I}) = L^{(2)}(\mathrm{A}) = \text{const.} + \log|\det \mathrm{B}| - \tfrac{1}{2}\log\det \bar{S}(\mathrm{A}).$$

In the following we use

$$\bar{S}_{\mathrm{I\,I}} = A_\mathrm{I}\bar{M}_{xx}A_\mathrm{I}', \qquad T_{\mathrm{I\,I}} = A_\mathrm{I}\overline{W}_{xx}A_\mathrm{I}'.$$

Expanding $L^{(2)}(A_{\mathrm{I},0} + h\Delta A_{\mathrm{I},0})$ in a Taylor series, we have, suppressing the subscript zero on the right-hand side (although A_I, $\bar{S}_{\mathrm{I\,I}}$, and $T_{\mathrm{I\,I}}$ are to be evaluated at $A_\mathrm{I} = A_{\mathrm{I},0}$),

$$\begin{aligned} L^{(2)}(A_{\mathrm{I},0} + h\Delta A_{\mathrm{I},0}) &= \text{const.} + \tfrac{1}{2}\log\det T_{\mathrm{I\,I}} - \tfrac{1}{2}\log\det \bar{S}_{\mathrm{I\,I}} \\ &+ h\,\mathrm{tr}\,\{(T_{\mathrm{I\,I}}^{-1}A_\mathrm{I}\overline{W}_{xx} - \bar{S}_{\mathrm{I\,I}}^{-1}A_\mathrm{I}\bar{M}_{xx})\,\Delta A_\mathrm{I}\} \\ &+ \tfrac{1}{2}h^2\,\mathrm{tr}\,\{(T_{\mathrm{I\,I}}^{-1}(\Delta A_\mathrm{I})\overline{W}_{xx} - \bar{S}_{\mathrm{I\,I}}^{-1}(\Delta A_\mathrm{I})\bar{M}_{xx})\Delta A_\mathrm{I}' \\ &- T_{\mathrm{I\,I}}^{-1}((\Delta A_\mathrm{I})\overline{W}_{xx}A_\mathrm{I}' + A_\mathrm{I}\overline{W}_{xx}\Delta A_\mathrm{I}')\,T_{\mathrm{I\,I}}^{-1}A_\mathrm{I}\overline{W}_{xx}\Delta A_\mathrm{I}' \\ &+ \bar{S}_{\mathrm{I\,I}}^{-1}((\Delta A_\mathrm{I})\bar{M}_{xx}A_\mathrm{I}' + A_\mathrm{I}\bar{M}_{xx}\Delta A_\mathrm{I}')\,\bar{S}_{\mathrm{I\,I}}^{-1}A_\mathrm{I}\bar{M}_{xx}\Delta A_\mathrm{I}'\} \\ &+ 0(h^3), \end{aligned} \tag{48}$$

which can also be written

$$\begin{aligned} L^{(2)}(A_{\mathrm{I},0} + h\Delta A_{\mathrm{I},0}) &= \text{const.} + \tfrac{1}{2}\log\det T_{\mathrm{I\,I}} - \tfrac{1}{2}\log\det \bar{S}_{\mathrm{I\,I}} \\ &+ h\{a_0^\star\Phi^\star(T_{\mathrm{I\,I}}^{-1}\otimes\overline{W}_{xx})({}_\oplus\Phi^\star)' - a_0^\star\Phi^\star(\bar{S}_{\mathrm{I\,I}}^{-1}\otimes\bar{M}_{xx})({}_\oplus\Phi^\star)'\}({}_\oplus d^\star)' \\ &+ \tfrac{1}{2}h^2\cdot{}_\oplus d^\star\cdot{}_{\oplus\oplus}L_0^{\star\star}\cdot({}_\oplus d^\star)' + 0(h^3), \end{aligned} \tag{49}$$

where $L_0^{\star\star} = \left[\dfrac{\partial^2 L^{(2)}(\mathrm{A_I})}{\partial(\mathrm{vec}\,\mathrm{A_I})^2}\right]_{\mathrm{A_I} = A_{\mathrm{I},0}}$ will be examined later. Also,

$$\bar{s}_{ij} = a^i V^{(i,j)}(a^j)', \qquad t_{ij} = a^i Z^{(i,j)}(a^j)', \tag{50}$$

where

$$V^{(i,j)} = \Phi_x^i\bar{M}_{xx}(\Phi_x^j)', \qquad Z^{(i,j)} = \Phi_x^i\overline{W}_{xx}(\Phi_x^j)'.$$

The direction of steepest ascent is given by ${}_{\oplus}d^{\star} = {}_{\oplus}n^{\star}({}_{\oplus\oplus}U^{\star\star})^{-1}$, where

$$(51)\qquad {}_{\oplus}n^{\star} = a_0^{\star}\Phi^{\star}(T_{\mathrm{I\,I}}^{-1} \otimes \overline{W}_{xx})({}_{\oplus}\Phi^{\star})' - a_0^{\star}\Phi^{\star}(\bar{S}_{\mathrm{I\,I}}^{-1} \otimes \bar{M}_{xx})({}_{\oplus}\Phi^{\star})'.$$

${}_{\oplus\oplus}U^{\star\star}$ is determined by the concept of distance adopted. Two useful methods called the $\mathcal{R}_h$ and $\mathcal{L}_h$ methods have been used. In the $\mathcal{R}_h$ method, $U^{\star\star} = R^{\star\star}$ as defined in the F.I.N.D. case, except that the superscripts i, j in $\bar{s}^{ij}N^{(i,j)}$ assume values corresponding to the equations in the subsystem only. In the $\mathcal{L}_h$ method, $U^{\star\star} = -L^{\star\star}$.

9. Computations in the Limited-Information Subsystem Method

Here we shall treat Model (*b*), in which the three equations form a subsystem of a complete system. [See (1) and (2).] The L.I.S.E. estimates have been obtained and are

$$(52)\qquad \begin{array}{lll} a_0 = 16.038869, & a_4 = 25.780463, & a_8 = 1.726865, \\ a_1 = 0.062699, & a_5 = -0.022994, & a_9 = 0.395823, \\ a_2 = 0.824882, & a_6 = 0.764704, & a_{10} = 0.140874, \\ a_3 = 0.163679, & a_7 = -0.181972, & a_{11} = 0.187339. \end{array}$$

These equations have been transformed (see Section 5), by eliminating three jointly dependent variables in the identities, to

$$(53.\mathrm{i})\qquad \overset{1}{\alpha}_1\pi + \overset{1}{\alpha}_2W_1 + \overset{1}{\alpha}_3Z + \overset{1}{\alpha}_2W_2 + \overset{1}{\alpha}_4\pi_{-1} - \overset{1}{\alpha}_3Z_{-1} + \overset{1}{\alpha}_3(G + F) - \overset{1}{\alpha}_3\tau + \alpha_0 + u_1 = 0,$$

$$(53.\mathrm{ii})\qquad \overset{2}{\alpha}_1\pi + \overset{2}{\alpha}_2Z + \overset{2}{\alpha}_3\pi_{-1} + \overset{2}{\alpha}_4Z_{-1} + \alpha_4 + u_2 = 0,$$

$$(53.\mathrm{iii})\qquad \overset{3}{\alpha}_1\pi + (\overset{3}{\alpha}_1 - \overset{3}{\alpha}_2)W_1 + \overset{3}{\alpha}_3t + \overset{3}{\alpha}_1\tau + \overset{3}{\alpha}_4(T + \tau - W_2)_{-1} + \alpha_8 + u_3 = 0,$$

where the $\overset{i}{\alpha}_j$ are defined as in equations (26.i), (26.ii), (26.iii). Using the L.I.S.E. estimates for our initial approximation we have

$$(54)\qquad \begin{aligned} a^{\star} &= [\overset{1}{a}_1 \;\; \overset{1}{a}_2 \;\; \overset{1}{a}_3 \;\; \overset{1}{a}_4 \;\; \overset{2}{a}_1 \;\; \overset{2}{a}_2 \;\; \overset{2}{a}_3 \;\; \overset{2}{a}_4 \;\; \overset{3}{a}_1 \;\; \overset{3}{a}_2 \;\; \overset{3}{a}_3 \;\; \overset{3}{a}_4] \\ &= [-0.937300 \quad -0.175117 \quad 1 \quad 0.163679 \quad -0.022994 \quad -1 \\ &\qquad 0.764704 \quad 0.818027 \quad 0.395823 \quad 1 \quad 0.140874 \quad 0.187339]. \end{aligned}$$

The jointly dependent variables are

$$(55.\mathrm{i})\qquad y_1 = \pi, \quad y_2 = W_1, \quad y_3 = Z, \quad y_4 = \tau, \quad y_5 = G + F.$$

The predetermined variables are

$$(55.\text{ii})\qquad \begin{aligned} z_1 &= t, \qquad Z_2 = \pi_{-1}, \qquad z_3 = Z_{-1}, \\ z_4 &= (Y + \tau - W_2)_{-1}, \qquad z_5 = W_2 . \end{aligned}$$

Thus the Φ matrices are as in Table 15. The reader should note that these are obtained from the Φ matrices in the F.I.N.D. case of Model (a) by mere rearrangement of columns and relabeling of variables.

Here again certain matrices to be used in the iterations must be calculated. We obtain $\bar{M}_{xx}$ (Table 16.1), which is a rearrangement of $\bar{M}_{xx}$ in F.I.N.D. of Model (a). Then we compute $\bar{M}_{yz}\bar{M}_{zz}^{-1}\bar{M}_{zy}$ (Table 16.1) and $\bar{W}_{yy} = \bar{M}_{yy} - \bar{M}_{yz}\bar{M}_{zz}^{-1}\bar{M}_{zy}$ (Table 16.2) exactly as in the L.I.S.E. method except that a few of our y's are slightly different in this case.[32]

Then $\Phi_x^i\bar{M}_{xx}$ and $\Phi_y^i\bar{W}_{yy}$ are computed in Table 17. In Table 18 we compute

$$(56)\qquad \begin{aligned} V^{(i,j)} &= \Phi_x^i\bar{M}_{xx}(\Phi_x^j)', \\ Z^{(i,j)} &= \Phi_y^i\bar{W}_{yy}(\Phi_y^j)', \\ N^{(i,j)} &= V^{(i,j)} - Z^{(i,j)} = (\Phi_x^i)(\bar{M}_{xz}\bar{M}_{zz}^{-1}\bar{M}_{zx})(\Phi_x^j)'. \end{aligned}$$

Table 19 shows the computation of $n^\star$. First our approximation $a^\star$ is listed. Then we compute, in the following order,[33]

$$(57)\qquad \begin{aligned} p_i^j &= a^i V^{(i,j)}, \\ k_i^j &= a^i Z^{(i,j)}, \\ \bar{s}_{ij} &= a^i V^{(i,j)} (a^j)' = p_i^j(a^j)', \\ t_{ij} &= a^i Z^{(i,j)} (a^j)' = k_i^j(a^j)', \\ n^i &= \sum_{j=1}^{3} (t^{ij}k_j^i - \bar{s}^{ij}p_j^i), \end{aligned}$$

where $[\bar{s}^{ij}] = \bar{S}^{-1}$ and $[t^{ij}] = T^{-1}$.

In the $\mathcal{R}_h$ method we use again

$$U^{\star\star} = R^{\star\star} = [R^{(i,j)}] = [\bar{s}^{ij}N^{(i,j)}].$$

Table 20 illustrates the computation of ${}_{\oplus\oplus}R^{\star\star}$ and ${}_{\oplus}d^\star = ({}_{\oplus}n^\star)({}_{\oplus\oplus}R^{\star\star})^{-1}$. Table 21 illustrates the summary sheet.

[32] In L.I.S.E. the y's were C, π, $W_1 + W_2$, I, W_1, and $Y + \tau - W_2$, while here the y's are π, W_1, Z, τ, $G + F$.

[33] As an example of the sum checking of $\bar{S}$ and T we have $(-0.937300) \cdot (-0.175847) + (-0.175117)(-0.131555) + (1.0)(-0.139781) + (0.163679) \cdot (-0.008300) + 1 = 1.046719$.

The $\mathcal{R}_h$ and $\mathcal{L}_h$ methods in L.I.S. are analogous in their properties to $\mathcal{R}_h$ and $\mathcal{L}_h$ in F.I.N.D. Again $\mathcal{L}_h$ is rather difficult to apply because $L^{\star\star}$ is complicated, but again $\mathcal{L}_h$ converges better than $\mathcal{R}_h$ when near the maximum.

As before, when the final approximation is obtained it is deadjusted as in the L.I.S.E. method.

To find $L^{\star\star}$ we compute, in the order given,

$$f_i^j = \sum_n \bar{s}^{in} p_n^j, \qquad g_i^j = \sum_n t^{in} k_n^j; \tag{58}$$

$$G^{(i,j)} = \sum_n (p_n^i)' f_n^j, \qquad H^{(i,j)} = \sum_n (k_n^i)' g_n^j; \tag{59}$$

$$\begin{aligned} {}^1L^{(i,j)} &= (g_i^j)' g_i^j - (f_i^j)' f_i^j, \\ {}^2L^{(i,j)} &= t^{ij}(Z^{(i,j)} - H^{(i,j)}), \\ {}^3L^{(i,j)} &= \bar{s}^{ij}(V^{(i,j)} - G^{(i,j)}); \end{aligned} \tag{60}$$

$$- L^{\star\star} = {}^1L - {}^2L + {}^3L. \tag{61}$$

Here again the matrix of the estimated covariances of the estimates of the parameters is given by $(1/T)(-{}_{\oplus\oplus}L^{\star\star})^{-1}$.

The fact that only ${}_{\oplus\oplus}L^{\star\star}$ is necessary introduces considerable saving in the computations illustrated in Tables 22, 23, and 24. In Table 24.1 we also computed $({}_{\oplus}d^{\star})' = (-{}_{\oplus\oplus}L^{\star\star})^{-1}({}_{\oplus}n^{\star})'$. In Table 24.2 we computed $(1/T)(-{}_{\oplus\oplus}L^{\star\star})^{-1}$ evaluated at the last estimate, which is the estimate of the covariances of the estimates of the parameters. This is now deadjusted as in the L.I.S.E. method.

10. Mathematical Considerations Concerning the Full-Information Method in the Diagonal Case

The full-information diagonal method is applicable to the case in which the matrix of the covariances of the residuals is known or assumed to be a diagonal matrix (i.e., disturbances in different equations are uncorrelated). It may be expected that, if this is approximately true, the F.I.D. method would give results that have only a small bias. The advantage of the F.I.D. method is that less work is required per iteration than in the F.I.N.D. method. Indeed, the matrix $U^{\star\star}$, which corresponds to $P^{\star\star}$ in this case, consists only of small diagonal blocks, with zeros elsewhere.

In treating the F.I.D. case a different normalization is found to be convenient. The original likelihood function in both F.I.D. and F.I.N.D. is a function of the coefficients A and of the covariance matrix Σ, $L = L(\text{A}, \Sigma)$. In F.I.N.D. it was found to be convenient to maximize first with respect to the covariance matrix. This gives the estimated covariance matrix $\bar{S}(A)/T^2 = A\bar{M}_{xx}A'/T^2$ as a function of the coefficients alone. Since the likelihood function is unaltered by multiplying all the coefficients of an equation by some constant, one may normalize by setting a given coefficient of each equation equal to a fixed number.

In the F.I.D. case the covariance matrix has one element for each row. If a row is multiplied by a constant, the likelihood function is unaltered and the corresponding element of the covariance matrix is multiplied by the square of the constant. Here we may proceed as in the F.I.N.D. case, but it is more convenient to normalize by fixing the elements of the covariance matrix. Let us fix them at chosen numbers σ_{ii}, i.e.,

(62) $$\Sigma = \begin{bmatrix} \sigma_{11} & 0 & \cdots & 0 \\ 0 & \sigma_{22} & \cdots & 0 \\ \cdots & \cdots & \cdots & \cdots \\ 0 & 0 & \cdots & \sigma_{GG} \end{bmatrix}.$$

In our example we choose $\sigma_{11} = \sigma_{22} = \sigma_{33} = 1/T^2$. It will be convenient to use $\bar{\Sigma} = T^2\Sigma$ as a parameter corresponding to $\bar{S}(A)$, which gives us $\bar{\sigma}_{11} = \bar{\sigma}_{22} = \bar{\sigma}_{33} = 1$.

Then the parameters which were formerly fixed by normalizations (i.e., $\overset{1}{\alpha_3}$, $\overset{2}{\alpha_2}$, and $\overset{3}{\alpha_2}$) are now free parameters, and the likelihood function can be shown to be given by

(63) $$\begin{aligned} L(A) &= \log |\det B| - \tfrac{1}{2}\operatorname{tr}(\bar{\Sigma}^{-1}A\bar{M}_{xx}A') \\ &= \log |\det B| - \tfrac{1}{2}\operatorname{tr}\{\bar{\Sigma}^{-1}(A)\}. \end{aligned}$$

It can be seen that $\bar{s}_{ii} = \bar{\sigma}_{ii}$ when the maximum is attained. It is wise then to modify all approximations used as initial values in iterative methods by multiplying each row by a constant, which makes $\bar{s}_{ii} = \bar{\sigma}_{ii}$. Again we obtain the Taylor expansion:

$$\begin{aligned} L(A_0 + h\Delta A_0) &= \log |\det B_0| - \tfrac{1}{2}\operatorname{tr}(\bar{\Sigma}^{-1}\bar{S}_0) \\ &+ h\{\operatorname{tr}(B_0'^{-1}\Delta B_0') - \operatorname{tr}(\bar{\Sigma}^{-1}A_0\bar{M}_{xx}\Delta A_0')\} \\ &+ \tfrac{1}{2}h^2\{\operatorname{tr}(B_0'^{-1}(\Delta B_0')B_0'^{-1}\Delta B_0') + \operatorname{tr}(\bar{\Sigma}^{-1}(\Delta A_0)\bar{M}_{xx}\Delta A_0')\} + 0(h^3). \end{aligned}$$

And, in more convenient form, this is

(64) $$\begin{aligned} L(A_0 + h\Delta A_0) &= \log |\det B_0| - \tfrac{1}{2}\operatorname{tr}(\bar{\Sigma}^{-1}\bar{S}_0) \\ &+ h\{\operatorname{vec}[B_0'^{-1} \quad 0_{yz}]\Phi^{\star\prime} - a_0^{\star}\Phi^{\star}(\bar{\Sigma}^{-1} \otimes \bar{M}_{xx})\Phi^{\star\prime}\}d^{\star\prime} \\ &+ \tfrac{1}{2}h^2 d^{\star}L^{\star\star}d^{\star\prime} + 0(h^3). \end{aligned}$$

The direction of steepest ascent is given by $d^{\star} = n^{\star}(U^{\star\star})^{-1}$, where

$$n^\star = \text{vec}\,[B_0'^{-1} \quad 0_{yz}]\Phi^{\star\prime} - a_0^\star\Phi^\star(\bar{\Sigma}^{-1} \otimes \bar{M}_{xx})\Phi^{\star\prime} \tag{65}$$

and $U^{\star\star}$ defines the measure of distance. The $\mathcal{P}_h$ method in the F.I.D. case is the gradient method given by

$$U^{\star\star} = P^{\star\star} = \begin{bmatrix} \bar{\sigma}^{11}V^{(1,1)} & 0 & \cdots & 0 \\ 0 & \bar{\sigma}^{22}V^{(2,2)} & \cdots & 0 \\ \cdots & \cdots & \cdots & \cdots \\ 0 & 0 & \cdots & \bar{\sigma}^{GG}V^{(G,G)} \end{bmatrix}, \tag{66}$$

where $\bar{\sigma}^{ii} = 1/\bar{\sigma}_{ii}$ and $\bar{\sigma}^{ij} = 0$ if $i \neq j$, and, as before, $V^{(i,j)} = (\Phi_x^i)\bar{M}_{xx}(\Phi_x^j)'$. The main simplicity of this method is that $(P^{\star\star})^{-1}$ may be evaluated once and for all; it is a constant matrix and very easy to invert:[34]

$$(P^{\star\star})^{-1} = \begin{bmatrix} \bar{\sigma}_{11}(V^{(1,1)})^{-1} & 0 & \cdots & 0 \\ 0 & \bar{\sigma}_{22}(V^{(2,2)})^{-1} & \cdots & 0 \\ \cdots & \cdots & \cdots & \cdots \\ 0 & 0 & \cdots & \bar{\sigma}_{GG}(V^{(G,G)})^{-1} \end{bmatrix}. \tag{67}$$

Indeed, if this method is applied, we have, omitting subscripts 0 from here on,

$$n^\star = \text{vec}\,[B'^{-1} \quad 0_{yz}]\Phi^{\star\prime} - a^\star P^{\star\star} \tag{68}$$

and

$$d^\star = n^\star(P^{\star\star})^{-1} = \text{vec}\,[B'^{-1} \quad 0_{yz}](\Phi^\star)'(P^{\star\star})^{-1} - a^\star; \tag{69}$$

i.e., we may evaluate in one step $a^\star + d^\star = \text{vec}\,[B_0'^{-1} \quad 0_{yz}]\Phi^{\star\prime}(P^{\star\star})^{-1} = l^\star(P^{\star\star})^{-1}$.

One may simplify even on this, since

$$a + d = (a^\star + d^\star)\Phi^\star = \text{vec}\,[B'^{-1} \quad 0_{yz}]\Phi^{\star\prime}(P^{\star\star})^{-1}\cdot\Phi^\star. \tag{70}$$

Let

$$J^{(i)} = (\Phi_y^i)'\bar{\sigma}_{ii}(V^{(i,i)})^{-1}(\Phi_x^i) \tag{71}$$

and $(A + \Delta A)_{iz} = (B'^{-1})_{iy}J^{(i)}$ or

$$a_{iz} + (\Delta A)_{iz} = \sum_k a^{ki}J_{kz}^{(i)}, \tag{72}$$

[34] One must keep in mind that $\bar{\sigma}_{11}(V^{(1,1)})^{-1}$ is a diagonal block of $(P^{\star\star})^{-1}$, not in general a single element. A similar statement holds for other capital letters with superscripts.

where $J^{(i)}_{kx}$ is the kth row of $J^{(i)}$. Now in successive iterations the only nonconstant terms that appear are the elements of B; only $(B + \Delta B)$ need be calculated from iteration to iteration until the last step, and only then do we want the complete $(A + \Delta A)$.

In the F.I.D. case the Newton method ($\mathfrak{L}_h$) consists again of using $U^{\star\star} = -L^{\star\star}$, $d^\star = n^\star(U^{\star\star})^{-1}$.

11. Computations in the Full-Information Method in the Diagonal Case

The F.I.D. computation will be illustrated in Model (a). We use $V^{(1,1)}$, $V^{(2,2)}$, and $V^{(3,3)}$, which were obtained previously (see Table 8.1), and compute $\bar{\sigma}_{11}(V^{(1,1)})^{-1}$, $\bar{\sigma}_{22}(V^{(2,2)})^{-1}$, and $\bar{\sigma}_{33}(V^{(3,3)})^{-1}$. (See Table 25.) Then in Table 26 we compute $J^{(i)} = (\Phi^i_y)'\bar{\sigma}_{ii}(V^{(i,i)})^{-1}(\Phi^i_x)$, where the Φ^i_x are taken from Table 7.1.

Ordinarily the original approximation would be obtained from L.I.S.E. estimates, but because of previous computation on a slightly different model the original approximation was obtained otherwise.

Applying the $\mathcal{P}_h$ method we start with our original approximation $A_{(0)}$. We take only $B_{(0)}$ and compute $(B_{(0)})^{-1}$. Then we compute

$$\Delta B_{(0)iy} = (B'^{-1}_{(0)})_{iy} J^{(i)}_{yy} - B_{(0)iy} \qquad (i = 1, \cdots, G). \tag{73}$$

That is, the ith row of $\Delta B_{(1)}$ is obtained by multiplying the ith column of $B^{-1}_{(0)}$ (or ith row of $B'^{-1}_{(0)}$) by the columns of $J^{(i)}_{yy}$ and subtracting the ith row of $B_{(0)}$. In this manner we obtain $\Delta B_{(0)}$, and the next approximation to B is given by $B_{(1)} = B_{(0)} + h_1 \Delta B_{(0)}$. We continue in this fashion to obtain $B_{(n)} = B_{(n-1)} + h_{n-1}\Delta B_{(n-1)}$ until the contribution of $\Delta B_{(n-1)}$ is negligible. Then for the last iteration we compute $B^{-1}_{(n)}$ and get

$$A_{(n+1)} = A_{(n)} + \Delta A_{(n)}, \tag{74}$$

where

$$A_{(n)} = (B'^{-1}_{(n)})_{iy} J^{(i)} \qquad (i = 1, 2, \cdots, G). \tag{75}$$

Then $A_{(n+1)}$ is our final approximation to A. This is done in Table 27, and the successive iterates $B_{(n)}$ are shown (in part) in Table 28.[35] Again the final approximation is deadjusted as in the L.I.S.E. method.

Using the terminology of Section 4, it was normalized by making $\bar{\sigma}_{ii} = 1$. This is convenient (but not necessary) as long as the h_i's are

[35] Table 28 shows results obtained by successive approximations to the column vector $[(\alpha_1 - 1) \quad (\alpha_2 - 1) \quad \alpha_5 \quad \alpha_9]$. Substituting these values in (22.i)–(22.iii), we obtain the equations on page 68 of Klein [1950] insofar as endogenous variables are concerned.

taken to be less than one. It is just as convenient to do something else, such as normalizing after each iteration by dividing each row of the approximation by a scale factor to make $\bar{s}_{ii} = \bar{\sigma}_{ii}$. Making $\bar{s}_{ii} = \bar{\sigma}_{ii}$ in this way would be necessary if $h_i = 1$ were used for every i.

It can be shown that all the λ's are between 0 and 2, and so to minimize $| 1 - \lambda h |$ it is wise to use $h_i > \frac{1}{2}$. Also, in order not to overshoot, it is wise to take $h_i \leq 1$. Taking $h_i < 1$ for every i insures convergence for large samples in the $\mathcal{P}_h$ method for this case.

In the F.I.D. case it is also possible to use the Newton method, where $U^{\star\star} = -L^{\star\star}$, $d^\star = n^\star(-L^{\star\star})^{-1}$ and $-L^{\star\star} = {}^1L^{\star\star} + {}^2L^{\star\star}$. Of course, if we use this method $n^\star$ must be computed and a good many of the short cuts of $\mathcal{P}_h$ in F.I.D. must be abandoned.

The vector $n^\star$ is computed very much as in the F.I.N.D. method. One computes

$$B' = [(a^1\Phi_y^1)' \quad (a^2\Phi_y^2)' \quad (a^3\Phi_y^3)'], \tag{76}$$

B^{-1}, and $l^\star = [l^1 \quad l^2 \quad l^3]$, where

$$l^i = \{\Phi_y^i(B^{-1})_i\}' \qquad (i = 1, 2, 3) \tag{77}$$

as in formulae (41) and (43). Then we find $m^\star = [m^1 \quad m^2 \quad m^3]$, where

$$m^i = a^i(\bar{\sigma}^{ii}V^{(i,i)}). \tag{78}$$

Then $n^\star = l^\star - m^\star$ and $d^\star = n^\star(-L^{\star\star})^{-1}$ are computed. To compute $-L^{\star\star}$ we need

$$C_y^j = \Phi_y^j B^{-1}, \tag{79}$$

$${}^1L^{(i,j)} = (c_j^i)'c_i^j, \tag{80}$$

where $(c_j^i)'$ is the jth column of C_y^i, and

$${}^2L^{(i,j)} = \bar{\sigma}^{ij}V^{(i,j)}, \tag{81}$$

where $\bar{\sigma}^{ij} = 1/\bar{\sigma}_{ii}$ if $i = j$, $\bar{\sigma}^{ij} = 0$ if $i \neq j$. Then $-L^{\star\star} = {}^1L^{\star\star} + {}^2L^{\star\star}$. This computation resembles that of $-L^{\star\star}$ in the F.I.N.D. case, but it is considerably simpler. An example is given in Tables 29 and 30. Again $(1/T)(-L^{\star\star})^{-1}$ is the matrix of the estimates of the covariances of the estimates of the parameters. This is deadjusted as in the L.I.S.E. method.

Appendix 1

L.I.S.E. METHOD, det $R_{\Delta\Delta} = 0$

If $R_{\Delta\Delta}$ is singular, as will happen when $K^{**} = G^{\Delta} - 1$, then $l_1^{\dagger} = 0$ and so b_{Δ} is a solution of the equation

$$R_{\Delta\Delta}\, b_{\Delta}' = 0. \tag{82}$$

Since b_{Δ}' may be multiplied by a nonvanishing scalar, we may fix $b_1 = 1$. Thus we must solve[36]

$$({}_{11}R_{\Delta\Delta})({}_{1}b_{\Delta}') + {}_{1}R_{\Delta 1} = 0,$$

where $b_{\Delta} = [1 \quad {}_{1}b_{\Delta}]$, by

$${}_{1}b_{\Delta}' = -\,({}_{11}R_{\Delta\Delta})^{-1}({}_{1}R_{\Delta 1}).$$

To obtain this we write down $R_{\Delta\Delta}$ except for the first row and column; next to it we write down the first column except for the first element; we apply the Doolittle method and so obtain $-{}_{1}b_{\Delta}'$, and then $b_{\Delta} = [1 \quad {}_{1}b_{\Delta}]$.

Appendix 2

L.I.S.E. METHOD, NO ELEMENTS OF z^*

If there are no z^*'s, the procedure is the same except that $P_{\Delta *}^{*\prime}$ and $\bar{M}_{\Delta *}\bar{M}_{**}^{-1}\bar{M}_{*\Delta}$ are not computed, and

$$R_{\Delta\Delta} = \bar{M}_{\Delta z}\bar{M}_{zz}^{-1}\bar{M}_{z\Delta}\,. \tag{83}$$

Appendix 3

TO OBTAIN ESTIMATED COVARIANCES OF THE ESTIMATES OF THE PARAMETERS INCLUDING THE CONSTANTS

In the F.I.N.D., F.I.D., and L.I.S. methods, a method was described for estimating the covariances of the estimates of the parameters. In each of these cases the constants were ignored. If it is desired to compute the estimates of the covariances of the estimates of the constants also, the problem is slightly more complicated since the likelihood function depends on more parameters.

Consider the F.I.N.D. method. The estimates e of ϵ are given by[37] $Am' + e' = 0$, where m is the vector of the means of $x = [y \quad z]$ (and is therefore not related to $m^* = [m^1 \quad m^2 \quad m^3]$ above). Consider the matrix

---

[36] ${}_{1}R_{\Delta 1}$ represents the first column of $R_{\Delta\Delta}$ with the first element deleted.

[37] See also Chapter VI, Section 5.6.

(84)
$$-L = \begin{bmatrix} -L^{**} + {}^5L^{**} & L_y^i \\ (L_y^i)' & L_{yy} \end{bmatrix},$$

where

$${}^5L^{(i,j)} = s^{ij}(\Phi_x^i m_x')(m_x\Phi_x^j)', \qquad L_y^i = (\Phi_x^i m_x')s^{iy}, \qquad L_{yy} = S^{-1}, \qquad S = \frac{1}{T^2}\bar{S}.$$

Then $(1/T)(-L)^{-1}$ is the estimate of the covariance matrix of the estimates $[a^* \quad e]$.

To invert the partitioned matrix $(-L)$, we may use methods given by Hotelling [1943, p. 4] or Frazer, Duncan, and Collar [1938, pp. 112–118]. The result is

(85)
$$(-L)^{-1} = \begin{bmatrix} (-L^{**})^{-1} & (L^{**})^{-1}L_y^i L_{yy}^{-1} \\ L_{yy}^{-1}(L_y^i)'(L^{**})^{-1} & L_{yy}^{-1} + \{I\,(L_y^i)'(-L^{**})^{-1}L_y^i L_{yy}^{-1}\} \end{bmatrix}.$$

For the F.I.D. method the procedure is the same except that s^{ij} is replaced everywhere by

$$\sigma^{ij} = 1/\sigma_{ii} \text{ when } i = j, \qquad \sigma^{ij} = 0 \text{ when } i \neq j, \qquad \sigma_{ii} = \frac{1}{T^2}\bar{\sigma}_{ii}.$$

In the L.I.S. case the method is the same as in the F.I.N.D. case.

APPENDIX 4

SAMPLE COMPUTATIONS FOR MAXIMUM-LIKELIHOOD ESTIMATION

* Not reproduced.

* Not reproduced.

TABLE 1.2—Computation of Moments $\bar{M}_{xx}^{(0)}$ for L.I.S.E. Method

	y_1	y_2	y_3	. . .	z_5	
	62166.63	19566.35	48054.11	. . .	5977.33	*564132.44*
	1305499.23	410893.35	1009136.31		125523.93	*11846781.24*
	1285729.21	402194.33	987740.29		121894.25	*11689942.05*
y_1	19770.02	8699.02	21396.02		3629.68	*156839.19*
		6347.25	15117.72	. . .	1821.11	*177310.01*
		133292.25	317472.12		38243.31	*3723510.21*
		125812.09	308979.17		38130.25	*3656779.65*
y_2		7480.16	8492.95		113.06	*66730.56*
			37275.87	. . .	4670.94	*435780.35*
			782793.27		98089.74	*9151387.35*
			758815.21		93643.25	*8980605.45*
y_3			23978.06		4446.49	*170781.90*
					. . .	. . .
					626.87	*54027.15*
					13164.27	*1134570.15*
					11556.25	*1108271.25*
z_5					1608.02	*26298.90*

TABLE 3—Matrix $\bar{W}_{yy}$

$\bar{M}_{zz}$

	z_1	z_2	z_3	z_4	z_5	
z_1	1.617000	−0.024990	1.240260	1.040760	0.499800	*4.372830*
z_2		0.681488	0.258778	1.261959	−0.029863	*2.147372*
z_3			4.131854	1.767609	0.272878	*7.671379*
z_4				3.340734	0.275028	*7.686090*
z_5					0.160802	*1.178645*
	1.617000	−0.024990	1.240260	1.040760	0.499800	*4.372830*
	1.	−0.015454	0.767012	0.643636	0.309090	*2.704285*
		0.681101	0.277945	1.278043	−0.022138	*2.214952*
		1.	0.408082	1.876435	−0.032504	*3.252013*
			3.067133	0.447785	−0.101440	*3.413478*
			1.	0.145994	−0.033073	*1.112921*
				0.207322	0.009690	*0.217013*
				1.	0.046740	*1.046740*
					0.001790	*0.001790*
					1.	*1.*

$\bar{M}_{zy}$

	y_1	y_2	y_3	y_4	y_5	y_6	
z_1	1.213170	0.039690	1.467690	−0.221760	0.967890	1.377180	*4.843860*
z_2	0.756856	0.549140	0.740566	0.461419	0.770429	1.337046	*4.615456*
z_3	0.894242	−0.354650	1.054910	−0.545839	0.782032	0.669891	*2.500586*
z_4	2.237085	0.972105	2.397327	0.606291	2.122299	3.410184	*11.745291*
z_5	0.362968	0.011306	0.444649	−0.067970	0.283847	0.416445	*1.451245*
	1.213170	0.039690	1.467690	−0.221760	0.967890	1.377180	*4.843860*
	0.750259	0.024545	0.907662	−0.137142	0.598571	0.851688	*2.995584*
	0.775604	0.549753	0.763248	0.457991	0.785387	1.358329	*4.690315*
	1.138750	0.807153	1.120608	0.672427	1.153112	1.994312	*6.886365*
	−0.352785	−0.609437	−0.382295	−0.562644	−0.280854	−0.940734	*−3.128752*
	−0.115021	−0.198699	−0.124642	−0.183443	−0.091569	−0.306714	*−1.020090*
	0.052376	0.003957	0.076295	−0.028225	0.066604	0.112305	*0.283314*
	0.252634	0.019086	0.368001	−0.136140	0.321260	0.541693	*1.366536*
	−0.000917	−0.003433	−0.000401	−0.001828	−0.002192	−0.001439	*−0.010212*
	−0.512166	−1.917294	−0.224252	−1.021075	−1.224252	−0.803897	*−5.702940*

$\bar{M}_{yy}$

	y_1	y_2	y_3	y_4	y_5	y_6	
y_1	1.977002	0.869902	2.139602	0.509747	1.776634	2.946711	*10.219598*
y_2		0.748016	0.849295	0.581308	0.837989	1.568955	*5.455465*
y_3			2.397806	0.458486	1.953157	3.174702	*10.973048*
y_4				0.529886	0.526456	1.064490	*3.670373*
y_5					1.669310	2.758257	*9.521803*
y_6						4.734474	*16.247589*

$\bar{M}_{yz}\bar{M}_{zz}^{-1}\bar{M}_{zy}$

	y_1	y_2	y_3	y_4	y_5	y_6	
y_1	1.847693	0.728666	2.033750	0.413682	1.670782	2.717355	*9.411931*
y_2		0.572462	0.730271	0.478990	0.718965	1.322010	*4.551367*
y_3			2.263286	0.372099	1.818637	2.931077	*10.149123*
y_4				0.447302	0.440069	0.883260	*3.035403*
y_5					1.534790	2.514632	*8.697878*
y_6						4.232390	*14.600726*

$\bar{W}_{yy} = \bar{M}_{yy} - \bar{M}_{yz}\bar{M}_{zz}^{-1}\bar{M}_{zy}$

	y_1	y_2	y_3	y_4	y_5	y_6	
y_1	0.129308	0.141235	0.105851	0.096064	0.105851	0.229355	*0.807666*
y_2		0.175553	0.119023	0.102317	0.119023	0.246944	*0.904097*
y_3			0.134519	0.086386	0.134519	0.243624	*0.823924*
y_4				0.082583	0.086386	0.181229	*0.634969*
y_5					0.134519	0.243624	*0.823924*
y_6						0.502083	*1.646862*

TABLE 4—L.I.S.E.: Estimation of the Coefficients of Equation (2), $\beta_1 y_4 + \beta_2 y_2 + \gamma_1 z_2 + \gamma_2 z_3 + \epsilon = u$

TABLE 4.1

	$\bar{M}_{**}$		I		
	z_2	z_3			
z_2	0.681488	0.258778	1.		*1.940266*
z_3		4.131854		1.	*5.390632*
	0.681488	0.258778	1.		*1.940266*
	1.	0.379724	1.467377		*2.847102*
		4.033589	−0.379724	1.	*4.653864*
		1.	−0.094140	0.247918	*1.153777*

	$\bar{M}_{**}^{-1}$		
	z_2	z_3	
z_2	1.503124	−0.094140	*2.408984*
z_3		0.247918	*1.153777*

TABLE 4.2

	$\bar{M}_{*\Delta}$		
	y_4	y_2	
z_2	0.461419	0.549140	*1.010559*
z_3	−0.545839	−0.354650	*−0.900489*

	$(P^*_{\Delta *})' = \bar{M}_{**}^{-1}\bar{M}_{*\Delta}$		
	y_4	y_2	
z_2	0.744956	0.858812	*1.603769*
z_3	−0.178761	−0.139620	*−0.318382*

	$\bar{M}_{\Delta *}(P^*_{\Delta *})'$		
	y_4	y_2	
y_4	0.441311	0.472482	*0.913794*
y_2		0.521125	*0.993607*

TABLE 4.3 $(R_{\Delta\Delta} = \bar{M}_{\Delta z}\bar{M}_{zz}^{-1}\bar{M}_{z\Delta} - \bar{M}_{\Delta *}(P^*_{\Delta *})')$

	$R_{\Delta\Delta}$		$\bar{W}_{\Delta\Delta}$		
	y_4	y_2	y_4	y_2	
y_4	0.005990	0.006507	0.082583	0.102317	*0.197399*
y_2		0.051337	0.102317	0.175553	*0.335716*
	0.005990	0.006507	0.082583	0.102317	*0.197399*
	1.	1.086368	13.786435	17.080739	*32.953543*
		0.044268	0.012600	0.064398	*0.121267*
		1.	0.284651	1.454743	*2.739394*

	$Q_{\Delta\Delta} = R_{\Delta\Delta}^{-1}\bar{W}_{\Delta\Delta}$		
	y_4	y_2	
y_4	13.477199	15.500352	*28.977551*
y_2	0.284651	1.454743	*2.739394*

TABLE 4.4

$q'_{(0)}$	$q'_{(1)}\times 10^{-1}$	$q'_{(2)}\times 10^{-2}$	$q'_{(3)}\times 10^{-4}$	$q'_{(4)}\times 10^{-5}$	$q'_{(5)}\times 10^{-6}$	$q'_{(6)}\times 10^{-7}$
4.0925	5.92155	8.31132	1.15130	1.592775	2.203401	3.048104
0.2612	0.21345	0.1996	0.02656	0.036636	0.050668	0.070090

$k^\dagger_1$	$k^\dagger_2$	$k^\dagger_3$	$k^\dagger_4$	$k^\dagger_5$	$k^\dagger_6$
14.47	14.035	13.85	13.835	13.834	13.833635
8.171	9.35	13.31	13.794	13.830	13.833378

$q'_{(7)}\times 10^{-8}$	$q'_{(8)}\times 10^{-9}$	$q'_{(9)}\times 10^{-10}$	$q'_{(10)}\times 10^{-11}$
4.216634	5.833135	8.069342	11.162828
0.096961	0.134132	0.185553	0.256688

$k^\dagger_7$	$k^\dagger_8$	$k^\dagger_9$	$k^\dagger_{10}$
13.833628	13.833628	13.833626	13.833628
13.833608	13.833626	13.833628	13.833628

	b'_Δ
y_4	11.162828
y_2	0.256688

	$c'_* = -P^{*\prime}_{\Delta *}b'_\Delta$
z_2	− 8.536263
z_3	2.031325
	− 6.504938

TABLE 4 (*continued*)

TABLE 4.5

	$[b_\Delta \;\; c_*]'$	m'	$[b_\Delta \;\; c_* \;\; e]'$	k'	$10^2 \times [b_\Delta^{(0)} \;\; c_*^{(0)} \;\; e^{(0)}]'$	$[b^{(0)} \;\; c^{(0)} \;\; e^{(0)}]'$(norm)
y_4	11.162828	0.012666	11.162828	0.01	11.162828	1.
y_2	0.256688	0.168904	0.256688	0.01	0.256688	0.022994
z_2	− 8.536263	0.163761	− 8.536263	0.01	− 8.536263	− 0.764704
z_3	2.031325	2.013952	2.031325	0.01	2.031325	0.181972
1		$e = -[b_\Delta \; c_*]m' =$	− 2.877828	1.	−287.782899	−25.780463
	4.914578	*2.359285*			*−282.868320*	*−25.340200*

TABLE 5—Sampling Covariances of the L.I.S.E. Estimated Coefficients

TABLE 5.1

b_Δ

	y_4	y_2	
	11.162828	0.256688	*11.419516*

$(b_\Delta \overline{W}_{\Delta\Delta})'$

y_4	0.948132
y_2	1.187214
	2.135346

$\overline{W}_{\Delta\Delta}$

	y_4	y_2	
y_4	0.082583	0.102317	*0.184901*
y_2		0.175553	*0.277870*

$b_\Delta \overline{W}_{\Delta\Delta} b_\Delta' = 10.888585$

${}_{11}[(b_\Delta \overline{W}_{\Delta\Delta})'(b_\Delta \overline{W}_{\Delta\Delta})] = 1.409477$

TABLE 5.2

$k_1^\dagger = 13.833628$ $\quad l_1^\dagger = 0.072287$ $\quad l_1^\dagger / b_\Delta \overline{W}_{\Delta\Delta} b_\Delta' = 10^{-2} \times 0.663884$

$T = 21$

$F = 4$

$k_1 = 10^{-2}$

$C = (1 + l_1^\dagger) b_\Delta \overline{W}_{\Delta\Delta} b_\Delta' = 11.675695$

$C^* = C/(T\text{-}F)(b_1 k_1)^2 = 55.116965$

TABLE 5.3

y_2

${}_{11}R_{\Delta\Delta}$

y_2	0.051337

$${}_{11}H = {}_{11}R_{\Delta\Delta} - \frac{l_1^\dagger}{b_\Delta \overline{W}_{\Delta\Delta} b_\Delta'} \, {}_{11}\{(b_\Delta W_{\Delta\Delta})'(b_\Delta W_{\Delta\Delta})\}$$

y_2	0.041980

$F_{\beta\beta} = ({}_{11}H)^{-1}$

y_2	23.820590

$({}_{10}P_{\Delta *}^*)'$

z_2	0.858812
z_3	− 0.139620
	0.719192

	z_2	z_3	

$F_{\beta\gamma} = F_{\beta\beta} \cdot {}_{10}P_{\Delta *}^*$

y_2	20.457431	−3.325844	*17.131587*

$\overline{M}_{**}^{-1}$

z_2	1.503124	−0.094140	*1.408984*
z_3		0.247918	*0.153777*

$F_{\gamma\gamma}^\dagger = ({}_{10}P_{\Delta *}^*)' F_{\beta\gamma}$

z_2	17.569108	−2.856278	*14.712829*
z_3		0.464356	*− 2.391922*

$F_{\gamma\gamma} = F_{\gamma\gamma}^\dagger + \overline{M}_{**}^{-1}$

z_2	19.072232	−2.950419	*16.121813*
z_3		0.712274	*− 2.238144*

TABLE 5 (*continued*)

TABLE 5.4

$$10^{-3} \times V^*(b_\Delta, c_*)/(b_1^{(0)})^2 = 10^{-3} \times C^* \begin{bmatrix} F_{\beta\beta} & -F_{\beta\gamma} \\ -F_{\gamma\beta} & F_{\gamma\gamma} \end{bmatrix}$$

	y_2	z_2	z_3	
y_2	1.312918	− 1.127551	0.183310	*0.368677*
z_2		1.051203	−0.162618	− *0.238966*
z_3			0.039258	*0.059950*

	${}_1m'$	$10^{-3} \times [V^*(b_\Delta, c_*)/(b_1^{(0)})^2] \cdot {}_1m'$
y_2	0.168904	0.406286
z_2	0.163761	−0.345806
z_3	2.013952	0.083395
	2.346619	*0.143875*

$10^{-3} \times {}_1m \cdot [V^*(b_\Delta, c_*)/(b_1^{(0)})^2] \cdot {}_1m' =$ 0.179949

$C^*/T^2 = \sum_t u_t^{*2}/T(T\text{-}F) =$ 0.124981

$V^*(e)/(b_1^{(0)})^2 =$ 180.074171

	$[k \quad 1]'$
y_2	10^{-2}
z_2	10^{-2}
z_3	10^{-2}
1	1

$$V^*(b_\Delta^{(0)}, c_*^{(0)}, e^{(0)})^{(\text{norm})} = \frac{1}{(b_1^{(0)})^2} \{V^*(b_\Delta, c_*, e) \text{ deadjusted}\}$$

	y_2	z_2	z_3	1
y_2	0.131291	− 0.112755	0.018331	− 4.062867
z_2		0.105120	−0.016261	3.458069
z_3			0.003925	− 0.833959
1				180.074171

TABLE 7.1*—F.I.N.D.: Basic Matrices Φ_x^i

		π	W_1	Z	W_2	π_{-1}	Z_{-1}	t	τ	$G+F$	$(Y+\tau-W_2)_{-1}$
		y_1	y_2	y_3	z_1	z_2	z_3	z_4	z_5	z_6	z_7
		1	0	0	0	0	0	0	0	0	0
Φ_x^1		0	1	0	1	0	0	0	0	0	0
		0	0	1	0	0	–1	0	–1	1	0
		0	0	0	0	1	0	0	0	0	0
		1	*1*	*1*	*1*	*1*	*–1*	*0*	*–1*	*1*	*0*
	⊕	*1*	*1*	*0*	*1*	*1*	*0*	*0*	*0*	*0*	*0*
		1	0	0	0	0	0	0	0	0	0
Φ_x^2		0	0	1	0	0	0	0	0	0	0
		0	0	0	0	1	0	0	0	0	0
		0	0	0	0	0	1	0	0	0	0
		1	*0*	*1*	*0*	*1*	*1*	*0*	*0*	*0*	*0*
	⊕	*1*	*0*	*0*	*0*	*1*	*1*	*0*	*0*	*0*	*0*
		1	1	0	0	0	0	0	1	0	0
Φ_x^3		0	–1	0	0	0	0	0	0	0	0
		0	0	0	0	0	0	1	0	0	0
		0	0	0	0	0	0	0	0	0	1
		1	*0*	*0*	*0*	*0*	*0*	*1*	*1*	*0*	*1*
	⊕	*1*	*1*	*0*	*0*	*0*	*0*	*1*	*1*	*0*	*1*

* Check row marked by ⊕ represents column sums with the elements used for normalization omitted.

TABLE 7.2—F.I.N.D.: "Semireduced" Matrices $\Phi_x^i \bar{M}_{xx}$ and $\Phi_x^i \bar{M}_{xz} \bar{M}_{zz}^{-1} \bar{M}_{zx}$

		y_1	y_2	y_3	z_1	z_2	z_3	z_4	z_5	z_6	z_7	
$\Phi_x^1 \bar{M}_{xx}$	1	0.748016	0.837989	0.226658	0.011306	0.549140	−0.354650	0.039690	−0.017050	0.129051	0.972105	*3.142255*
	2	0.849295	1.953157	1.513396	0.444649	0.740566	1.054910	1.467690	0.372250	1.021263	2.397327	*11.814503*
	3	0.727409	1.014512	0.336065	0.092987	0.532850	−0.193982	0.294210	0.055025	0.327384	1.132347	*4.318807*
	4	0.549140	0.770429	0.720197	−0.029863	0.681488	0.258778	−0.024990	0.017477	0.088908	1.261959	*4.293523*
		2.873860	*4.576087*	*2.796316*	*0.519079*	*2.504044*	*0.765056*	*1.776600*	*0.427702*	*1.566606*	*5.763738*	*23.569088*
$\Phi_x^2 \bar{M}_{xx}$	1	0.748016	0.837989	0.226658	0.011306	0.549140	−0.354650	0.039690	−0.017050	0.129051	0.972105	*3.142255*
	2	0.226658	1.308488	3.570062	0.204908	0.720197	3.586015	1.018500	0.199235	0.551253	2.373900	*13.759216*
	3	0.549140	0.770429	0.720197	−0.029863	0.681488	0.258778	−0.024990	0.017477	0.088908	1.261959	*4.293523*
	4	−0.354650	0.782032	3.586015	0.272878	0.258778	4.131854	1.240260	0.242509	0.594366	1.767609	*12.521651*
		1.169164	*3.698938*	*8.102932*	*0.459229*	*2.209603*	*7.621997*	*2.273460*	*0.44217i*	*1.363578*	*6.375573*	*33.716645*
$\Phi_x^3 \bar{M}_{xx}$	1	1.568955	2.758257	1.734381	0.416445	1.337046	0.669891	1.377180	0.407262	1.139718	3.410184	*14.819319*
	2	−0.837989	−1.669310	−1.308488	−0.283847	−0.770429	−0.782032	−0.967890	−0.250958	−0.739014	−2.122299	*− 9.732256*
	3	0.039690	0.967890	1.018500	0.499800	−0.024990	1.240260	1.617000	0.369600	0.885570	1.040760	*7.654080*
	4	0.972105	2.122299	2.373900	0.275028	1.261959	1.767609	1.040760	0.315780	0.841836	3.340734	*14.312010*
		1.742761	*4.179136*	*3.818293*	*0.907426*	*1.803586*	*2.895728*	*3.067050*	*0.841684*	*2.128110*	*5.669379*	*27.053153*
$\Phi_x^1 \bar{M}_{xz} \bar{M}_{zz}^{-1} \bar{M}_{zx}$	1	0.617920	0.750680	0.132373	0.011306	0.549140	−0.354650	0.039690	−0.017050	0.129051	0.972105	*2.830566*
	2	0.761986	1.869141	1.433761	0.444649	0.740566	1.054910	1.467690	0.372250	1.021263	2.397327	*11.563544*
	3	0.633124	0.934877	0.254947	0.092987	0.532850	−0.193982	0.294210	0.055025	0.327384	1.132347	*4.063770*
	4	0.549140	0.770429	0.720197	−0.029863	0.681488	0.258778	−0.024990	0.017477	0.088908	1.261959	*4.293523*
		2.562171	*4.325128*	*2.541279*	*0.519079*	*2.504044*	*0.765056*	*1.776600*	*0.427702*	*1.566606*	*5.763738*	*22.751404*
$\Phi_x^2 \bar{M}_{xz} \bar{M}_{zz}^{-1} \bar{M}_{zx}$	1	0.617920	0.750680	0.132373	0.011306	0.549140	−0.354650	0.039690	−0.017050	0.129051	0.972105	*2.830566*
	2	0.132373	1.228853	3.488944	0.204908	0.720197	3.586015	1.018500	0.199235	0.551253	2.373900	*13.504179*
	3	0.549140	0.770429	0.720197	−0.029863	0.681488	0.258778	−0.024990	0.017477	0.088908	1.261959	*4.293523*
	4	−0.354650	0.782032	3.586015	0.272878	0.258778	4.131854	1.240260	0.242509	0.594366	1.767609	*12.521651*
		0.944784	*3.531994*	*7.927530*	*0.459229*	*2.209603*	*7.621997*	*2.273460*	*0.442171*	*1.363578*	*6.375573*	*33.149920*
$\Phi_x^3 \bar{M}_{xz} \bar{M}_{zz}^{-1} \bar{M}_{zx}$	1	1.351551	2.586933	1.560462	0.416445	1.337046	0.669891	1.377180	0.407262	1.139718	3.410184	*14.256672*
	2	−0.750680	−1.585294	−1.228853	−0.283847	−0.770429	−0.782032	−0.967890	−0.250958	−0.739014	−2.122299	*− 9.481297*
	3	0.039690	0.967890	1.018500	0.499800	−0.024990	1.240260	1.617000	0.369600	0.885570	1.040760	*7.654080*
	4	0.972105	2.122299	2.373900	0.275028	1.261959	1.767609	1.040760	0.315780	0.841836	3.340734	*14.312010*
		1.612665	*4.091827*	*3.724008*	*0.907426*	*1.803586*	*2.895728*	*3.067050*	*0.841684*	*2.128110*	*5.669379*	*26.741464*

TABLE 8.1 *—F.I.N.D.: Reduced Moment Matrices $V^{(i,j)} = \Phi_x^i \bar{M}_{xx} (\Phi_x^j)'$

$V^{(1,1)}$

	1	2	3	4	
1	0.748016	0.849295	0.727409	0.549140	
2		2.397806	1.107499	0.740566	
3			0.802406	0.532850	
4				0.681488	
	2.873860	5.095166	3.170164	2.504044	13.643234
⊕	2.146451	3.987667		1.971194	8.105312

$V^{(1,2)}$

	1	2	3	4	
	0.748016	0.226658	0.549140	−0.354650	1.169164
	0.849295	1.513396	0.740566	1.054910	4.158167
	0.727409	0.336065	0.532850	−0.193982	1.402342
	0.549140	0.720197	0.681488	0.258778	2.209603
	2.873860	2.796316	2.504044	0.765056	8.939276
⊕	2.146451		1.971194	0.959038	5.076683

$V^{(1,3)}$

	1	2	3	4	
1	1.568955	−0.837989	0.039690	0.972105	1.742761
2	3.174702	−1.953157	1.467690	2.397327	5.086562
3	1.796946	−1.014512	0.294210	1.132347	2.208991
4	1.337046	−0.770429	−0.024990	1.261959	1.803586
	7.877649	−4.576087	1.776600	5.763738	10.481900
⊕	6.080703		1.482390	4.631391	12.194484

$V^{(2,2)}$

	1	2	3	4	
	0.748016	0.226658	0.549140	−0.354650	
		3.570062	0.720197	3.586015	
			0.681488	0.258778	
				4.131854	
	1.169164	8.102932	2.209603	7.621997	19.103696
⊕	0.942506		1.489406	4.035982	6.467894

$V^{(2,3)}$

	1	2	3	4	
1	1.568955	−0.837989	0.039690	0.972105	1.742761
2	1.734381	−1.308488	1.018500	2.373900	3.818293
3	1.337046	−0.770429	−0.024990	1.261959	1.803586
4	0.669891	−0.782032	1.240260	1.767609	2.895728
	5.310273	−3.698938	2.273460	6.375573	10.260368
⊕	3.575892		1.254960	4.001673	8.832525

$V^{(3,3)}$

	1	2	3	4	
	4.734474	−2.758257	1.377180	3.410184	
		1.669310	−0.967890	−2.122299	
			1.617000	1.040760	
				3.340734	
	6.763581	−4.179136	3.067050	5.669379	11.320874
⊕	9.521838		4.034940	7.791678	21.348456

* Check row marked by ⊕ represents column sums with the elements used for normalization omitted.

TABLE 8.2*—F.I.N.D.: The Matrices $N^{(i,j)} = \Phi_x^i \bar{M}_{xz} \bar{M}_{zz}^{-1} \bar{M}_{zx} (\Phi_x^j)'$

	$N^{(1,1)}$					$N^{(1,2)}$				
	1	2	3	4		1	2	3	4	
1	0.617920	0.761986	0.633124	0.549140		0.617920	0.132373	0.549140	−0.354650	*0.944784*
2		2.313790	1.027864	0.740566		0.761986	1.433761	0.740566	1.054910	*3.991223*
3			0.721288	0.532850		0.633124	0.254947	0.532850	−0.193982	*1.226940*
4				0.681488		0.549140	0.720197	0.681488	0.258778	*2.209603*
	2.562171	*4.844207*	*2.915127*	*2.504044*	*12.825550*	*2.562171*	*2.541279*	*2.504044*	*0.765056*	*8.372551*
⊕	*1.929047*	*3.816343*		*1.971194*	*7.716584*	*1.929047*		*1.971194*	*0.959038*	*4.859279*
	$N^{(1,3)}$					$N^{(2,2)}$				
1	1.351551	−0.750680	0.039690	0.972105	*1.612665*	0.617920	0.132373	0.549140	−0.354650	
2	3.003378	−1.869141	1.467690	2.397327	*4.999253*		3.488944	0.720197	3.586015	
3	1.623027	−0.934877	0.294210	1.132347	*2.114706*			0.681488	0.258778	
4	1.337046	−0.770429	−0.024990	1.261959	*1.803586*				4.131854	
	7.315002	*−4.325128*	*1.776600*	*5.763738*	*10.530211*	*0.944784*	*7.927530*	*2.209603*	*7.621997*	*18.703914*
⊕	*5.691975*		*1.482390*	*4.631391*	*11.805756*	*0.812410*		*1.489406*	*4.035982*	*6.337798*
	$N^{(2,3)}$					$N^{(3,3)}$				
1	1.351551	−0.750680	0.039690	0.972105	*1.612665*	4.345746	−2.586933	1.377180	3.410184	
2	1.560462	−1.228853	1.018500	2.373900	*3.724008*		1.585294	−0.967890	−2.122299	
3	1.337046	−0.770429	−0.024990	1.261959	*1.803586*			1.617000	1.040760	
4	0.669891	−0.782032	1.240260	1.767609	*2.895728*				3.340734	
	4.918950	*−3.531994*	*2.273460*	*6.375573*	*10.035988*	*6.546177*	*−4.091827*	*3.067050*	*5.669379*	*11.190778*
⊕	*3.358488*		*1.254960*	*4.001673*	*8.615121*	*9.133110*		*4.034940*	*7.791678*	*20.959728*

* Check row marked by ⊕ represents column sums with the elements used for normalization omitted.

TABLE 9—F.I.N.D.: First Iteration, Direction of Steepest Ascent; Computation of $\oplus n^\star = \oplus l^\star - \oplus m^\star$

	$a^{1\prime}$	$10 \times p_1^{1\prime}$	$10 \times p_2^{1\prime}$	$10 \times p_3^{1\prime}$	$10 \times p_\Sigma^{1\prime}$	$m^{1\prime}$	$l^{1\prime}$	$\oplus n^{1\prime}$
1	−0.979914	−0.518544	−0.563761	−0.136536	*−1.218841*	−1.598634	− 1.118965	0.479668
2	−0.200001	−0.376318	−0.120226	−0.272196	*−0.768742*	−2.511302	− 0.810861	1.700441
3	1.	−0.119717	−0.423157	−0.337018	*−0.879893*	−1.024884	− 0.258664	
4	0.225058	0.000000	0.000000	−0.046318	*−0.046318*	−0.195079	0.	0.195079
		−1.014581	*−1.107145*	−0.792069	−2.913794	*−5.329901*	− *2.188490*	*2.375189*

	$a^{2\prime}$	$10 \times p_1^{2\prime}$	$10 \times p_2^{2\prime}$	$10 \times p_3^{2\prime}$	$10 \times p_\Sigma^{2\prime}$	$m^{2\prime}$	$l^{2\prime}$	$\oplus n^{2\prime}$
1	0.231163	−0.518544	−0.563761	−0.136536	*−1.218841*	−0.296459	− 1.118965	−0.822506
2	−1.	−0.266356	−0.634175	−0.522006	*−1.422539*	0.136309	− 1.258664	
3	0.546429	0.000000	0.000000	−0.046318	*−0.046318*	0.144861	0.	−0.144861
4	0.853513	0.008011	0.000001	−0.427214	*−0.419201*	1.318882	0.	−1.318882
		−0.776890	*−1.197935*	*−1.132075*	*−3.106899*	*1.303594*	− *2.377629*	*−2.286249*

	$a^{3\prime}$	$10 \times p_1^{3\prime}$	$10 \times p_2^{3\prime}$	$10 \times p_3^{3\prime}$	$10 \times p_\Sigma^{3\prime}$	$m^{3\prime}$	$l^{3\prime}$	$\oplus n^{3\prime}$
1	0.420172	−0.745277	−0.693330	−0.227158	*−1.665766*	−3.072645	− 1.058990	2.013654
2	1.	0.238885	0.263152	0.309930	*0.811968*	3.051238	1.444959	
3	0.134945	−0.438473	0.355983	0.000000	*−0.082490*	−2.960079	0.	2.960079
4	0.164330	−0.156874	0.490653	0.000000	*0.333779*	−2.195244	0.	2.195244
		−1.101740	*0.416458*	*0.082772*	*−0.602509*	*−5.176730*	*0.385968*	*7.257918*

$10\bar{S} = 10[p_i^j(a^j)']$				I			B		
0.463675	0.153325	−0.159209	1.			*1.457792*	−0.979914	−0.200001	1.
	0.503855	0.100501		1.		*1.757683*	0.231163	0.	−1.
		0.214484			1.	*1.155777*	0.420172	−0.579827	0.
0.463675	0.153325	−0.159209	1.			*1.457792*	*−0.328577*	*−0.779828*	*0.*
1.	0.330674	−0.343363	2.156678			*3.143989*	det B = 0.518181		
	0.453154	0.153148	−0.330674	1.		*1.275628*	(adjoint B)′		
	1.	0.337960	−0.729717	2.206752		*2.814996*	−0.579827	−0.579827	0.200001
		0.108059	0.455118	−0.337960	1.	*1.225218*	−0.420172	−0.420172	−0.748750
		1.	4.211728	−3.127532	9.254128	*11.338325*	−0.134034	−0.652216	0.046233
				$10^{-1} \times \bar{S}^{-1}$			$B^{-1} = (\det B)^{-1}(\text{adj } B)'$		
							−1.118965	−1.118965	0.385968
			4.314815	−2.153116	4.211728	*7.373427*	−0.810861	−0.810861	−1.444959
				3.263736	−3.127532	− *1.016912*	−0.258664	−1.258664	0.089221
	$10^3 \det \bar{S}$ =	0.022705			9.254128	*11.338325*	check: $BB^{-1} = I$		

TABLE 10—F.I.N.D.: First Iteration, Direction of Steepest Ascent; Computation of Metric $_{\oplus\oplus}R^{\star\star}$ from Blocks $R^{(i,j)} = \bar{s}^{ij}N^{(i,j)}$

	$10^{-2} \times {}_{\oplus\oplus}R^{\star\star}$									$10^{-1} \times ({}_{\oplus}n^{\star})'$	
	1	2	4	5	7	8	9	11	12		
1	0.266621	0.328783	0.236943	–0.133045	–0.118236	0.076360	0.569236	0.016716	0.409424	0.047966	*1.700770*
2		0.998358	0.319540	–0.164064	–0.159452	–0.227134	1.264941	0.618151	1.009689	0.170044	*4.158856*
4			0.294049	–0.118236	–0.146732	–0.055717	0.563127	–0.010525	0.531502	0.019507	*1.633460*
5				0.201673	0.179224	–0.115748	–0.422701	–0.012413	–0.304028	–0.082250	*– 0.971591*
7					0.222419	0.084458	–0.418165	0.007815	–0.394681	–0.014486	*– 0.757835*
8						1.348528	–0.209510	–0.387895	–0.552825	–0.131888	*– 0.171373*
9							4.021609	1.274460	3.155828	0.201365	*10.000190*
11								1.496392	0.963132	0.296007	*4.261843*
12									3.091558	0.219524	*8.129123*
	0.266621	0.328783	0.236943	–0.133045	–0.118236	0.076360	0.569236	0.016716	0.409424	0.047966	*1.700770*
	1.	1.233145	0.888689	–0.499005	–0.443461	0.286399	2.134999	0.062696	1.535601	0.179906	*6.378973*
		0.592920	0.027354	0.000000	–0.013649	–0.321297	0.562989	0.597537	0.504809	0.110893	*2.061557*
		1.	0.046134	0.000000	–0.023021	–0.541889	0.949519	1.007786	0.851394	0.187030	*3.476953*
			0.082217	0.000000	–0.041027	–0.108755	0.031279	–0.052948	0.144362	–0.028235	*0.026892*
			1.	0.000000	–0.499005	–1.322770	0.380441	–0.643997	1.755849	–0.343425	*0.327090*
				0.135282	0.120224	–0.077644	–0.138649	–0.004071	–0.099724	–0.058314	*– 0.122897*
				1.	0.888689	–0.573940	–1.024889	–0.030097	–0.737153	–0.431060	*– 0.908451*
					0.042357	0.125656	–0.013945	0.006182	–0.040835	0.047072	*0.166487*
					1.	2.966576	–0.329224	0.145949	–0.964062	1.111314	*3.930552*
						0.591359	–0.064293	–0.159597	–0.141670	–0.295996	*– 0.070198*
						1.	–0.108722	–0.269882	–0.239566	–0.500534	*– 0.118706*
							2.106137	0.672051	1.616406	–0.072048	*4.322548*
							1.	0.319091	0.767474	–0.034208	*2.052357*
								0.600512	–0.029366	0.097539	*0.668685*
								1.	–0.048902	0.162427	*1.113525*
									0.390769	0.092577	*0.483346*
									1.	0.236910	*1.236910*

	$10 \times ({}_{\oplus}d^{\star})' = 10 \times ({}_{\oplus\oplus}R^{\star\star})^{-1}({}_{\oplus}n^{\star})'$	
1	0.139564	*1.139564*
2	–0.112105	*0.887894*
4	0.134384	*1.134384*
5	–2.986748	*–1.986748*
7	2.489680	*3.489680*
8	–0.426340	*0.573659*
9	–0.271557	*0.728442*
11	0.174012	*1.174012*
12	0.236910	*1.236910*

TABLE 11—F.I.N.D.: Summary of Successive Approximations $a^{\star}_{(j)} = a^{\star}_{(j-1)} + h_j d^{\star}_{(j-1)}$

	$a^{\star\prime}_{(0)}$	$a^{\star\prime}_{(1)}$	$a^{\star\prime}_{(2)}$	$a^{\star\prime}_{(3)}$	$a^{\star\prime}_{(4)}$	$a^{\star\prime}_{(5)}$	$a^{\star\prime}_{(6)}$	$a^{\star\prime}_{(7)}$	....	$a^{\star\prime}_{(17)}$	$a^{\star\prime}_{(18)}$	$a^{\star\prime}_{(19)}$	$a^{\star\prime}_{(20)}$
	− 0.979914	− 0.969447	− 0.927177	− 0.908995	− 0.946930	− 0.960014	− 0.975487	− 1.012009	....	− 1.228441	− 1.232267	− 1.232388	− 1.232388
	− 0.200001	− 0.208409	− 0.211977	− 0.226075	− 0.216264	− 0.215232	− 0.214029	− 0.211227	....	− 0.198239	− 0.198160	− 0.198155	− 0.198155
	1.	1.	1.	1.	1.	1.	1.	1.	....	1.	1.	1.	1.
	0.225058	0.235137	0.218517	0.228232	0.247426	0.254867	0.265148	0.285413	....	0.383916	0.385619	0.385673	0.385673
	0.231163	0.007157	− 0.077684	− 0.211279	− 0.262112	− 0.318214	− 0.369432	− 0.483559	....	− 0.796225	− 0.800852	− 0.801006	− 0.801006
	− 1.	− 1.	− 1.	− 1.	− 1.	− 1.	− 1.	− 1.	....	− 1.	− 1.	− 1.	− 1.
	0.546429	0.733155	0.794088	0.881065	0.891581	0.916489	0.932657	0.971018	....	1.049516	1.051801	1.051852	1.051852
	0.853513	0.821538	0.814132	0.808009	0.814258	0.816142	0.821040	0.826179	....	0.851961	0.851894	0.851900	0.851900
	0.420172	0.399806	0.366558	0.345257	0.336999	0.325181	0.312609	0.287883	....	0.234167	0.234133	0.234117	0.234117
	1.	1.	1.	1.	1.	1.	1.	1.	....	1.	1.	1.	1.
	0.134945	0.147996	0.166842	0.177744	0.183097	0.187826	0.194518	0.206407	....	0.234854	0.234827	0.234834	0.234834
	0.164330	0.182099	0.209650	0.221592	0.225284	0.233655	0.241121	0.255504	....	0.284659	0.284668	0.284676	0.284676
	2.395698	*2.349033*	*2.352950*	*2.315552*	*2.273341*	*2.240701*	*2.208146*	*2.125611*	....	*1.816170*	*1.811663*	*1.811504*	*1.811504*
det B	0.518181	0.660883	0.714223	0.811546	0.874477	0.932562	0.991392	1.125827	....	1.596976	1.603494	1.603733	
$10^3 \times \det \bar{S}$	0.022705	0.026875	0.028039	0.034615	0.038971	0.043701	0.048826	0.062035	....	0.122710	0.123713	0.123749	
$10^{-3} \times (\det B)^2/\det \bar{S}$	11.826005	16.251588	18.192903	19.026339	19.622374	19.900266	20.129598	20.431793	....	20.783346	20.783542	20.783543	
	use R_1	use R_1	use R_1	use R_2	use R_2	use R_2	use R_2	use R_3	....	use L_1	use L_1	use L_2	
	$d^{\star\prime}_{(0)}$	$d^{\star\prime}_{(1)}$	$d^{\star\prime}_{(2)}$	$d^{\star\prime}_{(3)} \times 10^2$	$d^{\star\prime}_{(4)} \times 10^2$	$d^{\star\prime}_{(5)} \times 10^2$	$d^{\star\prime}_{(6)} \times 10^2$	$d^{\star\prime}_{(7)} \times 10^2$	....	$d^{\star\prime}_{(17)} \times 10^2$	$d^{\star\prime}_{(18)} \times 10^2$	$d^{\star\prime}_{(19)} \times 10^6$	
	0.013956	0.042269	0.009090	− 4.310712	− 1.046707	− 0.859623	− 0.730437	− 1.151240	....	− 0.382544	− 0.011491	0.162767	
	− 0.011210	− 0.003567	− 0.007048	1.114891	0.082505	0.066831	0.056049	0.162636	....	0.007849	0.000476	− 0.008837	
	0.	0.	0.	0.	0.	0.	0.	0.	....	0.	0.	0.	
	0.013438	− 0.016619	0.004857	2.181144	0.595316	0.571153	0.405301	0.403008	....	0.170320	0.005034	− 0.081898	
	− 0.298674	− 0.084842	− 0.066797	− 5.776520	− 4.488152	− 2.845423	− 2.282551	− 0.711181	....	− 0.462673	− 0.014534	0.299046	
	0.	0.	0.	0.	0.	0.	0.	0.	....	0.	0.	0.	
	0.248968	0.060933	0.043488	1.195005	1.992613	0.898239	0.767207	− 1.237166	....	0.228417	0.004831	− 0.122665	
	− 0.042634	− 0.007405	− 0.003061	0.710035	0.150764	0.272075	0.102793	0.578967	....	− 0.006750	0.000645	− 0.004040	
	− 0.027155	− 0.033247	− 0.010650	− 0.938426	− 0.945468	− 0.698423	− 0.494512	− 0.380874	....	− 0.003483	− 0.001457	0.009783	
	0.	0.	0.	0.	0.	0.	0.	0.	....	0.	0.	0.	
	0.017401	0.018846	0.005450	0.608285	0.378283	0.371767	0.237794	0.359441	....	− 0.002753	0.000697	0.000107	
	0.023691	0.027551	0.005970	0.419620	0.669657	0.414767	0.287668	0.112922	....	0.000911	0.000789	− 0.000771	
	− 0.062219	*0.003916*	*− 0.018699*	*− 4.796675*	*− 2.611186*	*− 1.808635*	*− 1.650685*	*− 1.863486*	....	*− 0.450708*	*− 0.015007*	*0.253492*	
	$h_1 = 0.75$	$h_2 = 1.0$	$h_3 = 2.0$	$h_4 = 0.88$	$h_5 = 1.25$	$h_6 = 1.8$	$h_7 = 5.0$	$h_8 = 0.8$	....	$h_{18} = 1.0$	$h_{19} = 1.06$	$h_{20} = 1.0$	

TABLE 12—F.I.N.D.: Estimated Sampling Covariances of Estimated Coefficients; Computation of Matrices

$$c_y^j = \Phi_y^j B^{-1},\ f_i^j = \Sigma_n \bar{s}^{in} p_n^j,\ G^{(i,j)} = \Sigma_n (p_n^i)'(f_n^j)$$

			C_y^1		
	$c_1^{1\prime}$	$c_2^{1\prime}$	$c_3^{1\prime}$		
1	−1.118965	−1.118965	0.385968		
2	−0.810861	−0.810861	−1.444959		
4	0.	0.	0.		
	−1.929826	*−1.929826*	*−1.058990*		
			f_1^1		
	1	2	3	4	
	−1.598634	−2.511302	−1.024884	−0.195079	*0.329901*
			f_2^1		
	1	2	3	4	
	−0.296459	1.269173	−0.069270	0.144861	*1.048305*
			f_3^1		
	1	2	3	4	
	−1.684311	−3.727882	−2.299595	−0.428635	*0.140424*
	−3.579404	*−4.970011*	*−3.393750*	*−0.478853*	
			$G^{(1,1)}$		
		1	2	4	
1		1.226064	1.095702	0.078014	*2.399782*
2			1.807178	0.172669	*3.075550*
4				0.019853	*0.270537*
			$G^{(3,3)}$		
		9	11	12	
9		2.658815	1.193557	0.446011	*4.298384*
11			1.915312	1.450312	*4.559182*
12				1.223355	*3.119679*

			C_y^2		
		$c_1^{2\prime}$	$c_2^{2\prime}$	$c_3^{2\prime}$	
5		−1.118965	−1.118965	0.385968	
7		0.	0.	0.	
8		0.	0.	0.	
		−1.118965	*−1.118965*	*0.385968*	
			f_1^2		
	5	6	7	8	
	−1.598634	−1.982378	−0.195079	−1.764746	*− 5.540839*
			f_2^2		
	5	6	7	8	
	−0.296459	0.136309	0.144861	1.318882	*1.303594*
			f_3^2		
	5	6	7	8	
	−1.684311	−3.969137	−0.428635	−3.919758	*−10.001843*
	−3.579404	*−5.815206*	*−0.478853*	*−4.365623*	
			$G^{(1,2)}$		
		5	7	8	
1		1.226064	0.078014	0.706754	*2.010833*
2		1.095702	0.172669	1.572487	*2.840859*
4		0.078014	0.019853	0.181556	*0.279424*
			$G^{(2,2)}$		
		5	7	8	
5		1.226064	0.078014	0.706754	*2.010833*
7			0.019853	0.181556	*0.279424*
8				1.660440	*2.548751*

			C_y^3		
		$c_1^{3\prime}$	$c_2^{3\prime}$	$c_3^{3\prime}$	
9		−1.929826	−1.929826	−1.058990	
11		0.	0.	0.	
12		0.	0.	0.	
		−1.929826	*−1.929826*	*−1.058990*	
			f_1^3		
	9	10	11	12	
	−2.679641	1.769491	−2.658405	−1.733318	*−5.301874*
			f_2^3		
	9	10	11	12	
	0.052266	−0.624804	2.105919	1.939132	*3.472513*
			f_3^3		
	9	10	11	12	
	−3.072645	3.051238	−2.960079	−2.195244	*−5.176730*
	−5.700020	*4.195925*	*−3.512565*	*−1.989431*	
			$G^{(1,3)}$		
		9	11	12	
1		1.779575	0.595424	0.105326	*2.480325*
2		1.838479	1.552943	1.016682	*4.408106*
4		0.142319	0.137105	0.101679	*0.381105*
			$G^{(2,3)}$		
		9	11	12	
5		1.779575	0.595424	0.105326	*2.480325*
7		0.142319	0.137105	0.101679	*0.381105*
8		1.291210	1.243294	0.923956	*3.458461*

TABLE 13—F.I.N.D.: Estimated Sampling Covariances of Estimated Coefficients; Computation of $\oplus\oplus L^{**}$; ${}^1L^{(i,j)} = (c^i_j)'c^j_i$, ${}^2L^{(i,j)} = (f^i_j)'(f^j_i)$, $-{}^3L^{(i,j)} + {}^4L^{(i,j)} = \bar{s}^{ij}(V^{(i,j)} - G^{(i,j)})$

	$^1L^{(1,1)}$			
	1	2	4	
1	1.252084	0.907325	0.	*2.159409*
2		0.657495	0.	*1.564821*
4			0.	*0.*
	$^1L^{(3,3)}$			
	9	11	12	
9	1.121461	0.	0.	*1.121461*
11		0.	0.	*0.*
12			0.	*0.*
	$^2L^{(1,1)}$			
1	2.555631	4.014653	0.311861	*6.882147*
2		6.306638	0.489904	*10.811197*
4			0.038056	*0.839822*
	$^2L^{(3,3)}$			
9	9.441147	9.095273	6.745208	*25.281629*
11		8.762070	6.498099	*24.355443*
12			4.819100	*18.062408*
	$-{}^3L^{(1,1)} + {}^4L^{(1,1)}$			
1	26.985265	31.917756	23.357757	*82.260779*
2		95.663258	31.209019	*158.790034*
4			29.319283	*83.886061*
	$-{}^3L^{(3,3)} + {}^4L^{(3,3)}$			
9	413.529297	116.400672	311.455366	*841.385337*
11		131.914714	82.891888	*331.207275*
12			297.834734	*692.181990*

	$^1L^{(1,2)}$			
	5	7	8	
1	1.252084	0.	0.	*1.252084*
2	0.907325	0.	0.	*0.907325*
4	0.	0.	0.	*0.*
	$^1L^{(2,2)}$			
	5	7	8	
5	1.252084	0.	0.	*1.252084*
7		0.	0.	*0.*
8			0.	*0.*
	$^2L^{(1,2)}$			
1	0.473929	0.057833	0.523175	*1.054938*
2	− 2.028943	− 0.247590	− 2.239769	*− 4.516303*
4	− 0.231580	− 0.028259	− 0.255643	*− 0.515483*
	$^2L^{(2,2)}$			
5	0.087888	− 0.042945	− 0.390994	*− 0.346052*
7		0.020984	0.191055	*0.169094*
8			1.739450	*1.539510*
	$-{}^3L^{(1,2)} + {}^4L^{(1,2)}$			
1	−13.465796	−11.655649	9.157752	*− 15.963693*
2	−15.927136	−15.573472	− 19.327693	*− 50.828302*
4	−11.655649	−14.630483	− 5.180879	*− 31.467013*
	$-{}^3L^{(2,2)} + {}^4L^{(2,2)}$			
5	20.411716	17.667861	− 13.881499	*24.198078*
7		22.177173	7.853278	*47.698313*
8			129.433572	*123.405351*

	$^1L^{(1,3)}$			
	9	11	12	
1	− 0.744852	0.	0.	*− 0.744852*
2	2.788521	0.	0.	*2.788521*
4	0.	0.	0.	*0.*
	$^1L^{(2,3)}$			
	9	11	12	
5	− 0.744852	0.	0.	*− 0.744852*
7	0.	0.	0.	
8	0.	0.	0.	
	$^2L^{(1,3)}$			
1	4.513350	4.477582	2.919448	*11.910382*
2	9.989388	9.910222	6.461608	*26.361219*
4	1.148589	1.139486	0.742961	*3.031037*
	$^2L^{(2,3)}$			
5	− 0.088032	− 3.547024	− 3.266102	*− 6.901159*
7	− 0.022403	− 0.902671	− 0.831180	*− 1.756255*
8	− 0.204870	− 8.254697	− 7.600931	*− 16.060498*
	$-{}^3L^{(1,3)} + {}^4L^{(1,3)}$			
1	58.585040	− 0.836130	40.498821	*98.247730*
2	125.966660	55.274544	96.686918	*277.928124*
4	55.713338	− 1.629962	52.722043	*106.805419*
	$-{}^3L^{(2,3)} + {}^4L^{(2,3)}$			
5	− 43.503895	0.620891	−30.073487	*− 72.956491*
7	− 41.371436	1.210372	−39.150169	*− 79.311233*
8	− 16.912755	−34.901090	−52.392838	*−104.206683*

TABLE 14—F.I.N.D.: Estimated Sampling Covariances of Estimated Coefficients

TABLE 14.1

	$-10^{-2} \times (\oplus\oplus L^{\star\star})$ at first estimate									$(\oplus n^{\star})'$		$10^2(\oplus d^{\star})' = -10^2 \times (\oplus\oplus L^{\star\star})^{-1}(\oplus n^{\star})'$	
	1	2	4	5	7	8	9	11	12				
1	0.256817	0.288104	0.230458	−0.126876	−0.117134	0.086345	0.533268	−0.053137	0.375793	0.479668	*1.953308*	13.074294	*14.074294*
2		0.900141	0.307191	−0.129908	−0.153258	−0.170879	1.187657	0.453643	0.902253	1.700441	*5.285385*	− 0.114607	*0.885393*
4			0.292812	−0.114240	−0.146022	−0.049252	0.545647	−0.027694	0.519790	0.195079	*1.753770*	− 7.257781	*− 6.257781*
5				0.215759	0.177108	−0.134905	−0.441607	0.041679	−0.268073	−0.822506	*− 1.603571*	−33.810072	*−32.810072*
7					0.221561	0.076622	−0.413490	0.021130	−0.383189	−0.144861	*− 0.861534*	26.934683	*27.934683*
8						1.276941	−0.167078	−0.266463	−0.447919	−1.318882	*− 1.115471*	− 4.895655	*− 3.895655*
9							4.052096	1.073053	3.047101	2.013654	*11.430303*	− 8.055470	*− 7.055470*
11								1.231526	0.763937	2.960079	*6.197755*	5.063908	*6.063908*
12									2.930156	2.195244	*9.635095*	7.132693	*8.132693*
	0.256817	0.288104	0.230458	−0.126876	−0.117134	0.086345	0.533268	−0.053137	0.375793	0.479668	*1.953308*		
	1.	1.121826	0.897365	−0.494033	−0.456102	0.336214	2.076451	−0.206906	1.463273	1.867743	*7.605833*		
		0.576938	0.048656	0.012424	−0.021853	−0.267744	0.589423	0.513253	0.480677	1.162336	*3.094112*		
		1.	0.084335	0.021535	−0.037879	−0.464077	1.021640	0.889616	0.833153	2.014663	*5.362987*		
			0.081902	−0.001433	−0.039066	−0.104155	0.017401	−0.023296	0.142028	−0.333384	*− 0.260004*		
			1.	−0.017508	−0.476984	−1.271700	0.212465	−0.284439	1.734107	4.070484	*− 3.174544*		
				0.152785	0.119026	−0.088304	−0.190543	0.003966	−0.090283	−0.616402	*− 0.709756*		
				1.	0.779042	−0.577967	−1.247132	0.025961	−0.590920	−4.034437	*− 4.645453*		
					0.055948	0.124975	0.008802	0.002133	−0.055501	0.439129	*0.575487*		
					1.	2.233769	0.157338	0.038140	−0.992018	7.848854	*10.286084*		
						0.660997	−0.180495	−0.042508	−0.098780	−2.701877	*− 2.362664*		
						1.	−0.273064	−0.064310	−0.149441	−4.087573	*− 3.574389*		
							2.050609	0.656982	1.614691	−1.674625	*2.647658*		
							1.	0.320384	0.787420	−0.816647	*1.291156*		
								0.543901	−0.064741	2.292483	*2.771643*		
								1.	−0.119032	4.214888	*5.095856*		
									0.331179	2.362198	*2.693377*		
									1.	7.132693	*8.132693*		

TABLE 14.2

$(1/T)(-_{\oplus\oplus}L^{\star\star-1})$ at final estimate (T = 21)

	a_1^1	a_2^1	a_4^1	a_1^2	a_3^2	a_4^2	a_1^3	a_3^3	a_4^3
a_1^1	0.337121	–0.012400	–0.164261	0.457631	–0.194285	–0.015718	0.036795	–0.016007	–0.021393
a_2^1		0.001979	0.004079	–0.013768	0.002878	0.001109	–0.002322	0.000343	0.001217
a_4^1			0.091050	–0.224170	0.114377	0.006705	–0.015064	0.006862	0.009502
a_1^2				0.705917	–0.302978	–0.015097	0.049430	–0.022464	–0.025341
a_3^2					0.180082	0.003419	–0.011976	0.003102	0.009623
a_4^2						0.002189	–0.003497	0.001698	0.002380
a_1^3							0.009027	–0.004424	–0.005087
a_3^3								0.003195	0.002025
a_4^3									0.003951
	0.407480	*–0.016883*	*–0.170918*	*0.609157*	*–0.195755*	*–0.016811*	*0.052880*	*–0.025668*	*–0.023120*

TABLE 15*—L.I.S.: Basic Matrices Φ^{i}_{x}

		π	W_1	Z	τ	$G+F$	t	π_{-1}	Z_{-1}	$(Y+\tau-W_2)_{-1}$	W_2
		y_1	y_2	y_3	y_4	y_5	z_1	z_2	z_3	z_4	z_5
		1	0	0	0	0	0	0	0	0	0
Φ^1_x		0	1	0	0	0	0	0	0	0	1
		0	0	1	–1	1	0	0	–1	0	0
		0	0	0	0	0	0	1	0	0	0
		1	*1*	*1*	*–1*	*1*	*0*	*1*	*–1*	*0*	*1*
	⊕	*1*	*1*	*0*	*0*	*0*	*0*	*1*	*0*	*0*	*1*
		1	0	0	0	0	0	0	0	0	0
Φ^2_x		0	0	1	0	0	0	0	0	0	0
		0	0	0	0	0	0	1	0	0	0
		0	0	0	0	0	0	0	1	0	0
		1	*0*	*1*	*0*	*0*	*0*	*1*	*1*	*0*	*0*
	⊕	*1*	*0*	*0*	*0*	*0*	*0*	*1*	*1*	*0*	*0*
		1	1	0	1	0	0	0	0	0	0
Φ^3_x		0	–1	0	0	0	0	0	0	0	0
		0	0	0	0	0	1	0	0	0	0
		0	0	0	0	0	0	0	0	1	0
		1	*0*	*0*	*1*	*0*	*1*	*0*	*0*	*1*	*0*
	⊕	*1*	*1*	*0*	*1*	*0*	*1*	*0*	*0*	*1*	*0*

* Check row marked by ⊕ represents column sums with the elements used for normalization omitted.

TABLE 16.1—Moment Matrix $\bar{M}_{xx}$ and L.I.S. Computation of $\bar{M}_{yz}\bar{M}_{zz}^{-1}\bar{M}_{zy}$

	t	π_{-1}	Z_{-1}	$(Y + \tau - W_2)_{-1}$	W_2	π	W_1	Z	τ	$G + F$		$\bar{M}_{yz}$ only
	z_1	z_2	z_3	z_4	z_5	y_1	y_2	y_3	y_4	y_5		
z_1	1.617000	−0.024990	1.240260	1.040760	0.499800	0.039690	0.967890	1.018500	0.369600	0.885570	*7.654080*	
z_2		0.681488	0.258778	1.261959	−0.029863	0.549140	0.770429	0.720197	0.017477	0.088908	*4.293523*	
z_3			4.131854	1.767609	0.272878	−0.354650	0.782032	3.586015	0.242509	0.594366	*12.521651*	
z_4				3.340734	0.275028	0.972105	2.122299	2.373900	0.315780	0.841836	*14.312010*	
z_5					0.160802	0.011306	0.283847	0.204908	0.121292	0.282249	*2.082247*	
y_1						0.748016	0.837989	0.226658	−0.017050	0.129051	*1.924664*	$\bar{M}_{yy}$ only
y_2							1.669310	1.308488	0.250958	0.739014	*4.805759*	
y_3								3.570062	0.199235	0.551253	*5.855696*	
y_4									0.173354	0.271653	*0.878150*	
y_5										0.642150	*2.333121*	
	1.617000	−0.024990	1.240260	1.040760	0.499800	0.039690	0.967890	1.018500	0.369600	0.885570	*7.654080*	
	1.	−0.015454	0.767012	0.643636	0.309090	0.024545	0.598571	0.629870	0.228571	0.547662	*4.733506*	*2.029220*
		0.681101	0.277945	1.278043	−0.022138	0.549753	0.785387	0.735937	0.023189	0.102594	*4.411813*	
		1.	0.408082	1.876435	−0.032504	0.807153	1.153112	1.080510	0.034046	0.150629	*6.477465*	*3.225452*
			3.067133	0.447785	−0.101440	−0.609437	−0.280854	2.504489	−0.050442	−0.126744	*4.850488*	
			1.	0.145994	−0.033073	−0.198699	−0.091569	0.816556	−0.016445	−0.041323	*1.581440*	*0.468518*
				0.207322	0.009690	0.003957	0.066604	−0.028225	0.041743	0.097843	*0.398937*	
				1.	0.046740	0.019086	0.321260	−0.136140	0.201346	0.471939	*1.924233*	*0.877492*
					0.001790	−0.003433	−0.002192	−0.001828	0.004186	0.003096	*0.001619*	
					1.	−1.917294	−1.224252	−1.021075	2.337649	1.729345	*0.904372*	*−0.095627*

TABLE 16.2—Matrix $\bar{W}_{yy} = \bar{M}_{yy} - \bar{M}_{yz}\bar{M}_{zz}^{-1}\bar{M}_{zy}$

	y_1	y_2	y_3	y_4	y_5	
y_1	0.175553	0.119023	0.102317	−0.047632	0.003391	*0.352653*
y_2		0.134519	0.086386	−0.009917	0.051386	*0.381398*
y_3			0.082583	−0.007474	0.002581	*0.266395*
y_4				0.069063	0.036719	*0.040758*
y_5					0.084933	*0.179012*

$\bar{M}_{yz}\bar{M}_{zz}^{-1}\bar{M}_{zy}$

	y_1	y_2	y_3	y_4	y_5	
y_1	0.572462	0.718965	0.124340	0.030582	0.125659	*1.572010*
y_2		1.534790	1.222101	0.260875	0.687627	*4.424360*
y_3			3.487478	0.206709	0.548671	*5.589300*
y_4				0.104290	0.234933	*0.837391*
y_5					0.557216	*2.154108*

TABLE 18—L.I.S.: "Reduced" Matrices $V^{(i,j)} = \Phi_x^i \bar{M}_{xx} (\Phi_x^j)'$, $Z^{(i,j)} = \Phi_y^i \bar{W}_{yy} (\Phi_y^j)'$, $N^{(i,j)} = V^{(i,j)} - Z^{(i,j)} = \Phi_x^i (\bar{M}_{xz} \bar{M}_{zz}^{-1} \bar{M}_{zx}) (\Phi_x^j)'$

	$V^{(1,1)}$				$V^{(1,2)}$					$V^{(1,3)}$				
	1	2	3	4	1	2	3	4		1	2	3	4	
1	0.748016	0.849295	0.727409	0.549140	0.748016	0.226658	0.549140	−0.354650	*1.169164*	1.568955	−0.837989	0.039690	0.972105	*1.742761*
2		2.397806	1.107499	0.740566	0.849295	1.513396	0.740566	1.054910	*4.158167*	3.174702	−1.953157	1.467690	2.397327	*5.086562*
3			0.802406	0.532850	0.727409	0.336065	0.532850	−0.193982	*1.402342*	1.796946	−1.014512	0.294210	1.132347	*2.208991*
4				0.681488	0.549140	0.720197	0.681488	0.258778	*2.209603*	1.337046	−0.770429	−0.024990	1.261959	*1.803586*
	2.873860	*5.095166*	*3.170164*	*2.504044*	*2.873860*	*2.796316*	*2.504044*	*0.765056*	*8.939276*	*7.877649*	*−4.576087*	*1.776600*	*5.763738*	*10.841900*
	$V^{(2,2)}$				$V^{(2,3)}$					$V^{(3,3)}$				
1	0.748016	0.226658	0.549140	−0.354650	1.568955	−0.837989	0.039690	0.972105	*1.742761*	4.734474	−2.758257	1.377180	3.410184	
2		3.570062	0.720197	3.586015	1.734381	−1.308488	1.018500	2.373900	*3.818293*		1.669310	−0.967890	−2.122299	
3			0.681488	0.258778	1.337046	−0.770429	−0.024990	1.261959	*1.803586*			1.617000	1.040760	
4				4.131854	0.669891	−0.782032	1.240260	1.767609	*2.895728*				3.340734	
	1.169164	*8.102932*	*2.209603*	*7.621997*	*5.310273*	*−3.698938*	*2.273460*	*6.375573*	*10.260368*	*6.763581*	*−4.179136*	*3.067050*	*5.669379*	
	$Z^{(1,1)}$				$Z^{(1,2)}$					$Z^{(1,3)}$				
1	0.175553	0.119023	0.153340	0.	0.175553	0.102317	0.	0.	*0.277870*	0.246944	−0.119023	0.	0.	*0.127921*
2		0.134519	0.147691	0.	0.119023	0.086386	0.	0.	*0.205410*	0.243624	−0.134519	0.	0.	*0.109105*
3			0.183254	0.	0.153340	0.092640	0.	0.	*0.245981*	0.261213	−0.147691	0.	0.	*0.113522*
4				0.	0.	0.	0.	0.	*0.*	0.	0.	0.	0.	*0.*
	0.447917	*0.401234*	*0.484287*	*0.*	*0.447917*	*0.281344*	*0.*	*0.*	*0.729262*	*0.751782*	*−0.401234*	*0.*	*0.*	*0.350548*
	$Z^{(2,2)}$				$Z^{(2,3)}$					$Z^{(3,3)}$				
1	0.175553	0.102317	0.	0.	0.246944	−0.119023	0.	0.	*0.127921*	0.502082	−0.243624	0.	0.	
2		0.082583	0.	0.	0.181229	−0.086386	0.	0.	*0.094842*		0.134519	0.	0.	
3			0.	0.	0.	0.	0.	0.	*0.*			0.	0.	
4				0.	0.	0.	0.	0.	*0.*				0.	
	0.277870	*0.184901*	*0.*	*0.*	*0.428174*	*−0.205410*	*0.*	*0.*	*0.222763*	*0.258458*	*−0.109105*	*0.*	*0.*	*0.149352*
	$N^{(1,1)}$				$N^{(1,2)}$					$N^{(1,3)}$				
1	0.572462	0.730271	0.574068	0.549140	0.572462	0.124340	0.549140	−0.354650	*0.891293*	1.322010	−0.718965	0.039690	0.972105	*1.614839*
2		2.263286	0.959807	0.740566	0.730271	1.427009	0.740566	1.054910	*3.952756*	2.931077	−1.818637	1.467690	2.397327	*4.977456*
3			0.619151	0.532850	0.574068	0.243424	0.532850	−0.193982	*1.156360*	1.535732	−0.866820	0.294210	1.132347	*2.095468*
4				0.681488	0.549140	0.720197	0.681488	0.258778	*2.209603*	1.337046	−0.770429	−0.024990	1.261959	*1.803586*
	2.425942	*4.693931*	*2.685876*	*2.504044*	*2.425942*	*2.514971*	*2.504044*	*0.765056*	*8.210013*	*7.125866*	*−4.174852*	*1.776600*	*5.763738*	*10.491351*
	$N^{(2,2)}$				$N^{(2,3)}$					$N^{(3,3)}$				
1	0.572462	0.124340	0.549140	−0.354650	1.322010	−0.718965	0.039690	0.972105	*1.614839*	4.232391	−2.514632	1.377180	3.410184	
2		3.487478	0.720197	3.586015	1.553151	−1.222101	1.018500	2.373900	*3.723450*		1.534790	−0.967890	−2.122299	
3			0.681488	0.258778	1.337046	−0.770429	−0.024990	1.261959	*1.803586*			1.617000	1.040760	
4				4.131854	0.669891	−0.782032	1.240260	1.767609	*2.895728*				3.340734	
	0.891293	*7.918030*	*2.209603*	*7.621997*	*4.882098*	*−3.493527*	*2.273460*	*6.375573*	*10.037604*	*6.505122*	*−4.070030*	*3.067050*	*5.669379*	*11.171521*

TABLE 19—L.I.S.: First Iteration, Direction of Steepest Ascent; Computation of $n^{\star}$; $p_i^j = a^i V^{(i,j)}$, $k_i^j = a^i Z^{(i,j)}$, $\bar{s}_{ij} = a^i V^{(i,j)}(a^j)'$, $t_{ij} = a^i Z^{(i,j)}(a^j)'$, $n^i = \Sigma_{j=1}^{3} (t^{ij} k_j^i - \bar{s}^{ij} p_j^i)$

a^1				
1	2	3	4	
−0.937300	−0.175117	1.	0.163679	

	$p_1^{1\prime}$	$p_2^{1\prime}$	$p_3^{1\prime}$	
1	−0.032550	−0.114042	−0.029254	− *0.175847*
2	0.012771	−0.103665	−0.040661	− *0.131555*
3	0.013878	−0.104001	−0.049658	− *0.139781*
4	−0.000000	0.000000	−0.008300	− *0.008300*
	−0.005900	*−0.321709*	*−0.127875*	− *0.455485*

	$k_1^{1\prime}$	$k_2^{1\prime}$	$k_3^{1\prime}$	
1	−0.032048	−0.106354	−0.021277	− *0.159679*
2	0.012574	−0.089123	−0.038086	− *0.114636*
3	0.013664	−0.096166	−0.044297	− *0.126798*
4	0.	0.	0.	*0.*
	−0.005809	*−0.291644*	*−0.103661*	− *0.401114*

a^2				
5	6	7	8	
− 0.022994	− 1.	0.764704	0.818027	

	$p_1^{2\prime}$	$p_2^{2\prime}$	$p_3^{2\prime}$	
5	− 0.032550	− 0.114042	−0.029254	*−0.175847*
6	− 0.023522	− 0.091076	−0.033773	*−0.148372*
7	0.000000	0.000000	−0.008300	*−0.008300*
8	− 0.003945	0.000000	−0.011008	*−0.014954*
	− *0.060018*	− *0.205118*	*−0.082337*	*−0.347474*

	$k_1^{2\prime}$	$k_2^{2\prime}$	$k_3^{2\prime}$	
5	− 0.032048	− 0.106354	−0.021277	*−0.159679*
6	− 0.018389	− 0.084936	−0.014652	*−0.117978*
7	0.	0.	0.	*0.*
8	0.	0.	0.	*0.*
	− *0.050438*	− *0.191290*	*−0.035929*	*−0.277658*

a^3				
9	10	11	12	
0.395823	1.	0.140874	0.187339	*2.335035*

	$p_1^{3\prime}$	$p_2^{3\prime}$	$p_3^{3\prime}$	
9	− 0.010736	− 0.200024	− 0.051369	− *0.262130*
10	− 0.013135	0.098883	0.043585	*0.129333*
11	− 0.004100	− 0.023955	0.000000	− *0.028055*
12	0.007934	0.014725	0.000000	*0.022659*
	− *0.020037*	− *0.110371*	− *0.007783*	− *0.138192*

	$k_1^{3\prime}$	$k_2^{3\prime}$	$k_3^{3\prime}$	
9	− 0.012910	− 0.186908	− 0.044888	− *0.244707*
10	− 0.012574	0.089123	0.038086	*0.114636*
11	0.	0.	0.	*0.*
12	0.	0.	0.	*0.*
	− *0.025484*	− *0.097784*	− *0.006801*	− *0.130070*

$\bar{S}$			I			
0.042152	0.021044	−0.016476	1.			*1.046719*
	0.093698	0.019092		1.		*1.133835*
		0.023252			1.	*1.025868*
0.042152	0.021044	−0.016476	1.			*1.046719*
1.	0.499239	−0.390873	23.723596			*24.831962*
	0.083192	0.027318	− 0.499239	1.		*0.611271*
	1.	0.328372	− 6.000993	12.020266		*7.347645*
		0.007841	0.554809	− 0.328372	1.	*1.234279*
		1.	70.750291	−41.874608	127.521682	*157.397365*

T			I			
0.041501	0.019126	−0.017684	1.			*1.042943*
	0.087382	0.015141		1.		*1.121650*
		0.020318			1.	*1.017775*
0.041501	0.019126	−0.017684	1.			*1.042943*
1.	0.460867	−0.426114	24.095443			*25.130196*
	0.078567	0.023291	− 0.460867	1.		*0.640990*
	1.	0.296452	− 5.865902	12.727946		*8.158496*
		0.005878	0.562740	− 0.296452	1.	*1.272165*
		1.	95.728831	−50.430145	170.111943	*216.410629*

$\bar{S}^{-1}$				
	65.972491	−29.233440	70.750291	*108.489342*
		25.770734	− 41.874608	− *44.337314*
det S = 0.0000274992			127.521682	*157.397365*

T^{-1}				
	80.669312	−34.244972	95.728831	*143.153170*
		27.678098	− 50.430145	− *55.997019*
det T = 0.0000191677			170.111943	*216.410629*

n^1			
1	2	4	
−0.096652	−0.575883	0.587268	− *0.085267*

n^2			
5	7	8	
− 0.010836	−0.347583	−0.576330	*−0.934750*

n^3			
9	11	12	
− 0.511833	− 0.713022	0.055252	*−1.169602*

TABLE 20—**L.I.S.: First Iteration,** Direction of Steepest Ascent; Computation of Metric $_{\oplus\oplus}R^{\star\star}$ from Blocks $R^{(i,j)} = \bar{s}^{ij} N^{(i,j)}$ and Direction $_{\oplus}d^{\star} = (_{\oplus}n^{\star})(_{\oplus\oplus}R^{\star\star})^{-1}$

	$10^{-2} \times {}_{\oplus\oplus}R^{\star\star}$									$(_{\oplus}n^{\star})'$	
	1	2	4	5	7	8	9	11	12		
1	0.377667	0.481778	0.362281	−0.167350	−0.160532	0.103676	0.935326	0.028080	0.687767	−0.096652	*2.552042*
2		1.493146	0.488569	−0.213483	−0.216492	−0.308386	2.073745	1.038394	1.696115	−0.575883	*5.957505*
4			0.449594	−0.160532	−0.199222	−0.075649	0.945963	−0.017680	0.892839	0.587268	*3.273432*
5				0.147527	0.141517	−0.091395	−0.553586	−0.016620	−0.407065	−0.010836	*− 1.331825*
7					0.175624	0.066688	−0.559882	0.010464	−0.528440	−0.347583	*− 1.617859*
8						1.064809	−0.280514	−0.519354	−0.740179	−0.576330	*− 1.356635*
9							5.397216	1.756203	4.348724	−0.511833	*13.551362*
11								2.062025	1.327194	−0.713022	*4.955686*
12									4.260160	0.055252	*11.592369*
	0.377667	0.481778	0.362281	−0.167350	−0.160532	0.103676	0.935326	0.028080	0.687767	−0.096652	*2.552042*
	1.	1.275666	0.959258	−0.443115	−0.425062	0.274517	2.476583	0.074353	1.821089	−0.255919	*6.757371*
		0.878558	0.026419	0.	−0.011706	−0.440642	0.880581	1.002573	0.818754	−0.452586	*2.701950*
		1.	0.030071	0.	−0.013325	−0.501552	1.002302	1.141157	0.931929	−0.515147	*3.075436*
			0.101278	0.	−0.044878	−0.161851	0.022263	−0.074766	0.208471	0.693592	*0.744110*
			1.	0.	−0.443115	−1.598081	0.219823	−0.738224	2.058398	6.848369	*7.347170*
				0.073372	0.070382	−0.045455	−0.139129	−0.004176	−0.102304	−0.053664	*− 0.200975*
				1.	0.959258	−0.619516	−1.896208	−0.056928	1.394326	−0.731399	*− 2.739120*
					0.019830	0.076770	−0.007250	0.006636	−0.034672	−0.035877	*0.025437*
					1.	3.871360	−0.365630	0.334676	−1.748442	−1.809231	*1.282731*
						0.231323	−0.118164	−0.171983	−0.114330	0.437273	*0.264119*
						1.	−0.510817	−0.743476	−0.494246	1.890314	*1.141774*
							1.866470	0.604866	1.513873	0.137186	*4.122396*
							1.	0.324069	0.811089	0.073500	*2.208659*
								0.534306	−0.074194	0.612261	*1.072373*
								1.	−0.138860	1.145899	*2.007038*
									0.317569	−0.722332	*− 0.404763*
									1.	−2.274564	*− 1.274564*

	$10^2 \times (_{\oplus}d^{\star})' = 10^2 \times (_{\oplus\oplus}R^{\star\star})^{-1}(_{\oplus}n^{\star})'$	
1	− 8.877012	*− 7.877012*
2	− 0.340692	*0.659307*
4	9.099448	*10.009448*
5	14.154998	*15.154998*
7	−14.077695	*−13.077695*
8	2.225777	*3.225777*
9	1.649380	*2.649380*
11	0.830051	*1.830051*
12	− 2.274564	*− 1.274564*
	2.389692	

TABLE 21—L.I.S.: Summary of Successive Approximations $\overset{\star}{a}_{(j)} = \overset{\star}{a}_{(j-1)} + h_j d_{(j-1)}$ Using R_h and L_h Methods

	$\overset{\star\prime}{a}_{(0)}$	$\overset{\star\prime}{a}_{(1)}$	$\overset{\star\prime}{a}_{(2)}$	$\overset{\star\prime}{a}_{(3)}$	$\overset{\star\prime}{a}_{(4)}$	$\overset{\star\prime}{a}_{(5)}$	$\overset{\star\prime}{a}_{(6)}$	$\overset{\star\prime}{a}_{(7)}$	$\overset{\star\prime}{a}_{(8)}$	$\overset{\star\prime}{a}_{(9)}$	$\overset{\star\prime}{a}_{(10)}$
	– 0.937300	–0.981685	–1.004801	–1.005926	–1.008160	–1.010929	–1.011386	–1.011690	–1.011861	–1.011957	–1.011957
	– 0.175117	–0.176821	–0.178442	–0.178574	–0.178262	–0.177878	–0.177714	–0.177602	–0.177542	–0.177510	–0.177510
	1.	1.	1.	1.	1.	1.	1.	1.	1.	1.	1.
	0.163679	0.209176	0.234785	0.236182	0.237652	0.239390	0.239484	0.239530	0.239560	0.239581	0.239581
	– 0.022994	0.047780	0.092506	0.065835	0.070662	0.068734	0.069855	0.070309	0.070494	0.070614	0.070613
	– 1.	–1.	–1.	–1.	–1.	–1.	–1.	–1.	–1.	–1.	–1.
	0.764704	0.694315	0.647516	0.673241	0.668621	0.670349	0.669316	0.668913	0.668755	0.668651	0.668651
	0.818027	0.829156	0.837273	0.834116	0.835328	0.835558	0.835824	0.835968	0.836040	0.836082	0.836082
	0.395823	0.404070	0.404419	0.401880	0.401437	0.400770	0.400746	0.400680	0.400632	0.400606	0.400606
	1.	1.	1.	1.	1.	1.	1.	1.	1.	1.	1.
	0.140874	0.145025	0.148545	0.147547	0.147705	0.147619	0.147630	0.147621	0.147615	0.147614	0.147614
	0.187339	0.175966	0.173672	0.176780	0.177289	0.178114	0.178165	0.178263	0.178331	0.178366	0.178366
	2.335035	*2.346984*	*2.355476*	*2.351084*	*2.352275*	*2.351728*	*2.351921*	*2.351994*	*2.352026*	*2.352049*	*2.352049*
$10^4 \times \det \bar{S}$	0.274992	0.258411	0.254885	0.264089	0.263970	0.266469	0.266423	0.266493	0.266557	0.266587	
$10^4 \times \det T$	0.191677	0.190677	0.189889	0.197011	0.196963	0.198846	0.198813	0.198866	0.198914	0.198936	
$\det T/\det \bar{S}$	0.697028	0.737881	0.744998	0.746002	0.746157	0.746225	0.746231	0.746232	0.746233	0.746233	
	use R_1	use R_1	use R_1	use R_1	use R_2	use R_2	use R_2	use R_2	use L_1	use L_2	
	$10^2 \times \overset{\star\prime}{d}_{(0)}$	$10^2 \times \overset{\star\prime}{d}_{(1)}$	$10^2 \times \overset{\star\prime}{d}_{(2)}$	$10^2 \times \overset{\star\prime}{d}_{(3)}$	$10^2 \times \overset{\star\prime}{d}_{(4)}$	$10^3 \times \overset{\star\prime}{d}_{(5)}$	$10^3 \times \overset{\star\prime}{d}_{(6)}$	$10^3 \times \overset{\star\prime}{d}_{(7)}$	$10^4 \times \overset{\star\prime}{d}_{(8)}$	$10^6 \times \overset{\star\prime}{d}_{(9)}$	
	– 8.877012	–2.568418	–0.187475	–0.319219	–0.276922	–0.761754	–0.379138	–0.171764	–0.954336	–0.115382	
	– 0.340692	–0.180147	–0.021910	0.044563	0.038363	0.272571	0.140196	0.060435	0.320815	0.014626	
	0.	0.	0.	0.	0.	0.	0.	0.	0.	0.	
	9.099448	2.845499	0.232679	0.210035	0.173849	0.156832	0.057453	0.029944	0.202674	0.070118	
	14.154998	4.969600	–4.445148	0.689488	–0.192782	1.868384	0.567369	0.185256	1.196090	–0.080635	
	0.	0.	0.	0.	0.	0.	0.	0.	0.	0.	
	–14.077695	–5.199967	4.287601	–0.660003	0.172755	–1.721611	–0.503265	–0.157962	–1.041166	0.059592	
	2.225777	0.901850	–0.526189	0.173251	0.022991	0.443234	0.179217	0.071979	0.420164	0.004062	
	1.649380	0.038868	–0.423233	–0.063309	–0.066727	–0.039949	–0.081764	–0.048594	–0.255078	–0.012221	
	0.	0.	0.	0.	0.	0.	0.	0.	0.	0.	
	0.830051	0.391211	–0.166365	0.022523	–0.008599	0.018715	–0.011249	–0.006233	–0.008954	0.002367	
	– 2.274564	–0.254945	0.518036	0.072768	0.082463	0.085236	0.121668	0.068594	0.352979	0.014035	
	2.389692	*0.943553*	*–0.732007*	*0.170097*	*–0.054607*	*0.321660*	*0.090488*	*0.031656*	*0.233188*	*–0.043437*	
	$h = 0.5$	$h = 0.9$	$h = 0.6$	$h = 0.7$	$h = 1.0$	$h = 0.6$	$h = 0.8$	$h = 1.0$	$h = 1.0$	$h = 1.0$	

TABLE 22—L.I.S.: Estimated Sampling Covariances of Estimated Coefficients; Computation of the Matrices $f_i^j = \sum_n \bar{s}^{in} p_n^j$, $g_i^j = \sum_n t^{in} k_n^j$, $G^{(i,j)} = \sum_n (p_n^i)'(f_n^j)$, $H^{(i,j)} = \sum_n (k_n^i)'(g_n^j)$

	1	2	4			5	7	8			9	11	12	
		f_1^1					f_1^2					f_1^3		
	−1.226174	0.188690	0.000238	*−1.037245*		−1.226174	0.000238	0.758378	*−0.467557*		0.467939	−0.347010	0.491766	*0.612696*
		b_2^1					b_2^2					b_2^3		
	−0.601681	−0.901100	−0.000112	*−1.502894*		−0.601681	0.000112	0.000462	*−0.601331*		−2.387437	0.176985	0.054099	*−2.156352*
		b_3^1					b_3^2					b_3^3		
	−1.718628	−0.864094	−0.585737	*−3.168460*		−1.718628	−0.585737	−0.163997	*−2.468363*		−0.202036	0.000047	−0.000889	*−0.202877*
		g_1^1					g_1^2					g_1^3		
	−1.226794	0.188561	0.	*−1.038233*		−1.226794	0.	0.			0.470658	0.	0.	
		g_2^1					g_2^2					g_2^3		
	−0.601376	−0.999118	0.	*−1.600495*		−0.601376	0.	0.			−2.493856	0.	0.	
		g_3^1					g_3^2					g_3^3		
	−1.632154	−1.081217	0.	*−2.713371*		−1.632154	0.	0.			−0.202723	0.	0.	
		$G^{(1,1)}$					$G^{(1,2)}$					$G^{(1,3)}$		
	1	2	4			5	7	8			9	11	12	
1	0.173718	0.109886	0.017688	*0.301293*	1	0.173718	0.017688	−0.032038	*0.159369*	1	0.229661	−0.001360	−0.029511	*0.198790*
2		0.100794	0.021737	*0.232418*	2	0.109886	0.021737	0.005918	*0.137541*	2	0.189624	−0.013449	−0.004180	*0.171994*
4			0.007856	*0.047282*	4	0.017688	0.007856	0.008998	*0.034543*	4	0.029320	−0.004775	0.003916	*0.028460*
		$G^{(2,2)}$					$G^{(2,3)}$					$G^{(3,3)}$		
	5	7	8			9	11	12			9	11	12	
5	0.173718	0.017688	−0.032038	*0.159369*	5	0.229661	−0.001360	−0.029511	*0.198790*	9	0.399045	−0.018228	−0.025829	*0.354987*
7		0.007856	0.008998	*0.034543*	7	0.029320	−0.004775	0.003916	*0.028460*	11		0.005138	−0.005918	*−0.019008*
8			0.032539	*0.009499*	8	−0.017626	−0.010824	0.020365	*−0.008086*	12			0.013381	*−0.018365*
		$H^{(1,1)}$					$H^{(1,2)}$					$H^{(1,3)}$		
1	0.142607	0.103018	0.	*0.245625*	1	0.142607	0.	0.		1	0.206994	0.	0.	
2		0.118477	0.	*0.221495*	2	0.103018	0.	0.		2	0.203583	0.	0.	
4			0.	*0.*	4	0.	0.	0.		4	0.	0.	0.	
		$H^{(2,2)}$					$H^{(2,3)}$					$H^{(3,3)}$		
5	0.142607	0.	0.		5	0.206994	0.	0.		9	0.402137	0.	0.	
7		0.	0.		7	0.	0.	0.		11		0.	0.	
8			0.		8	0.	0.	0.		12			0.	

TABLE 23—L.I.S.: Estimated Sampling Covariances of Estimated Coefficients; Computation of $\oplus\oplus L^{**}$;
$^1L^{(i,j)} = (g^i_i)'(g^j_i) - (f^i_i)'(f^j_i)$, $^2L^{(i,j)} = t^{ij}(Z^{(i,j)} - H^{(i,j)})$, $^3L^{(i,j)} = \bar{s}^{ij}(V^{(i,j)} - G^{(i,j)})$

$^1L^{(1,1)}$

	1	2	4	
1	0.001520	0.000041	0.000292	*0.001854*
2		−0.000048	−0.000044	*−0.000052*
4			0.000000	*0.000247*

$^1L^{(1,2)}$

	5	7	8	
1	0.000000	0.000143	0.456302	*0.456444*
2	0.120806	0.000214	0.683375	*0.804396*
4	−0.000138	0.000000	0.000085	*−0.000052*

$^1L^{(1,3)}$

	9	11	12	
1	0.036027	−0.596381	0.845164	*0.284810*
2	−0.104540	−0.299849	0.424933	*0.020543*
4	0.274090	−0.203256	0.288046	*0.358879*

$^1L^{(2,2)}$

	5	7	8	
5	−0.003366	−0.000067	0.000278	*−0.003156*
7		0.000000	0.000000	*−0.000067*
8			0.000000	*0.000277*

$^1L^{(2,3)}$

	9	11	12	
5	−0.032760	0.304171	0.092976	*0.364388*
7	−1.398412	0.103666	0.031688	*−1.263057*
8	−0.391533	0.029025	0.008872	*−0.353635*

$^1L^{(3,3)}$

	9	11	12	
9	0.000278	0.000009	−0.000179	*0.000108*
11		0.000000	0.000000	*0.000009*
12			0.000000	*−0.000180*

$^2L^{(1,1)}$

	1	2	4	
1	2.021928	0.982251	0.	*3.004180*
2		0.984498	0.	*1.966750*
4			0.	

$^2L^{(1,2)}$

	5	7	8
1	−1.089819	0.	0.
2	−0.529433	0.	0.
4	0.	0.	0.

$^2L^{(1,3)}$

	9	11	12
1	2.812110	0.	0.
2	2.818543	0.	0.
4	0.	0.	0.

$^2L^{(2,2)}$

	5	7	8
5	1.124451	0.	0.
7		0.	0.
8			0.

$^2L^{(2,3)}$

	9	11	12
5	−1.920359	0.	0.
7	0.	0.	0.
8	0.	0.	0.

$^2L^{(3,3)}$

	9	11	12
9	13.720959	0.	0.
11		0.	0.
12			0.

$^3L^{(1,1)}$

	1	2	4	
1	31.235758	40.216095	28.905375	*100.357229*
2		124.933347	39.096751	*204.246194*
4			36.638514	*104.640640*

$^3L^{(1,2)}$

	5	7	8	
1	−17.653904	−16.336813	9.917088	*− 24.073629*
2	−22.729434	−22.096801	−32.246019	*− 77.072255*
4	−16.336813	−20.707448	− 7.678220	*− 44.722481*

$^3L^{(1,3)}$

	9	11	12	
1	77.551613	2.377006	57.998459	*137.927079*
2	172.850512	85.765214	139.058985	*397.674711*
4	75.723707	− 1.170514	72.846809	*147.400003*

$^3L^{(2,2)}$

	5	7	8	
5	19.040921	17.620349	− 10.696245	*25.965025*
7		22.334373	8.281475	*48.236198*
8			135.913461	*133.498691*

$^3L^{(2,3)}$

	9	11	12	
5	−58.632804	− 1.797132	−43.849665	*−104.279602*
7	−57.250818	0.884965	−55.075743	*−111.441595*
8	−30.098784	−54.771129	−76.492416	*−161.362330*

$^3L^{(3,3)}$

	9	11	12	
9	490.310987	157.812322	388.592480	*1036.715789*
11		182.291891	118.373044	*458.477258*
12			376.303545	*883.269070*

TABLE 24.2—L.I.S.: Estimated Sampling Covariances of Estimated Coefficients

	$(1/T)(-_{\oplus\oplus}L^{**})^{-1}$ evaluated at final estimate								
	a_1^1	a_2^1	a_4^1	a_1^2	a_3^2	a_4^2	a_1^3	a_3^3	a_4^3
a_1^1	0.021707	–0.002374	–0.014175	0.009846	–0.008375	–0.000665	–0.002047	0.001386	0.001702
a_2^1		0.001755	–0.000038	0.002595	–0.002284	0.000723	–0.000020	–0.000556	0.000039
a_4^1			0.014316	–0.011076	0.011348	–0.000370	0.001437	–0.000143	–0.001693
a_1^2				0.053637	–0.044588	0.007194	–0.000749	0.001325	0.001186
a_3^2					0.042537	–0.006389	0.001359	–0.001685	–0.001184
a_4^2						0.001922	–0.000601	0.000405	0.000694
a_1^3							0.001608	–0.000618	–0.001428
a_3^3								0.000961	0.000343
a_4^3									0.001647

TABLE 25—F.I.D.: with $\bar{\sigma}_{11} = \bar{\sigma}_{22} = \bar{\sigma}_{33} = 1$; Computation of $\bar{\sigma}_{ii}(V^{(i,i)})^{-1}$

	$\bar{\sigma}_{11}(V^{(1,1)})^{-1}$			
	1	2	3	4
1	21.114503	3.783108	–21.494899	– 4.318347
2		1.828398	– 5.427387	– 0.791682
3			26.633397	2.393940
4				3.935593
	– 0.915636	*– 0.607563*	*2.105051*	*1.219503*
	$\bar{\sigma}_{22}(V^{(2,2)})^{-1}$			
	5	6	7	8
5	10.731345	–13.184889	0.605944	12.326253
6		27.489386	– 9.155030	–24.416219
7			7.802827	7.508922
8				22.020451
	10.478653	*–19.266752*	*6.762663*	*17.439408*
	$\bar{\sigma}_{33}(V^{(3,3)})^{-1}$			
	9	10	11	12
9	10.042576	20.917537	2.517486	2.252839
10		47.596437	6.199208	6.953360
11			1.631338	0.860185
12				2.149008
	35.730440	*81.666545*	*11.208219*	*12.215395*

TABLE 26—F.I.D.: Reduced Matrices $J^{(i)} = (\Phi^i_y)' \bar{\sigma}_{ii} (V^{(i,i)})^{-1} (\Phi^i_x)$

	$(\Phi^1_y)'\bar{\sigma}_{11}(V^{(1,1)})^{-1}$				$(\Phi^2_y)'\bar{\sigma}_{22}(V^{(2,2)})^{-1}$				$(\Phi^3_y)'\bar{\sigma}_{33}(V^{(3,3)})^{-1}$			
	1	2	3	4	5	6	7	8	9	10	11	12
y_1	21.114503	3.783108	–21.494899	–4.318347	10.731345	–13.184889	0.605944	12.326253	10.042576	20.917537	2.517486	2.252839
y_2	3.783108	1.828398	– 5.427387	–0.791682	0.	0.	0.	0.	–10.874961	–26.678899	–3.681722	–4.700521
y_3	–21.494899	– 5.427387	26.633397	2.393940	–13.184889	27.489386	– 9.155030	–24.416219	0.	0.	0.	0.
	3.402711	*0.184119*	*– 0.288888*	*–2.716090*	*– 2.453544*	*14.304497*	*– 8.549085*	*–12.089966*	*– 0.832385*	*– 5.761361*	*–1.164236*	*–2.447681*

$J^{(1)}$

	y_1	y_2	y_3	z_1	z_2	z_3	z_4	z_5	z_6	z_7	
y_1	21.114503	3.783108	–21.494899	3.783108	–4.318347	21.494899	0.	21.494899	–21.494899	0.	*24.362371*
y_2	3.783108	1.828398	– 5.427387	1.828398	–0.791682	5.427387	0.	5.427387	– 5.427387	0.	*6.648221*
y_3	–21.494899	– 5.427387	26.633397	–5.427387	2.393940	–26.633397	0.	–26.633397	26.633397	0.	*–29.955733*

$J^{(2)}$

	y_1	y_2	y_3	z_1	z_2	z_3	z_4	z_5	z_6	z_7	
y_1	10.731345	0.	–13.184889	0.	0.605944	12.326253	0.	0.	0.	0.	*10.478653*
y_2	0.	0.	0.	0.	0.	0.	0.	0.	0.	0.	*0.*
y_3	–13.184889	0.	27.489386	0.	–9.155030	–24.416219	0.	0.	0.	0.	*–19.266752*

$J^{(3)}$

	y_1	y_2	y_3	z_1	z_2	z_3	z_4	z_5	z_6	z_7	
y_1	10.042576	–10.874961	0.	0.	0.	0.	2.517486	10.042576	0.	2.252839	*13.980516*
y_2	–10.874961	15.803937	0.	0.	0.	0.	– 3.681722	–10.874961	0.	–4.700521	*–14.328229*
y_3	0.	0.	0.	0.	0.	0.	0.	0.	0.	0.	*0.*

TABLE 27—F.I.D.: Last Iteration; Final Approximation to A

$B_{(13)}$			$(\text{adjoint } B_{(13)})'$			$B^{-1}_{(13)}$			check: $BB^{-1} = I$		
−0.979914	− 0.200001	1.	−0.579827	− 0.579827	0.200001	− 1.118965	− 1.118965	0.385968	1.000	0.000	0.000
0.231163	0.	− 1.	−0.420172	− 0.420172	− 0.748750	− 0.810861	− 0.810861	−1.444959	0.000	1.000	0.000
0.420172	− 0.579827	0.	−0.134034	− 0.652216	0.046233	− 0.258664	− 1.258664	0.089221	0.000	0.000	1.000
−0.328577	*− 0.779828*	*0.*	det B = 0.518181								

$A_{(13)} + \Delta A_{(13)}$

	y_1	y_2	y_3	z_1	z_2	z_3	z_4	z_5	z_6	z_7	
y_1	−21.134019	− 4.311874	21.563806	−4.311874	4.854801	−21.563806	0.	−21.563806	21.563806	0.	*−24.902967*
y_2	4.587340	0.	−19.846466	0.	10.845077	16.939165	0.	0.	0.	0.	*12.525117*
y_3	19.589995	−27.033440	0.	0.	0.	0.	6.291610	19.589995	0.	7.661587	*26.099748*

$A_{(13)} + \Delta A_{(13)}$

normalized: first row divided by 21.563806, second row by 19.846466, third row by 46.623436

	y_1	y_2	y_3	z_1	z_2	z_3	z_4	z_5	z_6	z_7	
y_1	− 0.980069	− 0.199958	1.	−0.199958	0.225136	− 1.	0.	− 1.	1.	0.	*− 1.154850*
y_2	0.231141	0.	− 1.	0.	0.546448	0.853510	0.	0.	0.	0.	*0.631100*
y_3	0.420174	− 0.579825	0.	0.	0.	0.	0.134945	0.420174	0.	0.164329	*0.559798*

TABLE 28—F.I.D.: Summary of Successive Approximations to B

	L.I.S.E.	F.I.D.						
	$B_{(0)}$	$B_{(1)}$	$B_{(2)}$	$B_{(3)}$	$B_{(4)}$	$B_{(5)}$	$B_{(6)}$	$B_{(7)}$
(1,1)	−1.22	−0.94741	−0.96788	−0.95457	−0.95642	−0.95550	−0.95565	−0.955580
(1,2)	−0.18	−0.21369	−0.21449	−0.21442	−0.21438	−0.21436	−0.21436	−0.214357
(2,1)	0.21	0.30967	0.25231	0.26043	0.25604	0.25669	0.25637	0.256420
(3,1)	0.53	0.52640	0.53136	0.53036	0.53062	0.53059	0.53056	0.421668

	$B_{(8)}$	$B_{(9)}$	$B_{(10)}$	$B_{(11)}$	$B_{(12)}$	$B_{(13)}$	$(B_{(14)})$
(1,1)	−0.985812	−0.978368	−0.980587	−0.979775	−0.979970	−0.979914	(−0.980069)
(1,2)	−0.200040	−0.200197	−0.199967	−0.200011	−0.199997	−0.200001	(−0.199959)
(2,1)	0.226041	0.233740	0.230565	0.234407	0.231086	0.231163	(0.231141)
(3,1)	0.421670	0.420026	0.420242	0.420155	0.420180	0.420172	(0.420175)

TABLE 29—F.I.D.: Estimated Sampling Covariances of Estimated Coefficients; Computation of ${}^1L^{(i,j)} = (c_j^i)' c_i^j$

$a^1_{(13)}$				$a^2_{(13)}$				$a^3_{(13)}$				
1	2	3	4	5	6	7	8	9	10	11	12	
−0.979914	−0.200001	1.	0.225058	0.231163	−1.	0.546429	0.853513	0.420172	1.	0.134945	0.164330	*2.395698*

$B = B_{(13)}$			(adjoint B)′			B^{-1}			check: $BB^{-1} = I$		
−0.979914	−0.200001	1.	−0.579827	−0.579827	0.200001	−1.118965	−1.118965	0.385968	1.000	0.000	0.000
0.231163	0.	−1.	−0.420172	−0.420172	−0.748750	−0.810861	−0.810861	−1.444959	0.000	1.000	0.000
0.420172	−0.579827	0.	−0.134034	−0.652216	0.046233	−0.258664	−1.258664	0.089221	0.000	0.000	1.000
−0.328577	*−0.779828*	*0.*	det A_{yy} = 0.518181								

	1	2	3	4	5	6	7	8	9	10	11	12	
m^*	−0.051854	−0.037631	−0.011971	0.000000	−0.056376	−0.063417	0.000000	0.000000	−0.022715	0.030993	0.000000	0.000000	*−0.212974*
l^*	−1.118965	−0.810861	−0.258664	0.	−1.118965	−1.258664	0.	0.	−1.058990	1.444959	0.	0.	*−4.180152*
n^*	−1.067111	−0.773229	−0.246692	0.000000	−1.062589	−1.195246	0.000000	0.000000	−1.036275	1.413966	0.000000	0.000000	*−3.967177*

	1	2	3
	$c_1^{1\prime}$	$c_2^{1\prime}$	$c_3^{1\prime}$
1	−1.118965	−1.118965	0.385968
2	−0.810861	−0.810861	−1.444959
3	−0.258664	−1.258664	0.089221
4	0.	0.	0.
	−2.188490	*−3.188490*	*−0.969769*

	5	6	7
	$c_1^{2\prime}$	$c_2^{2\prime}$	$c_3^{2\prime}$
5	−1.118965	−1.118965	0.385968
6	−0.258664	−1.258664	0.089221
7	0.	0.	0.
8	0.	0.	0.
	−1.377629	*−2.377629*	*0.475190*

	9	10	11
	$c_1^{3\prime}$	$c_2^{3\prime}$	$c_3^{3\prime}$
9	−1.929826	−1.929826	−1.058990
10	0.810861	0.810861	1.444959
11	0.	0.	0.
12	0.	0.	0.
	−1.118965	*−1.118965*	*0.385968*

${}^1L^{(1,1)}$

	1	2	3	4
1	1.252084	0.907325	0.289436	0.
2		0.657495	0.209740	0.
3			0.066907	0.
4				0.
	2.448846	*1.774562*	*0.566084*	*0.*

${}^1L^{(1,2)}$

	5	6	7	8
1	1.252084	0.289436	0.	0.
2	0.907325	0.209740	0.	0.
3	1.408402	0.325571	0.	0.
4	0.	0.	0.	0.
	3.567811	*0.824748*	*0.*	*0.*

${}^1L^{(1,3)}$

	9	10	11	12
1	−0.744852	0.312966	0.	0.
2	2.788521	−1.171661	0.	0.
3	−0.172182	0.072346	0.	0.
4	0.	0.	0.	0.
	1.871486	*−0.786348*	*0.*	*0.*

${}^1L^{(2,2)}$

	5	6	7	8
5	1.252084	1.408402	0.	0.
6		1.584235	0.	0.
7			0.	0.
8				0.
	2.660486	*2.992637*	*0.*	*0.*

${}^1L^{(2,3)}$

	9	10	11	12
5	−0.744852	0.312966	0.	0.
6	−0.172182	0.072346	0.	0.
7	0.	0.	0.	0.
8	0.	0.	0.	0.
	−0.917035	*0.385313*	*0.*	*0.*

${}^1L^{(3,3)}$

	9	10	11	12
9	1.121461	−1.530198	0.	0.
10		2.087907	0.	0.
11			0.	0.
12				0.
	−0.408737	*0.557708*	*0.*	*0.*

TABLE 30—F.I.D.: Estimated Sampling Covariances of Estimated Coefficients; Computation of $-L^{\star\star} = {}^1L^{(i,j)} + {}^2L^{(i,j)}$ and $(1/T)(-L^{\star\star})^{-1}$

$$-L^{(i,j)} = (c^{i}_{j})c^{j\prime}_{i} + \bar{\sigma}^{ij}V^{(i,j)}$$

	1	2	3	4	5	6	7	8	9	10	11	12	
1	2.000100	1.756620	1.016845	0.549140	1.252084	0.289436	0.	0.	−0.744852	0.312966	0.	0.	*6.432339*
2		3.055301	1.317239	0.740566	0.907325	0.209740	0.	0.	2.788521	−1.171661	0.	0.	*9.603651*
3			0.869313	0.532850	1.408402	0.325571	0.	0.	−0.172182	0.072346	0.	0.	*5.370384*
4				0.681488	0.	0.	0.	0.	0.	0.	0.	0.	*2.504044*
5					2.000100	1.635060	0.549140	−0.354650	−0.744852	0.312966	0.	0.	*6.965575*
6						5.154297	0.720197	3.586015	−0.172182	0.072346	0.	0.	*11.820480*
7							0.681488	0.258778	0.	0.	0.	0.	*2.209603*
8								4.131854	0.	0.	0.	0.	*7.621997*
9									5.855935	−4.288455	1.377180	3.410184	*7.309297*
10										3.757217	−0.967890	−2.122299	− *4.022464*
11											1.617000	1.040760	*3.067050*
12												3.340734	*5.669379*

$$(1/T)(-L^{\star\star})^{-1} \times 10^2 = 0.047619(-L^{\star\star})^{-1} \times 10^2$$

	1	2	3	4	5	6	7	8	9	10	11	12	
1	4.382355	1.056607	−5.029688	−0.746813	−1.125159	1.000276	0.221139	−0.978560	−1.521864	−1.115355	0.105943	0.811935	− *2.939184*
2		−0.382852	0.148313	−0.551332	−0.120714	0.107316	0.023725	−0.104986	2.267318	1.661688	−0.157837	−1.209644	*2.737602*
3			3.699112	0.999423	5.246104	−4.663830	−1.031073	4.562580	−0.524593	−0.384468	0.036519	0.279877	*3.338276*
4				7.406976	−3.064059	2.723974	0.602212	−2.664838	−0.827384	−0.606379	0.057597	0.441420	*3.770797*
5					−1.276011	0.301774	0.871046	−0.425986	−0.622583	−0.456283	0.043340	0.332156	− *0.296375*
6						3.333542	−2.742510	−2.695499	0.553482	0.405639	−0.038530	−0.295290	− *2.009656*
7							8.452721	1.925581	0.122363	0.089678	−0.008518	−0.065282	*8.461082*
8								3.334733	−0.541466	−0.396833	0.037693	0.288879	*2.341298*
9									−0.473168	1.008835	0.354567	1.013437	*0.808944*
10										3.965689	0.695236	1.272920	*6.140367*
11											3.762115	−1.092304	*3.795821*
12												1.539853	*3.317957*

CORRECTIONS TO *Statistical Inference in Dynamic Economic Models*, COWLES COMMISSION MONOGRAPH 10

Page 8, lines 3, 11: *for* equation (1.1) *read* equations (1.1).
Page 74, line 5: *for* $S^{\oplus\oplus\oplus}$ *read* $S^{\oplus\oplus}$.
Page 148, equation (3.132): insert subscripts $\bar{\zeta} = \zeta$ to right of closing bracket.
Page 153, equation (3.156): insert superscript $^{-1}$ to right of closing parenthesis in right-hand member.
Page 158, equation (4.15): *for* $\Phi^{g\prime}$ *read* $\mathrm{X}^{g\prime}$.
Page 159, line 1: *for* Φ^{g} *read* X^{g}.
Page 159, line 2: *for* $\alpha(g)\Phi^{g\prime}$ *read* $\beta(g)\mathrm{X}^{g\prime}$; *for* α *read* $\beta(g)$.
Page 164, equation (4.34): *for* $-$ *read* $=$.
Page 193, line 1: *for* in that notation, *read* , in the notation of (4.15),.
Page 193, equations (4.130) and (4.131): *for* Φ'^{g} *read* X'^{g}.
Page 197, equation (4.138): insert subscripts $_{xx}$ to right of M in second member.
Page 274, first line of footnote 3: change second "$\supset$" to "$\supseteq$".
Page 301, equation (1.0): *for* y_0 *read* y_{0t}.
Page 316, bottom line: *for* W_{yy} *read* W.
Page 425, line 23: *for* Bank *read* Rank.
Page 438, line 29: *after* variables, endogenous *insert* p. 8.
Page 438, line 34: *after* variables, exogenous, *insert* p. 8.

REFERENCES

AITKEN, A. C., *Determinants and Matrices*, New York: 1948 (5th ed.), 143 pp.

ALBERT, A. A., *Introduction to Algebraic Theories*, Chicago: University of Chicago Press, 1941, 137 pp.

ANDERSON, T. W. [1950], "Estimation of the Parameters of a Single Equation by the Limited-Information Maximum-Likelihood Method," Chapter IX in *Statistical Inference in Dynamic Economic Models*, Cowles Commission Monograph 10, New York: John Wiley & Sons, Inc., 1950, pp. 311–322.

——— [1951], "The Asymptotic Distribution of Certain Characteristic Roots and Vectors," *Proceedings of the Second Berkeley Symposium on Mathematical Statistics and Probability*, Jerzy Neyman, ed., Berkeley and Los Angeles: University of California Press, 1951, pp. 103–130.

ANDERSON, T. W., AND LEONID HURWICZ, "Errors and Shocks in Economic Relationships," presented at the Washington, D. C., meeting of the Econometric Society, September 6–18, 1947 (abstract in *Econometrica*, Vol. 16, January, 1948, pp. 36–37).

ANDERSON, T. W., AND HERMAN RUBIN [1949], "Estimation of the Parameters of a Single Equation in a Complete System of Stochastic Equations," *Annals of Mathematical Statistics*, Vol. 20, March, 1949, pp. 46–63 (included in Cowles Commission Paper, New Series, No. 36).

——— [1950], "The Asymptotic Properties of Estimates of the Parameters in a Complete System of Stochastic Equations," *Annals of Mathematical Statistics*, Vol. 21, December, 1950, pp. 570–582 (included in Cowles Commission Paper, New Series, No. 36).

ANGELL, JAMES, Review of *Planning and Paying for Full Employment*, edited by Abba P. Lerner and Frank D. Graham, and *Economic Policy for Full Employment*, by Alvin H. Hansen, *Review of Economic Statistics*, Vol. 29, November, 1947, pp. 290–292.

BIRKHOFF, GARRETT, AND SAUNDERS MACLANE, *A Survey of Modern Algebra*, New York: The Macmillan Co., 1941, 450 pp.

BÔCHER, Maxime, *Introduction to Higher Algebra*, New York: The Macmillan Co., 1907.

CANNON, WALTER B., *The Wisdom of the Body*, New York: W. W. Norton & Co., 1939 (revised ed.), 333 pp.

COCHRANE, D., *see* Orcutt and Cochrane.

COCHRANE, D., AND G. H. ORCUTT, "Application of Least Squares Regression to Relationships Containing Auto-Correlated Error Terms," *Journal of the American Statistical Association*, Vol. 44, March, 1949, pp. 32–61.

COLLAR, A. R., *see* Frazer, Duncan, and Collar.

COURANT, R., *Differential and Integral Calculus*, Vol. II, New York: Interscience Publishers, 1936, 682 pp.

CRAMÉR, HARALD [1937], *Random Variables and Probability Distributions*, Cambridge Tracts in Mathematics and Mathematical Physics No. 36, Cambridge, England: The University Press, 1937, 120 pp.

——— [1946], *Mathematical Methods of Statistics*, Princeton: Princeton University Press, 1946, 575 pp.

DAVID, F. N., AND J. NEYMAN, "Extension of the Markoff Theorem on Least Squares," *Statistical Research Memoirs*, Vol. II, London: Department of Statistics, University College, 1938, pp. 105–116.

DERKSEN, J. B. D., "Long Cycles in Residential Building: An Explanation," *Econometrica*, Vol. 8, April, 1940, pp. 97–116.

DUNCAN, W. J., *see* Frazer, Duncan, and Collar.

DWYER, P. S., *Linear Computations*, New York: John Wiley & Sons, Inc., 1951.

EZEKIEL, M. [1942], "Statistical Investigations of Saving, Consumption, and Investment, I and II," *American Economic Review*, Vol. 32, March, 1942, pp. 22–49; June, 1942, pp. 272–307.

——— [1944], "The Statistical Determination of the Investment Schedule," *Econometrica*, Vol. 12, January, 1944, pp. 89–90.

FRAZER, ROBERT, W. J. DUNCAN, AND A. R. COLLAR, *Elementary Matrices and Some Applications to Dynamics and Differential Equations*, Cambridge, England: The University Press, 1938, 410 pp.

FRISCH, RAGNAR [1933a], "Propagation Problems and Impulse Problems in Dynamic Economics," in *Economic Essays in Honour of Gustav Cassel*, London: George Allen & Unwin, 1933, pp. 171–205.

——— [1933b], "Pitfalls in the Statistical Construction of Demand and Supply Curves," *Veröffentlichungen der Frankfurter Gesellschaft für Konjunkturforschung*, Neue Folge, Heft 5, Leipzig: Hans Buske, 1933, 39 pp.

——— [1934], *Statistical Confluence Analysis by Means of Complete Regression Systems*, Oslo: Universitetets Økonomiske Institutt, 1934, 192 pp.

——— [1938], "Statistical Versus Theoretical Relations in Economic Macrodynamics," mimeographed document prepared for a League of Nations conference in Cambridge, England, July 18–20, 1938, concerning Tinbergen's work.

GEARY, R. C. [1948], "Studies in Relations Between Economic Time Series," *Journal of the Royal Statistical Society*, Vol. 10, 1948, pp. 1–19.

——— [1949], "Determination of Linear Relations Between Systematic Parts of Variables With Errors of Observation the Variances of Which Are Unknown," *Econometrica*, Vol. 17, January, 1949, pp. 30–58.

GOODWIN, RICHARD M., "Dynamical Coupling with Especial Reference to Markets Having Production Lags," *Econometrica*, Vol. 15, July, 1947, pp. 181–204.

HAAVELMO, TRYGVE [1943], "The Statistical Implications of a System of Simultaneous Equations," *Econometrica*, Vol. 11, January, 1943, pp. 1–12.

——— [1944], "The Probability Approach in Econometrics," *Econometrica*, Vol. 12, Supplement, July, 1944, 118 pp. (reprinted as Cowles Commission Paper, New Series, No. 4).

HANSEN, ALVIN H., *Fiscal Policy and Business Cycles*, New York: W. W. Norton & Co., 1941, 462 pp.

HART, ALBERT, " 'Model Building' and Fiscal Policy," *American Economic Review*, Vol. 35, September, 1945, pp. 531–558.

HOTELLING, HAROLD [1940], "The Selection of Variates for Use in Prediction with Some Comments on the Problem of Nuisance Parameters," *Annals of Mathematical Statistics*, Vol. 11, September, 1940, pp. 271–283.

——— [1943], "Some New Methods in Matrix Calculation," *Annals of Mathematical Statistics*, Vol. 14, March, 1943, pp. 1–34.

HSU, P. L., "On the Limiting Distribution of the Roots of a Determinantal Equation," *Journal of the London Mathematical Society*, Vol. 16, 1941, pp. 183–194.

HURWICZ, LEONID [1945], "Aspects of the Theory of Economic Fluctuations" (abstract), *Econometrica*, Vol. 13, January, 1945, p. 79.

Hurwicz Leonid [1950a], "Generalization of the Concept of Identification," Chapter IV in *Statistical Inference in Dynamic Economic Models*, Cowles Commission Monograph 10, T. C. Koopmans, ed., New York: John Wiley & Sons, Inc., 1950, pp. 245–257.

——— [1950b], "Prediction and Least Squares," Chapter VI in *Statistical Inference in Dynamic Economic Models*, Cowles Commission Monograph 10, T. C. Koopmans, ed., New York: John Wiley & Sons, Inc., 1950, pp. 266–300.

——— [1950c], "Least-Squares Bias in Time Series," Chapter XV in *Statistical Inference in Dynamic Economic Models*, Cowles Commission Monograph 10, T. C. Koopmans, ed., New York, John Wiley & Sons, Inc., 1950, pp. 365–383.

———, *see* Anderson and Hurwicz.

Klein, L. [1943], "Pitfalls in the Statistical Determination of the Investment Schedule," *Econometrica*, Vol. 11, July–October, 1943, pp. 246–258.

——— [1944], "The Statistical Determination of the Investment Schedule: A Reply," *Econometrica*, Vol. 12, January, 1944, pp. 91–92.

——— [1950], *Economic Fluctuations in the United States, 1921–1941*, Cowles Commission Monograph 11, New York: John Wiley & Sons, Inc., 1950, 174 pp.

Knopp, Konrad, *Theory and Application of Infinite Series*, London: Blackie & Son, Ltd., 1928.

Koopmans, Tjalling C. [1937], *Linear Regression Analysis of Economic Time Series*, Haarlem: De Erven F. Bohn N.V., 1937, 150 pp.

——— [1941], "The Logic of Econometric Business-Cycle Research," *Journal of Political Economy*, Vol. 49, April, 1941, pp. 157–181.

——— [1945], "Statistical Estimation of Simultaneous Economic Relations," *Journal of the American Statistical Association*, Vol. 40, December, 1945, pp. 448–466 (reprinted as Cowles Commission Paper, New Series, No. 11).

——— [1947], "Measurement Without Theory," *Review of Economic Statistics*, Vol. 29, August, 1947, pp. 161–172 (included in Cowles Commission Paper, New Series, No. 25).

——— [1950a], "The Equivalence of Maximum-Likelihood and Least-Squares Estimates of Regression Coefficients," Chapter VII in *Statistical Inference in Dynamic Economic Models*, Cowles Commission Monograph 10, T. C. Koopmans, ed., New York: John Wiley & Sons, Inc., 1950, pp. 301–304.

——— [1950b], "Models Involving a Continuous Time Variable," Chapter XVI in *Statistical Inference in Dynamic Economic Models*, Cowles Commission Monograph 10, T. C. Koopmans, ed., New York: John Wiley & Sons, Inc., 1950, pp. 384–389.

——— [1950c], "When Is an Equation System Complete for Statistical Purposes?" Chapter XVII in *Statistical Inference in Dynamic Economic Models*, Cowles Commission Monograph 10, T. C. Koopmans, ed., New York: John Wiley & Sons, Inc., 1950, pp. 393–409.

Koopmans, T. C., and O. Reiersøl, "The Identification of Structural Characteristics," *Annals of Mathematical Statistics*, Vol. 21, June, 1950, pp. 165–181 (included in Cowles Commission Paper, New Series, No. 39).

Koopmans, T. C., H. Rubin, and R. B. Leipnik, "Measuring the Equation Systems of Dynamic Economics," Chapter II in *Statistical Inference in Dynamic Economic Models*, Cowles Commission Monograph 10, T. C. Koopmans, ed., New York: John Wiley & Sons, Inc., 1950, pp. 53–237.

Leipnik, Roy B., "Distribution of the Serial Correlation Coefficient in a Circularly Correlated Universe," *Annals of Mathematical Statistics*, Vol. 18,

March, 1947, pp. 80–87 (included in Cowles Commission Paper, New Series, No. 21).

LEIPNIK, ROY B., *see* Koopmans, Rubin, and Leipnik.

LEONTIEF, W. W., "Verzoegerte Angebotsanpassung," *Zeitschrift für Nationalökonomie*, 1934, pp. 670–676.

LERNER, ABBA P., "The Economic Steering Wheel," *The University Review* (University of Kansas City), June, 1941.

LUNDBERG, ERIK, *Studies in the Theory of Economic Expansion*, London: P. S. King, 1937, 265 pp.

MACDUFFEE, CYRUS COLTON [1933], *The Theory of Matrices*, Berlin: J. Springer, 1933, 110 pp.

——— [1943], *Vectors and Matrices*, Menasha, Wisc.: Mathematical Association of America, 1943, 192 pp.

MACLANE, SAUNDERS, *see* Birkhoff and MacLane.

MANN, H. B., AND A. WALD, "On the Statistical Treatment of Linear Stochastic Difference Equations," *Econometrica*, Vol. 11, July–October, 1943, pp. 173–220.

MARSCHAK, J. [1942], "Economic Interdependence and Statistical Analysis," in *Studies in Mathematical Economics and Econometrics, in memory of Henry Schultz*, O. Lange, F. McIntyre, and T. O. Yntema, eds., Chicago: The University of Chicago Press, 1942, pp. 135–150.

——— [1947a], "Statistical Inference from Nonexperimental Observations: An Economic Example," presented September 10, 1947; *Proceedings of the International Statistical Conferences*, Washington, D. C.: International Statistical Institute, 1951, Vol. III, pp. 289–298.

——— [1947b], "Economic Structure, Path, Policy, and Prediction," *American Economic Review, Proceedings Supplement*, Vol. 37, pp. 81–84.

——— [1949], Comment on "Mitchell on What Happens During Business Cycles" by Arthur F. Burns, presented in November, 1949; *Conference on Business Cycles*, New York: National Bureau of Economic Research, Inc., 1951, pp. 14-24.

——— [1950], "Statistical Inference in Economics: An Introduction," Chapter I in *Statistical Inference in Dynamic Economic Models*, Cowles Commission Monograph 10, T. C. Koopmans, ed., New York: John Wiley & Sons, Inc., 1950, pp. 1-50.

MILNE, WILLIAM EDMUND, *Numerical Calculus*, Princeton: Princeton University Press, 1949, 393 pp.

MOOD, A. M., *Introduction to the Theory of Statistics*, New York: McGraw-Hill Book Co., 1950, 433 pp.

MOSAK, JACOB L., "Forecasting Postwar Demand: III," *Econometrica*, Vol. 13, January, 1945, pp. 25–53.

NEYMAN, J., *see* David and Neyman.

ORCUTT, GUY H. [1952], "Toward Partial Redirection of Econometrics," *Review of Economics and Statistics*, Vol. 34, August, 1952.

———, *see* Cochrane and Orcutt.

ORCUTT, GUY H., AND DONALD COCHRANE, "A Sampling Study of the Merits of Autoregressive and Reduced Form Transformations in Regression Analysis," *Journal of the American Statistical Association*, Vol. 44, September, 1949, pp. 356–372.

PIGOU, A. C., "A Method of Determining the Numerical Values of Elasticities of Demand," *Economic Journal*, Vol. 20, 1910, pp. 636–640 (reprinted as Appendix II in his *Economics of Welfare*, London: Macmillan & Co., 1929, 835 pp.).

Reiersøl, Olav, *see* Koopmans and Reiersøl.

Rubin, Herman [1948], "Systems of Linear Stochastic Equations" (unpublished Ph.D. dissertation, University of Chicago), 1948, 50 pp.

——— [1950], "Consistency of Maximum-Likelihood Estimates in the Explosive Case," Chapter XIV in *Statistical Inference in Dynamic Economic Models*, Cowles Commission Monograph 10, T. C. Koopmans, ed., New York: John Wiley & Sons, Inc., 1950, pp. 356–364.

———, *see* Anderson and Rubin.

———, *see* Koopmans, Rubin, and Leipnik.

Samuelson, Paul A. [1933], "Full Employment After the War," in *Postwar Economic Problems*, S. E. Harris, ed., New York and London: McGraw-Hill Book Co., 417 pp.

——— [1947], *Foundations of Economic Analysis*, Cambridge, Mass.: Harvard University Press, 1947, 447 pp.

Schultz, Henry, *The Theory and Measurement of Demand*, Chicago: The University of Chicago Press, 1938, 817 pp.

Simon, Herbert A. [1947], "The Axioms of Newtonian Mechanics," *Philosophical Magazine*, Vol. 37, December, 1947, pp. 888–905.

——— [1952], "On the Definition of the Causal Relation," *Journal of Philosophy*, Vol. 49, July 31, 1952.

Smithies, Arthur [1945], "Forecasting Postwar Demand: I," *Econometrica*, Vol. 13, January, 1945, pp. 1–14.

——— [1951], "Business Cycle Analysis and Public Policy," with comments by J. M. Clark, L. Hurwicz, and C. Christ, presented in November, 1949; *Conference on Business Cycles*, New York: National Bureau of Economic Research, Inc., 1951, pp. 405–422.

Snedecor, George W., *Statistical Methods Applied to Experiments in Agriculture and Biology*, Ames: The Iowa State College Press, 1940 (3rd ed.), 442 pp.

Sverdrup, Erling [1949], "Some Aspects of Links Between Prediction Problems and Problems of Statistical Estimation" (abstract), *Annals of Mathematical Statistics*, Vol. 20, September, 1949, p. 468.

——— [1951], "Prediction Problems and the Theory of Statistical Decision Functions" (abstract), *Econometrica*, Vol. 19, January, 1951, p. 61.

Tinbergen, Jan [1939], *Statistical Testing of Business-Cycle Theories*, Vol. II: Business Cycles in the United States of America, 1919–1932, Geneva: League of Nations, 1939, 244 pp.

——— [1940], "Econometric Business Cycle Research," *Review of Economic Studies*, Vol. 7, 1939–40, pp. 73–90.

Tintner, G. [1945], "A Note on Rank, Multicollinearity, and Multiple Regression," *Annals of Mathematical Statistics*, Vol. 16, September, 1945, pp. 304–308.

——— [1946a], "Multiple Regression for Systems of Equations," *Econometrica*, Vol. 14, January, 1946, pp. 5–32.

——— [1946b], "Some Applications of Multivariate Analysis to Economic Data," *Journal of the American Statistical Association*, Vol. 41, December, 1946, pp. 472–500.

Wald, Abraham [1939], "Contributions to the Theory of Statistical Estimation and Testing Hypotheses," *Annals of Mathematical Statistics*, Vol. 10, December, 1939, pp. 299–326.

——— [1940], "The Fitting of Straight Lines If Both Variables Are Subject to Error," *Annals of Mathematical Statistics*, Vol. 11, September, 1940, pp. 284–300.

——— [1945], "Statistical Decision Functions Which Minimize the Maximum Risk," *Annals of Mathematics*, Vol. 46, 1945, pp. 265–280.

——— [1948], "Asymptotic Properties of the Maximum-Likelihood Estimate of an Unknown Parameter of a Discrete Stochastic Process," *Annals of Mathematical Statistics*, Vol. 19, March, 1948, pp. 40–46.

——— [1949], "Note on the Consistency of the Maximum-Likelihood Estimate," *Annals of Mathematical Statistics*, Vol. 20, December, 1949, pp. 595–601.

——— [1950a], "Note on the Identification of Economic Relations," Chapter III in *Statistical Inference in Dynamic Economic Models*, Cowles Commission Monograph 10, T. C. Koopmans, ed., New York: John Wiley & Sons, Inc., 1950, pp. 238–244.

——— [1950b], "Remarks on the Estimation of Unknown Parameters in Incomplete Systems of Equations," Chapter VIII in *Statistical Inference in Dynamic Economic Models*, Cowles Commission Monograph 10, T. C. Koopmans, ed., New York: John Wiley & Sons, Inc., 1950, pp. 305–310.

——— [1950c], *Statistical Decision Functions*, New York: John Wiley & Sons, Inc., 1950, 179 pp.

———, *see* Mann and Wald.

Wilks, S. S., *Mathematical Statistics*, Princeton: Princeton University Press, 1943, 284 pp.

Wold, Herman O. A., "Statistical Estimation of Economic Relationships," *Econometrica*, Vol. 17, Supplement, July, 1949, pp. 1–22.

Wolfowitz, J., "On Wald's Proof of the Consistency of the Maximum Likelihood Estimate," *Annals of Mathematical Statistics*, Vol. 20, December, 1949, pp. 601–602.

INDEX OF NAMES

SUBJECT INDEX

COWLES FOUNDATION MONOGRAPHS

1. Charles F. Roos, *Dynamic Economics* (out of print)
2. Charles F. Roos, *NRA Economic Planning* (out of print)
3. Alfred Cowles and Associates, *Common-Stock Indexes* (2d edition)
4. Dickson H. Leavens, *Silver Money* (out of print)
5. Gerhard Tintner, *The Variate Difference Method* (out of print)
6. Harold T. Davis, *The Analysis of Economic Time Series* (out of print)
7. Jacob L. Mosak, *General Equilibrium Theory in International Trade* (out of print)
8. Oscar Lange, *Price Flexibility and Employment*
9. George Katona, *Price Control and Business* (out of print)
10. Tjalling C. Koopmans, ed., *Statistical Inference in Dynamic Economic Models*
11. Lawrence R. Klein, *Economic Fluctuations in the United States, 1921-1941* (out of print)
12. Kenneth J. Arrow, *Social Choice and Individual Values* (2d edition)
13. Tjalling C. Koopmans, ed., *Activity Analysis of Production and Allocation*
14. William C. Hood and Tjalling C. Koopmans, eds., *Studies in Econometric Method*
15. Clifford Hildreth and F. G. Jarrett, *A Statistical Study of Livestock Production and Marketing*
16. Harry M. Markowitz, *Portfolio Selection: Efficient Diversification of Investments*
17. Gerard Debreu, *Theory of Value: An Axiomatic Analysis of Economic Equilibrium*
18. Alan S. Manne and Harry M. Markowitz, eds., *Studies in Process Analysis: Economy-Wide Production Capabilities*
19. Donald D. Hester and James Tobin, eds., *Risk Aversion and Portfolio Choice*
20. Donald D. Hester and James Tobin, eds., *Studies of Portfolio Behavior*
21. Donald D. Hester and James Tobin, eds., *Financial Markets and Economic Activity*